An Introduction to Applied Behavioral Neuroscience

An Introduction to Applied Behavioral Neuroscience explores the connection between neuroscience and multiple domains, including psychological disorders, forensics, education, consumer behavior, economics, leadership, health, and robotics and artificial intelligence.

The book ensures students have a solid foundation in the history of behavioral neuroscience; its applicability to other facets of science and policy, and a good understanding of major methodologies and their limitations to aiding critical thinking skills. Written in a student-friendly style, it provides a highly accessible introduction to the major structural and functional features of the human nervous system. It then discusses applications across a variety of areas in society, including how behavioral neuroscience is used by the legal system, in educational practice, advertising, economics, leadership, the development of and recovery from health challenges, and in robotics. Each of the application-specific chapters presents the problems that neuroscience is being asked to address, the methods being used, and the challenges and successes experienced by scholars and practitioners in each domain.

It is a must-read for all advanced undergraduate and postgraduate students in biological psychology, neuroscience, and clinical psychology who want to know what neuroscience can really do to address real-world problems.

Laura A. Freberg is a Professor of Psychology at California Polytechnic State University, San Luis Obispo. She served as the 2018–2019 President of the Western Psychological Association.

An Introduction to Applied Behavioral Neuroscience

Biological Psychology in Everyday Life

Laura A. Freberg

Routledge
Taylor & Francis Group

NEW YORK AND LONDON

Cover image: © Getty Images

First published 2022
by Routledge
605 Third Avenue, New York, NY 10158

and by Routledge
4 Park Square, Milton Park, Abingdon, Oxon, OX14 4RN

Routledge is an imprint of the Taylor & Francis Group, an informa business

© 2022 Laura A. Freberg

The right of Laura A. Freberg to be identified as author of this work has been asserted in accordance with sections 77 and 78 of the Copyright, Designs and Patents Act 1988.

All rights reserved. No part of this book may be reprinted or reproduced or utilised in any form or by any electronic, mechanical, or other means, now known or hereafter invented, including photocopying and recording, or in any information storage or retrieval system, without permission in writing from the publishers.

Trademark notice: Product or corporate names may be trademarks or registered trademarks, and are used only for identification and explanation without intent to infringe.

Library of Congress Cataloging-in-Publication Data
A catalog record for this title has been requested

ISBN: 978-1-032-04928-1 (hbk)
ISBN: 978-1-032-04930-4 (pbk)
ISBN: 978-1-003-19521-4 (ebk)

DOI: 10.4324/9781003195214

Typeset in Optima
by codeMantra

Access the support material: www.routledge.com/9781032049304

Contents

1	Introduction to Applied Behavioral Neuroscience	1
2	**Foundations of Behavioral Neuroscience**	28
3	Behavioral Neuroscience for Psychotherapists and Neuropsychologists	53
4	Forensic Neuroscience	78
5	Neuroeducation	101
6	**Consumer Neuroscience**	132
7	**Neuroeconomics**	160
8	Leadership	184
9	Health Neuroscience	210
10	Robotics and Artificial Intelligence	241

Index   *265*

1 | Introduction to Applied Behavioral Neuroscience

LEARNING OBJECTIVES

After completing this chapter, you will be able to:

▶ 1. Distinguish between basic and applied research.
▶ 2. Define behavioral neuroscience and explain its relationship to the field of neuroscience.
▶ 3. Discuss the challenges of applying behavioral neuroscience.
▶ 4. Compare major methodologies used in behavioral neuroscience.
▶ 5. Evaluate ethical constraints in applied behavioral neuroscience.

What Can Applied Neuroscience Actually Do?

A quick search of the internet results in many claims for how you can use neuroscience to make a better you and a better world. But how is the public supposed to know what neuroscience can and cannot deliver? To help answer that question, the non-profit Institute for Applied Neuroscience (n.d.) has an ambitious agenda—bridging gaps between academic researchers and policy-makers to provide evidence-based practices based on brain science. The group focuses on healthcare, education, law enforcement, juvenile justice, business, and leadership. These and several additional topics will all be featured in this book. We share the Institute's goal—using "brain science for good."

Evaluating neuroscience applications requires us to engage in the very best critical thinking practices. In this book, we hope to explore both the remarkable potential of the brain sciences as well as the limits to our knowledge and our ability to apply that knowledge to practical, real-world situations. You will see situations where neuroscience is applied very effectively, and other situations where the promises simply aren't

DOI: 10.4324/9781003195214-1

FIGURE 1.1 Applied neuroscience attempts to build bridges between the best academic research and practices and policies for the greater good.
Source: www.flickr.com/photos/davidstanleytravel/31099123226

as well supported by the current state of knowledge. We will begin that journey with a tour of basic principles of behavioral neuroscience and the strengths and weaknesses of neuroscience research methods.

The Basic and Applied Science of the Brain

When you hear the term "neuroscience," what comes to mind? A person in a white lab coat poring over images of the brain? Another scientist carefully placing recording electrodes on the scalp of a research participant? A preserved brain in a tray waiting to be examined? A rat freezing in place as it hears a tone that has been previously paired with electric shock?

These are images of **basic research**, or the pursuit of knowledge for knowledge's sake. Scientists conducting basic research are driven by their own curiosity, spending relatively little time wondering how their findings might be used by others. Astrophysicists spend entire careers carefully examining black holes on the edge of our galaxy, with no real expectations that their results will fundamentally change the way people live today. Basic research provides the foundation of what is "known." In contrast, **applied research** is directed at solving particular problems. The explicit goal is to improve the human condition rather than just gaining knowledge. While a scientist conducting basic research might be curious about the chemical composition of an asteroid, a scientist conducting applied research wants to learn how the path of the asteroid could be altered so that catastrophic collisions with Earth can be prevented.

The distinction between basic and applied research is usually somewhat blurred. You might be driven by the curiosity of basic science to find out what causes schizophrenia, but in the pursuit of this information, you are likely to learn things that will lead to new preventive or treatment strategies. Many scientists, although not all, carefully consider the "so what" factors driving their work as an important motivation, even if applications are not yet clearly in view. Their funding sources are likely to take a similar perspective. Nobody wants their work to be the example of useless research raised in Congressional budget hearings or perhaps the recipient of an Ig Nobel Prize. At the same time, the applied researcher cannot function without a firm understanding of the basic science of a field. It's all fine and good to say that you want to revolutionize education, but you are going to need a solid foundation in cognition, learning, memory, and development before you meet your goals.

Where does neuroscience fall in this continuum from basic to applied science? The answer clearly depends on which scientist you're asking. Libraries are full of books outlining the basic science of neuroscience. The purpose of this book is to introduce and evaluate some of the current and potential applications of neuroscience, and behavioral neuroscience in particular.

Neuroscience is the interdisciplinary study of the nervous system, whose ultimate goal is to understand brain and nervous system function and neurological disease at many levels (UCLA, 2021). Neuroscientists zoom in to the molecular level of the very building blocks of the system, and then zoom out again to look at cells, connections, networks, and ultimately behavior. **Behavioral neuroscience** is the study of the relationships between the nervous system and behavior, emotions, and mental processes (Freberg, 2019).

When considering applications of behavioral neuroscience, it is critical to recall that the relationship between brain and behavior is not a one-way street (see Figure 1.2). Most of us are very familiar with the concept that changes in our brains can have profound effects on our behavior. Reading about the famous case of Phineas Gage, the unfortunate railway construction foreman whose iron tamping rod shot through his brain, makes this point in a dramatic fashion. Many people take medications or know those who do which are designed to change how the brain manages mood or attention.

What is less familiar, and perhaps less comfortable, is the opposite process—your behavior, emotions, and mental processes are perfectly capable of changing the way

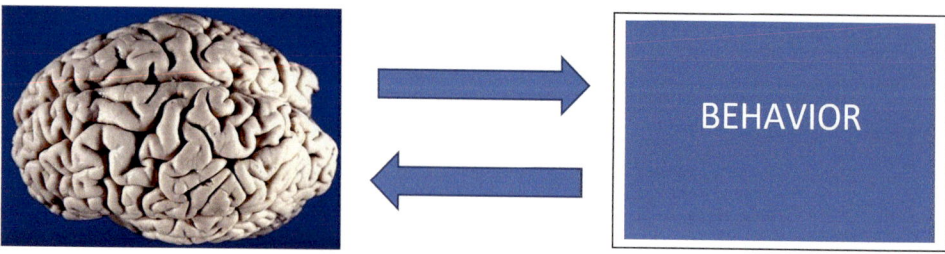

FIGURE 1.2 The relationship between the brain and behavior is reciprocal. Changes in the brain can affect behavior while changes in behavior can affect the brain.
Source: author.

your brain and nervous system operate. This ability to change brain function by changing the way people think forms the basis of cognitive behavioral therapy (CBT; see Chapter 3). CBT changes the unrealistic ways a person thinks through cognitive restructuring, such as learning that you are unlikely to be killed by a spider. After undergoing CBT, patients with phobias and obsessive–compulsive disorder (OCD) showed changes in brain activity that were very similar to those that resulted from medication (Linden, 2006).

Why do we sometimes consider this part of the brain–behavior relationship uncomfortable? In some instances, people prefer a more deterministic perspective of the brain and nervous system. For example, it might be more comfortable to think of depression as a "brain disease" resulting from disruptions in serotonin systems well outside our personal control rather than something we can influence ourselves through our own thoughts and behavior. Psychology's own William James (1899), who suffered from profound depression most of his life, wrote that "To feel cheerful, sit up cheerfully, look around cheerfully, and act as if cheerfulness were already there" (p. 153). James's approach might feel empowering to some (I'm not a victim of my biochemistry and there's something I can do to feel better) but to others, this might be an example of blaming the victim (If you just controlled your thoughts better, you wouldn't be depressed).

The solution to this dilemma is to avoid either–or thinking. Our outcomes are rarely a simple matter of our biology operating in isolation. There are fortunately very few human afflictions like Huntington's disease, where a single allele has a 100% probability of producing the disease. If you inherit the allele from a parent, you get Huntington's disease, regardless of your inheritance from your other parent, your lifestyle, or any other factors. There is no variation.

Our thoughts, emotions, and behaviors are also inseparable from our biology. Neuroscientists follow the philosophy of **monism**—the mind is the work of the brain—rather than the **dualism** proposed by Renaissance philosopher René Descartes, shown in Figure 1.3. For Descartes, the mind represented something more or different from the workings of the physical body. Western thought has been heavily influenced by this Cartesian approach, and you might find yourself rebelling against the idea that the "you" that includes your memories, hopes, and dreams is nothing more than patterns of firing in some special cells. We do not propose talking you out of following the dualistic approach, as long as you recognize that this is not the way neuroscientists think about the mind.

As is so often the case, taking an either-or approach in thinking about the relationship between brain and behavior (the brain causes behavior OR behavior controls the brain) is likely to fail. The relationship between the brain and behavior is reciprocal, intertwined, and nuanced. Attempting to separate these functions is not likely to lead to useful conclusions. Perhaps you have already learned something new or thought about the brain differently from reading these first few pages. While you think about what you have read, the connections between nerve cells in your brain are being shifted and strengthened and physical changes are taking place in the structure of your nerve cells. These processes will support your memories for what you have read, which then become changed again when you respond to a question asked by your professor or share what you have learned with your roommate. Then you must repeat the physical changes to reconsolidate your memories yet again. Over the course of this process, as you read, think, remember, and explain, physical processes in your brain interact with each step, both influencing and being influenced.

FIGURE 1.3 Renaissance philosopher René Descartes viewed the mind as neither physical nor subject to scientific inquiry. This dualistic approach is rejected by most neuroscientists, who view the mind as "what the brain does."

Source: https://en.wikipedia.org/wiki/Ren%C3%A9_Descartes#/media/File:Frans_Hals_-_Portret_van_Ren%C3%A9_Descartes.jpg

The reciprocal relationship between brain and behavior is a major theme that will inform our discussion of applications throughout this book. If one route in this relationship is neglected, the efficacy of an application is likely to be impacted negatively. For example, if we only consider the effects of brain factors on a child's educational outcomes, we miss the very real possibility that the educational setting and experience impacts the development of the child's brain.

Because of the great variety of human behavior, the applications of our understanding of the interactions between brain and behavior are seemingly infinite. The neurosciences have experienced an explosion of growth over the past few decades, driven for the most part by technological innovations discussed later in this chapter. We are only starting to scratch the surface of potential applications of this wealth of knowledge. This book provides a sampling, but by no means an exhaustive survey, of some of the more common applications of modern neuroscience. A quick review of the table of contents will demonstrate the wide variety of applications we'll cover, from courts of law to schools to advertising to robotics.

As we explore these applications, be prepared to experience a bit of skepticism on the part of your author. When asked about the implications of his research on the different processing conducted by the right and left hemispheres of the brain, Roger Sperry (1982, p. 1225) observed that this was "an idea with which it is very easy to run wild." Strolling through the self-help sections of any bookstore proves Sperry's point, as non-scientific titles like "Right-Brained Children in a Left-Brained World" fill the shelves. We believe that many applications of today's behavioral neuroscience run the risk of proving Sperry correct. One of our goals for this book is to leave you with a sense of awe about what the neurosciences can do, tempered by a big dose of humility resulting from how much we still do not know or understand.

Challenges in Applied Behavioral Neuroscience

The public is fascinated with neuroscience (we share this view, of course). This is a good thing, as neuroscience can benefit from public support, but it also raises potential challenges. Throughout this book, we will return to these challenges to moderate our enthusiasm for specific applications.

Why could the public's interest in neuroscience ever be anything but a good thing? It appears that under some circumstances, bringing neuroscience into a conversation has an outsized influence on an audience's trust and beliefs. This challenge was demonstrated in a study by Weisberg et al. (2008), who provided participants with explanations of scientific phenomena. Each participant saw either a good explanation (one the original researchers might use) and a bad explanation (a circular argument that really doesn't explain anything). In some cases, neuroscience information would also be included.

The neuroscience information included an area of interest that supposedly was known to be involved in the phenomenon and was the same in both the good and bad explanations. A sample item is shown in Figure 1.4.

The good news is that adding neuroscience language did not change people's evaluation of the good argument. They thought it was good with or without the neuroscience part. What was concerning was the finding that adding neuroscience language to the bad argument made it more satisfying. It appears the neuroscience information had the capacity to cloud an otherwise sound evaluation of the bad argument.

Along similar lines, you might have heard that including brain images that are not relevant to a topic can also sway belief. Please do not start adding brain images to your term paper on the use of light and dark imagery in *Wuthering Heights* just yet. On the surface, it seems reasonable that brain images would produce this type of boost in believability. People have a general tendency to assign "truthiness" to any statement accompanied by an illustration, even when the illustration adds nothing to the statement (Marsh et al., 2016). When that illustration is an image of the brain, the scientific merit of a statement might reasonably be further inflated (McCabe & Castel, 2008). However, a careful replication and extension of the work by McCabe and Castel (2008) did not find a boosting effect of brain images (Michael et al., 2013). This discrepancy raises yet another issue, the presentation of neuroscience results in the popular press. The McCabe and Castel study received wide, enthusiastic coverage, and you might have a sense of surprise when reading that the results did not replicate.

Kedia et al. (2017) identify several additional challenges faced in our quest to apply neuroscience effectively. First on their list is something known as **reverse inference**. In real English, this means that we can predict a cognitive process by observing brain activity. If we see your brain behave in a certain way, we're pretty sure you will select Coca Cola over Pepsi (McClure et al., 2004). Although reverse inference is a staple in many areas of behavioral neuroscience, it is not without its flaws (Poldrack, 2006). The

Sample Item

	Good Explanation	Bad Explanation
Without Neuroscience	The researchers claim that this "curse" happens because subjects have trouble switching their point of view to consider what someone else might know, mistakenly projecting their own knowledge onto others.	The researchers claim that this "curse" happens because subjects make more mistakes when they have to judge the knowledge of others. People are much better at judging what they themselves know.
With Neuroscience	**Brain scans indicate** that this "curse" happens because **of the frontal lobe brain circuitry known to be involved in self-knowledge.** Subjects have trouble switching their point of view to consider what someone else might know, mistakenly projecting their own knowledge onto others.	**Brain scans indicate** that this "curse" happens because **of the frontal lobe brain circuitry known to be involved in self-knowledge.** Subjects make more mistakes when they have to judge the knowledge of others. People are much better at judging what they themselves know.

FIGURE 1.4 Sample item from the study by Weisberg et al. (2008).

large bulk of neuroscience research remains correlational—observed nervous system activity accompanies certain emotions, cognitions, or behavior. And we all know that we cannot use the magic word "cause" when discussing correlational data. We simply do not know enough about the links between neural activity and cognitive processes to simply assume that observed activity in Area X *causes* behavior Y. It is possible that the observed activity in Area X might be performing multiple roles or have a role that is only peripheral to the task at hand, such as maintaining attention. Researchers are not abandoning reverse inferences, but they are recognizing a need to interpret their data more cautiously (Hutzler, 2013; Nathan & Del Pinal, 2017).

A second concern voiced by Kedia et al. (2017) relates to **ecological validity**. A study has ecological validity if it models behavior in real world contexts well. All laboratory studies are artificial to some extent, due to the controls required to maintain internal validity. Internal validity refers to the quality of the study's data and the study's ability to represent "truths" about the larger population. Laboratory study participants are aware that they are being observed, which might make them behave in socially appropriate rather than authentic ways. The context of the lab itself can be dramatically different from real world settings. Ethical concerns restrict the methods that can be used. For example, a major flaw in research attempting to link exposure to violent video games with subsequent aggression is the artificial nature of these studies. Some use the "hot sauce paradigm" as a measure of aggression (Lieberman et al., 1999; Figure 1.5). This paradigm involves having the participant measure out some hot sauce (5 parts Heinz chili sauce plus 3 parts Tapatio salsa picante hot sauce, if you'd like to try this at home) into a little paper cup ostensibly to be given to another person. It's hard to imagine that serving hot sauce to another person captures the types of aggression that psychologists have tried to explain, such as mass school shootings.

If you have ever undergone a brain imaging test, like **magnetic resonance imaging (MRI)** and **functional magnetic resonance imaging (fMRI**; described in detail later in this chapter), you are aware of some of the further constraints and challenges to ecological validity these procedures involve. Participants being scanned must hold extremely still for long periods of time. Tasks must be repeated frequently to reduce the "noise" in the data. Available stimuli are usually limited to still or video images. Sound stimuli do not work well due to the loud pounding of the magnets essential to this process. The participant is usually lying down in a tube, which might raise anxiety for those who do not like enclosed places. The psychological literature regarding context-dependent memory suggests that the effects of these contextual features are not trivial. For example, your ability to recall information is best when recall takes place in the same context in which it was learned. Godden and Baddeley (1975) famously compared the memory performance of participants who learned and recalled words either on dry land or under water. Those who learned and recalled in the same contexts (land–land or water–water) outperformed those who switched (water–land or land–water). Students preparing for

INTRODUCTION TO APPLIED BEHAVIORAL NEUROSCIENCE

FIGURE 1.5 Using the amount of hot sauce participants are willing to serve to another person as a measure of "aggression" probably does not capture the types of aggression that we really want to understand in the real world.
Source: Karla Freberg[1].

challenging standardized exams like the SAT, GRE, or MCAT are encouraged to actually take a practice test in the same setting where they will take the official test. These findings suggest that the settings of fMRI and other neuroscience studies must be considered.

Contemporary science is engaged in a bout of self-reflection stimulated by the failure of many classic studies to replicate and leading to new practices collectively known as "open science." Questionable statistical practices, searching for positive results when the original hypothesis fails, and the biased publication of positive results (while excluding papers that support a null hypothesis) have been common features of scientific practice that we now hope to correct. Neuroscience has not been immune to these global scientific challenges.

Behavioral neuroscience studies fall prey to many of the same problems identified across all fields of science, but some are amplified even further. Participants in many published studies are not representative of "people," but instead comprise convenience samples, usually nearby college students needing extra credit or a few extra dollars. College students typically do not represent the larger population in terms of age, gender, race and ethnicity, socioeconomic status, culture, country of origin, and so on. This is a significant problem for a field that seeks to understand the "human" brain.

Sampling problems are even more acute for neuroscience due to the high cost of many procedures, which makes large, representative samples unaffordable in many cases. At the UC Santa Barbara Brain Imaging Center, hourly rates of $600 per hour for internal users and $933 for external users are charged for using the MRI facility. The typical experiment requires about two hours per participant, so the cost adds up quickly. Largely due to these costs, fMRI samples are typically small. Between 1990 and 2012, the median sample size in highly cited fMRI studies was 12. By 2018, this number had grown to 24 (Szucs & Ioannidis, 2020). Small samples are not necessarily bad, but sample size should be chosen thoughtfully. Researchers can estimate the minimum size of their samples using power calculations. Statistical **power** estimates the likelihood of finding an effect, such as the idea that coffee enhances memory, if in fact there is an effect to be found. Szucs and Ioannidis (2020) found that only 3% of fMRI papers published in 2017–2018 conducted these essential analyses.

A further casualty of the high cost of fMRI research is the exclusion in most studies of people with left-handedness or ambiguous handedness. Handedness is correlated with the lateralization of several functions in the brain, notably language. The variations in brain activity resulting from atypical lateralization (at least 90% of humans are right-handed, so everyone else is considered atypical) introduce too much noise when the researcher is looking for subtle changes related to cognitive processing in a small sample. Nonetheless, atypical lateralization, while characterizing 10% or less of the human population, is still a very real part of the human condition deserving of study.

Other exclusions occur due to safety concerns. Because research scanning raises the ethical bar higher than medical scanning due to the relatively lower benefit to the participant, potential participants can be screened out for tattoo ink, metal piercings that cannot be removed, and welding experience. Because tattoo ink usually contains metal, some people report a pulling sensation when exposed to the powerful magnets used in fMRI. The inks can also absorb energy during the fMRI procedure, raising the risk of a burn. When people perform welding, those little sparks that fly are actually tiny bits of metal that can become embedded in the skin. Like the tattoo ink, this can lead to potential burns. As a result, we don't know much about the brain structure and function of people who took shop class in high school or sport elaborate tattoos. If we wish to generalize results to "the human brain," a knowledge of that brain and all its variations is essential. Szucs and Ioannidis (2020) found that a minority of fMRI papers reported the reasons for excluding participants and encouraged neuroscientists to begin providing this information in their papers.

We do not want to leave you with the impression that neuroscientists do not know what they're talking about. Instead, we wish to instill a healthy sense of skepticism that is so critical for good science. Science is a moving target rather than a finished product. It moves along step-wise in a positive direction by identifying flaws in previous work and striving to correct them. Szucs and Ioannidis (2020) have shown that neuroscientists are attempting to improve their sample sizes in response to criticisms about low-powered studies. Most scientific conferences feature panels and presentations admonishing researchers to avoid relying on WEIRD (Western, Educated, Industrial, Rich, Democratic) samples. Researchers are pre-registering their studies by publicly presenting their hypotheses and research plans, in the hopes of reducing the temptation to search after the fact for positive results. Journal editors are striving to be more friendly toward papers showing null results or replications.

The importance of considering the challenges involved with conducting good science is especially acute when we move from basic to applied realms. Mistakes and misinterpretations in basic research have the potential to set science back for a period of time; mistakes in applied research have the potential to hurt living human beings.

Negotiating Theory and Practice

The medical newsfeed service Medscape Psychiatry summarized research by Read et al. (2020) that cast doubt on the efficacy of electroconvulsive therapy (ECT) for major depressive disorder and suicidal ideation (Viessides, 2020). While the summary is fascinating, the comments were even more so. Many of the self-identified medical doctors responding to the article had difficulty accepting the findings. A number mentioned that they had used ECT with their patients for years with positive results. One medical doctor pointed out derisively, "A PhD attacking a medical psychiatric [MD] procedure? How shocking." Another stated, "Let us be sure all the 'experts' have all had close personal long term clinical responsibility for treating patients with chronic treatment resistant major depression." We might counter that the M.D. degree provides little if any preparation in research, while statistics and research methods make up a sizeable chunk of any Ph.D. curriculum in scientific fields.

This type of problem has plagued all fields with both research and practitioner branches, whether that is psychology, medicine, law, social work, education, communication, business, or many others. Practitioners are concerned that academic researchers lack the practical experience needed to understand the field. Academic researchers often find that practitioners, like some of the medical doctors described above, give too much weight to their personal impressions of what does and doesn't work.

Academic researchers and practitioners often come to very different conclusions. Psychometrics experts are baffled by the continued use in various practitioner domains of flawed personality instruments, such as the Rorschach Inkblot Test and the Myers-Briggs Type Indicator. By purely scientific standards, these instruments fail spectacularly in areas such as validity and reliability, yet many clinical psychologists and practitioners in other fields still use them. The Rorschach, astonishingly, is still admitted to U.S. courts of law, where it is used to make significant decisions such as those related to probation and custody. Practitioners defend their use of flawed instruments in two different ways. First, they refer to history—"we've always done it this way"—as if that is a reasonable criterion for any practice based on science. Second, they acknowledge that the practice is flawed, but argue that they are somehow immune to any negative effects. "I know the Rorschach has problems when used by others, but the way I use it in my practice has always worked well."

A robust solution to academic–practitioner disputes is the use of **evidence-based practice (EBP).** As shown in Figure 1.6, we can visualize EBP as three intersecting Venn diagrams. The first circle is a good understanding of the best science available. We might argue that this circle is a weak spot for some of the medical doctors criticizing Read et al. (2020). Instead of evaluating the data carefully, they reject the conclusion out of hand.

The second circle is practitioner experience. We do not want to appear dismissive of the practitioner. Years of experience and careful observation can lead to significant wisdom. When hearing about the trials and tribulations of new faculty, the senior members of a department usually recognize the exact nature of the problem and can recommend effective solutions. This is the "oh, I've seen that before many times" advantage that comes from experience. The problem with this second circle is that it cannot exist in isolation. When a practitioner's experience conflicts with the best scientific data available, the practitioner must re-evaluate even the most beloved of approaches.

The third and final circle is the preferences of the person served, usually a patient or client depending on the field. When some individuals are told that their cancer is terminal, they reject any further treatment and perhaps take a last trip to a beloved holiday destination. Others in this situation fight to the bitter end, even engaging in experimental treatments. It is incumbent on practitioners to assess what the targets of their solutions really want. In other cases, we are using neuroscience information to make

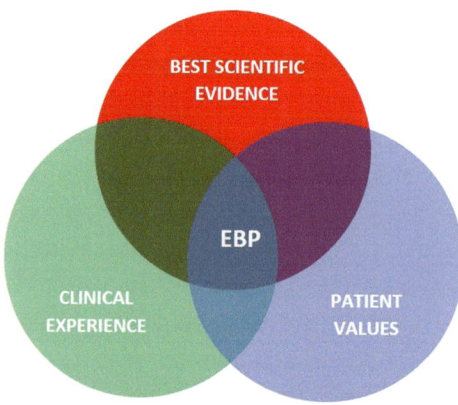

FIGURE 1.6 Evidence-based practice combines scientific evidence and practitioner experience with the goals and values of the recipient of the treatment.

critical decisions for an individual, such as a person being evaluated for parole. Their choices in these cases are not the point, but we must act in their best interests.

This final circle is complicated by the **group-to-individual (G2i) problem**. Science works on the basis of statistical probabilities. If you know that 85% of convicted criminals with a particular pattern of brain activity reoffend, is that sufficient to deny parole to one such individual? How can we tell if our one person is part of the 85% majority or the 15% minority? There are no easy answers to such dilemmas that we know of. This issue will be featured prominently in our chapter on Forensic Neuroscience, where expert scientific testimony must be evaluated in court.

Methods in Behavioral Neuroscience

The history of advances in the neurosciences is intimately tied to the development of new technologies with which to observe the structure and function of the nervous system. An exhaustive review of the basic science methodologies used in the neurosciences is beyond the scope of this book. Instead, we will focus on classic and emerging technologies that you will see applied in upcoming chapters. We learn applicable results by studying both humans and other animals, but this discussion will highlight methods used primarily with human participants. Following our survey of methods, we will address the ethical constraints on neuroscience research.

One of the advantages of human research is that you can actually ask people what they think or how they feel. Although self-report is notoriously subjective and biased, these reports help the researcher obtain a more complete picture of the participant's experience. Neuroscience data alone cannot give us all the information we need. Combining different methodologies designed to assess the same question is usually the best strategy.

The architect Louis Sullivan (1856–1924) famously said "form follows function," meaning that the design of a building should flow from its purpose. We take much the same approach when selecting methodologies in science. We start with the purpose of our research—what questions are we trying to answer? That leads to a set of appropriate tools for answering the question. Subdomains, such as cognitive and social neuroscience, generally feature a set of shared, typical methods, although innovations are common and frequent.

Peripheral Measures

A variety of tools allows us to observe the activity of the autonomic nervous system (described in more detail in Chapter 2). The autonomic nervous system (ANS) communicates with glands and organs to manage such functions as digestion, heart rate, and breathing. These processes typically occur at a non-conscious level. You would not have much of a social life if you had to consciously will yourself to inhale and exhale at appropriate intervals. Of course, you can take more conscious control of these functions, like holding your breath while under water, but this requires significant cognitive resources. More often, we simply put the ANS on cruise control. As such, the ANS can provide us with information about the general arousal level of a person, regardless of what they might tell you about their current state. Some researchers use peripheral measures to assess emotion, but this is less than precise. These measures provide insight into the valence, or positive or negative quality, of an emotion, but usually cannot be used to distinguish between emotions on one side of the continuum from another, such as joy and pride.

Peripheral measures of ANS activity include **facial electromyography (fEMG)**, **heart rate variability (HRV)**, the **skin conductance response (SCR**; also known as the Galvanic skin response or GSR), eye tracking, and pupil dilation (Niedziela & Ambroze, 2021). It is conventional for researchers to combine these methods for the most accurate snapshot of ANS activity. Because these measures tend to be relatively inexpensive and non-invasive, they feature prominently in applied settings such as consumer research and forensics.

Facial Electromyography (fEMG)

As shown in Figure 1.7, surface electrodes are placed on three of the forty-three muscles of the face that participate in emotional expression. We apologize in advance for the names of these muscles. The corrugator supercilii participates in lowering the eyebrow while producing a frown, so its activity is correlated with negatively valenced emotions. The zygomatic major muscle is involved in both smiling and grimacing, so a third recording of the orbicularis oculi, which is only correlated with positively valenced emotions, is needed to distinguish between positive and negative states.

Not only can fEMG help distinguish between positive and negative emotional states, but it can also measure intensity, as in a more positive response to one stimulus compared to another. The technique is complicated by individual differences in muscle structure and the spread of electrical activity from one muscle to another. Again, this suggests that multiple methods are needed for accuracy.

Heart Rate/Heart Rate Variability (HRV)

The ANS directly controls heart rate. Because blood flow is essential to the brain's functioning, the action of the heart can provide insight into how the brain will function in particular circumstances. Heart activity measures can indicate changes in attention, arousal, stress, and physical and mental activity.

FIGURE 1.7 Electrode arrays commonly used for peripheral measures of ANS activity.
Source: Karla Freberg.

As we will see in Chapter 2, when the sympathetic division of the ANS communicates with the heart, heart rate speeds up. When the parasympathetic division of the ANS communicates with the heart, the heart slows down. As a result, heart rate can provide insights into a person's general state of arousal. A person's pulse rate can be taken without any special equipment simply by placing fingers at an appropriate place on the wrist, but for research purposes, these data are usually collected with electrocardiogram (EKG) electrodes placed in several locations on the body. Alternately, photoplethysmography (PPG) is an inexpensive method that measures changes in light absorption related to blood flow. Several commercial heart rate sensors, such as WHOOP, are marketed to the public to enhance athletic training.

HRV is a measure of the variation of the time between heart beats, or how regularly the heart is beating. If your heart beats 60 times per minute, it is not beating exactly once every second—there is variance. This variance reflects the competing inputs from the sympathetic (speed up) and parasympathetic (slow down) divisions of the ANS. Overall, higher HRV (more variance between beat intervals) is considered to be an indicator of better health and autonomic balance. However, transient variations in HRV can reflect changes in focus and attention. When a person is vigilant, HRV decreases (intervals become more regular) due to dominance of the sympathetic division, which prepares the person for fight or flight. Without any competing inputs from the parasympathetic division, heart rate becomes more regular. When a person is more relaxed, we see the HRV increase as more balance between the parasympathetic and sympathetic divisions occurs.

Correct interpretation of HRV requires sensitive evaluation of participants. It is usually more meaningful to track HRV over time, but researchers rarely have the luxury of doing this. HRV is sensitive to health conditions, gender, and age. Females have slightly lower (average 37 ms) HRV rates compared to males (average 40 ms). Young adults usually have HRV rates between 55 and 105 ms, while individuals between 60 and 65 have HRV rates between 25 and 45. Alcohol consumption can lower HRV for several days. Sleep quality and quantity prior to measurement can influence HRV. Many illnesses can influence HRV. So again, it is essential to use HRV thoughtfully in conjunction with other measures.

Skin Conductance Response (SCR)

This method takes advantage of the fact that skin becomes a better conductor of electricity when you are aroused. Sweat glands are controlled by the sympathetic division of the ANS, so they become more active during arousal. Active sweat glands produce local changes in ions, or electrically charged particles, that impact the conductance of electrical signals. The SCR is taken by placing two electrodes next to the skin, usually on the palm of the hand or sole of the foot, which are rich in sweat glands. A small charge that can't usually be felt by the participant is sent from one electrode to the other, and its speed and characteristics can be measured.

Like the other measures we have explored, SCR is highly sensitive to factors other than arousal. SCR is influenced by demographic variables such as age, gender, and ethnicity, as well as environmental factors such as temperature and humidity. Some medications, particularly those used to treat allergies, cold, and flu, can impact the SCR.

Eye Tracking and Pupillometry

Eye tracking, usually using wearable technology, can assess what participants are looking at as well as how the eyes are moving relative to the head. The same technology can be used to measure pupil size (**pupillometry**). These methods provide information about visual attention and arousal. When the sympathetic division of the ANS is active, the pupils will dilate. Pupil dilation might be sensitive to emotional valence as well as overall arousal. Increased dilation was associated with positive stimuli compared to neutral or negative stimuli (Nunnally et al., 1967). Changes in pupil dilation also reflect changes in lighting, so researchers must be careful to consider the lighting of the laboratory.

Central Measures

While the peripheral measures can be very useful, they lack precision. Directly observing the activity of the brain itself provides researchers with much more detail. Among the most powerful methods in the neuroscientists' toolkit are recording technologies (electroencephalogram and magnetoencephalography) and brain imaging technologies (magnetic resonance imaging and functional magnetic resonance imaging).

Recording the Brain's Activity

The brain operates using electrochemical signaling, and it is possible to record the tiny bits of electricity it generates during information processing. Any time electricity is present, we also have magnetic fields, so it has more recently become possible to record the magnetic output from the brain. Recording the electrical output of the brain is known as **electroencephalography (EEG)** and the recording of the brain's magnetic output is known as **magnetoencephalography (MEG)**.

Hans Berger recorded the first electroencephalogram using a human subject in 1924. Electroencephalograms are now conducted by placing a cap with up to 256 surface electrodes on the head of a participant. One of the significant advantages of EEG is its excellent temporal resolution, or ability to tell you *when* something happened. In contrast, the brain imaging technologies discussed later in this chapter have much poorer temporal resolution. However, this advantage in temporal resolution is offset by relatively poor *spatial* resolution, or the ability to tell you *where* something happened. Due to the nature of the technology, EEG recordings reflect activity from the surface of the brain rather than from structures deep within the brain. More contemporary EEG methods, however, are improving spatial resolution.

EEG data have been classified according to the frequencies of waveforms. Higher frequency waveforms are associated with more brain activity while lower frequency waveforms are associated with less processing. During normal waking, people alternate between beta (13–30 Hz or cycles per second) and alpha (8–13 Hz) waves with occasional bursts of gamma waves (30–100 Hz). Beta waves are associated with focused attention, but this waveform is also seen during Rapid Eye Movement (REM) sleep. Alpha waves are associated with relaxed, unfocused thought or mind wandering. Gamma is correlated with processing of sensory stimuli, especially when modalities are combined (sound plus vision, etc.) and with associative learning (such as operant or classical conditioning). Theta (4–8 Hz) and delta (0.5–4 Hz) waves are prominent during sleep, with delta waves being characteristic of deeper stages of sleep. Theta waves are seen during waking in children under the age of 13 and in drowsy adults.

A modification of the EEG technique involves the recording of **event-related potentials (ERPs)**. Hundreds of recordings are made after exposing a participant to the same stimulus, perhaps a tone or light. The results of all of these recordings are then averaged, removing "noise" and highlighting regular components or waves. These waves are named according to their direction (P for positive or N for negative) and their approximate latency. The P300 component, therefore, is a positive wave appearing approximately 300 ms after the presentation of a stimulus. The P300 wave is correlated with cognitive functioning and shows lower amplitude and longer latency in several conditions, including alcohol abuse and Alzheimer's disease.

EEG has been used traditionally to assess sleep and seizure activity. More recently, the use of EEG has been expanded to assess more complex brain functions. Methods have been developed to identify brain microstates, or stable, non-overlapping patterns of activity in an EEG. You might think about these as separate steps in what William James described as a "stream of consciousness." Thus, microstates have been nicknamed as "atoms of thought" (Koenig et al., 1999, p. 209). Cacioppo et al. (2014) were able to identify distinct microstates during an experiment in which participants watched a series of reversing checkerboards. Separate microstates were associated with viewing a checkerboard, waiting for the next one to arrive, and then viewing the next checkerboard. Unusual patterns of brain microstates have been observed in patients with schizophrenia (Koenig et al., 1999) and other types of psychological disorder.

For the purpose of applications, a major advantage of EEG is its relatively low cost. Commercial EEG devices can be obtained for as little as $100. These devices are often restricted to a very small number of electrodes, even as few as two, which are dry rather than the more accurate gel-assisted electrodes used in medicine and research. A novel application of EEG technology is the Necomimi headband complete with motorized cat ears that turn up during beta wave activity and turn down during alpha activity. The Necomimi uses the MindWave platform developed by NeuroSky, which is also marketed for health and wellness, educational, and entertainment applications.

One of the challenges in recording an EEG is that much of the electricity one would want to record is blocked by the scalp and skull bones that separate the brain from your electrodes. When recording the magnetic output of the brain, we do not experience this problem. Magnetism moves freely through the skull and scalp, a fact that we might want to remind ourselves about when holding our cellphones up next to our heads for hours at a time. However, the size of the magnetic fields generated by the brain is tiny, and easily lost against the other sources of magnetism surrounding us in the environment. Fortunately, special signal detectors known as SQUIDs (superconducting quantum interference devices) can record these signals. This allows MEG to localize the source of activity in a way that is much superior to EEG. MEG recordings are usually superimposed on structural images, such as those acquired using magnetic resonance imaging (MRI). Together, this provides information about both the structure and function of the brain.

Like MRI, the cost of MEG is a potential barrier to application. UC San Diego advertises rates of $510 per hour for UC users and $740 per hour for non-UC users. The initial cost of the machinery and the necessary shielding in the facility are high, as is the cost of the liquid helium required by the SQUID sensors.

In 2018, Boto et al. reported the development of an exciting new MEG technology that recorded data from a freely moving participant wearing a helmet, illustrated in Figure 1.8. The participants nodded their heads, stretched, took a drink, and played a ball game while being scanned. The wearable technology was made possible by a new type of quantum sensor that does not require the expensive liquid helium. Although like standard MEG, this pilot equipment still requires use in a room shielded to eliminate the Earth's magnetic field, it holds the promise of developing MEG technology that will provide data as participants perform more naturally.

Brain Imaging

Several brain imaging technologies have been developed for medical and research purposes since the 1970s. Some are less likely to be used in the types of applications we discuss in this book due to their expense, less available equipment, or invasiveness. For example, **positron emission tomography (PET)** and **single photon emission computerized tomography (SPECT)** require the administration of a radioactive tracer to the

FIGURE 1.8 Mobile MEG technology has the potential to revolutionize our ability to assess the activity of the brain during more natural movements.
Source: Karla Freberg.

patient or participant. While the risks associated with this exposure to radiation make sense to a medical patient because the information provided by the scan will result in better diagnosis and treatment, the risk–benefit ratio for a research participant or consumer panel is quite different.

The "gold standard" of contemporary behavioral neuroscience is functional magnetic resonance imaging (fMRI). This technology is also the most commonly used brain imaging technology in consumer applications, despite its cost. Functional MRI assesses brain activity by looking at changes in blood flow. It differs from magnetic resonance imaging (MRI), which is a single image at one point in time, in that a time series of images is used to capture these changes in blood flow. This approach assumes that busy neurons need more oxygen and nutrients than quiet neurons do, resulting in increased blood flow to a busy area. Red blood cells carrying oxygen respond differently to bombardment with magnetism than cells carrying less or no oxygen, resulting in blood oxygenation level dependent (BOLD) contrast. Brain activity recorded during fMRI is represented using color-coded units known as voxels, which are essentially 3D pixels that represent the activity of neurons in a particular area.

A significant advantage for the application of fMRI is its relative safety. No dye contrasts are needed, which increases the safety of the procedure. As far as we know, exposure to the rather powerful magnetic fields used in fMRI has no lasting detrimental effects on participants. We discussed some of the challenges associated with fMRI, such as cost, small non-representative samples, and low power, earlier in this chapter. In the heady early days of fMRI, researchers occasionally jumped to unwarranted conclusions about their data, as in an opinion piece in the *New York Times* (Iacobini et al., 2007) that claimed that activity in the anterior cingulate cortex (see Chapter 2) meant that participants who expressed unfavorable views of Hillary Clinton "were battling unacknowledged impulses to like Mrs. Clinton." Researchers using fMRI have learned, sometimes the hard way, to be a bit more guarded in their interpretations of their data. The use of machine learning to evaluate data might improve the interpretation of these complex data. When performed accurately, fMRI can provide considerable insight into the real-time functioning of the human brain as a function of the tasks performed by healthy participants.

Some lesser known types of brain imaging, now used primarily for medical and research purposes, might eventually make their way into more widespread application. **Functional magnetic resonance spectroscopy (fMRS)** allows researchers to study brain metabolism during brain activation without being invasive. This approach does not require the radiation used in PET or SPECT. Other methods used to assess the brain's biochemistry require surgery, which obviously limit their use in research and application. **Functional near-infrared spectroscopy (fNIRS)** is, like fMRI, a non-invasive method for measuring blood flow. In the case of fNIRS, the scatter of near-infrared light projected on the head is assessed. Blood rich in oxygen will respond differently to this light than blood that has already delivered its oxygen to an active area of the brain. Because fNIRS and fMRI provide similar information, why would you use fNIRS? Functional NIRS is portable, requiring a cap similar to that used in EEG, and it is not as disturbed by movement and sound as fMRI. This means that the fNIRS technology might be more useful in realistic settings important to our applications. Its temporal resolution is significantly better than fMRI. On the downside, however, the spatial resolution of fNIRS is not as good as that of fMRI, and it cannot assess activity deep within the brain.

What Method Do We Use?

If you are seeing these methods described for the first time, the array of possibilities might seem a bit overwhelming. As shown in Figure 1.9, each method provides trade-offs between strengths and weaknesses, and researchers need to decide which are most important. In an ideal world, our research questions would guide our choice of methods, but this is not always possible. The choice of method is often a question of access and cost as much as it is scientific convention.

Relying on a single method is probably not a great idea either. When we see researchers arriving at the same conclusions using multiple, combined methods such as concurrent fNIRS—fMRI recordings, we can have more confidence in their findings.

A Word about Ethics

No discussion of methodology is complete without a word or two (or more) about the ethics involved.

Academic researchers are bound by government regulations regarding the treatment of research participants and their data. These regulations developed in response to some exceedingly uncomfortable history, such as the infamous Tuskegee Syphilis Study. In this study,

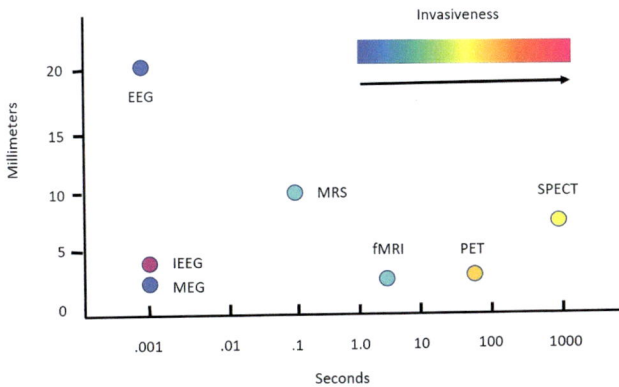

FIGURE 1.9 Research methods provide several trade-offs between strengths and weaknesses. In this case, the various imaging methods differ in temporal and spatial resolution, as well as invasiveness.

Source: adapted from MIT.

conducted by the government agency that is now the CDC, low income African-American men who had been infected with syphilis were studied without their even knowing they were in a study. Even worse, when penicillin was discovered to be an effective treatment for syphilis during the study, the men were not offered this life-saving treatment.

Emerging from these research debacles, standards have been set in place regarding informed consent and volunteerism, confidentiality, and avoidance of harm. Participants must freely volunteer to participate, and they require sufficient information on an informed consent form to make a decision. Their personal data should never be matched to their identities. Obviously, "do no harm" is a very important aspect of ethical research. Comparable regulations exist for the protection of animals used in research. Special committees at colleges and universities review proposed research to ensure that it meets government regulations.

But this is a book about applications. What about the corporation marketing consumer neuroscience to clients? Currently, U.S. regulations do not cover organizations that do not receive government research funds. While we hope that private corporations would follow the same sets of rules as academic researchers do, there is no way to ensure that. Tech giants like Google and Facebook employ armies of behavioral scientists, who have no formal restrictions on the use of data provided by the public for research purposes (which we sign up for when we click on "agree" to the terms of service, which all of us read thoroughly, of course). If you're okay with the Nest Hub's ability to tell Google when you cough or snore and how long you sleep each night, well, then you have nothing to worry about.

Chapter Summary

In this chapter, we explored the differences between basic and applied science and the positioning of behavioral neuroscience within the larger field of neuroscience. We described some of the methodologies we are likely to meet in applied areas of behavioral neuroscience and laid out the ethical concerns related to neuroscience research. You might find it useful to revisit these foundational concepts as needed as you proceed to the remaining chapters. Finally, we hope that this chapter has piqued your interest in the chapters to come.

Review Questions

1. Which of the following is the clearest example of basic research (LO 1.1)?
    a. Using fMRI to assess the truthfulness of courtroom witnesses.
    b. Using EEG to monitor the attention of children with ADHD before and after an intervention.

c. Using fMRI to correlate brain activity and a memory task.

d. Using eye-tracking to evaluate participant responses to a website.

2. Which of the following is the best description of behavioral neuroscience (LO 1.2)?

    a. A branch of neuroscience that looks at correlations between neural activity and behavior.

    b. A branch of psychology that looks at correlations between brain and behavior.

    c. A branch of psychology that looks at correlations between the brain and psychological disorders.

    d. A branch of neuroscience that uses mathematical models to learn about the activity of the nervous system.

3. Which of the following is NOT a challenge related to applying behavioral neuroscience (LO 1.3)?

    a. People tend to give more weight to neuroscience explanations.

    b. Reverse inference is difficult to do well.

    c. Methods in neuroscience can be artificial and lacking in ecological validity.

    d. Neuroscience research tends to be over-powered due to very large samples.

4. Which of the following methodologies provide good information about brain activity (LO 1.4)?

    a. MRI and fMRI

    b. PET and fMRI

    c. PET and MRI

    d. EEG and MRI

5. Which of the following is the most accurate statement regarding ethics in behavioral neuroscience research (LO 1.5)?

    a. Private organizations like Google and Facebook must adhere to the same ethical guidelines as academic researchers follow.

    b. Behavioral neuroscience does not have the potential to cause harm to participants.

    c. Research in behavioral neuroscience requires volunteers.

Thought Questions

1. Of the methods described in this chapter, which seem to have the most ethical challenges?

2. What are the implications of the group-to-individual (G2i) problem when we attempt to apply our knowledge of behavioral neuroscience? Are there ways to work around this problem?

Answer Key for Review Questions

1. c
2. a
3. d
4. b
5. c

Note

[1] Karla is the author's daughter, and she has autism spectrum disorder. Karla has contributed many illustrations to this text.

References

Boto, E., Holmes, N., Leggett, J., Roberts, G., Shah, V., Meyer, S. S., Muñoz, L. D., Mullinger, K. J., Tierney, T. M., Bestmann, S., Barnees, G. R., Bowtell, R., & Brookes, M. J. (2018). Moving magnetoencephalography towards real-world applications with a wearable system. *Nature, 555,* 657–661. https://doi.org/10.1038/nature26147

Cacioppo, S., Weiss, R. M., Runesha, H. B., & Cacioppo, J. T. (2014). Dynamic spatiotemporal brain analyses using high performance electrical neuroimaging: Theoretical framework and validation. *Journal of Neuroscience Methods, 238,* 11–34. http://dx.doi.org/10.1016/j.jneumeth.2014.09.009

Freberg, L. A. (2019). *Discovering behavioral neuroscience: An introduction to biological psychology* (4th ed.). Boston, MA: Cengage.

Godden, D. R., & Baddeley, A. D. (1975). Context-dependent memory in two natural environments: On land and underwater. *British Journal of Psychology, 66,* 325–331. https://doi.org/10.1111/j.2044-8295.1975.tb01468.x

Hutzler, F. (2014). Reverse inference is not a fallacy per se: Cognitive processes can be inferred from functional imaging data. *Neuroimage, 84,* 1061–1069. https://doi.org/10.1016/j.neuroimage.2012.12.075

Iacoboni, M., Freedman, J., & Kaplan, J. (2007). This is your brain on politics. *New York Times.* www.nytimes.com/2007/11/11/opinion/11freedman.html?_r=0

Institute for Applied Neuroscience (n.d.). *About.* www.appliedneuro.org/about.html

James, W. (1899). *Talks to teachers on psychology: And to students on some of life's ideals*. New York, NY: Holt.

Kedia, G., Harris, L., Lelieveld, G-J., & van Dillen, L. (2017). From the brain to the field: The applications of social neuroscience to economics, health and law. *Brain Sciences, 7*(8), 94. https://doi.org/10.3390/brainsci7080094

Koenig, T., Lehmann, D., Merlo, M. C. G., Kochi, K., Hell, D., & Koukkou, M. (1999). A deviant EEG brain microstate in acute, neuroleptic-naïve schizophrenics at rest. *European Archives of Psychiatry and Clinical Neuroscience, 249*(4), 205–211. https://doi.org/10.1007/s004060050088

Lieberman, J. D., Solomon, S., Greenberg, J., & McGregor, H. A. (1999), A hot new way to measure aggression: Hot sauce allocation. *Aggressive Behavior, 25*, 331–348. https://doi.org/10.1002/(SICI)1098-2337(1999)25:5<331::AID-AB2>3.0.CO;2-1

Linden, D. (2006). How psychotherapy changes the brain: The contribution of functional neuroimaging. *Molecular Psychiatry, 11*, 528–538. https://doi.org/10.1038/sj.mp

Marsh, E. J., Cantor, A. D., & M. Brashier, N. (2016). Believing that humans swallow spiders in their sleep: False beliefs as side effects of the processes that support accurate knowledge. In B. H. Ross (Ed.), *Psychology of learning and motivation* (Vol. 64, pp. 93–132): Academic Press.

McCabe, D. P., & Castel, A. D. (2008) Seeing is believing: The effect of brain images on judgments of scientific reasoning. *Cognition, 107*(1), 343–352. https://doi.org/10.1016/j.cognition.2007.07.017

McClure, S. M., Li, J., Tomlin, D., Cypert, K. S., Montague, L. M., & Montague, P. R. (2004). Neural correlates of behavioral preference for culturally familiar drinks. *Neuron, 44*(2), 379–387. https://doi.org/10.1016/j.neuron.2004.09.019

Michael, R. B., Newman, E. J., Vuorre, M., Cumming, G., & Garry, M. (2013). On the (non) persuasive power of a brain image. *Psychonomic Bulletin Reviews, 20*, 720–725. https://doi.org/10.3758/sl13423-013-0391-6

Nathan, M. J., & Del Pinal, G. (2017). The future of cognitive neuroscience? Reverse inference in focus. *Philosophy Compass, 12*(7), e12427. https://doi.org/10.1111/phc3.12427

Niedziela, M. M., & Ambroze, K. (2021). Neuroscience tools: Using the right tool for the right question. In H. L. Meiselman (Ed.), *Emotion measurement* (2nd ed., pp. 559–592). Woodhead Publishing. https://doi.org/10.1016/B978-0-12-821124-3.00017-X

Nunnally, K., Knott, P., Duchnowski, A., & Parker, R. (1967). Pupillary response as a general measure of activation. *Perception and Psychophysics, 2*(4), 149–155. https://doi.org/10.3758/BF03210310

Poldrack, R. A. (2006). Can cognitive processes be inferred from neuroimaging data? *Trends in Cognitive Science, 10*(2), 59–63. https://doi.org/10.1016/j.tics.2005.12.004

Read, J., Kirsch, I., & McGrath, L. (2020). Electroconvulsive therapy for depression: A review of the quality of ECT vs sham ECT trials and meta-analyses. *Ethical Human Psychology and Psychiatry*. https://doi.org/10.1891/EHPP-D-19-00014

Szucs, D., & Ioannidis, J. P. A. (2020). Sample size evolution in neuroimaging research: An evaluation of highly-cited studies (1990–2012) and of latest practices (2017–2018) in high-impact journals. *NeuroImage, 221*(1), 117164. https://doi.org/10.1016/j.neuroimage.2020.117164

Sperry, R. (1982). Some effects of disconnecting the cerebral hemispheres. *Science, 217*, 1223–1226. https://doi.org/10.1126/science.7112125

UCLA (2021). *UCLA undergraduate interdepartmental program for neuroscience*. www.neurosci.ucla.edu/.

Viessides, M. (2020). *Experts call for immediate suspension of ECT, others push back*. Medscape Psychiatry. www.medscape.com/viewarticle/934536

Weisberg, D. S., Keil, F. C., Goodstein, J., Rawson, E., & Gray, J. R. (2008). The seductive allure of neuroscience explanations. *Journal of Cognitive Neuroscience, 20*, 470–477. https://doi.org/10.1162/jocn.2008.20040

Glossary

Applied research	Research directed at solving particular problems.
Basic research	The pursuit of knowledge for its own sake.
Behavioral neuroscience	The study of relationships between the nervous system and behavior, emotions, and mental processes.
Dualism	A philosophy of mind and body that maintains that the body and mind are quite separate, with the mind not being subject to scientific study.
Ecological validity	A quality of a study that refers to its "real world" applicability.
Electroencephalography (EEG)	Recording the brain's electrical output through surface electrodes on the scalp.
Event-related potentials (ERPs)	Averaged data from many EEG recordings in response to a stimulus.
Evidence-based practice (EBP)	A combination of clinical expertise, the best science available, and client/patient preferences.
Eye tracking	An assessment of eye movement and gaze using wearable technology.
Facial electromyography (fEMG)	A measure of muscle activity associated with facial expressions of emotion.
Functional magnetic resonance imaging (fMRI)	A popular brain imaging technology based on magnetism that provides information about the activity of different parts of the brain.
Functional magnetic resonance spectroscopy (fMRS)	A non-invasive method for studying brain metabolism.
unctional near-infrared spectroscopy (fNIRS)	A non-invasive method to track blood flow in the brain using light projected on the head.
Group-to-individual problem (G2i)	The challenge faced when applying research results based on statistical probabilities to one individual.
Heart rate variability (HRV)	A measure of the time between heart beats used to assess attention and stress levels.

Magnetic resonance imaging (MRI)	A brain imaging technology using magnetism that features excellent spatial resolution. When MRI images are taken quickly over time and compared, we refer to the process as a functional MRI (fMRI).
Magnetoencephalography (MEG)	Recording the brain's magnetic output using external SQUID devices.
Monism	A philosophy of mind and body that maintains that the mind is the result of activity in the brain.
Neuroscience	The interdisciplinary study of the nervous system, whose ultimate goal is to understand brain and nervous system function and neurological disease at many levels.
Positron emission tomography (PET)	A brain imaging technology based on the detection of radioactive tracers. Similar to SPECT.
Power	The ability of a study to detect an effect if one is there to be found.
Pupillometry	Measures of the pupil's dilation.
Reverse inference	A logical interpretation of brain imaging studies that assumes that patterns of activity observed in response to a stimulus can be used to predict what a person is thinking when observed on another similar occasion.
Single photon emission computerized tomography (SPECT)	A brain imaging technology based on the detection of radioactive tracers; similar to PET.
Skin conductance response (SCR)	A measure of the conductance of electricity on the surface of the skin as a function of arousal; also known as a Galvanic skin response.

2 Foundations of Behavioral Neuroscience

LEARNING OBJECTIVES

After completing this chapter, you will be able to:

▶ 1. Describe the major structures of the nervous system and identify their functions.

▶ 2. Explain the structures and processes involved with neural signaling.

▶ 3. Identify the key neurochemicals and the systems they influence.

▶ 4. Discuss how neurochemical function can be manipulated with therapeutic and recreational drugs.

Learning about the Structure of the Nervous System

Before we can evaluate how behavioral neuroscience can be applied appropriately, it is necessary to spend some time reviewing the nuts and bolts of how the system works. Contemporary neuroscientists take our abilities to view the structure of the nervous system for granted, but scientists were not able to do this well until quite recently. The development of more powerful microscopes and technologies such as MRI (see Chapter 1) opened whole new windows for scientists interested in the structure of the brain. As recently as 1900, scientists were still debating whether the nervous system was made of separate cells like any other organ or was made up of an interconnected reticulum ("network" in Latin). It took the development of special stains for scientists like Santiago Ramón y Cajal to convince others that the former explanation is true. One of Cajal's beautiful drawings can be seen in Figure 2.1. Ironically, Cajal used a stain developed by his rival, Camillo Golgi, to prove that Golgi's reticulum theories were wrong. Much to Cajal's chagrin, he shared the 1906 Nobel Prize with Golgi.

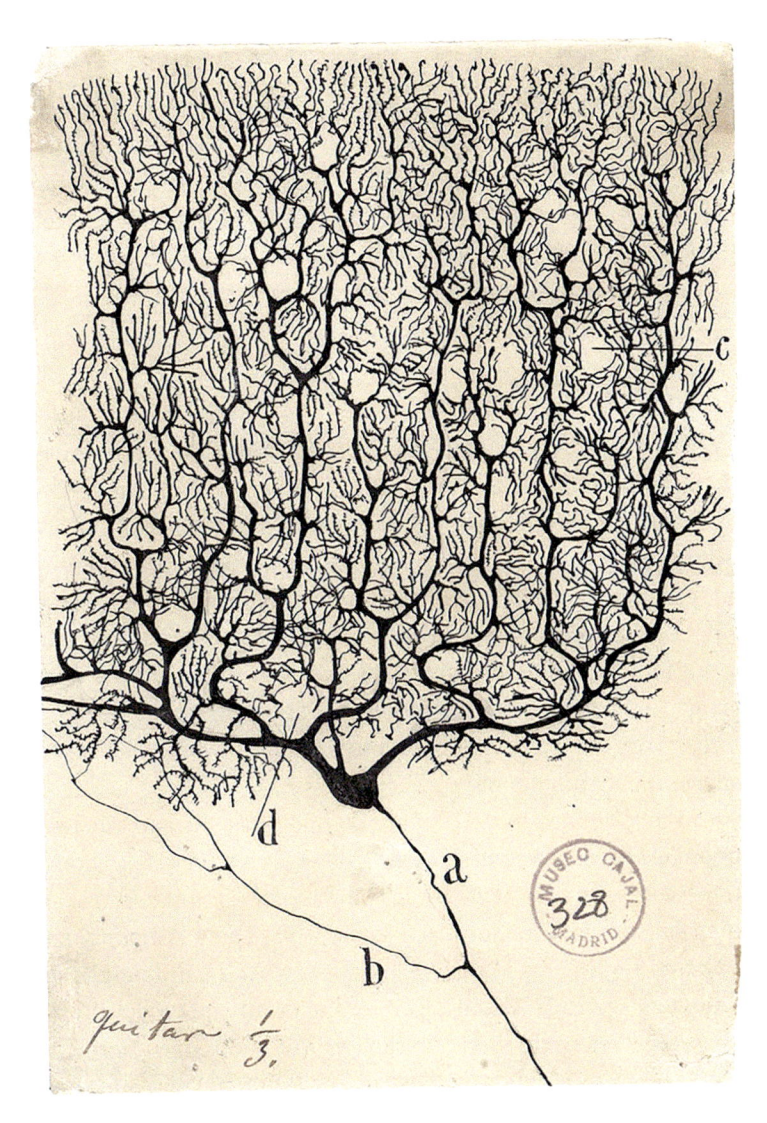

FIGURE 2.1 Santiago Ramón y Cajal (c. 1900) drew a Purkinje cell from the human cerebellum.
Source: https://commons.wikimedia.org/wiki/Category:Santiago_Ram%C3%B3n_y_Cajal

This chapter is not intended to be a substitute for more comprehensive descriptions of the structure and function of the nervous system, which can be the subject of entire books on their own. If you are quite new to the study of neuroscience, it might be especially useful to make use of a general textbook, such as *Discovering Behavioral Neuroscience* (Freberg, 2019) and internet resources as backup, such as the 3D Brain provided by Cold Spring Harbor Laboratory at www.g2conline.org/3dbrain/. The 3D Brain is also available as an app for your phone.

The Larger Picture: Structures and Functions of the Nervous System

Like Google Earth, we can zoom in and out to explore the structure and functions of the nervous system. We will start our journey by looking at large-scale structures and their network connections. Then we will zoom in to the microscopic level to see the cells that make up these larger structures and learn how they function.

Overview of the Nervous System

The nervous system is divided into two main components: the **central nervous system (CNS)** and the **peripheral nervous system (PNS**; see Figure 2.2). The CNS contains the brain and spinal cord, leaving everything else to form the PNS. The CNS is protected by the bones of the skull and vertebrae. As soon as nerves peek out from this protection, they fall into the category of PNS. You might be wondering why anyone would bother with the distinction between CNS and PNS. Among the many useful features of this distinction is the understanding that the CNS and PNS differ in how they respond to damage. Damage to the CNS is still considered permanent, but some repair is possible in the PNS. Otherwise, we would not bother to reattach severed digits or limbs or even transplant cadaver parts onto people.

The PNS is further divided into two more components: the **somatic nervous system** and the **autonomic nervous system**. "Soma" is the Greek word for "body," so the somatic nervous system serves the body by carrying motor commands to skeletal muscles and transmitting sensory information back to the CNS. The autonomic nervous system (ANS) serves glands and organs to manage processes like heart rate and digestion. The **sympathetic nervous system** division of the ANS coordinates arousal while the **parasympathetic nervous system** division coordinates rest and repair. Normally, these divisions of the ANS work as an either/or type of toggle switch. When one is on, the other

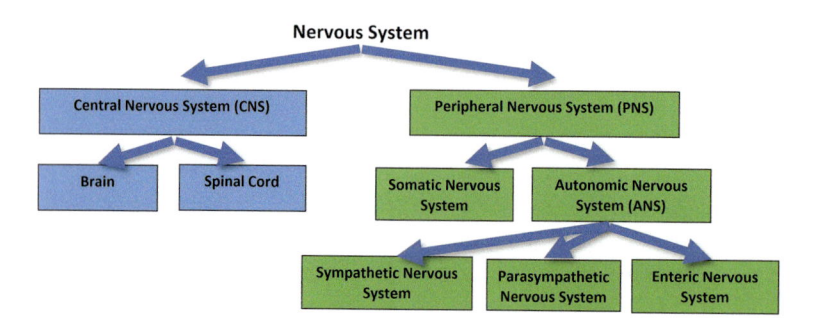

FIGURE 2.2 The nervous system can be divided into the central nervous system (CNS) and the peripheral nervous system (PNS).

is off. You cannot typically be relaxed and aroused simultaneously. The two divisions do manage, however, to work together during sex. The **enteric nervous system** makes up the third part of the ANS. This system includes the many neurons found in the gut. Recent discoveries about the communication between the gut and the brain have led to renewed interest in the enteric nervous system. Finally, the nervous system is influenced by hormones released into the blood by the **endocrine system**.

The Central Nervous System

As we mentioned previously, the central nervous system (CNS) includes the brain and spinal cord. We often speak of these as if they are quite separate things, but of course, they are intimately connected. It is more accurate to view the spinal cord as a tail extending from the brain. If you place your hand on the back of your neck and bend your head backwards, the junction of the brain and spinal cord will fall just under the flexion point.

The **spinal cord** is relatively small, amounting to only about 2% of the nervous system by weight. Its importance to our ability to function, however, is far greater than its size suggests. The spinal cord gives rise to the peripheral nervous system serving the body through 31 pairs of spinal nerves. Twelve pairs of **cranial nerves** extend from the brain to perform similar functions primarily in the head and neck. As a result, the spinal cord is the original information superhighway, transmitting vast amounts of data to and from the brain. In addition, the spinal cord can behave on its own without help from the brain by managing several essential reflexes. When you touch a hot stove or step on a sharp object, you immediately pull back from the source of your pain. This withdrawal reflex is purely spinal. If you stretch a muscle, the spinal cord automatically contracts it to maintain steady tension. This process is usually very subtle but can be observed in the more obvious patellar or knee-jerk reflex tested by your healthcare provider.

Moving upward from the spinal cord, we find the **brainstem**, which is a combination of the hindbrain and midbrain. These categories reflect the embryological development of the nervous system, during which the developing brain forms three bulges. The first two bulges form the hindbrain and midbrain, and the third bulge becomes the forebrain.

The brainstem continues the "information superhighway" function of the spinal cord, with vast tracts of nerve fiber pathways traveling to and from higher levels of the brain. We will be referring to these pathways as white matter due to their coloration. Suspended within these fiber pathways are collections of nerve cell bodies, or gray matter. These clusters, usually referred to as nuclei, perform a variety of functions. Some receive and process information from the twelve pairs of cranial nerves, nerves that perform similar functions as the spinal nerves but that extend directly from the brain. Other brainstem nuclei participate in the processing of sleep and waking, pain, vigilance, and movement. Running along the center core of the brainstem is the reticular formation, a collection of nuclei that participate in the regulation of awareness and consciousness. As a result of activity in this structure, you are more aware of stimuli such as noise when you are awake compared to when you are sound asleep. Clusters of cells in the midbrain give rise to the brain's major circuit for processing reward. This circuit projects forward to communicate with structures in the forebrain and is implicated in cases of addiction. Yet another group of cells, the substantia nigra (named after its dark pigmentation), forms tight connections with forebrain structures associated with movement.

Attached to the back of the brainstem is the **cerebellum**, which literally means little brain. The cerebellum is notable for containing more nerve cells than the rest of the brain combined, although it makes up about 10% of the total volume of the brain. The cerebellum plays important roles in balance and motor coordination, especially during the performance of learned, complex movements like your golf swing or making a free throw in basketball. The incapacitation of the cerebellum by alcohol is the main reason that we do not want people to drive a car after drinking. The cerebellum, through rich connections with the forebrain, also participates in much more complex, cognitive processes, including language, attention, emotion, and mental imagery. The structural abnormalities observed in the cerebellum of individuals diagnosed with autism spectrum disorder might be associated with some of the cognitive deficits that characterize this condition.

The forebrain consists of the two large cerebral hemispheres. Several fiber pathways, known as commissures, connect the right and left hemispheres. The largest of these is the corpus callosum ("tough body" in Latin). When the brain is sliced in relatively equal halves, the corpus callosum can be seen making a "C" shape on its side near the middle of the brain.

Within the hemispheres, we find the remnants of a fluid-filled, embryological neural tube, which in the adult brain takes the form of the cerebral **ventricles**. The lining of the ventricles produces cerebrospinal fluid, a heavy, clear substance that cushions the weight of the brain and provides a means of transport for various substances traveling from one part of the brain to another. Cerebrospinal fluid circulates through the ventricle system as well as through the central canal at the center of the spinal cord. At the base of the skull, an opening allows the cerebrospinal fluid to enter a space within the meninges, a set of three membranes that separate the brain from the bones of the skull and the spinal cord from their surrounding vertebrae.

Hugging the surface of the cerebral hemispheres is the relatively thin layer of gray matter known as the **cerebral cortex** (cortex literally means "bark" as in the bark of a tree). It is customary to divide the cortex into four lobes, just as we divide the globe into continents: frontal, parietal, occipital, and temporal (see Figure 2.3). Each appears twice, once in each hemisphere. These are very large areas of cortex, but we can identify some general types of processing that take place primarily in each lobe. The **frontal lobe** contains areas devoted to movement and to some of our highest cognitive processes,

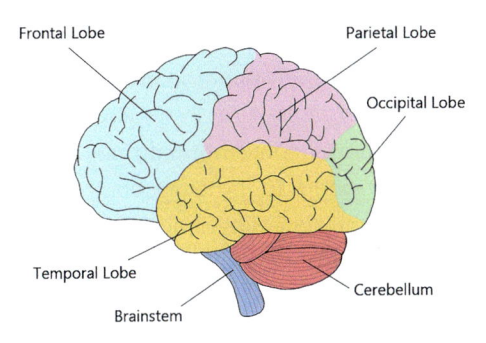

FIGURE 2.3 Lobes of the brain.
Source: Karla Freberg.

including decision-making, attention, impulse control, and executive function. The **parietal lobe** receives information about touch and body position and location. This information is combined with visual input to help us maneuver through the environment. The **occipital lobe** processes input from vision, while the **temporal lobe** processes sound. The temporal lobe also participates in object and face recognition.

In addition to the traditional four lobes, some anatomists identify a "fifth lobe"—the **insula**. The insula lines the depths of the large lateral sulcus, a deep "valley" that divides the temporal lobes from the rest of the cerebral cortex. The roles of the insula are many and varied. It provides sensory information from internal organs along with assessments of the general physiological state of the body, such as awareness of thirst or a rapid heartbeat. The insula appears to play important roles in the processing of pain, taste, smell, and hearing. The insula is also involved with craving, subjective emotion, and empathy. Higher level cognitive processes such as speech and the ability to detect novel stimuli are associated with activity in the insula.

The parts of the cortex described above are often referred to as "neocortex," or new cortex. An older cortical area ("archicortex") is the cingulate cortex, which is found just above the arc formed by the corpus callosum (see Figure 2.4). The **cingulate cortex** is divided into the front two-thirds, the anterior cingulate cortex or ACC, and the back one-third, the posterior cingulate cortex or PCC. The ACC participates in control of the autonomic nervous system, decision-making, anticipation of reward, and empathy. The posterior cingulate cortex processes memory and visual input.

Much has been made, most of it highly exaggerated, of the differences in functioning in the right and left hemispheres. We can draw several conclusions about the lateralization of functions to one side of the cortex or the other. Movement and sensation from one side of the body are processed by the opposite side of the brain. For about 96% of the population, language is processed primarily in the left hemisphere. Tasks requiring spatial reasoning, such as navigating through an environment, are typically associated with activity on the right hemisphere. The right hemisphere is also involved in decoding emotional stimuli. However, connectivity between the hemispheres is strong and fast, and most behavioral outcomes of hemisphere lateralization are subtle. We are sorry to disappoint you, but you simply cannot "activate your right hemisphere to improve your artistic abilities," as claimed by some self-help books and popular press outlets. Communication from one hemisphere to the other via the corpus callosum and other commissures is quick and efficient, ensuring that the observable behaviors related to hemisphere lateralization are subtle.

Most of the bulk of the cerebral hemispheres is made up of extensive fiber pathways connecting the cortex to the rest of the brain and to the spinal cord. Suspended in this white matter are several structures representing a wide range of functions. At the very center of the forebrain, we find the **thalamus**. The thalamus is the target of incoming sensory information, which it then relays to appropriate parts of the cortex. It also participates in learning, memory, consciousness, and the selection of motor programs. Cupping the thalamus are structures that are grouped together as the **basal ganglia**. These structures provide a checkpoint for planned behavior, which will be implemented only if the basal ganglia "agree." In cases of Parkinson's disease, which makes the initiation of voluntary movement very difficult, we see an associated degeneration of the basal ganglia.

Other forebrain structures are grouped together as a **limbic system**, shown in Figure 2.4. You might have heard the limbic system described as "your emotional brain," but only some of these structures actually participate in the processing of emotion. Primary among these is the **amygdala**, located toward the front of the temporal lobe. These small, almond-shaped structures receive sensory information from the thalamus and evaluate its positive or negative significance. Psychologists are especially interested in the ability of the amygdala to detect threat. Damage to the amygdala reduces a person's ability to experience fear. The nucleus accumbens, which receives input from the reward pathway mentioned previously, normally processes reward and pleasure but is also implicated in addiction.

Several limbic structures, including the **hippocampus**, are essential to the processing of memory. Memories are stored permanently in the cerebral cortex, not the hippocampus, but processing by the hippocampus is required for the formation of some types of new memories. Damage to the hippocampus results in little loss of memories for events prior to the damage but leads to profound difficulties when the patient tries to learn new things. The hippocampus, like most brain structures, is involved with multiple functions. In addition to its role in memory formation, the hippocampus can sense the amount of stress hormones a person has released. If the amount gets too high, the hippocampus issues commands to reduce the stress response. This role is tough on the hippocampus. Severe, chronic stress seems to damage the structure. Fortunately, neuroscientists believe that some recovery in the form of the growth of new neurons can take place, even in adulthood.

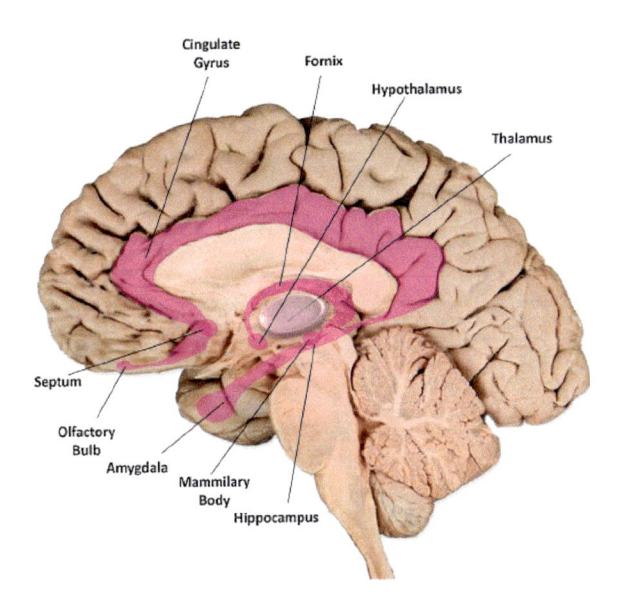

FIGURE 2.4 Structures of the limbic system.
Source: https://commons.wikimedia.org/wiki/File:Limbic_System.png

The **hypothalamus**, which literally means "below the thalamus," regulates body states and maintains homeostasis or equilibrium. Separate areas of the hypothalamus regulate hunger, thirst, body temperature, and daily biorhythms. Other areas contribute to sexual, parenting, attachment, and aggressive behaviors. The hypothalamus provides instructions to the autonomic nervous system and to the body's endocrine system.

Discussions of the major parts of the brain and their functions usually take the form of "this structure performs this function," but in reality, the structures of the brain are intimately connected in complex networks. It is more accurate to say that a structure participates in a circuit that relates to a function. Notable networks in the brain govern processes like movement, language, sensory processing, and memory. A **default mode network (DMN)**, named for its higher level of activity during unfocused than focused thought, links areas in the frontal and parietal lobes with the cingulate cortex. Differences in the activity and connectivity of the DMN occur in people diagnosed with several disorders, including Alzheimer's disease and autism spectrum disorder.

The Peripheral Nervous System

As we mentioned earlier, everything outside the central nervous system (CNS) falls into the category of the peripheral nervous system (PNS; see Figure 2.5).

The somatic component of the PNS manages the delivery of motor commands to skeletal muscles and returns sensory information to the CNS. This information flows through

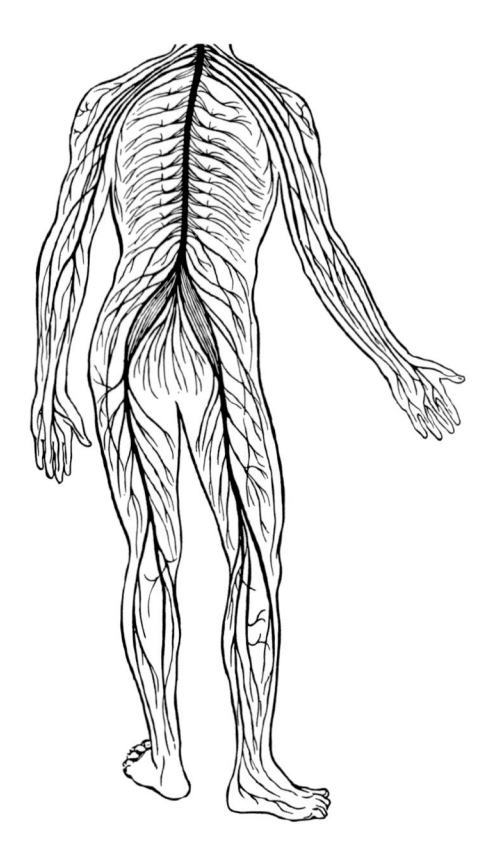

FIGURE 2.5 Peripheral nerves exit the brain as 12 pairs of cranial nerves and the spinal cord as 31 pairs of spinal nerves.
Source: www.publicdomainpictures.net/en/view-image.php?image=130383&picture=nervous-system

the 12 pairs of cranial nerves and the 31 pairs of spinal nerves. The cranial nerves exit the brainstem directly, and most serve the area of the head and neck. One exception is cranial nerve X, the vagus nerve. Like its Latin namesake, the "vagabond," the vagus nerve travels far from the head and neck to interact with the viscera. Some of the cranial nerves carry exclusively sensory or motor information, while others carry both. Spinal nerves contain both a ventral root (on the belly side), which carries motor information, and a dorsal root (on the back—think dorsal fins of sharks), which carries sensory information.

The autonomic nervous system (ANS) connects the CNS with internal organs and glands. It gets its name from the Latin for "autonomous" or independent because many of its functions simply run in the background like your antivirus software. You can consciously control some autonomic functions, like holding your breath, but as soon as you direct your attention elsewhere, your autonomic nervous system goes back on cruise control. As mentioned previously, the sympathetic division of the ANS is associated with arousal while the parasympathetic division is associated with rest and repair. For example, as you climb a flight of stairs, your sympathetic nervous system tells your heart to speed up. When you relax at the top of the stairs, your parasympathetic nervous system tells your heart to slow down. How does the heart know which system is talking to it? The two systems use different neurochemicals at each organ. The sympathetic division releases norepinephrine onto the heart while the parasympathetic division releases acetylcholine.

Under extreme duress, which psychologist Walter Cannon (1915, p. 211) dubbed "fight-or-flight," the sympathetic division goes into overdrive. The body's resources are mobilized, heart rate increases, breathing speeds up, and blood is driven from the surface of the body into the muscles. Most people report mental clarity and a sense that time is moving more slowly. An alternate response to threat is freezing. Freezing has been characterized as a "braking" mechanism controlled by the parasympathetic division that allows the animal to gather information and plan a response and usually precedes the more active defensive responses of fight or flight. An increased understanding of the trajectory of threat detection to freezing to fight-or-flight should illuminate individual differences in anxiety and aggression.

The enteric nervous system serving the gut is also part of the ANS. Its ability to communicate directly with the vagus nerve (cranial nerve X) forms a gut–brain axis. Not only is information about the gut itself transmitted in this fashion, but also information about the gut's microbiome, or bacteria population. Observations that differences in the microbiome are associated with a variety of conditions like obesity and autism spectrum disorder has led to renewed interest in the enteric system.

The endocrine system, which answers directly to the hypothalamus, is responsible for the manufacture and release of a wide range of hormones into the blood circulation. Endocrine hormones are especially important to arousal, metabolism, growth, and sex. In many cases, the hormones are the same chemicals that are used to communicate between neurons, but because of their release into the blood, they can influence distant cells in a very coordinated fashion. For example, your experience of an "adrenalin rush" results from the release of adrenalin (we call it epinephrine in neuroscience) and cortisol from the adrenal glands above your kidneys into the blood supply.

Cells of the Nervous System

Now that you have a general idea of the larger scope of the nervous system, we will zoom in to the microscopic level and explore the structures and functions of the cells that make up these larger structures.

Neurons and Glia

We find two major types of cells within the nervous system—neurons and glia. The **neurons** process and communicate information while the **glia** perform support functions.

Neurons

Neurons, like the one illustrated in Figure 2.6, have many features in common with other body cells but are uniquely configured for their communication functions. The bulk of the neuron, its soma or cell body, contains the cell's nucleus and other organelles that characterize animal cells. Extending from the cell body are two types of branches—dendrites and axons. **Dendrites** provide locations for input from other cells, while the neuron's **axon** is used to transmit information to other cells. Most human neurons have many dendrites but only one axon. The end of the axon, its terminal, features a bulge to accommodate many small vesicles or packages of neurochemical waiting to be released.

In vertebrates like ourselves, most axons are insulated by glial cells (described below) that form segments of **myelin**. The myelin segments are separated by sections of bare axon known as nodes of Ranvier. As we will see later in this chapter, electrical signals travel from node to node. In general, myelin enhances the speed and energy efficiency of neural signaling. The human nervous system requires nearly 23 to 25 years to become completely myelinated. The very last areas of the brain to be myelinated are the frontal lobes, which means that adolescents and emerging young adults will make decisions differently than older adults.

Surrounding the neuron is a very thin plasma membrane. The cell's structure is provided by a cytoskeleton made up of protein fibers. Dysfunction in one type of these fibers is associated with some of the cellular degeneration found in Alzheimer's disease. Embedded in the membrane are many channels that allow substances to enter and exit the cell. Some of these respond to the electrical current in their vicinity while others interact with neurochemicals. Certain channels require substantial energy to operate, contributing to the overall large energy requirements of the nervous system.

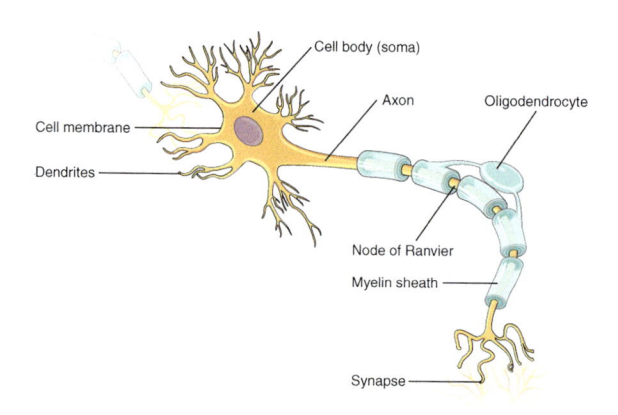

FIGURE 2.6 Features of a neuron.
Source: https://commons.wikimedia.org/wiki/File:1206_The_Neuron.jpg

Glia

Glia get their name from the Greek word for "glue," due to one of their many functions—providing structure and support for the nervous system. Glia are divided into macroglia and microglia based on their size. Among the macroglia are the astrocytes, oligodendrocytes, Schwann cells, satellite cells, and ependymal cells.

The astrocytes, named after their star-like shape, perform numerous support functions in addition to providing structural support. Their branches not only reach out to hold neurons in place, but also form connections with the capillaries serving the nervous system to help form a **blood–brain barrier (BBB)**. The BBB protects the central nervous system from many circulating toxins that successfully escape the circulation to impact other organs, like the liver. Psychoactive drugs, by their very nature, move right through the BBB to influence the brain. The astrocytes also provide nutrients to neurons, regulate the chemical environment in their vicinity, and influence the signaling of nearby neurons. They participate in some minor repair functions, although we must consider damage to the central nervous system as permanent.

The oligodendrocytes and Schwann cells form the segments of myelin mentioned previously in the CNS and PNS respectively. Although they both serve the same function, they do so slightly differently. In particular, they respond differently to damage to an axon. The oligodendrocytes tend to inhibit axon regrowth by forming scar tissue, which is one of the reasons we consider CNS damage to be permanent. In contrast, the Schwann cells are actually helpful in guiding a regrowing axon back to its target. As a result, PNS damage can be repaired somewhat, allowing us to reattach severed digits or limbs or even transplant cadaver parts onto people. Satellite cells cover the cell bodies of some neurons in the PNS. They perform duties similar to the astrocytes found in the CNS, including the provision of nutrients, structural support, and monitoring of the local neurochemical environment. The ependymal cells line the ventricles and the central canal of the spinal cord. They participate in the development of cerebrospinal fluid (CSF). Their cilia, which extend into the CSF, contribute to its circulation.

The microglia are the clean-up crew of the CNS. They are mobile and will congregate in areas of damage, where they ingest debris and regulate inflammation. Microglia also play significant roles in synaptic pruning, or the destruction of junctions where two neurons communicate. While this sounds like a negative process, synaptic pruning is an important feature of an efficient nervous system, just like decluttering your house. Errors in microglia function are suspected to contribute to several neurodevelopmental conditions, like autism spectrum disorder, and psychological disorders such as schizophrenia.

Neural Communication

Neural communication takes place in two steps: (1) the development of an electrical signal within a nerve cell or neuron, and (2) the use of neurochemicals to transmit information from one cell to another.

Electrical Signaling

The process of **electrical signaling** begins when a neuron receives input from one or more other cells at synapses, or points of communication. In most cases, two neurons do not physically touch at a synapse, but are separated by tiny fluid-filled gaps. Incoming signals take the form of interactions between neurochemicals in the fluid at the synapse and receptors located in the membrane of the receiving cell. These receptors identify and bind specific neurochemicals and then open channels in the membrane. Inflowing or outflowing charged particles, or ions, set up a current that flows to the junction of the receiving cell's cell body and axon. If the current is sufficient, an electrical signal known as an **action potential** will be generated in this initial segment of the axon.

What do we mean by "sufficient?" At rest, or when no information is being processed, electrical recordings show that the interior of an axon segment is negatively charged compared to its exterior by a factor of approximately 70 millivolts (a millivolt is 1/1000th of a volt). Thus, we refer to the resting potential of a neuron as –70 mV. Incoming signals and the currents they generate within the cell can move this recording in either a more negative or more positive direction. Neurons have a threshold, or minimum change needed, before they respond. Typically, if the incoming signals produce a positive change of 5 to 15 mV (e.g., our recording moves from –70 mV to –65/–55 mV), an electrical signal, called an action potential, will be produced.

When this threshold is reached, special channels in the axon membrane open, providing the ability of certain ions to move in or out of the cell. Initially, positively charged sodium ions move rapidly into the axon, which is reflected in our recording as a sharp upward spike or rise. Subsequently, positively charged potassium ions leave the cell, which results in a "fall" as our recording moves back in a negative direction again. Following the rise and fall of the spike, the axon segment experiences a refractory period, or "time out," in which it is unlikely to fire again. Housekeeping mechanisms go into high gear to return the sodium and potassium ions to their pre-firing locations and the neuron becomes capable of firing a second time. This entire process takes about a single millisecond, or 1/1000th of a second. We talk about the action potential as "all-or-none," which reflects its binary nature—you either make an action potential or you do not. In other instances, we observe so-called "graded potentials," which can vary in height and duration, but the action potential always looks the same.

So far, we have produced a very localized disturbance in the initial segment of the axon. Our goal, of course, is to get our signal to the axon terminal, where it will initiate the release of chemical messengers. Some human axons are only a millimeter (1/1000th of a meter) in length whereas others can be about one meter long, depending on your height. The sciatic nerve, which stretches from your spinal cord to your big toe, contains the longest axons in the body. So, by itself, making an action potential adjacent to a cell body at the base of the spinal cord is not going to influence an axon terminal in your big toe. We need to propagate, or replicate, our action potential down the whole length of the axon.

This is where myelin becomes especially useful. In an unmyelinated axon, the action potential must be replicated along the entire length of an axon in small increments. This is analogous to crossing a room while shuffling your feet. You will eventually arrive at the other side, but it is going to take some time. In contrast, action potentials jump from node of Ranvier to node of Ranvier in a myelinated axon. No action potentials must be made to cover the distance under a segment of myelin. This is analogous to a triple jumper in track and field who can cover long distances in just a few steps.

Our world is full of marvelous invertebrates who manage quite well without myelin. We ourselves retain some deliberately unmyelinated axons, such as the fibers in the pain system that deliver the dull, achy feeling that lingers after the initial shock of an injury. However, myelin provides remarkable advantages. Normally, we see a positive correlation between the diameter of an axon and its speed of transmission, much like any electronic cable. To obtain the speed of processing we enjoy, we would need some very large diameter axons, which would take up precious space within our skulls. Instead, our myelinated axons are capable of transmitting signals at a rate of about 150 m/sec compared to 0.5 to 10 m/sec in an unmyelinated axon, despite having small diameters. Myelinated axons are also energy efficient. The housekeeping that must occur at the end of an action potential to return sodium and potassium to their rightful places requires about 20% of the total calories you consume during a day. The fewer the action potentials needed to cover a length of axon, the less energy you need to clean up. On average, the metabolic cost to cover the same distance is about 70% cheaper in a myelinated axon compared to an unmyelinated one.

Whether propagated along a myelinated or unmyelinated axon, our action potential eventually reaches the axon terminal. Current can flow directly from one neuron to another in synapses known as gap junctions, but in most cases, we now need to switch to chemical signaling to pass information along to the next cells.

Chemical Signaling

As we mentioned previously, the axon terminal contains numerous vesicles that contain **neurochemicals**. Why must these be packaged as opposed to being allowed to float freely in the terminal? First, these are very active chemicals which might start producing unwanted effects in the terminal. Second, the terminal contains enzymes that would break the chemicals apart. Finally, the vesicles ensure a coordinated release of known quantities of neurochemical at the right time.

As illustrated in Figure 2.7, when our action potential reaches the terminal, it signals the opening of calcium channels. We have not discussed these previously because few if any are found along the axon, unlike the numerous sodium and potassium channels.

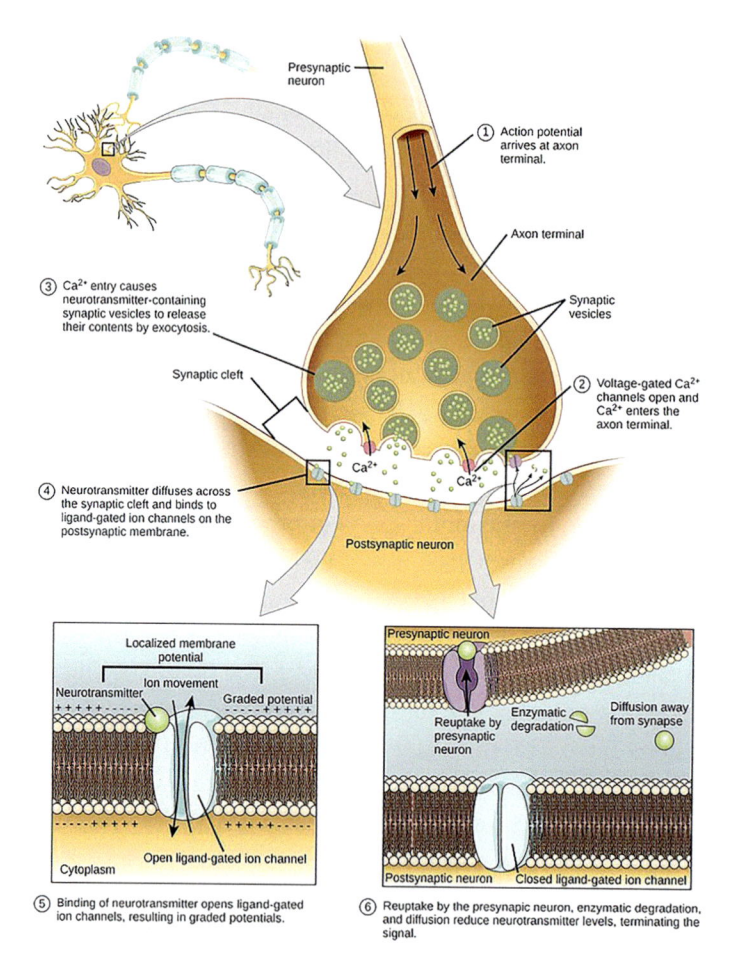

FIGURE 2.7 Chemical signaling at the synapse.
Source: https://commons.wikimedia.org/wiki/File:Figure_35_02_07.jpg

However, the axon terminal is richly supplied with calcium channels. When calcium enters the axon terminal, it signals the release of the vesicles, which otherwise are docked like boats in a bay. The vesicles are propelled with mechanical force to the release site on the axon terminal. Because the vesicles are made of the same plasma material as the cell membrane, they fuse with the membrane and break open, spilling their contents into the extracellular fluid separating the two cells at a synapse.

Before we follow the released molecules of neurochemicals on their journey, we still have some work to do at the axon terminal. If we continually release neurochemicals, the vesicle material could accumulate near the release site or active zone, which would eventually interfere with the release process. Instead, the material is budded off and used to form fresh vesicles, just one of the many sustainable recycling efforts we see in the nervous system. The new vesicles are refilled and ready to be released in a short period of time.

In some cases, the axon terminal also features special channels that recapture molecules of the neurochemical that were just released, a process known as reuptake. The recaptured molecules are then reinserted in vesicles, reducing the need to synthesize more neurochemicals. Many drugs, both therapeutic and recreational, act as reuptake inhibitors. In other words, these drugs interfere with this recycling process by blocking the recapture of neurochemicals. As a result, the molecules of neurochemicals remain for a longer than normal time in the synaptic gap, giving them additional opportunities to interact with other cells.

The releasing cell is referred to as presynaptic, meaning "before the synapse." We will now turn our attention to the postsynaptic cell, or the "after the synapse" cell that is receiving our message. How will the molecules of neurochemical just released influence the activity of this cell?

Embedded in the membrane of the dendrites, cell body, and even axon are special receptors. These structures can recognize particular types of neurochemicals. Once they bind molecules of released neurochemicals, they can either directly open a channel contained within their structure or influence adjacent channels by releasing internal second messengers. The released neurochemicals in the synapse interact with these receptors in a lock-and-key fashion, with the structure of the neurochemical serving as a key that interacts with the lock formed by the receptor. The neurochemical molecule is not bound for long but is rapidly released by the receptor. Until its activity is terminated by reuptake, or the actions of enzymes, or its simply diffusing away from the synapse, it can continue to interact with receptors.

Many psychoactive drugs produce behavioral effects by mimicking the action of neurochemicals at receptor sites. It is fascinating to consider the inventiveness of our ancestors as they discovered naturally occurring substances from plants and other sources that had the capability of modifying neural functions. We would not respond to opioids, tobacco, and cannabis without having endogenous, natural neurochemicals that were so similar that the receptors cannot tell them apart. Still other chemicals interact with receptors in harmful ways. Most snake venoms and the dart poison curare act by occupying a recognition site on a receptor and blocking the ability of normal neurochemicals to activate muscle fibers, often leading to death.

The interaction between a specific neurochemical and its receptor determines the type of effect that the neurochemical can have. The effect can take two forms, excitatory and inhibitory. Excitatory synapses result in current that makes the production of an action potential more likely. These synapses are usually found on dendrites and involve receptors that control sodium channels. Be careful to keep the effects of these postsynaptic, ligand-controlled (responding to neurochemicals) channels separate from the effects of the presynaptic, voltage-controlled (responding to the local current) channels we discussed in the context of the action potentials. Postsynaptic potentials differ from action potentials in important ways. They are more variable in size and duration. Activity at inhibitory synapses makes an action potential less likely. These synapses are usually found on the cell body and involve receptors that control either potassium channels or chloride channels. If you allow more positive potassium ions to leave the cell or allow more negative chloride ions to enter, you produce a hyperpolarizing current that will move our recording in the initial segment of the axon in a more negative direction, or farther away from the threshold for firing.

The need for excitatory input seems quite intuitive. This is a green light for activating the next cell and passing a message along. The need for inhibition, however, might be confusing. Why would we want to send a red light, "no go" message to the next cell? The need for inhibition is illustrated dramatically by tetanus, for which you have probably been vaccinated. Tetanus refers to maximum contraction of a muscle, and we usually do not need or want to reach that state. Instead, muscle tension is finely tuned to provide just the right amount of force to get a job done. This requires a delicate balance between excitatory and inhibitory inputs to muscles. The tetanus toxin invades the nervous system and selectively destroys inhibitory motor neurons. Left with just excitation alone, the muscles contract too much, leading to the colloquial name "lockjaw" for the condition. At this point, you are probably ensuring that your tetanus vaccinations are up to date.

Now we circle around to finish the story we started in this section. Imagine a cortical neuron with about 1000 synapses across its dendrites and cell body. How does this cell know what to do? The convergence of currents flowing toward the initial segment of the axon determines whether the cell forms an action potential or not. In spatial summation, the effects of input across the cell are summed at the initial segment. If the input results in reaching threshold, an action potential will result. If not, the cell will stand down until more input occurs. In temporal summation, a very active synapse might be sufficient to cause the postsynaptic cell to reach threshold and fire.

The Neurochemicals

Over 40 different chemicals have been shown to serve as chemical messengers. In many cases, these chemicals are multitaskers. For example, the brain contains receptors for the neurochemical oxytocin, which is believed to have an impact on bonding and social behavior. However, oxytocin plays many other roles in the body, such as uterine contractions related to childbirth and the let-down reflex of the nursing mother. A comprehensive survey of **neurochemicals** is beyond the scope of this book, but we will outline some of the key systems that we will refer to in our upcoming discussions.

A single neuron can release several neurochemicals in response to the arrival of an action potential at its axon terminal, but we often speak of neurons as "serotonergic" or "dopaminergic" depending on the primary chemical that is released. Many neurochemicals can have either excitatory or inhibitory effects, depending on their interaction with receptors, while others have one effect or the other more consistently.

We can classify neurochemicals as small molecules, peptide neurochemicals, and gasotransmitters. The small molecule neurochemicals include acetylcholine, adenosine, dopamine, epinephrine, norepinephrine, serotonin, melatonin, histamine, and several amino acid neurochemicals, such as GABA and glutamate. Peptide neurochemicals are much larger chains of proteins and include the oxytocin mentioned earlier along with many others. The gasotransmitters, such as nitric oxide or NO, break all the rules we have presented to you so far. They defuse through membranes, often from postsynaptic to presynaptic cells, and interact with receptors located in the interior of cells instead of the outer membranes.

It is helpful to link specific neurochemicals with the systems and behaviors they influence, especially when we want to predict the main and side effects of therapeutic and recreational drugs. We have supplied a table to assist you with this process.

Acetylcholine is found in the neuromuscular junction, or the synapse between the nervous system and skeletal muscle fibers, as well as in the autonomic nervous system and the brain. As a result, it is central to movement, the control of glands and organs, alertness, and memory. One of the notable drugs that interacts with acetylcholine is nicotine, found in tobacco products. Nicotine is chemically similar enough to acetylcholine that it is recognized by receptors and can activate channels. Because of the importance of acetylcholine to the neuromuscular junction, this neurochemical is a major target for bioweapons, such as sarin gas. Interfering with acetylcholine action quickly suppresses respiration, leading to death.

Adenosine is a byproduct of the ATP energy molecule. It has a general inhibitory action on the brain, and participates in tracking sleep debt, or the amount of time we have been awake. Caffeine competes with molecules of adenosine at receptors, which is why caffeine can keep us going even when sleep debt is high, at least for a while.

Neurons releasing dopamine are numerous in the midbrain, especially in the substantia nigra, in the basal ganglia, and in the frontal lobe. As a result, we think of dopamine as being essential for voluntary movement, reward, and planning. Dopamine systems in the substantia nigra and basal ganglia degenerate in the movement disorder Parkinson's disease. The reward and planning functions of dopamine are distorted in cases of addiction. Most addictive drugs either directly or indirectly promote greater dopamine activity.

Epinephrine (adrenalin) is an important neurohormone, which is a chemical released by glands into the blood supply that has effects on the nervous system, but it plays only minor roles when released from cells in the brain. However, the related neurochemical norepinephrine (noradrenalin) has important effects on arousal in the brain. If you know how it feels to be vigilant, you are experiencing behavior associated

TABLE 2.1 Major neurochemicals

Neurochemical	Found In	Associated Behaviors
Acetylcholine	▶ Neuromuscular junction ▶ Autonomic nervous system ▶ Brain	▶ Movement ▶ Control of glands and organs ▶ Alertness ▶ Memory
Adenosine	▶ Brain	▶ Brain inhibition ▶ Sleep debt
Dopamine	▶ Substantia nigra ▶ Basal ganglia ▶ Frontal lobe	▶ Reward ▶ Planning ▶ Voluntary movement
Norepinephrine	▶ Locus coeruleus	▶ Arousal and vigilance ▶ Sleep/waking cycles
Serotonin	▶ Enteric nervous system ▶ Raphe nuclei	▶ Mood ▶ Appetite ▶ Sleep/waking cycles ▶ Dominance and aggression
Melatonin	▶ Pineal gland	▶ Sleep/waking cycles
Histamine	▶ Hypothalamus	▶ Appetite ▶ Wakefulness
GABA	▶ Brain	▶ General inhibition
Glutamate	▶ Brain	▶ General excitation
Glycine	▶ Hypothalamus ▶ Retina ▶ Spinal cord	▶ General inhibition ▶ Sleep
Substance P	▶ Spinal cord	▶ Pain
Endorphins	▶ Hypothalamus ▶ Pituitary gland	▶ Pain ▶ "Runner's high"
Insulin	▶ Pancreas	▶ Hunger and satiety
Cholecystokinin (CCK)	▶ Gut	▶ Satiety
Oxytocin and Vasopressin	▶ Hypothalamus	▶ Social cognition and behavior ▶ Anxiety and fear
Gasotransmitters	▶ Brain	▶ Signaling

with the release of norepinephrine. Norepinephrine is also critical to the management of sleep–waking cycles.

Serotonin plays important roles in many discussions related to behavioral neuroscience, as it is involved with mood, appetite, sleep, dominance, and aggression. About 95% of the serotonin in our bodies is outside the central nervous system and cannot cross the blood–brain barrier. The remaining 5% is released by fewer than 200,000 neurons in the brainstem that make up structures known as the raphe nuclei. Because of its role in mood, serotonin is the target of most antidepressant medications. Because of the related behaviors, however, we would expect any manipulation of serotonin to affect appetite, sleep, dominance, and aggression as well. For example, serotonin reuptake inhibitors like Prozac specifically suppress the rapid eye movement (REM) component of sleep in many patients. Antidepressants are also notorious for causing sexual dysfunction. Increasing serotonin levels in the circulation has the effect of reducing sensitivity of the genitalia.

Melatonin is released by the pineal gland in darkness and helps regulate our sleep–waking cycles. Many people attempt to use melatonin as a sleep aid, but it breaks down rapidly in the presence of light. Histamine, which we usually associate with allergic reactions and itching, participates in appetite and wakefulness. If you have ever taken an older antihistamine medication (the newer ones do not cross the blood–brain barrier), you know that drowsiness is a side effect.

At least eight amino acids, or protein building blocks, also serve as neurochemicals. Notable among this group are glutamate, gamma aminobutyric acid (GABA), and glycine. Glutamate is the most significant excitatory neurochemical in the brain. The food additive monosodium glutamate (MSG) is a combination of sodium and glutamate that causes adverse reactions in some people. However, dietary MSG cannot cross the blood–brain barrier, so these adverse effects do not involve the effects of MSG on the brain. Glutamate is especially important to processes of learning and memory.

GABA is the major inhibitory neurochemical in the brain. GABA interacts with several psychoactive drugs, including alcohol, benzodiazepines (e.g., Valium and other tranquilizers), and barbiturates. Each of these drugs enhances the inhibition produced by GABA, which is why we are warned about combining them. Glycine is found in the retina of the eye, the spinal cord, and in cells in the hypothalamus that regulate sleep.

There are more than 40 known neuropeptides. Substance P and our endorphins (short for "endogenous morphine") participate in the sensation of pain. Insulin and the gut hormone cholecystokinin (CCK) not only participate in the digestive process, but also act as neurochemicals involved with appetite and satiety. Oxytocin, mentioned previously, and vasopressin, also known as antidiuretic hormone, participate in bonding and parenting in addition to their many other duties.

Gasotransmitters include nitric oxide (NO), carbon monoxide (CO), and hydrogen sulfide (H_2S). NO is involved with learning and memory, anxiety, addiction, penile erection, and the maintenance of blood pressure. Because of its roles, NO is the common target for medications for erectile dysfunction. NO is particularly important to the communication between the thalamus and the cerebral cortex, placing it in a position to regulate the processing of sensory information.

Manipulating Neurochemicals

Before a drug can produce psychoactive effects, by definition it must be able to enter the brain by crossing the blood–brain barrier described earlier in the chapter. A substance that merely circulates in the blood supply without crossing the blood–brain barrier might have significant effects on other organs, but it will not produce changes in brain activity.

The method of administration is very important to our understanding of drug effects. The brain's response to a drug is correlated with its concentration in the blood, usually stated in terms of milligrams per kilogram of body weight. Larger bodies contain more blood, which requires the consideration of body size. This is why messages from the Department of Motor Vehicles about drinking and driving provide charts based on weight. Methods that access the blood supply directly, such as injection, produce stronger effects with smaller amounts of the drug. Mucous membranes and the lungs are relatively permeable to many types of drugs, allowing individuals to chew, snort, or inhale a drug. Other drugs can be absorbed through the skin, but this is rarely done on purpose. Swallowing a drug is the least efficient method of administration. Our ancestors evolved systems to prevent poisoning via ingestion. If the area postrema of the brainstem detects unwanted substances in the circulation, it initiates a vomiting reflex, which is why consumption of large amounts of alcohol often makes people vomit. Ingested drugs are also subject to breakdown by the digestive system, allowing relatively less active substance to enter the blood supply.

In addition to body size, individual differences to the administration of psychoactive substances can result from genetics and gender. People have genetic differences in various liver enzymes that often influence their response to some drugs, such as alcohol. Gender matters because females typically have higher body fat percentages than males, affecting the movement of substances out of the blood supply into surrounding tissues.

Recreational and therapeutic drugs can influence a neurochemical's performance by enhancing or reducing its activity. Agonists are substances that result in increased neurochemical activity, while antagonists reduce neurochemical activity. Please do not think that one is somehow better or safer than the other. Both can kill. For example, the venom of the black widow spider and organophosphates like sarin gas can both be fatal. These agonists boost the activity of acetylcholine, leading to fatigue and potentially respiratory arrest as muscle fibers become unable to respond to abnormally high input.

Drugs can act as agonists or antagonists in one or more of the steps of synaptic activity previously described in this chapter. Some can affect the synthesis and storage of a neurochemical. Others either block or enhance a neurochemical's release from axon terminals. Many interact with postsynaptic receptors by either activating or blocking them. Still others act by influencing enzymes that normally deactivate a neurochemical or by inhibiting the process of reuptake.

It is beyond the scope of this book to describe the effects of psychoactive drugs in detail, but in upcoming chapters, a number will appear in context.

Chapter Summary

This chapter is meant to provide a brief overview of the structure and function of the nervous system that will form a reference for upcoming chapters. We explored the division of the nervous system into central and peripheral components and surveyed the key structures in each. Next, we zoomed in to look at the neurons and glia that make up the larger structures and saw how they function to support information processing. Finally, we discussed the ways psychoactive drugs, both therapeutic and recreational, can interact with our natural biochemistry to produce their effects on brain functions.

Review Questions

1. Which of the following structures helps us detect sources of danger in the environment (LO 2.1)?
    a. The amygdala
    b. The hippocampus
    c. The basal ganglia
    d. The cerebellum
2. Which of the following describes advantages of myelin (LO 2.2)?
    a. Myelin reduces the need for large quantities of neurochemicals.
    b. Myelin speeds reuptake of released neurochemicals.
    c. Myelin speeds up the propagation of action potentials along an axon.
    d. Myelin reduces the amount of input needed for a cell to reach its firing threshold.
3. Which of the following neurochemicals is associated with sleep, mood, appetite, and dominance (LO 2.3)?
    a. Dopamine
    b. Serotonin
    c. Glutamate
    d. Endorphins

4. Which of the following is NOT a mechanism by which a drug can influence the action of a neurochemical (LO 2.4)?

    a. A drug can enhance production of a neurochemical.
    b. A drug can inhibit the release of a neurochemical.
    c. A drug can interact with postsynaptic receptors.
    d. A drug can change cognitive behavior without crossing the blood-brain barrier.

Thought Questions

1. Where do you think consciousness occurs in the brain? Why?
2. The toxin produced by the bacteria responsible for tetanus, for which you have probably been vaccinated, selectively damages the inhibitory motor neurons of the spinal cord. How does this produce the symptoms of tetanus?

Answer Key for Review Questions

1. a
2. c
3. b
4. d

References

Cannon, W. B. (1915). *Bodily changes in pain, hunger, fear and rage.* New York, NY: Appleton & Company.

Freberg, L. (2019). *Discovering behavioral neuroscience: An introduction to biological psychology* (4th ed.). Boston, MA: Cengage.

Glossary

Action potential	An electrical signal that travels the length of an axon.
Amygdala	A small structure located toward the front of the temporal lobe that assigns value to stimuli, notably threat.
Autonomic nervous system (ANS)	Division of the PNS that provides instruction and obtains feedback from organs and glands.

Axon	A branch extending from the cell body of a neuron that transmits signals to other cells.
Basal ganglia	A collection of forebrain structures involved with the selection of voluntary movements and reward.
Blood–brain barrier (BBB)	A collaboration between glia and blood vessels that prevents many toxins and other invaders from entering the brain tissue.
Brainstem	The lower part of the brain consisting of the hindbrain and midbrain.
Central nervous system (CNS)	The brain and spinal cord.
Cerebellum	Hindbrain structure that participates in balance, motor coordination, and higher cognitive processing.
Cerebral cortex	Thin layer of cells on the surface of the cerebral hemispheres responsible for highest levels of processing in the brain.
Cingulate cortex	An area of cortex near the midline of the brain and above the corpus callosum. The anterior cingulate cortex (ACC; forward two-thirds) participates in decision-making, empathy, and control of the ANS. The posterior cingulate cortex (PCC; back one-third) participates in memory and visual input.
Cranial nerves	Twelve pairs of nerves extending from the brain that are part of the PNS.
Default mode network (DMN)	A cortical network whose activity correlates with unfocused thought or mind-wandering.
Dendrite	A branch extending from the cell body of a neuron that provides space for incoming synapses.
Endocrine system	The system of glands that produce or release hormones into the blood.
Enteric nervous system	A part of the ANS that serves the gut.
Frontal lobe	Area of cortex toward the front of the brain responsible for movement, planning, and executive functions.
Glia	Support cells in the nervous system.

Hippocampus	A structure that participates in the management of stress and the processing of memory.
Hypothalamus	A complex collection of structures that manage homeostasis.
Insula	An area of cortex lying within the lateral sulcus that separates the temporal lobe from the frontal and parietal lobes.
Limbic system	A collection of subcortical structures that participate in a variety of functions, including memory and emotional processing.
Myelin	Insulation of axons provided by glia that speeds up signaling.
Neurochemical	One of over 40 types of chemical messengers in the nervous system.
Neuron	A cell in the nervous system that processes and communicates information.
Occipital lobe	Area of cortex at the back of the brain that processes visual input.
Parasympathetic nervous system	Division of the ANS associated with rest, repair, and digestion.
Parietal lobe	Area of cortex behind the frontal lobe that processes body senses and movement.
Peripheral nervous system (PNS)	All neurons outside the brain and spinal cord.
Somatic nervous system	Component of the PNS containing sensory and motor nerves.
Spinal cord	Division of the CNS extending from the medulla of the brainstem to the lower back.
Sympathetic nervous system	Division of the ANS associated with arousal.
Temporal lobe	Area of cortex to the side of the brain that processes auditory input and visual recognition of faces and objects.
Thalamus	Forebrain structure involved with sensation, learning, memory, and consciousness.
Ventricles	Fluid-filled spaces within the brain containing cerebrospinal fluid.

3 Behavioral Neuroscience for Psychotherapists and Neuropsychologists

LEARNING OBJECTIVES

After reading this chapter, you should be able to:

▶ 1. Differentiate between the diagnostic approaches for medical conditions and those used to identify psychological disorders.

▶ 2. Explain the challenges faced by practitioners who wish to use neuroscience methods to improve diagnosis.

▶ 3. Compare and contrast the biological treatments available for psychological disorders.

▶ 4. Differentiate among the types of professionals who provide psychotherapy relative to their exposure to neuroscience information.

▶ 5. Describe the neuroscience principles relevant to psychotherapy, including neurogenesis, memory reconsolidation, epigenetics, genetics, sleep, mirror neurons, and brain changes associated with psychotherapy.

What Can Neuroscience Tell the Therapist?

Psychiatrist Daniel Amen has made a lucrative career out of offering single photon emission computed tomography (SPECT) scans (see Chapter 1) to thousands of children and adults at his six Amen Clinics, for problems ranging from ADHD, anxiety, and depression to marital disorder, healthy aging, and obesity. He has become quite a celebrity, with multiple books on the *New York Times* bestseller lists and programs distributed by PBS. He is a favorite of TV talk shows and motivational speakers. He also offers a wide variety of nutritional supplements from his website.

DOI: 10.4324/9781003195214-3

FIGURE 3.1 Dr. Daniel Amen.
Source: https://en.wikipedia.org/wiki/Daniel_Amen#/media/File:Daniel_Amen.jpg

All of this has taken place with a surprising lack of systematic peer review of Amen's work (Farah & Gillihan, 2012). Amen's major premise is that brain imaging, and SPECT in particular, can be used to diagnose a variety of psychological disorders. The lack of research validating this approach is especially surprising, given the Amen Clinic's claims to have scanned over 50,000 individuals. It should be a simple matter to share the collected data with the scientific community for review, but this has not occurred. Further criticism centers around the cost to patients, in the vicinity of $3000–$4000 for an initial visit (not reimbursed by insurance companies due to the lack of scientific validation), and the ethical concerns raised by exposing patients to the radiation involved with a SPECT scan without established benefit.

We can dispute Dr. Amen's specific methods, but we might also ask why more practitioners are not attempting to incorporate neuroscience methods into the diagnosis and treatment of psychological disorders. Psychological disorders are clearly centered in the brain, and psychiatry is largely based on the manipulation of the brain's chemistry. Neuroscientists know quite a bit about the brain. Nonetheless, many practitioners do not yet see a central role for the neurosciences in the diagnosis and treatment of psychological disorders. What should that role look like?

This chapter assumes some basic knowledge of major types of psychological disorder, such as ADHD and autism spectrum disorder. If you need more background on these disorders, we recommend reviewing the diagnostic books cited in the next section or a good introductory psychology textbook.

Diagnosis and Diagnostic Categories

The diagnosis of psychological disorders deviates dramatically from the usual practices in medicine. Suppose you wake up with a sore throat. Your healthcare provider is likely to take your temperature and other vital signs and swab your throat. The results suggest you have strep throat, and you are put on a course of antibiotics to clear up the condition. While observation of your overall health might be informative, such observations are secondary to the objective evaluation of your vital signs and swab results. In stark contrast, the current practice in psychiatry and psychology is to diagnose conditions solely on the basis of clinically observed symptoms, using as references diagnostic systems like the American Psychiatric Association's **Diagnostic and Statistical Manual of Mental Disorders (DSM-5**, APA, 2013) or the World Health Organization's **International Classification of Diseases (ICD-11**, WHO, 2021). In the United States, educational evaluations designed to meet **IDEA (Individuals with Disabilities Education Act)** may or may not conform to the criteria in the DSM or ICD systems. Psychological conditions covered by IDEA include ADHD, autism spectrum disorder, and emotional disturbance (e.g., depression and anxiety). Using IDEA criteria, it is possible for a child who has been diagnosed by a psychologist or medical professional to be found ineligible for special education while an educational assessment by school personnel might apply a label to a child that is not supported by a psychologist or medical professional.

There are few established objective measures incorporated in these systems, and those that do appear are subject to corroboration by observation. For example, a diagnosis of intellectual disability might refer to standardized IQ test scores, but deficits in several aspects of daily functioning must also be observed before a diagnosis is made. At present, none of the diagnostic categories refer to brain imaging, measures of brain activity obtained through EEG, or the results of other objective neuroscience measures like those discussed in Chapter 1.

Changes in this basic diagnosis by observation approach come slowly and gradually. Only in the most recent edition of the DSM, DSM-5 (APA, 2013), has there been an effort to incorporate the wealth of current understanding of the genetic contributions to psychological disorders. In response to this new understanding, the DSM-5 reconfigured its approach to schizophrenia and bipolar disorder. In previous versions, based on observation alone, the two disorders held widely separate positions in the diagnostic systems, with bipolar disorder grouped along with major depressive or unipolar disorder in an overarching section of mood disorders. While it is true that the depressive phase often found in bipolar disorder was evaluated with the same observational criteria used to evaluate major depressive disorder, bipolar disorder has been shown to share a more similar genetic substrate with schizophrenia (Potash & Bienvenu, 2009; Cross-Disorder Group of the Psychiatric Genomics Consortium, 2013). These findings were acknowledged in the DSM-5's references to bipolar disorder as a "bridge" condition linking schizophrenia and major depressive disorder. Bipolar disorder moved out of a category of mood disorders shared with major depressive disorder into its own new category situated between discussions of schizophrenia and major depressive disorder.

The use of observation as a mainstay in the diagnosis of psychological disorders might account for some cases of misdiagnosis or variations in rates of diagnosis. Similar behaviors characterize several categories in the DSM, and the DSM goes to great lengths to help practitioners distinguish one category from other similar categories. For example, a patient with grandiose ideation (exaggerated self-importance) might be diagnosed with schizophrenia or bipolar disorder, and one who talks incessantly might be diagnosed with ADHD or bipolar disorder. Given the disparate chemical treatments of these disorders, plus the fact that the wrong medication might exacerbate a condition, it is unquestionably important to get a diagnosis right.

Diagnoses often hinge on the DSM's typical statement of severity—clinically significant impairment. One of the DSM-5 criteria (APA, 2013, p. 59) for the inattentive subtype of attention deficit disorder (ADHD) is as follows: "Often avoids, dislikes, or is reluctant to engage in tasks that require sustained mental effort (e.g., schoolwork or homework; for older adolescents and adults, preparing reports, completing forms, reviewing lengthy papers)." It is hard to imagine anyone cherishing the opportunity to complete more forms, so how does the clinician know where to draw the line? At what point does one's reluctance to fill out forms represent a clinically significant impairment that merits a diagnosis of ADHD? Finally, we are assuming that clinicians do not deviate from the diagnostic systems, which does not always seem to be the case. In a 2005 survey of pediatricians, only 26% said that they used DSM criteria when diagnosing ADHD (Wolraich et al., 2010).

A surprising gap occurs between the prevalence rates of ADHD reported in the academic literature (around 5% of school-aged children) and actual parent-reported diagnoses (around 11%; Song et al., 2019). Parent reports to the Centers for Disease Control and Prevention indicate that more than 16% of children have received the diagnosis in some areas of the United States. As shown in Figure 3.2, the rates of ADHD diagnosis show some odd geographical variations. We know of no hypothesis suggesting that living in the western United States is somehow protective against a diagnosis of ADHD while living in the southeast is a risk factor. Yes, ADHD is sensitive to socioeconomic variables and the southeast has high rates of poverty, but this factor alone cannot account for the observed patterns of prevalence.

It appears that considerable confusion regarding the accurate diagnosis of ADHD exists among clinicians and the public. Some argue that ADHD is under-diagnosed while others argue that it is over-diagnosed. It is difficult to assess changes in prevalence rates over time, as we do not know if increases are due to real changes in case numbers or greater awareness. A good starting point, however, would be for clinicians responsible for diagnosing psychological disorders to "go by the book."

Is it possible that neuroscience might be the solution to these types of discrepancies? The neuroscience literature has contributed an extensive catalogue of the structural and functional brain correlates for a wide variety of psychological disorders. From the reduced frontal lobe activity and enlarged ventricles associated with schizophrenia to the reduced hippocampal volume seen in posttraumatic stress disorder (PTSD) to the differences in cerebellum and amygdala volume in autism spectrum disorder (ASD), neuroscience provides a very clear picture of how the brains of people with diagnosed disorders look and act differently compared to those of control participants.

In addition, the treatment for psychological disorders is typically biological, whether a patient receives medication or experiences biological change due to psychotherapies such as cognitive behavioral therapy. If the goal of diagnosis is to plot the best path to treat, it is logical to assume that a symmetry between the methods used for diagnosis and treatment would be ideal. Improved diagnosis would contribute to a greater

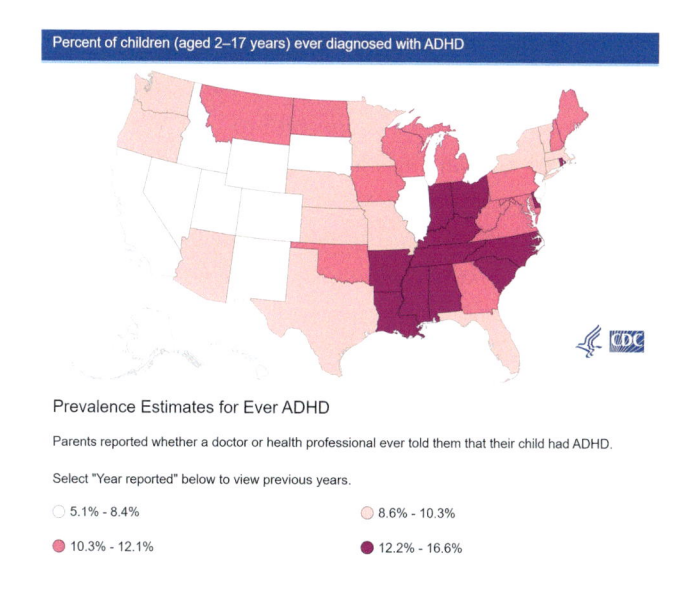

FIGURE 3.2 In spite of a consensus in the scientific literature that the prevalence rate of ADHD is approximately 5% of school-aged children, many more children are actually diagnosed. The geographical variations in diagnosis rates also speaks to an inconsistency in application of diagnostic criteria. The fact that about half of these children are likely to be medicated raises the stakes for diagnosing ADHD accurately.

Source: www.cdc.gov/ncbddd/adhd/data/diagnosis-treatment-data.html

understanding of the causes of psychological disorders as well as more effective treatments. For example, there might be very different causal factors leading to "classic" autism spectrum disorder than to cases of high functioning individuals who have been diagnosed under the much looser diagnostic criteria of the last 30 years. Many current approaches to psychopharmacology have emerged from accidental discoveries, including the use of stimulant drugs for ADHD, rather than from a strong understanding of the underlying differences in biological function that characterize a disorder. As a result, we see efforts in the scientific literature to "reverse engineer" the process by discovering why a particular medication might work. Instead, we could begin the process by understanding the underlying correlates of a disorder and then work to find solutions that resolve those correlates.

Objective methods like neuroimaging have the potential to resolve some of the validity issues that plague diagnosis by observation. Ideally, we could establish a set of metrics that characterized people with a specific disorder but no others. If we had a definitive test for ADHD, the geographic variations in prevalence rates seen in Figure 3.2 and the likelihood that ADHD is being diagnosed in inappropriately high numbers should be resolved. It is also likely that realignments, similar to the improved view of the relationships between schizophrenia, bipolar disorder, and major depressive disorder resulting from the incorporation of genetic analyses, would occur to the benefit of patients and their families.

So why don't we see greater incorporation of neuroscience assessments in the diagnosis of psychological disorders? Martha Farah and Seth Gillihan (2012) call this "the puzzle of neuroimaging and psychiatric diagnosis" (p. 31). We can safely assume that the brain is the seat of both normal and abnormal function, making information about the brain essential to the understanding of psychological disorders. We now have sophisticated methods that let us view the structure and function of the brain in detail. At the same time, except for a handful of highly criticized practitioners like Dr. Amen, brain imaging and other biological measures have no current role in the diagnosis of psychological disorders outside of their use in assessing tumors and other medical conditions that might result in symptoms.

Practitioners are not rejecting neuroscience as a tool for diagnosis because they generally believe the science is not mature enough. Treatments based on neuroscience, such as deep brain stimulation or transcranial magnetic or electrical stimulation, have moved easily from the experimental research laboratory into practice. This suggests no overall objections to neuroscience applications. So why is diagnosis different?

In Chapter 1, we covered some of the general challenges facing applications of neuroscience, and those certainly hold when we discuss applying neuroscience technologies, such as brain imaging, to individual diagnoses. The group-to-individual (G2i) problem is at the forefront—neuroimaging data collected from groups that differ by the presence or absence of a psychological condition (e.g., have ADHD or do not have ADHD) can be very tricky to apply to a given individual. Imaging data from separate groups are still very likely to show considerable overlaps, making it challenging to know where any individual is situated. Even when looking at data from just one group (e.g., all participants with ADHD), we see quite a bit of variability. Part of this latter problem is due to the natural variability we see in people with a particular psychological disorder. Individuals diagnosed with autism spectrum disorder have certain characteristics in common, to be sure, but they can range from having severe intellectual disabilities to average intellectual function to superior intellectual function.

Complicating matters further is the fact that neuroimaging research is task-dependent (Farah & Gillihan, 2012). Before we can apply Dr. Amen's SPECT methods to others, for example, we would need to know exactly what his participants were doing during their scans. Were they resting with closed eyes? Trying to solve problems? Switching from one stimulus to another? Task instructions would need to be standardized before neuroimaging data would begin to be useful in diagnosis. In addition, Farah and Gillihan (2012) point out that clinicians are rarely deciding about whether a person has a single disorder. Instead, they are usually trying to decide which of several disorders is the most likely in a particular case. Few research studies provide comparisons of brain structure and function across multiple types of disorders that could be used to guide this decision. Finally, many individuals have comorbid conditions, or multiple diagnosable conditions. What would those brains look like? The added variability would be difficult to interpret.

We do not want to leave you with the idea that using neuroscience, and brain imaging in particular, to inform better diagnostic practices is a lost cause. Instead, ongoing improvements in the methods themselves and in particular, the statistical methods available for the interpretation of brain imaging, continue to hold promise. At the same time, the diagnostic categories of the DSM and ICD are likely to be challenged by this progress, much as they have been by improved methods in genetics. Time will tell whether clinicians will embrace new categories based on neuroscience data even if they conflict with the way psychological disorders have been viewed in the past.

Beginning in 2009, the U.S. National Institute of Mental Health (NIMH) began to develop a research framework for mental health known as the Research Domain Criteria Initiative (RDoC). According to the NIMH, RDOC is not meant to replace current diagnostic systems but rather to gain more understanding of mental health and illness. As shown in Figure 3.3, the RDoC framework focuses on six domains of human functioning: negative valence, positive valence, cognitive systems, systems for social processes, arousal/regulatory systems, and sensorimotor systems. These domains can be investigated using a variety of methods with the goal of improving both diagnosis and treatment of disorders.

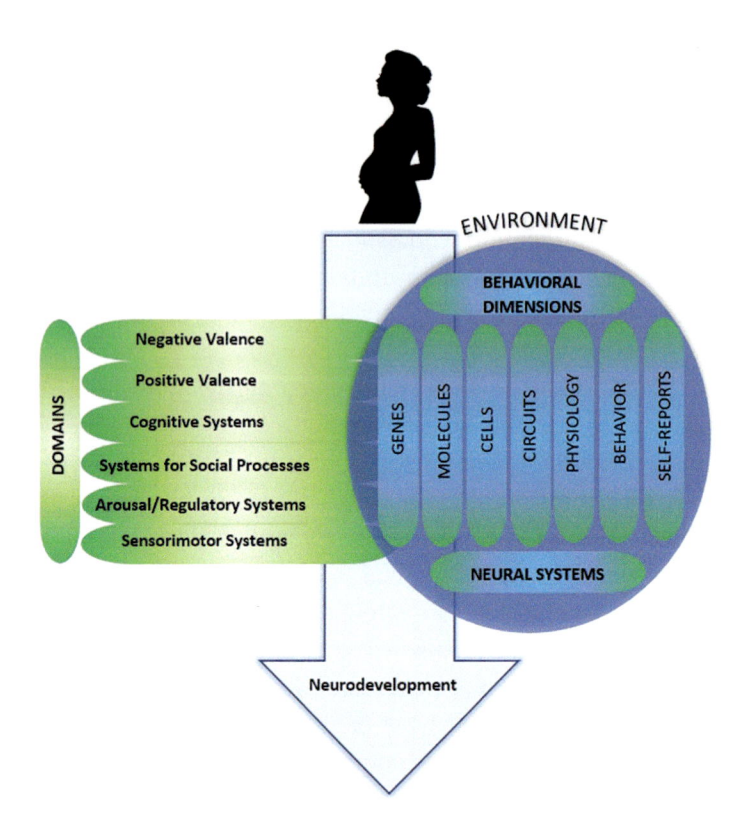

FIGURE 3.3 The RDoC matrix, developed by NIMH, features rows that represent specific dimensions of function (e.g., cognitive systems) while the columns represent different observations (e.g., genetics or self-report). The long-term goals of RDoC include the improvement of diagnosis and the development of new treatments for mental disorders.

Source: Adapted from www.nimh.nih.gov/research/research-funded-by-nimh/rdoc/about-rdoc

Neuroscience in Treatment

As mentioned previously, the practitioner community has been relatively open to innovations in treatment based on neuroscience research despite its caution about using neuroscience in diagnosis.

Medication

Neuroscience research, of course, has played a lengthy historical role in the treatment of psychological disorders in the form of therapeutic **medications**. It is difficult to pinpoint the exact beginning of humanity's attempts to "fix" mental problems with substances, but the use of psychiatric drugs jumped forward significantly in the aftermath of World

War II. The first major class of psychiatric drugs were the neuroleptics used to treat schizophrenia. These experiments were stimulated by observations of calm and sedation following the use of antihistamines. Today's antihistamines are configured to avoid the side effect of drowsiness. In the 1940s, Australian psychiatrist John Cade performed several unsophisticated experiments involving the injection of urine from psychiatric patients into guinea pigs. Urine from patients with mania was especially lethal to the animals. He further noted that lithium carbonate, used historically to treat gout, reduced the toxicity of the human urine and made the guinea pigs calm. After experimenting on himself to determine a safe dose (the effective dose of lithium is very close to the lethal dose), Cade began treating patients with bipolar disorder. In 1937, psychiatrist Charles Bradley experimented with the use of an amphetamine, Benzedrine sulfate, to reduce headaches in institutionalized children. We do not know how the children's headaches turned out, but the amphetamine boosted the children's school performance, social interactions, and emotional responses (Strohl, 2011). Bradley's experiments formed the basis for the later development beginning in the 1960s of amphetamine-based medications like Ritalin for the treatment of ADHD.

These early experiments might seem quite wild, particularly the experimentation with institutionalized children, but our ethical standards for research are relatively new. Attitudes toward drugs in general were considerably looser at this time, with amphetamines prescribed widely during the 1960s as "diet aids." Few government regulations existed to ensure that a marketed drug was safe and effective. Today's medications face many years and costs of many millions of dollars in development, and most do not make it all the way through the approval process.

Although most psychiatric medications involve serious side effects, they have also provided the opportunity for many to live more normal lives as opposed to being institutionalized and subject to physical restraint.

Psychosurgery

Psychosurgery, or surgery on the brain intended to treat psychological problems, has an unsavory history, primarily due to the relatively indiscriminate use of imprecise frontal lobotomy surgeries. Despite having no training in surgery, William Freeman (1895–1972) performed as many as 4000 lobotomies for $25 each, even on one child aged four. While we shudder today over Freeman's actions, he served as president of the American Board of Psychiatry and Neurology and was a member of the American Psychiatric Association in good standing. He nominated his mentor, Antonio Egas Moniz, for a Nobel Prize, which was awarded to Moniz in 1949.

You might be under the impression that psychosurgery is a thing of the past, but it is not. Several procedures are currently used in cases of obsessive–compulsive disorder (OCD) and depression, including the anterior cingulotomy (damaging the anterior cingulate cortex), the anterior capsulotomy (disconnecting the orbitofrontal cortex and the thalamus), the subcaudate tractotomy (separating the limbic system from the lower frontal lobes), and the limbic leucotomy, which combines the subcaudate tractotomy and anterior cingulotomy. The outcome studies report widely varying success rates for these procedures. Amygdalotomy, or damage to the amygdala, is still used on occasion for the treatment of aggression and has been described as a "valid surgical treatment option for carefully selected patients" (Mpakopoulou et al., 2008, p. E6).

Deep Brain Stimulation (DBS)

Deep brain stimulation (DBS) requires the surgical implantation of electrodes in the brain that are then connected to a battery-powered stimulator inserted under the skin near the collarbone, much like a cardiac pacemaker (see Figure 3.4). One of the great advantages of DBS is that the patient cannot feel the stimulation. This allows researchers to observe symptoms under both active stimulation and sham (fake) stimulation to evaluate the efficacy of the treatment.

Encouraged by the results of DBS in treating the movement disorder Parkinson's disease, researchers have attempted to use DBS to treat chronic pain, major depressive disorder, and obsessive–compulsive disorder (OCD). Obviously, the patients submitting to this procedure have been resistant to all other possible treatments. Nonetheless, results for patients with OCD have been good enough to gain FDA approval for the procedure. Outcomes for chronic pain and depression are mixed, although some patients show dramatic improvements.

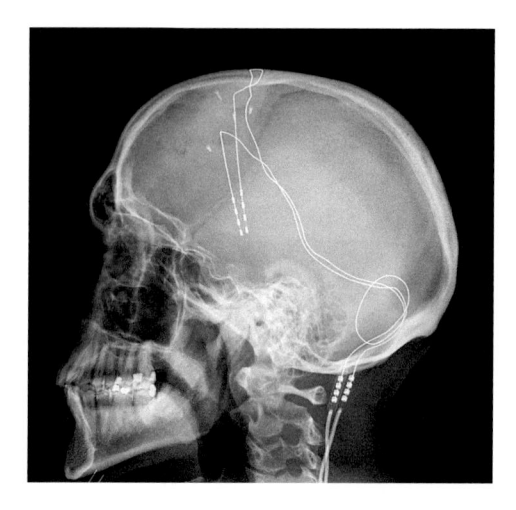

FIGURE 3.4 Placement of DBS electrodes in a 42-year-old male with OCD.
Source: By Jmarchn – Own work, CC BY-SA 3.0, https://commons.wikimedia.org/w/index.php?curid=99264875

Electroconvulsive Therapy (ECT)

Electroconvulsive therapy (ECT) shares a negative reputation with psychosurgery, probably due to depictions in entertainment such as "One Flew Over the Cuckoo's Nest." However, as many as one million patients per year are treated with ECT.

The procedure originated in the 1930s, when effective treatment options for schizophrenia and other serious disorders were nonexistent. Today, ECT is used most frequently to treat major depressive disorder, bipolar disorder, schizophrenia, and catatonia (the maintenance of odd postures for long periods of time). ECT is administered under anesthesia approximately two to three times per week until the patient's symptoms improve. Electricity is applied to the patient's head to produce a seizure lasting less than one minute. Possible side effects include memory loss, which is usually mild but can be severe.

As we mentioned in Chapter 1, the efficacy of ECT is not well established (Read et al., 2020), although most insurance companies in the U.S. offer coverage. The methodologies used in most ECT efficacy studies do not control for placebo effects, such as the patients' and physicians' expectations of improvement. Those that do attempt to control for placebo effects feature very small samples and result in very small effect sizes or in some cases, more "improvement" following sham ECT than following the real thing. In this case, the statistical measure of effect size would tell you how big an effect on symptoms results from having ECT treatments relative to sham ECT treatments. Given the questionable efficacy of ECT, it is not surprising that the mechanism of action of ECT has been elusive. Nobody can say for certain why ECT is supposed to be beneficial.

Vagus Nerve Stimulation (VNS)

In Chapter 2, we introduced the 12 pairs of cranial nerves as part of the peripheral nervous system. These nerves perform similar functions as the 31 pairs of spinal nerves but exit the brain itself rather than the spinal cord. The tenth pair is known as the vagus nerve, from the Latin root meaning "vagabond." Like its namesake, the vagus nerve does wander far from the head and neck area served by the other cranial nerves to contact the digestive tract and other major organs.

Vagus nerve stimulation (VNS) was originally developed to treat epilepsy, but during this treatment, patients also experienced positive mood. Subsequently, VNS was used to treat depression. Treatment is administered through an electrode implanted under the skin of the neck placed in proximity to the vagus nerve. A pulse generator is inserted near the collarbone, much like the DBS procedure discussed earlier. Although this procedure has FDA approval in the U.S., it is used infrequently, and its efficacy remains controversial.

Transcranial Electrical Stimulation (tES)

Unlike the previously mentioned methods for applying electrical stimulation to the brain and nervous system, **transcranial electrical stimulation (tES)** is non-invasive. Instead, small amounts of electrical stimulation are applied through electrodes on the head. The safety and cost of tES relative to other electrical stimulation treatments make it an attractive option. Transcranial ES also differs from other electrical stimulation procedure in that it uses very small amounts of electricity that bring underlying neurons closer to threshold (see Chapter 2) without directly producing action potentials. The effects of tES depend on the placement of electrodes, but the overall outcome of stimulation is a change in the connectivity of networks, such as the default mode network (DMN; Reed & Cohen Kadosh, 2018). Differences in network connectivity are associated with several psychological and neurological disorders.

Although still largely experimental, tES has been used to treat depression, schizophrenia, and brain injuries. Research about the potential for tES to enhance cognitive abilities in healthy individuals and people with Alzheimer's disease has produced mixed results.

Repeated Transcranial Magnetic Stimulation (rTMS)

We mentioned in Chapter 1 that one of the advantages of magnetoencephalography (MEG) is that the skull bones are transparent to magnetism while they block much of the electrical activity we try to record with EEG. Well, that transparency goes both ways, which means that any magnetism applied to the head will go right through the skull bones to influence the brain.

In **repeated transcranial magnetic stimulation (rTMS)**, pulses of magnetism are applied to a specific part of the head through an electromagnetic coil at a rate of about one pulse per second (Figure 3.5). The magnetism used is strong, like that used in magnetic

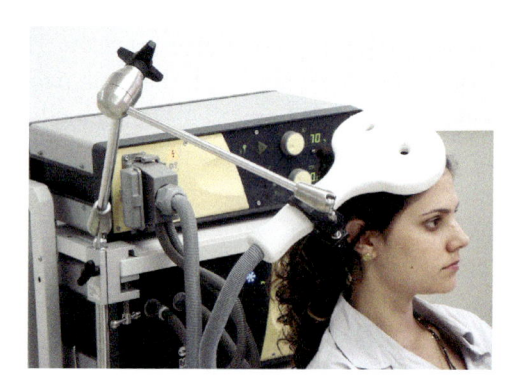

FIGURE 3.5 Repeated transcranial magnetic stimulation is applied through magnetic coils placed on the head.

Source: https://en.wikipedia.org/wiki/Transcranial_magnetic_stimulation#/media/File:Neuro-ms.png

resonance imaging (MRI). No anesthesia is required as the magnetism is not something we can detect. The magnetism impacts the activity of the brain to about a depth of two inches. Depending on the exact method employed, rTMS can either produce greater activation or inhibition in the areas of cortex exposed to the magnetic fields.

The FDA approved the use of rTMS for treatment-resistant depression in 2008. Efficacy trials appear to be positive so far. It is possible to control for placebo effects in rTMS efficacy studies by using a sham procedure that participants cannot distinguish from real rTMS, making quality efficacy studies possible. Few side effects have been reported, but because of the recent development of this procedure, we still know little about any long-term effects.

Magnetic Seizure Therapy (MST)

Magnetic seizure therapy (MST) is similar to ECT in its ability to produce a seizure and its need for anesthesia, but instead of using electricity, it uses magnetism like rTMS. The difference between MST and rTMS results from the higher frequency of pulses in MST. MST is still being evaluated as a treatment for major depressive disorder and bipolar disorder. The hope is that it would provide a safer alternative to ECT. Given the controversies regarding the efficacy of ECT, however, it is unclear whether a safer alternative that shares the same goal—seizures—is likely to be an improvement.

Eye Movement Desensitization and Reprocessing (EMDR)

During the 1980s, Francine Shapiro developed **eye movement desensitization and reprocessing (EMDR)** after noticing that she moved her own eyes rapidly when thinking about something unpleasant. The EMDR therapy involves asking the client to recall troubling memories while following the therapist's moving finger to produce side-to-side movement of the eyes. This might sound strange to you, but EMDR has gained its place as an "evidence-based" treatment in the views of professional organizations like the American Psychological Association. It is widely used for treating posttraumatic stress disorder (PTSD). However, outcome studies for EMDR are plagued by many of the same issues we have seen in studies of other methods, including small sample sizes and researcher bias.

Why would something like this be effective? De Voogd and her colleagues (2018) conducted fMRI (see Chapter 1) while participants either underwent EMDR or were engaged in a memory task (had this digit been presented earlier). Both tasks reduced activity in the amygdala, which we described in Chapter 2 as a structure that participates in the detection of threat. The amygdala also receives visual input directly from the thalamus. The results of this study suggest that there is nothing special about moving one's eyes. Any task that requires cognitive control has the potential to reduce amygdala activity and emotional responses. These findings are consistent with other research studies indicating that working memory tasks reduce the emotionality of other memories.

Advocates of EMDR often emphasize the unlearning and relearning of "appropriate emotions" as the basis of the efficacy of EMDR (EMDR Institute, 2021). Unfortunately for this perspective, the fMRI data collected by de Voogd et al. provide no support for any unlearning. Any emotional changes observed following EMDR are more likely to occur because of competition between cognitive control and emotional processing for limited brain resources. This is like rubbing your elbow to reduce pain after you bump it into the furniture.

Virtual Reality Therapy (VRT)

Virtual reality therapy (VRT) is not a directly biological approach to treatment, but it is based on the provision of more realistic sensory experiences than those obtained by simply imagining or remembering an event (Figure 3.6). VRT makes use of immersive technology to provide exposure therapy for phobias and PTSD, pain reduction for burn patients, and relief for patients experiencing phantom limb. Virtual rehabilitation can be very helpful in cases of traumatic brain injury (TBI) and stroke. Instead of engaging in less than an hour per day of rehabilitation with a therapist, a patient with TBI can participate in virtual therapy for as many hours as their pain and cognitive statuses allow. Because the VRT programs are entertaining, patient motivation is improved.

Initial efficacy studies of VRT appear promising, but the cost of the equipment continues to be a barrier to more widespread use. Few clinicians have the training needed to use VRT effectively.

Neuroscience from the Clinician's Perspective

Individuals who are licensed to provide therapy for psychological disorders come from several academic traditions and levels of training. On the more biological side are the psychiatrists, whose attainment of the MD degree ensures that their understanding of the physical side of psychological conditions is good and provides them with the option of using biological treatments, such as medication. The neuropsychologist is a clinical psychologist specializing in neuroscience. These professionals are often employed in rehabilitation settings alongside medical professionals. The neurologist might assess the extent of damage and develop a medical treatment plan for a patient with a traumatic brain injury (TBI) while the neuropsychologist assesses the cognitive outcomes of the injury and develops a rehabilitation plan. Clinical psychologists holding either the PhD or PsyD degree are trained in several psychotherapy methods, but usually experience less

FIGURE 3.6 "Virtual Iraq" provides realistic exposure therapy for veterans who have been diagnosed with posttraumatic stress disorder (PTSD).
Source: https://commons.wikimedia.org/wiki/File:Virtual_Iraq.jpg

training in neuroscience than the two previous groups. An exception would be prescribing psychologists, with either PhD or PsyD degrees, who practice in one of five states (Iowa, Idaho, Illinoi, New Mexico, and Louisiana) that allow psychologists with additional training to prescribe medication. This approach was pioneered by the military as a way of dealing with a shortage of psychiatrists. The states with prescribing psychologists also face a shortage of psychiatrists, although this practice is likely to spread regardless of the availability of psychiatrists in a state. Counselors with either doctoral or masters level degrees probably experience the least amount of exposure to neuroscience during their training.

Because of these wide variations in training, we would also expect wide variations in the endorsement of neuroscience by practitioners. Faculty charged with training many types of therapists often recognize the need to incorporate more neuroscience into their curricula, but find navigating the neuroscience literature challenging (Cabaniss, 2018). A National Neuroscience Curriculum Initiative (NNCI) was developed to improve the teaching of neuroscience in psychiatry programs (Arbuckle et al., 2017). Classroom learning does not guarantee application, however. Psychiatric residents are not being taught or encouraged to incorporate neuroscience into their practice (Cooper et al., 2019). However, the pressure to "go modern" by endorsing neuroscience in therapy continues to build.

Several themes emerge from discussions about *how* neuroscience should be used in therapy. In many cases, therapists take comfort in neuroscience results that reinforce the benefits of their existing methods. The following neuroscience concepts are especially relevant to the understanding of psychological disorders and their treatments.

Neuroplasticity

A basic finding in neuroscience is that the brain continues to be modifiable, or "plastic," throughout the lifespan, although plasticity in childhood exceeds plasticity later in life. **Neuroplasticity** refers to the brain's ability to grow and reorganize in response to experience and injury. Without neuroplasticity, we probably would not see any benefits of rehabilitation in cases of traumatic brain injury and stroke. Neuroplasticity encourages the therapist to think that the experience of therapy can assist the client or patient to literally "rewire" their brain networks in a more positive way.

Neurogenesis

Neurogenesis literally means the birth of new neurons. The vast majority of neurogenesis occurs prenatally during the embryonic stage but continues in a more limited fashion throughout the lifespan. In adult mammals, neurogenesis takes place in the hippocampus, the subventricular zone (SVZ; located in the lateral ventricles), and in the amygdala. The new cells in the SVZ migrate forward to the olfactory bulbs.

What makes neurogenesis exciting for therapists is the knowledge that rates of neurogenesis can change. For example, exercise changes the rate of neurogenesis in the SVZ of older mice (Blackmore et al., 2012), while depression might slow neurogenesis down (Schoenfeld & Cameron, 2015). Treatment with antidepressant medications might increase proliferation of new cells (Malberg et al., 2000). The connection between early life stress and early life enrichment on later neurogenesis helps explain the profound impact of child maltreatment and other early experiences on later risk for physical and mental health problems. Ongoing research is attempting to explain how various types of disorder and their treatments might be related to rates of neurogenesis.

Memory Reconsolidation

Contemporary cognitive neuroscience shows that every time you retrieve a memory, you have the potential to change it. To retain the memory after retrieval, it must go through a **memory reconsolidation** process that is similar to the processing required to establish the memory in the first place. This concept might be frightening to you as a student, as the implication is that answering a test question is enough to change your memory for the relevant information. Memories that are older and more established are less likely to be subject to reconsolidation, however.

During the reconsolidation process, a memory can be updated or changed. This can have either positive or negative implications. Elizabeth Loftus has demonstrated how this updating can produce distorted memories (e.g., Loftus & Palmer, 1974). One week after viewing a video, a question that mentions a car passing a barn prompted 20% of participants to report having seen a barn in the video, compared with fewer than 5% of participants who did not hear the "barn" question. There was, of course, no barn at all in the original stimulus. In response to the wording of the question, participants proceeded to update their memory of the video to be consistent with the new information. This obviously has serious implications for eyewitness testimony, as discussed in Chapter 4.

On the positive side, memory reconsolidation provides opportunities to update a traumatic memory with a version of events that downplays guilt and self-blame by revisiting the memory during the therapy process. Future research might help us evaluate the use of pharmacological agents, such as propranolol, in conjunction with memory reconsolidation. Propranolol administered immediately after exposure to images, stories, and word lists or before reconsolidation for these items reduces subsequent recall of negative items (Lonergan et al., 2013). Propranolol does not "erase" a memory. Propranolol reduced classically conditioned startle responses in human participants, but they were still able to tell the experimenters that shock usually followed the signal (Cogan et al., 2019). In other words, learned facts were not impacted by propranolol, but the emotional significance of the facts was diminished. The ethics of reducing the emotional impact of a person's memory for traumatic events, however, remains hotly debated. Would we become more tolerant of traumatic events if we could take medication that would reduce our emotional responses to the memories of those events?

Epigenetics

Perhaps you know a pair of identical twins. These individuals share the same DNA, yet as they mature, they become less "identical." In some twin pairs, one will develop cancer while the other remains healthy. One might be diagnosed with schizophrenia and the other with bipolar disorder. How can we account for these differences?

First, few human traits are exclusively genetic. But even among those traits that are heavily influenced by genetics, we still see variance in identical twins. One explanation is the process of **epigenetics**. "Epi" means "above" or "around," like the "epicenter" of an earthquake, so epigenetics refers to changes in the performance of genes that do not involve changes in the DNA itself. There are plenty of ways to change your DNA, such as radiation exposure, but epigenetics does not involve those types of changes. Instead, you can think of epigenetics as the relative ease with which genetic material can be expressed (leading to the construction of a protein) as a function of certain environmental influences (Figure 3.7). Nearly everything we do, from exercising to smoking to eating our veggies, has the potential to "tag" our DNA to make it more or less likely that a segment will be expressed.

FIGURE 3.7 A dramatic example of epigenetics was demonstrated by Randy Jirtle and his colleagues (Dolinoy et al., 2007). Cloned mice embryos were implanted into different mouse mothers, whose diet did or did not contain bisphenol A (BPA). BPA in the mother's diet changed the expression of the agouti gene during development, resulting in the offsprings' yellow fur and obesity.
Source: Karla Freberg.

Michael Meaney and his colleagues demonstrated that maternal care could influence the later resilience to stress in offspring through epigenetic mechanisms (Weaver et al., 2004). Nurturant rodent moms "lick and groom" their pups frequently, the rodent version of a hug from your mom. Pups that were nurtured generously by their moms not only showed changes in the expression of genes related to glucocorticoid receptors compared to pups who received less nurture, but they also showed lower responses to stress. Glucocorticoids, including cortisol, are released during stressful situations and the amount of glucocorticoid activity is monitored by the hippocampus. This phenomenon might help us explain why prenatal and childhood stress and maltreatment seem to have such wide-ranging and long-term effects on adult behavior.

The good news, of course, is that epigenetic changes are potentially reversible. Currently, however, we do not have ways to reverse the impact of child maltreatment or other traumatic experiences. Certain drugs appear to be promising in animal studies, but much work needs to be done before they are approved for use with humans. What we can do in the meantime, however, is work to improve public health measures and educational initiatives that prevent child maltreatment. We can recognize that a military recruit with a history of child maltreatment might be more likely to develop combat-related PTSD than a soldier without this history.

Genetics

Our genetic heritage from our parents is a giant roll of the dice. A single human being can produce eggs or sperm with over 8 million variations. Add this to the variation from the other parent, and it becomes surprising that we resemble our siblings at all.

Many human traits, including those related to psychological disorders, are somewhat heritable. Heritability refers to the amount of variance in a population that is explained by genetics. If we measured all the people living on your street, there would be variance in their height, with some being relatively tall or short and many in the middle. Heritability would tell us how much of that variance is due to genetics. We never use heritability to refer to individuals, like saying "50% of my height is due to genetics." Instead, heritability always refers to populations. Most human traits have a heritability between 30% and 60%. What else besides genetics can influence a trait? In addition to our genes, our traits are shaped by shared experience (our whole family had Thanksgiving at Grandma's every year) and unshared experiences (I played the piano, but my brother played the drums). As we make these evaluations, it is also important to remember that our genes and experiences interact in complex ways, as we saw in our discussion of epigenetics.

Although it is possible to manipulate epigenetics, we are stuck with our DNA. So how can genetics be useful to therapists? At the present, genetics can help us gain a better understanding of the risk factors and causality for specific conditions. Genetics can also be used to predict which individuals will benefit from a specific treatment, especially in the case of medications. Finally, many individuals with psychological disorders experience a sense of guilt (it's my fault) and isolation (I'm the only one with this problem). Helping individuals understand that at least some of the risk for a disorder was out of their control might be soothing.

Sleep

It is somewhat entertaining to listen in on discussions between therapists and sleep researchers as they discuss psychological disorders at conferences. The therapists typically argue that sleep disturbances are the outcome of psychological disorders, while the sleep researchers argue that sleep disturbances result in psychological disorders. As is the case with correlations in general, perhaps both are correct, or some third factor influences both sleep and a person's risk for psychological disorder.

What we do know is that sleep disturbances are common in people with psychological disorders. Chronic sleep problems affect between 50% and 80% of psychiatric patients, compared to about 10–18% of adults without any psychological disorders. In particular, sleep problems are associated with anxiety, depression, bipolar disorder, and ADHD. Individuals with poorly managed major depressive disorder enter rapid-eye-movement (REM) sleep too soon after going to sleep and spend far too much time in that component (as opposed to spending time in non-REM sleep). Those who continue to experience sleep disruption are less likely to respond to treatment and more likely to relapse later.

Good sleep hygiene is not a magic cure, but it can certainly help overall health, which in turn will help a person cope with a psychological disorder more effectively. Changes in lifestyle factors like reducing intake of caffeine and alcohol, having a regular sleep schedule and routine, increasing exercise during the day, and avoiding pre-sleep screen time (blue light is particularly damaging to the sleep hormone melatonin) can lead to improved sleep.

Mirror Neurons

While studying the brain correlates of movement in monkeys, a group of Italian neuroscientists noticed something odd—the same neurons fired when the monkey reached for a piece of food or when the experimenter reached for a piece of food (di Pellegrino et al., 1992). They concluded that these "**mirror neurons**" helped animals understand the actions and intentions of others (Rizzolatti & Sinigaglia, 2016). We typically do not do the single cell recordings that characterized these initial studies with monkeys in human participants, but rather use fMRI or EEG instead. Consequently, we speak of mirror "systems" in humans rather than single mirror neurons. These systems appear to support the same functions as the mirror neurons observed in monkeys, including the understanding of the actions, emotions, and intentions of others (Ortigue et al., 2010).

Like the discoveries of the lateralization of functions to one hemisphere or the other (right brain–left brain), the discovery of mirror neurons led to some unfortunate hyperbole, especially in the media. Overnight, mirror neurons were touted as the answer to questions of self-awareness, language, empathy, theory of mind, and a whole host of additional phenomena. While mirror systems are certainly important and intriguing, much additional research is needed before strong conclusions can be made. For example, early suggestions that the social deficits seen in autism spectrum disorder represented a "broken mirror" have not been supported (Yates & Hobson, 2020).

Psychotherapy Changes the Brain

In Chapter 1, we emphasized the reciprocal nature of the relationship between the brain and behavior. Not only can brain changes influence behavior, but behavioral changes can influence the brain as well. This simple principle suggests that psychotherapy should have the ability to produce real, measurable changes in brain structure and function.

A case in point is a comparison of the results of medication and cognitive behavioral therapy (CBT) for obsessive–compulsive disorder (OCD; Baxter et al., 1992). CBT for treating OCD usually takes the form of training the client to anticipate the need to engage in a compulsive behavior. The client then carries out a competing behavior, followed by self-congratulation. For example, a person with compulsive hand-washing behavior might leave the house when the urge to wash arises and pull some weeds in the garden. Abnormal activity in the basal ganglia (see Chapter 2), which participate in the selection of voluntary behaviors, often accompanies compulsive behavior in people with OCD. Similar "normalization" of this abnormal activity is seen following either medication or CBT.

Chapter Summary

It is highly likely that significant advances in the diagnosis and treatment of psychological disorders will emerge from continuing breakthroughs in the neurosciences. These advances will be gradual, as implementation within the therapeutic community will require changes in education and training. If you are considering a career as a therapist, we would advise you to continue your study of the neurosciences, as these are likely to play a greater role in your future career.

At the same time, we reviewed challenging obstacles still to be solved in the application of the neurosciences to therapy for psychological disorders. Use of evidence-based practice guides us as we attempt to incorporate new understanding and methods.

Review Questions

1. Which of the following is true of the diagnosis of psychological disorders (LO 3.1)?
    a. Blood tests are often helpful for diagnosing psychological disorders.
    b. Brain scans can be used to diagnose psychological disorders.
    c. Observed behaviors are used to diagnose psychological disorders.
    d. If a patient reacts to a drug, like a person with ADHD reacting to Ritalin or Adderall, that means they probably have that condition.
2. Which of the following might be a barrier to the use of neuroscience methods in the diagnosis of psychological disorders (LO 3.2)?
    a. Practitioners believe that neuroscience is not mature enough as a field to be helpful.
    b. The group-to-individual (G2i) problem makes it difficult to apply research to a given individual.
    c. Practitioners are usually deciding which single disorder a person might have, not multiple disorders.
    d. Neuroscience data are not very task specific.
3. Which of the following is true of contemporary psychosurgery (LO 3.3)?
    a. Deep brain stimulation is used to treat Parkinson's disease and in rare cases, depression.
    b. Psychosurgery is no longer performed.
    c. Frontal lobotomies are still conducted to treat cases of severe aggression.
    d. Results of psychosurgery for OCD are uniformly positive.

4. Which of the following individuals are licensed to prescribe medication (LO 3.4)?
    a. Psychiatrists only.
    b. All licensed psychotherapists.
    c. Psychiatrists and doctoral level psychologists.
    d. Psychiatrists and some specially trained doctoral level psychologists.
5. Which of the following is an example of the effects of epigenetics (LO 3.5)?
    a. A person experiences DNA damage due to radiation.
    b. A person's diet changes their risk for a disease.
    c. Identical twins share the same DNA.
    d. Twins have similar risks for some types of psychological disorders.

Thought Questions

1. Which of the technologies explored in Chapter 1 seems to have the most potential for helping practitioners to make better diagnoses of psychological disorders? Why?
2. How do you think today's psychotherapists should be trained to prepare for careers that might involve more neuroscience?

Answer Key for Review Questions

1. c
2. b
3. a
4. d
5. b

References

American Psychiatric Association (APA, 2013). *Diagnostic and statistical manual of mental disorders* (5th ed.). Washington, D.C.: Author.

Arbuckle, M. R., Travis, M. J., & Ross, D. A. (2017). Integrating a neuroscience perspective into clinical psychiatry today. *JAMA Psychiatry, 74*(4), 313–314. https://doi.org/10.1001/jamapsychiatry.2016.3849

Baxter, L. R., Schwartz, J. M., Bergman, K. S., Szuba, M. P., Guze, B. H., Mazziotta, J. C., Alazraki, A., Selin, C. E., Ferng, H-K., Munford, P., & Phelps, M. E. (1992). Caudate glucose metabolic rate changes with both drug and behavior therapy for obsessive-compulsive disorder. *Archives of General Psychiatry, 49*(9), 681–689. https://doi.org/10.1001/archpsyc.1992.01820090009002

Blackmore, D. G., Vukovic, J., Waters, M. J., & Bartlett, P. F. (2012) GH mediates exercise-dependent activation of SVZ neural precursor cells in aged mice. *PLoS ONE, 7*(11), e49912. https://doi.org/10.1371/journal.pone.0049912

Cabaniss, D. L. (2018). Teaching neuroscience: A primer for psychotherapists. *Frontiers in Behavioral Neuroscience*. https://doi.org/10.3389/fnbeh.2018.00307

Cogan, E. S., Shapses, M. A., Robinson, T. E., & Tronson, N. C. (2019). Disrupting reconsolidation: Memory erasure or blunting of emotional/motivational value? *Neuropsychopharmacology, 44*, 399–407. https://doi-org/10.1038/s41386-018-0082-0

Cooper, J. J., Korb, A. S., & Akil, M. (2019). Bringing neuroscience to the bedside. *Focus, 17*(1), 2–7. https://doi.org/10.1176/appi.focus.20180033

Cross-Disorder Group of the Psychiatric Genomics Consortium. (2013). Genetic relationship between five psychiatric disorders estimated from genome-wide SNPs. *Nature Genetics, 45*(9), 984–994. https://doi.org/10.1038/ng.2711

de Voogd, L. D., Kanen, J. W., Neville, D. A., Roelofs, K., Fernández, G., & Hermans, E. J. (2018). Eye-movement intervention enhances extinction via amygdala deactivation. *Journal of Neuroscience, 38*(40), 8694–8706. https://doi.org/10.1523/JNEUROSCI.0703-18.2018.

di Pellegrino, G., Fadiga, L., Fogassi, L., Gallese, V., & Rizzolatti, G. (1992). Understanding motor events: A neurophysiological study. *Experimental Brain Research, 91*(1), 176–180. https://doi.org/10.1007/bf00230027

Dolinoy, D. C., Huang, D., & Jirtle, J. L. (2007). Maternal nutrient supplementation counteracts bisphenol A-induced DNA hypomethylation in early development. *Proceedings of the National Academy of Sciences of the United States of America, 104*(32), 13056–13061. https://doi.org/10.1073/pnas.0703739104

EMDR Institute. (2019). *What is EMDR?* www.emdr.com/what-is-emdr/

Farah, M. J., & Gillihan, S. J. (2012). The puzzle of neuroimaging and psychiatric diagnosis: Technology and nosology in an evolving discipline. *AJOB Neuroscience, 3*(4), 31—41. https://doi.org/10.1080/21507740.2012.713072

Loftus, E. F., & Palmer, J. C. (1974). Reconstruction of automobile destruction: An example of the interaction between language and memory. *Journal of Verbal Learning & Verbal Behavior, 13*, 585–589. https://doi.org/10.1016/S0022-5371(74)80011-3

Lonergan, M. H., Olivera-Figueroa, L. A., Pitman, R. K., & Brunet, A. (2013). Propranolol's effects on the consolidation and reconsolidation of long-term emotional memory in healthy participants: A meta-analysis. *Journal of Psychiatry & Neuroscience, 38*(4), 222–231. https://doi.org/10.1503/jpn.120111

Malberg, J. E., Eisch, A. J., Nestler, E. J., & Duman, R. S. (2000). Chronic antidepressant treatment increases neurogenesis in adult rat hippocampus. *Journal of Neuroscience, 20*(24), 9104–9110. https://doi.org/10.1523/JNEUROSCI.20-24-09104.2000

Mpakopoulou, M., Gatos, H., Brotis, A., Paterakis, K. N., & Fountas, K. N. (2008). Stereotactic amygdalotomy in the management of severe aggressive behavioral disorders. *Neurosurgical Focus, 25*(1), E6. https://doi.org/10.3171/FOC/2008/25/7/E6

Ortigue, S., Sinigaglia, C., Rizzolatti, G., & Grafton, S. T. (2010). Understanding actions of others: The electrodynamics of the left and right hemispheres. A high-density EEG neuroimaging study. *PLoS ONE, 5*(8), e12160. https://doi.org/:10.1371/journal.pone.0012160

Potash, J., & Bienvenu, O. (2009) Shared genetics of bipolar disorder and schizophrenia. *Nature Reviews Neurology, 5*, 299–300. https://doi.org/10.1038/nrneurol.2009.71

Read, J., Kirsch, I., & McGrath, L. (2020). Electroconvulsive therapy for depression: A review of the quality of ECT vs sham ECT trials and meta-analyses. *Ethical Human Psychology and Psychiatry.* https://doi.org/10.1891/EHPP-D-19-00014

Reed, T., & Cohen Kadosh, R. (2018). Transcranial electrical stimulation (tES) mechanisms and its effects on cortical excitability and connectivity. *Journal of Inherited Metabolic Disease, 1*(6), 1123–1130. https://doi.org/10.1007/s10545-018-0181-4

Rizzolatti, G., & Sinigaglia, C. (2016). The mirror mechanism: A basic principle of brain function. *Nature Reviews Neuroscience, 17*(12), 757–765. https://doi-org/10.1038/nrn.2016.135

Schoenfeld, T. J., & Cameron, H. A. (2015). Adult neurogenesis and mental illness. *Neuropsychopharmacology, 40*(1), 113–128. https://doi.org/10.1038/npp.2014.230

Song, M., Dieckmann, N. F., & Nigg, J. T. (2019). Addressing discrepancies between ADHD prevalence and case identification estimates among US children utilizing NSCH 2007–2012. *Journal of Attention Disorders, 23*(14), 1691–1702. https://doi.org/10.1177/1087054718799930

Strohl, M. P. (2011). Bradley's Benzedrine studies on children with behavioral disorders. *The Yale Journal of Biology and Medicine, 84*(1), 27–33.

Weaver, I. C., Cervoni, N., Champagne, F. A., D'Alessio, A. C., Sharma, S., Seckl, J. R., Dymov, S., Szyf, M., & Meaney, M. J. (2004). Epigenetic programming by maternal behavior. *Nature Neuroscience, 7*(8), 847–854. https://doi.org/10.1038/nn1276

Wolraich, M. L., Bard, D. E., Stein, M. T., Rushton, J. L., & O'Connor, K. G. (2010). Pediatricians' attitudes and practices on ADHD before and after the development of ADHD pediatric practice guidelines. *Journal of Attention Disorders, 13*(6), 563–572. https://doi.org/10.1177/1087054709344194

World Health Organization (WHO). (2021). *International classification of diseases for mortality and morbidity statistics* (11th Revision). https://icd.who.int/browse11/l-m/en

Yates, L., & Hobson, H. (2020). Continuing to look in the mirror: A review of neuroscientific evidence for the broken mirror hypothesis, EP-M model and STORM model of autism spectrum conditions. *Autism.* https://doi.org/10.1177/1362361320936945

Glossary

Deep brain stimulation	A treatment including the surgical implantation of stimulating electrodes in the brain.
***Diagnostic and Statistical Manual of Mental Disorders* (DSM-5)**	A book describing diagnostic criteria for a wide range of psychological disorders.
Electroconvulsive therapy (ECT)	The use of electricity to stimulate a seizure to treat psychological disorders.
Epigenetics	Changes in gene expression resulting from external influences, leaving the underlying DNA unchanged.

Eye movement desensitization and reprocessing (EMDR)	A therapy method involving moving the eyes rapidly while recalling troubling memories.
Individuals with Disabilities Education Act (IDEA)	U.S. legislation providing guidance for the diagnosis and accommodation of disabilities affecting schoolchildren, including psychological and emotional disturbances.
***International Classification of Diseases* (ICD-11)**	A diagnostic system developed by the World Health Organization (WHO).
Magnetic seizure therapy (MST)	A method of producing a seizure similar to ECT but using magnetism instead of electricity.
Medication	The use of a wide variety of substances to treat medical or psychological conditions.
Memory reconsolidation	The process of reinforcing a weakened memory.
Mirror neurons	Neurons that respond to the perception of a particular movement without regard to the agent, or individual doing the movement. In humans, we usually refer to mirror systems.
Neurogenesis	The birth of new neurons.
Neuroplasticity	The brain's ability to be modified in response to experience or injury.
Psychosurgery	The use of surgical techniques to correct the symptoms of a psychological disorder.
Repeated transcranial magnetic stimulation (rTMS)	The application of magnetism to the brain through coils positioned on the head.
Transcranial electrical stimulation (tES)	An experimental treatment in which electricity is applied through surface electrodes on the head.
Vagus nerve stimulation (VNS)	Stimulation of the vagus nerve to treat depression.
Virtual reality therapy (VRT)	The use of virtual reality technologies to treat a variety of physical and psychological conditions.

4 Forensic Neuroscience

LEARNING OBJECTIVES

After reading this chapter, you should be able to:

▶ 1. Define forensic psychology and describe the neuroscience information that has been used in courtrooms.

▶ 2. Discuss the interactions between nature and nurture in the context of criminal behavior.

▶ 3. Evaluate neuroscience correlates of aggression.

▶ 4. Debate the use of neuroprediction.

▶ 5. Examine the evidence for a neuroscience of lie detection.

▶ 6. Recommend strategies for the use of neuroscience in courts of law.

▶ 7. Identify future directions for research in forensic neuroscience.

Shrunken Brains and the Insanity Defense

John Hinckley, a 25-year-old with known behavioral problems, opened fire on March 30, 1981, shooting President Ronald Reagan, Press Secretary James Brady, a Secret Service agent, and a police officer. His case went to trial the following year. Based on clinical evidence of schizophrenia, Hinckley's attorneys presented an insanity defense. The attorneys, however, did not stop there. They asked the court to review the results of a computerized tomography (CT) scan showing that Hinckley's brain was "shrunken" or atrophied. Although there are multiple reasons a person's brain might atrophy, Hinckley's legal team argued that the atrophy seen in his scan was common among people with schizophrenia. The jury found Hinckley not guilty by reason of insanity. He was

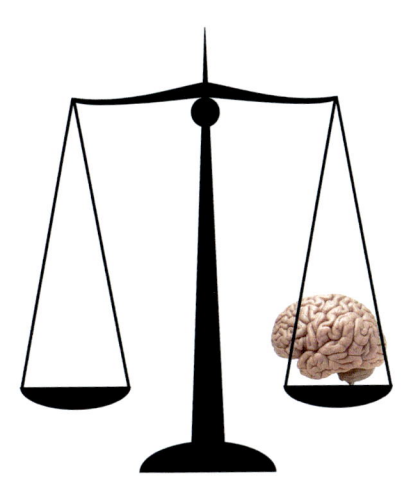

FIGURE 4.1 Neuroscience is being used more frequently to help decide legal outcomes.

committed for treatment at St. Elizabeth's hospital in Washington, D.C., from which he was released in 2016. Hinckley's verdict caused so much widespread dismay that several states outlawed the use of an insanity defense and federal laws for its use became more restrictive.

The insanity defense dates to the 1843 trial of Daniel M'Naghton, in which the defendant was acquitted by reason of insanity for shooting Edward Drummond, whom he mistook for his target, British Prime Minister Robert Peel. The resulting M'Naghton rules state that a person who is not guilty by reason of insanity must be so impacted that the nature and quality of the criminal act cannot be understood, or if it is understood, it is not recognized as wrong.

As we noted in Chapter 3, mental illness is traditionally diagnosed based on observable behavioral symptoms, such as the presence of hallucinations and delusions in schizophrenia. These, in turn, are evaluated by psychiatrists and clinical psychologists, and are therefore somewhat subjective. In some cases, defendants have faked the symptoms of psychological disorder in efforts to obtain the less restrictive not guilty by reason of insanity verdict or to reduce the severity of sentencing. Mental health professionals do not always agree on their diagnoses, potentially leading to battles between competing expert witnesses. Would the introduction of neuroscience data provide a more objective assessment tool?

Legal questions of intent, knowledge, responsibility, and punishment are among the most profound faced by contemporary societies. Neuroscience provides some, but not all answers sought by legal professionals in deciding issues of honesty, cognitive abilities, and level of responsibility. Although neuroscience is yet to become a staple in the courtroom, its rapid evolution suggests that it will influence legal judgments more frequently in the future. Imagine yourself as a juror in the Hinckley case. How would you evaluate the neuroscience testimony that was presented? What else would you need to know to come to any reasonable conclusions? How well prepared are legal professionals, judges, and jury members to respond appropriately to neuroscience evidence?

Introduction to Forensic Neuroscience

"**Forensic psychology** is a subfield of psychology in which psychological science or professional practice is applied to the law to help resolve legal, contractual, or administrative matters" (Neal et al., 2019, p. 139). As of 2017, 7% of licensed clinical psychologists listed a specialization in forensic psychology and 8% are board certified in forensic psychology (Lin et al., 2017). Forensic psychologists are joined in the courtroom by forensic psychiatrists and other mental health professionals. Forensic professionals use a wide array of interviews and structured instruments to provide insight into decisions of responsibility and dangerousness.

Increasingly, forensic professionals are looking to neuroscience for guidance about the prevention, prediction, causes, and treatment of criminal behavior, especially physical violence. **Forensic neuroscience** is the application of neuroscience principles to the understanding and management of criminal behavior. This application is closely related to neurolaw, or the interdisciplinary study of neuroscience implications for law and legal practice (Meynen, 2018) and to neuroethics. For example, using brain imaging technologies for lie detection raises significant privacy concerns.

In applying neuroscience to forensic practice, a mindset of skeptical humility is essential. Weisberg et al. (2008) warned of the "seductive allure" of neuroscience. The public tends to view neuroscience very positively as the source of many explanations for human behavior. Neuroscience novices are more likely to rate poor explanations of behavior positively when irrelevant neuroscience information is included (see Chapter 1). In contrast, neuroscience experts rate such explanations more negatively, due to the irrelevant inclusion of neuroscience concepts. Attorneys and judges must be aware of the risks of overstating the contributions of neuroscience to legal questions, and must be able to communicate these limitations to jurors.

Assessment

Forensic psychologists and psychiatrists are asked to provide many different types of assessments, illuminating future risk of criminal activity, whether a person is truly in pain or malingering, the cognitive capabilities and intelligence of defendants, and the presence of psychological disorders.

A wide variety of **psychological assessments** are used in the courtroom. Forensic psychologists and psychiatrists are frequently called on to provide expert testimony, and they use hundreds of different assessment tools. Interviews cover topics such as psychiatric history, personal history, prior trauma, medical history, family history, and substance use. Standardized tests of cognitive ability and psychological disorders are common. Interviews and standardized instruments can lose validity when the defendant is deliberately deceptive. In addition, some forensic psychologists and psychiatrists continue to use weakly supported assessments, such as the Rorschach Inkblot, and legal challenges to even the least scientifically supported of these assessments are rare (Neal et al., 2019). In an ideal world, the neurosciences could provide more objective means of assessing a defendant's ability to stand trial, responsibility for criminal activity, and likelihood of performing future criminal acts. However, the neurosciences are far from a "magic bullet" for meeting these goals.

As shown in Figure 4.2, neuroscience has been increasingly introduced to courts of law to support more lenient punishment due to reduced moral responsibility for an action. This evidence might include medical histories of head injury or brain damage, neuropsychological testing, and brain scans. As many as 10–12% of homicide cases and 25% of death penalty cases in recent years have featured these types of neuroscience evidence (Greely & Farahany, 2019). However, neuroscience evidence is introduced in other types of felonies as well. This practice is becoming so common that in many appeals, counsel has been found to be inadequate when relevant neuroscience data were not introduced during the initial trial.

Neuroscience is beginning to shed light on issues that are otherwise troublesome in the courtroom, such as distinguishing between states of mind (*mens rea*) associated with

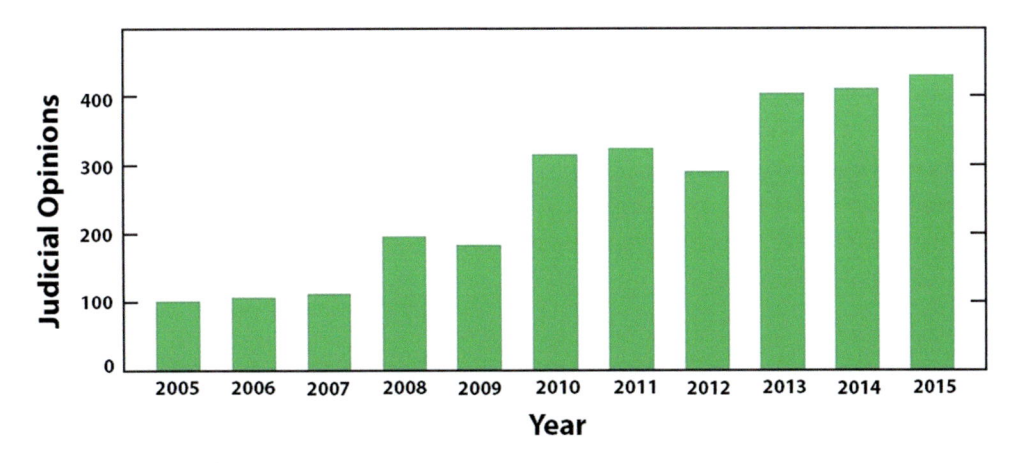

FIGURE 4.2 The number of judicial opinions including neuroscience data continues to grow, even for felonies other than homicide.

Source: Adapted from Greely & Farahany, 2019.

a criminal act that have consequences for sentencing. One of the important distinctions in these deliberations is the difference between knowledge and recklessness. Imagine that you transported a suitcase across the border that turned out to contain drugs. Did you know the suitcase contained drugs (knowledge)? Did you suspect the suitcase might contain drugs without knowing for certain (recklessness)? A jury will be called on to consider your state of mind when assessing your guilt and sentencing, yet this can be a very difficult distinction to make. Iris Vilares and her colleagues (2017) were able to use machine learning to evaluate brain images, reliably distinguishing between knowledge and reckless mental states.

Legal scholars are also aware, in large part due to the efforts of Elizabeth Loftus, of the malleability of memory. It is astonishingly easy to manipulate people to have significant confidence in a false memory. Many studies have demonstrated that similar patterns of brain activity accompany both remembering a real event and imagining the event, making real memories difficult to distinguish from imagined events. Can neuroscience help make the distinction between different types of memories? Tiffany Chow and her colleagues (2018) asked participants to wear a camera as they went about daily activities. They demonstrated very distinctive patterns of brain activity when viewing an image from their own lives as opposed to that of another participant's life. In an interesting twist, however, the researchers previewed some of the photos the day prior to testing. Could brain activity patterns be used to distinguish between people's own experiences (firsthand) and images they had previewed in the lab (secondhand)? The researchers claimed that the answer was "yes." As we learn more about the patterns of activity associated with variables such as first- and secondhand knowledge, neuroscience will have more to say regarding a person's testimony about remembered events.

Legal scholars remain unconvinced that neuroscience will provide insight into some of their more profound questions. Do we punish because perpetrators deserve it or because we are keeping society safe? What is free will? Why did the defendant act this way? Neuroscience assessments after the fact are not yet at a point where they can tell us what a defendant was thinking or feeling at the time of a crime. While neuroscience used properly can be a valuable tool for assessment, it remains one of several appropriate methods. As summarized by legal scholar Stephen Morse of the University of Pennsylvania, if there is a discrepancy between neuroscience and behavior, the courts will focus on the behavior.

Nature, Nurture, and Criminal Behavior

In 2005, 13-year-old Roberto Holguin murdered 87-year-old Gerald O'Malley by hitting him over the head with a skateboard. Holguin carefully padlocked O'Malley's mobile home to conceal the crime and then took O'Malley's car for a joyride. He later told law enforcement personnel that he knew what he had done was wrong, but he did it anyway. Expert testimony suggested that Holguin had structural and functional brain abnormalities and reduced intellectual ability. His family situation had been chaotic and potentially abusive. At sentencing, the judge needed to choose between a treatment-oriented option and incarceration in a juvenile facility. How a judge or jury views the intricate interplay between one's biology and experience is likely to push a decision like this in one way or the other. In Holguin's case, the judge decided on incarceration, from which he was released at age 25, the maximum amount of time he could be held in California. What choice would you have made?

As in all behavioral domains, it is essential to avoid either–or thinking when considering the contributions of biology (nature) and the environment (nurture) to criminal behavior. Historically, this pendulum has swung to extremes on several occasions. In the 19th century, Italian criminologist Cesare Lombroso attempted to outline the genetic and biological features of criminals, including a description of the outward physical characteristics he associated with criminal behavior. The association of these and similar efforts with eugenics, along with the rising dominance of Freudian approaches, pushed the "nature" explanation of criminal behavior into the background for most of the 20th century. Sociological explanations for criminal behavior, such as child maltreatment and low socioeconomic status, dominated the discussion. However, purely environmental reasoning also fails to capture reality. Not everyone experiencing poverty or child maltreatment responds by engaging in criminal behavior, and many criminals emerge from caring middle to upper income families.

Instead of engaging in either–or reasoning, it is essential to view nature and nurture as interacting in complex ways to produce the final behavioral product. In gene x environment interactions, we see that possessing a particular genotype does not, in itself, predict behavior, except under certain circumstances. For example, the MAOA gene produces a protein that is involved with clearing the synapse of important neurochemicals, including dopamine (see Chapter 2). This gene has unfortunately been referred to in popular culture as "the Warrior Gene." Although MAOA alleles are associated with individual differences in aggressiveness in animals, similar associations in humans do not occur reliably. Approximately 30% to 60% of individuals possess the low activity MAOA allele associated with higher levels of aggression, yet fewer than .01% of adults in the U.S. are arrested for violent crime. Clearly, many people with this allele do not behave violently. Instead, Avshalom Caspi and his colleagues (2002) reported that an interaction between having the low activity allele of MAOA and also being maltreated in childhood is predictive of youth violence. Youth with the high activity allele do not have a high risk of violence regardless of whether they were maltreated. This explains at least in part why some abused youth remain "resilient," or unlikely to engage in violence. Youth with the low activity allele who are nurtured prosocially also show reduced risk of violence. It is only the youth with both the low activity allele and the experience of child maltreatment that show a higher risk of being violent offenders.

In addition to gene x environment interactions, our improved understanding of epigenetics also reinforces the need to avoid either–or thinking about biological and environmental influences. Epigenetics refers to changes in gene expression, not the DNA of the genes themselves, that result from environmental influences. As we observed in Chapter 3, Robert Jirtle and his colleagues (Dolinoy et al., 2007) demonstrated that feeding a pregnant mouse food that contained the common plastic additive BPA resulted in the expression of the agouti gene at a point in the offsprings' development when it normally would remain silent. The resulting offspring were obese and sported yellow fur instead of the normal brown color. This effect could be prevented by adding folic acid as well as BPA to the mother's diet. The folic acid prevented the inappropriate activation of genes due to the presence of BPA. We now understand that epigenetic effects result from not only diet, but also behavioral components like stress, drinking alcohol, smoking tobacco, and exercising throughout the lifespan. This helps us understand why identical twins, who share the same underlying DNA, can have such different outcomes later in life. Even though our primary mission in this book is to explore applications of the "nature" side of the equation, phenomena like epigenetics require us to investigate nature within a framework of interactions with environmental influences.

The advent of a greater understanding of genetics and new neuroscience technologies in the last decades of the 20th century led to a renewed interest in the biological correlates of criminal behavior, largely influenced by the work of Adrian Raine. In his 1993 *The Psychopathology of Crime: Criminal Behavior as a Clinical Disorder*, Raine explored the influences of genetics, evolution, neurochemistry, brain imaging, and neurophysiology on criminal behavior, as well as the effects of head injury, pregnancy, birth complications, diet, cognition, and familial and non-familial influences. As technologies continue to improve in the 21st century, neuroscience provides increasing insights to forensic professionals.

The Neuroscience of Aggression

Criminal behavior can take many forms, but violent aggression remains one of the key plagues of modern human societies. **Aggression** is defined as the act of causing deliberate harm to another. We typically focus on physical harm, but aggression can also include social, reputational, and emotional harm, such as gossip, exclusion, and cyberbullying. In addition to the obvious psychological and physical costs of violent crime, many billions are lost in the form of direct costs to the victims, public money required for law enforcement, and the cost of incarceration. Understanding the correlates of violent aggression can direct policies and preventive efforts in positive ways.

Like most human behaviors, aggression has deep evolutionary roots. Our minds were shaped in the cauldron of the hunter–gatherer experience, which characterized human life up until the relatively recent development of agriculture only 10,000 years ago. Philosophers, including Hobbes, Locke, and Rousseau, debated the propensity of our early ancestors for violence and came to different conclusions. For Hobbes and Locke, human nature was inherently violent and in need of social control, while Rousseau believed in the benign, "noble" savage. We see these philosophical debates emerge again in several psychological perspectives, such as the rather pessimistic views of human nature held by Sigmund Freud and the more optimistic approaches of the humanistic psychology espoused by Abraham Maslow and Carl Rogers.

Reactive Versus Proactive Aggression

One answer to this philosophical dilemma might be found in viewing aggression in multiple ways rather than as a single entity (Wrangham, 2017). Aggression can be divided into proactive or premeditated aggression and reactive or impulsive aggression. Each type is correlated with different patterns of activity in the nervous system. If you own a cat, you know that different sets of aggressive behaviors are initiated when your cat is hunting a mouse or bird (proactive aggression) than when it is defending its territory against another feline interloper (reactive aggression). **Reactive aggression** does not engage specific targets—any individual in the immediate environment might be on the receiving end of the violent response. In contrast, **proactive aggression** is planned carefully with a specific target in mind. Reactive aggression is perceived as an aversive experience, whereas proactive aggression engages reward pathways. Consider the billions of dollars and many hours of time modern humans spend on hunting and fishing when food could easily be obtained at the local market. Rational minds regularly struggle against romanticized views of another type of proactive aggression, namely warfare. Activated reward pathways can lead to notions of wartime honor and glory while neglecting war's true horror. The Hobbes and Locke view is supported by the remarkably high rate of proactive aggression among humans compared to other primates, while Rousseau's position is supported by our species' relatively lower rate of reactive aggression.

The perception of offenders as engaged in impulsive or premeditated violence often influences the assignment of blame. Many people are less inclined to assign blame in impulsive violence due to its more reflexive, less cognitive nature. Because of the carefully laid plans featured in premeditated violence, these cases are more likely to be viewed as the conscious responsibility of the perpetrator.

Genetics, Culture, and Aggression

Aggression has likely been conserved across the course of evolution due to its ability to serve as an adaptation. Within-species aggression occurs in species from fruit flies to humans, and provides advantages in the form of acquiring territory, food, mates, and dominance. For predator species like our own, the ability to engage in premeditated aggression would provide advantages in war and hunting. As a result, it is relatively easy to breed strains of animals for higher aggressiveness, including fruit flies (Diereck & Greenspan, 2006), mice (Lagerspetz & Lagerspetz, 1971), and of course, the legendary fighting bulls of Spain (Figure 4.3).

Once again, though, we must caution you against thinking that genetics act independently of environment to produce aggressive behavior. An interesting case in point is the comparison of the Waorani and Yanomamö of the Amazon basin. These groups are almost constantly at war with their neighbors, resulting in the deaths of 30–54% of the adult males in combat (Chagnon, 1988; Beckerman et al., 2009). In both groups, the most aggressive males are likely to be at the front lines, placing them in the greatest danger of death. However, the two groups differ in the survival and reproductive success of their most aggressive males. The most aggressive Yanomamö males father the most children, whereas the least aggressive Waorani males have the greatest reproductive success. To the extent that aggressiveness is heritable, we would assume that the offspring of these two groups would then differ in their own aggressiveness.

How can we account for this discrepancy? A simple social norm of "standing down" between raids, characteristic of Yanomamö culture but not Waorani culture, seems to make all the difference. During these time outs, aggressive Yanomamö can heal and well, reproduce. Waorani warriors, in contrast, do not enjoy the luxury of a time out between raids. As a result, the aggressive Waorani, who are most at risk in combat, are less likely to survive and reproduce.

Cultural variations are also found in rates of homicide throughout the world. Homicide rates vary dramatically, from Singapore's 0.2 per 100,000 residents to South Africa's

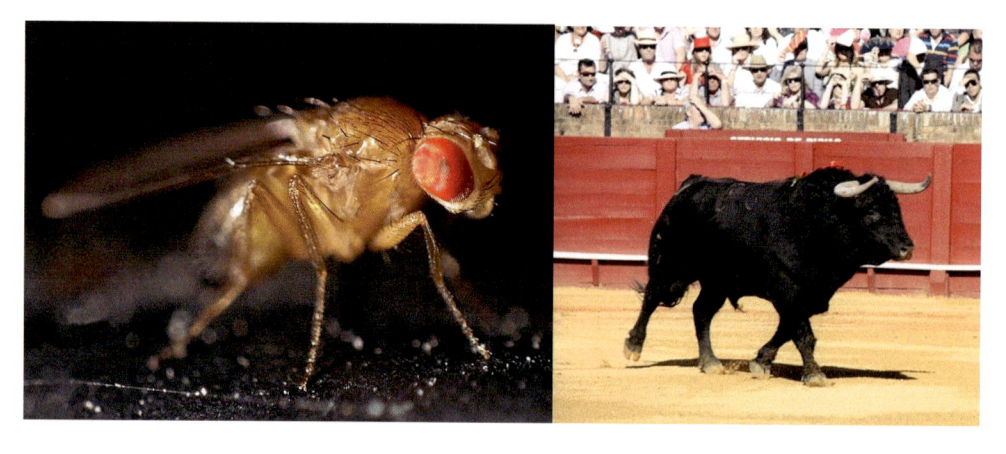

FIGURE 4.3 It is a simple matter to selectively breed for aggression, indicating that aggression is influenced by genetics.

Sources: https://commons.wikimedia.org/wiki/File:Drosophila_melanogaster.jpg; https://en.wikipedia.org/wiki/Spanish_Fighting_Bull#/media/File:El_Pilar_Bull_by_Alexander_Fiske-Harrison,_Seville_Feria_09.jpg

59.9 per 100,000. The United States has an overall rate of 5.1 homicides per 100,000 people, but this differs from city to city. Detroit, MI has a homicide rate of 40.74 per 100,000 while Pembroke Pines, FL has a homicide rate of only 0.6 per 100,000. Motivation for homicide differs substantially as well. Nations differ in the number of homicides occurring during a robbery as opposed to homicides perpetrated by intimate partners, family members, and others who are well known by the victim.

Brain Structure and Aggression

What do we know about the structural correlates of aggressive behavior? In the 19th century, John Hughlings Jackson proposed that the brain acts as a hierarchy, with "higher" parts of the brain controlling "lower," more primitive parts. While we view this model as overly simplistic today, Hughlings Jackson's approach is particularly relevant to our understanding of reactive or impulsive aggression. When researchers remove the cerebral cortex of an animal, the animal maintains a steady state of rage. While it's unsettling to believe that beneath our otherwise civilized demeaner is a raging beast, that's probably not too far-fetched. Aggression is often viewed as a failure in inhibitory control, and inhibitory control of lower structures is one of the main functions of the cerebral cortex.

At the "lower" levels of the impulsive aggressive response are networks that respond to threat. In particular, our ability to assess potential threat involves the amygdala, located toward the front of each temporal lobe (see Chapter 2). The amygdala receives sensory input from the thalamus. If the amygdala determines something is a threat, such as the sight of an angry face, it sets a series of processes into motion that result in further evaluation and action. An important part of the "further evaluation" is analysis by the frontal lobes, which can assess the threat message within the context of a situation. An angry expression on the face of an actor in a play will evoke different responses than an angry expression on the face of somebody you bump into in a dark alley. When both the amygdala and frontal lobes agree about the presence of threat, messages are relayed to behavioral response systems. Species specific aggressive responses, such as the hissing and arched back of a cat, can be elicited by electrical stimulation of the medial hypothalamus or the dorsolateral periaqueductal gray of the midbrain. As a result of activation in these areas, the sympathetic nervous system is kicked into high gear. Keep in mind that we have described one of the functions of the sympathetic nervous system as managing "fight or flight," with the "fight" part being especially relevant to our discussion of aggression.

The hierarchical approach helps us understand the rage of the decorticated animal. Without the guidance of the frontal lobes, a friendly pat on the head might be mistaken for an assault. We can use this model to understand impulsive, reactive aggression like bar fights. When interviewed later, a perpetrator might say that he assaulted another patron for "looking at me funny." A threatening look would certainly get the attention of the amygdala, but under normal circumstances, the frontal lobes would note that the individual was in a public place, no other threats seemed imminent, and the consequences for aggression would likely deter the other person from doing more than looking mean. However, we are talking about a bar fight, which means people are likely to be consuming alcohol, possibly large quantities of alcohol. Alcohol reduces cortical processing, leaving the amygdala and other subcortical structures with more influence than they normally would have. Impulsive aggression could easily result (Figure 4.4).

Premeditated aggression in human or animal is akin to hunting or predatory behavior. Unlike impulsive aggression, premeditated aggression does not involve much sympathetic arousal or outward emotion, leading to its characterization as "cold" aggression. Because premeditated aggression involves planning and strategizing (prey can attempt to escape or fight back), it requires activity in the frontal lobes. Once the plan is in place, lower structures again manage its implementation. Hunting behavior can be elicited in cats using electrical stimulation of the lateral hypothalamus, the ventral portion of periaqueductal gray in the midbrain, or the dopamine-releasing areas of the ventral midbrain that also give rise to the brain's major reward pathways (see Chapter 2).

The medial and lateral portions of the hypothalamus inhibit each other, which means that impulsive and premeditated aggression typically do not occur simultaneously. In addition to oversight by the cortex, the activity of the behavioral systems is also modified by the limbic system, including the hippocampus, amygdala, septal area, nucleus accumbens, the ventral striatum portion of the basal ganglia, and the anterior

FIGURE 4.4 Bar fights exemplify impulsive aggression and might occur due to alcohol's inhibition of cortical control systems.
Source: https://brobible.com/wp-content/uploads/2019/09/bar-fight.jpg

cingulate cortex. These structures can either suppress or enhance the activity of the hypothalamus and periaqueductal gray, leading to different likelihoods that premeditated aggression will be expressed.

Neurochemicals and Aggression

Aggression can be correlated with activity levels of several neurochemical systems, notably serotonin, testosterone, and cortisol.

High levels of serotonin suppress reactive aggression but are not well correlated with premeditated aggression. In primates with strong social hierarchies, such as rhesus monkeys, animals with the lowest serotonin levels are lower ranking and tend to be the more aggressive members of the group. In humans, low serotonin levels are typically associated with depression as well as with aggression. Why low serotonin levels are associated with depression in some individuals and aggression in others is unclear, although both depression and aggression coexist in cases of murder–suicide and suicide. Sigmund Freud's view of depression as "aggression toward the self" might well apply in these cases.

The relationship between testosterone and aggression is complex. Males are responsible for more violent crimes than females are. Adult testosterone levels are associated with the level of violence displayed by both male and female inmates. At the same time, however, testosterone fluctuates with competition and cognitive assessments of winning and losing (Booth et al., 1989). As a competition approaches, testosterone increases. Winning generally increases testosterone further, while losing often results in reduced testosterone. The exception, however, is that an athlete who assesses a performance positively despite a loss might also experience an increase in testosterone. It becomes challenging to know whether competitive circumstances or natural testosterone levels or some combination of related factors contributes to violent behavior.

Testosterone is associated with changes in emotions related to aggressive behavior. Testosterone reliably reduces fear through its actions on the amygdala (Bos et al., 2013), which in turn might enable aggression. If you are less fearful of possible consequences, you might be more likely to act. Laboratory manipulations designed to elicit anger increase testosterone levels at the same time (Angus et al., 2016).

Prenatal exposure to androgens is correlated with increased aggressiveness. Pregnant women are treated occasionally with synthetic progesterone for various health conditions. Children who were prenatally exposed to synthetic progesterone, which is structurally similar to androgens and produces androgen-related side effects, exhibit increased aggressiveness toward their peers (Figure 4.5).

Higher levels of cortisol, a glucocorticoid that helps regulate circadian rhythms and is released in response to stress, actually predict lower levels of aggressive behavior. Testosterone and cortisol are mutually inhibitory. When one is high, the other is relatively

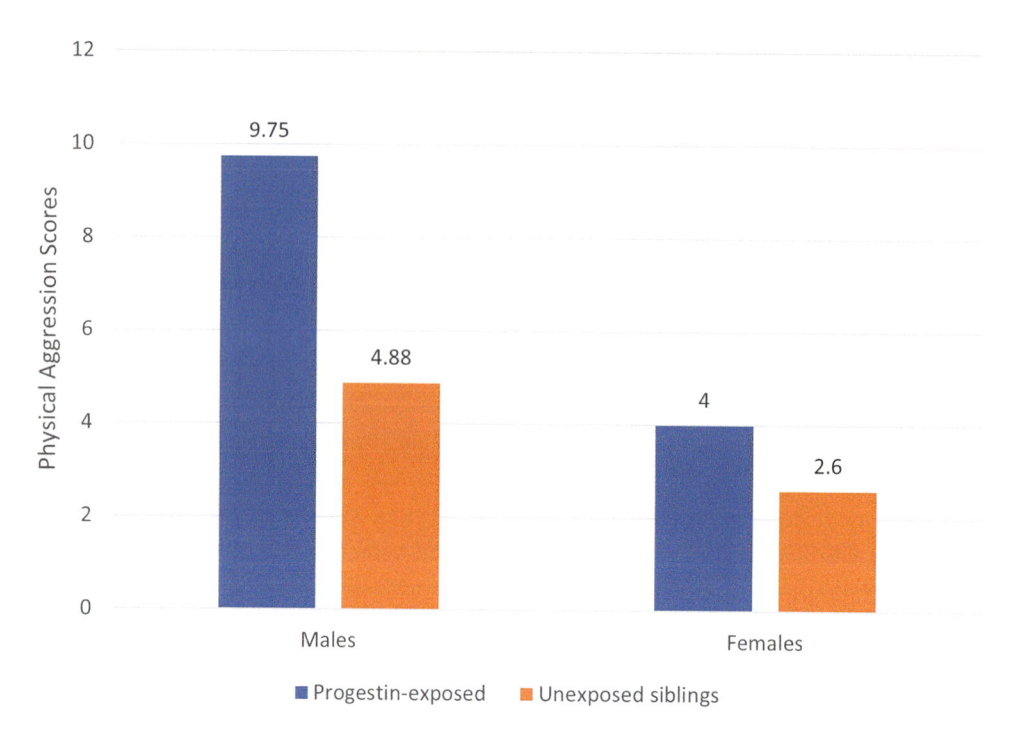

FIGURE 4.5 Children whose mothers were treated with synthetic progesterone during their pregnancies received higher physical aggression ratings later in childhood than their siblings who were not exposed to the hormone.

Source: Adapted from Reinisch (1981).

suppressed (Angus et al., 2016). The two hormones have different effects on the amygdala, with testosterone acting to enhance approach behaviors and cortisol enhancing withdrawal. The interaction between the two hormones helps us understand aggressive behavior. High testosterone is associated with violence only in youth who also have low cortisol levels. It is important to note that the effects of testosterone on aggression do not operate on a conscious, subjective level but rather in an unconscious, automatic manner.

Individual Differences in Aggression

How can we explain individual differences in aggressiveness? Any predispositions toward violence obviously interact with complex social factors, such as exposure to violent role models and poverty. Our focus, however, remains on the biological correlates of individual aggressiveness.

As mentioned previously, aggressive behavior can be bred easily in animals. This suggests that some portion of individual differences in aggression can be explained genetically. Evidence from human twin studies supports a genetic role in reactive aggressiveness that is relatively stable.

A critical factor in an individual's potential for aggression is psychopathy. Robert Hare characterizes the psychopath as having no remorse and no empathy. Psychopaths are 20 to 25 times more likely to be in prison than non-psychopaths (Yoder & Decety, 2018). Psychopaths differ from non-psychopath offenders in that they are more likely to engage in proactive aggression, more likely to reoffend, less likely to respond to pharmaceutical interventions, and more likely to continue aggressive behavior past adolescence (Wrangham, 2017). That being said, many violent criminals are not psychopaths at all. They maintain the ability to demonstrate remorse and empathy while relating to friends, associates, and family members, yet are capable of doing great harm to those deemed as belonging to outgroups without losing sleep at night.

Several brain areas appear to differentiate between psychopaths and non-psychopaths, including the prefrontal cortex, amygdala, and the striatum portion of the basal ganglia (Ling & Raine, 2018). Psychopaths tend to have lower volume, reduced cortical thickness, and less white matter integrity in the prefrontal cortex than non-psychopaths, particularly in areas connected to the amygdala. Damage to the prefrontal cortex can initiate negative personality and behavioral change, as in the case of the unfortunate Phineas Gage. When compared to non-psychopaths, the prefrontal cortex of psychopaths shows reduced activity during fear conditioning and while observing expressions of fear, pain, sadness, and happiness in others.

Disturbances of the function of the amygdala are associated with an inability to process emotional expressions of others and to form associations between responses and consequences. Psychopaths show clear reductions in the volume of the amygdala. This structural difference probably contributes to their inability to link their antisocial behaviors to their negative consequences and to recognize expressions of distress. Responding appropriately to consequences and to the distress of others provide deterrents to antisocial behavior.

The striatum, which consists of the nucleus accumbens and several other structures within the basal ganglia, is associated with reward-seeking and impulsive behavior. Unlike the cases of the prefrontal cortex and the amygdala, these structures appear to be larger in psychopaths than in non-psychopaths. Given the association between premeditated aggression and reward, this difference might explain some of the observed increase in premeditated aggression in psychopaths relative to non-psychopath offenders.

Prediction

The United States has a long tradition of supporting the "innocent until proven guilty" approach. Nonetheless, decisions regarding bail, sentencing, parole, probation, court-ordered treatments, and civil commitment are based on predictions of further violent behavior (Poldrack et al., 2018). Eventually, predicting the likelihood that an individual will behave in violent ways could lead to improved prevention and intervention approaches.

Violent behavior is not normally distributed in the population. A relatively small number of individuals perpetrate the vast majority of violent crimes. Identifying these individuals before they act could provide significant benefits to society. However, prediction efforts are based on group data, and any one individual may or may not conform to those group trends. When making major decisions about sentencing and parole, group assumptions might be anything but fair to a particular individual.

Efforts to predict future behavior are not new. These efforts generally fall into one of two categories: clinical assessments based on the subjective impressions of a trained clinician and actuarial approaches based on statistical models (Meehl, 1954). The actuarial approach, which combines factors such as education and employment, has consistently outperformed the clinical approach (Poldrack et al., 2018), but has been criticized on ethical grounds. Consequently, forensic experts are anxious to find additional insights that will lead to better predictions. It remains unclear whether the use of brain imaging technologies or other neuroscience approaches will provide these insights in the near future.

An important, ecologically valid contribution to our understanding of neuroprediction was a study conducted by Aharoni et al. (2013). Using mobile functional MRI equipment at several correctional institutions, the researchers assessed activity of the anterior cingulate cortex (ACC) during a go/no-go task of inhibitory control in 96 inmates about to be released. The inmates' rearrest rate for felony offenses was tracked for nearly four years; 40% of the inmates showing above the median ACC activity level during the task were rearrested in contrast to 60% of those with below median ACC activity. Additional efforts to replicate these findings would be useful.

Poldrack et al. (2018) identify several challenges facing neuroprediction. One is that brain imaging requires a compliant participant, and violent offenders might not be very cooperative. Kanwisher (2009) relates that nearly one in five cooperative brain imaging participants must be disqualified for moving too much, so we can only imagine how this would work with people who did not wish to be scanned. Individuals could learn to engage countermeasures meant to distort their data. Results could be complicated by confounding variables, such as gender and age. Finally, it might be difficult to generalize predictive accuracy to new samples. With an individual's future at stake, any use of neuroprediction must be stringently validated.

Lie Detection

In a court of law, we obviously seek truth. Unfortunately for this goal, human beings, along with many other animals, are usually quite good at deception, implying that deceptive abilities have evolved. Baboons hide fear, associated with a spontaneous baring of their teeth, by turning their backs to others until the expression passes. Why would the ability to deceive ever be adaptive? Deception as an adaptation implies that organisms that can deceive enjoy advantages in survival and reproductive success (Bond & Robinson, 1988). The adaptive value of deception produces conflict with our equally compelling need to build social trust.

To see the value of deception requires that we understand how it is used. Lewis (2015) identifies four different types of deception. As members of a social species, we often lie to protect the feelings of others. Your friend is seeking reassurance, not necessarily truth, when asking whether her outfit makes her look attractive. This type of deceptive ability emerges as early as three years of age, and girls are generally better at it than boys of the same age. A second type of deception is designed to avoid punishment. Again, this ability emerges quite early, as young as two and a half years of age, but its use increases in frequency with age. Interestingly, children with higher IQ scores and higher emotional intelligence scores are more likely to lie in this manner than children with lower scores. The third type is self-deception. If our survival depends on assessing our world accurately and learning from our mistakes, why would it ever be adaptive to deceive yourself? Robert Trivers (2011) argues that self-deception makes us better at deceiving others and shelters us from pain. Finally, people lie to hurt others. Although Lewis notes that this form is the least prosocial of the four, we must assume that it exists because it provides benefits in some circumstances. If a person can compete successfully with another by lying about that person without being caught, that's a win. A quick look at the news during an election cycle makes the "benefits" of this strategy obvious.

Even if our deceptive abilities have evolutionary, adaptive roots, they are also clearly influenced by experience and culture. Lewis notes that over the past 50 years in the U.S., "social tact," or the lying to protect the feelings of others, has been gradually pushed aside by moral imperatives to speak one's mind frankly, even if the result is harm to another. One need not read too far in social media before seeing this new social norm at work.

Despite our adaptive abilities to deceive, we have not evolved comparable abilities to detect deception. In face-to-face interactions, jurors are only slightly better than chance at detecting deception (Ekman & O'Sullivan, 1991). We seem to be better at implicit than explicit detection of lies. People report being less interested in further interaction with a person who has lied to them, even when they do not explicitly identify the person as having lied (ten Brinke et al., 2016). Trusting people are less likely to detect lies than more suspicious people, although most people improve in their ability to detect lies when they feel threatened (Schindler & Reinhard, 2015).

It is generally understood that traditional **polygraph measures**, which are simply measures of arousal, are unsatisfactory measures of deception. In the hands of experienced analysts, polygraph results are accurate about 65% of the time, which is the main reason that they are not universally admissible in courts of law. A primary source of the poor validity of these measures is that arousal can mean many things. About one-third of innocent people will "fail" a standard polygraph, simply because aspects of the situation ("they think I did something wrong") produce arousal. Perhaps worse, about one quarter of guilty people will sail through a polygraph. If you do not believe that lying is a bad thing, you will not be aroused by it. This presents a standard signal detection scenario, as diagrammed in Figure 4.6. Ideally, the polygraph would identify all of the guilty as guilty, and all of the innocent as innocent, but that is not what happens. The interesting ethical dilemma presented by the use of the polygraph is whether you are more bothered by misses than by false alarms. In other words, is it worse to accuse an innocent person or to fail to accuse a guilty one?

Rather than focusing on plain arousal, other researchers note that lying has cognitive costs (Suchotzki et al., 2017). To lie successfully, the truth must be held in working memory, communication of the truth must be inhibited, and comparing the truth with lies as they are constructed requires task switching. These executive functions (working memory, response inhibition, task switching) have relatively well-understood biological correlates that might form the basis of lie detection via brain imaging.

Brain imaging can be used to distinguish lies from truthful statements in law-abiding, prosocial university students under low-stakes situations. Using a version of the Guilty Knowledge Test, Daniel Langleben and his colleagues (2002) were able to identify brain regions that become more or less active depending on the truthfulness of a statement. Participants were asked whether they were holding a particular card from a deck of playing cards. Areas of the frontal lobe were more active during lying, whereas areas of the parietal lobe were more active during truthfulness.

While imaging technologies might become more useful in lie detection in the future, significant doubts have been raised by imaging experts regarding this application. This application suffers from the same G2i (group to individual) issues we have seen many times so far in this book. Imaging studies rely on the averaging of data from multiple participants to identify regions of interest related to specific behaviors. In contrast,

	The person is guilty.	The person is innocent.
The polygraph determines the person is guilty.	Hit (76%)	False alarm (37%)
The polygraph determines the person is innocent.	Miss (24%)	Correct rejection (63%)

FIGURE 4.6 Signal detection theory helps us understand the outcomes of traditional polygraph assessments of lying. Even in the hands of experienced investigators, about one third of innocent people will look guilty and one quarter of guilty people will look innocent.

Source: Kleinmuntz & Szucko, 1984.

imaging data from single individuals is "noisy" and thus difficult to interpret (Raichle, 2009). Multiple types of lying are recognized in legal codes, including lies of omission and half-truths. These subtleties probably lie outside the detection abilities of today's technology (Rakoff, 2009). Extrapolating from the behavior of prosocial college students lying about low-stakes situations (are you holding the Queen of spades?) to real-world testimony by antisocial people facing life in prison is risky at best. Many researchers worry that naïve judges and juries would be swayed by imaging data due to the public's trust in and respect for neuroscience in general.

Chapter Summary

Forensic neuroscience offers considerable potential for informing the legal process. Although neuroscience data are already being introduced in courts of law, this application of neuroscience raises serious questions about responsibility, using group data to assess individuals, and privacy. Legal professionals should avoid being "dazzled" by neuroscience, but instead view it with a critical eye as a potentially objective tool that can be used effectively or poorly.

Review Questions

1. Which of the following is NOT neuroscience evidence that is often admitted to courts of law (LO 4.1)?
    a. Medical history of head injury.
    b. Neuropsychological test results.
    c. Brain imaging data on truthfulness.
    d. Brain imaging results regarding brain structure and volume.
2. Which of the following illustrates the interaction of nature and nurture (LO 4.2)?
    a. Child maltreatment interacts with genetics to predict violence in youth.
    b. Aggression is more similar in identical than in fraternal twins.
    c. Child maltreatment is a risk factor for antisocial behavior due to modeling.
    d. Violent media exposure increases aggressiveness in children.
3. Which of the following is true of the neuroscience correlates of aggression (LO 4.3)?
    a. Aggression has few neuroscience correlates, as it is learned from others.
    b. Premeditated aggression does not produce much sympathetic arousal.

    c. Reactive aggression does not produce much sympathetic arousal.

    d. Premeditated aggression is experienced as an aversive event, but reactive aggression is rewarding.

4. Which of the following factors makes neuroprediction difficult to do well (LO 4.4)?

    a. Violent behavior is normally distributed.

    b. The G2i problem does not apply.

    c. We do not have any data about brain structure or function that predicts future offenses.

    d. Neuroscience methods require a cooperative participant.

5. Which of the following is true of traditional polygraph lie detector tests (LO 4.5)?

    a. Polygraph lie detectors are very accurate and results are typically admissible in courts of law in the U.S.

    b. Polygraph lie detectors are about 65% accurate when administered by experts.

    c. Polygraph lie detectors do not misjudge guilty individuals, but might judge some innocent people as guilty (false alarms).

    d. Polygraph lie detectors do not misjudge innocent individuals, but might judge some guilty people as innocent (misses).

6. Which of the following is NOT a recommendation for the use of neuroscience in courts of law (L.O. 4.6)?

    a. Neuroscience should not be used, as traditional methods like the Rorschach Inkblot test are much more reliable and valid.

    b. Neuroscience forensic applications require more research, but can be useful adjuncts to other sources of information.

    c. Neuroscience research should be presented to the level of understanding of judges, defendants, and juries.

    d. Forensic neuroscientists should be aware of the extra credibility many people assign to neuroscience-based information.

7. Which of the following is NOT a good future direction for forensic neuroscience (LO 4.7)?

    a. Mobile and inexpensive technologies should be developed.

    b. Additional research on lie detection using brain imaging should be conducted.

    c. Research correlating brain structure and function and dangerousness should be conducted.

    d. Youth should be prescreened for violent tendencies.

Thought Questions

1. Based on your reading in this chapter, where do you think forensic neuroscience will be in ten years?
2. If you were accused of a crime, would you want your defense attorneys to use neuroscience methods to evaluate you? Why or why not?

Answer Key for Review Sections

1. c
2. a
3. b
4. d
5. b
6. a
7. d

References

Aharoni, E., Vincent, G. M., Harenski, C. L., Calhoun, V. D., Sinnott-Armstrong, W., Gazzaniga, M. S., & Kiehl, K. A. (2013). Neuroprediction of future rearrest. *Proceedings of the National Academy of Sciences of the United States of America*, *110*(15), 6223–6228. https://doi.org/10.1073/pnas.1219302110

Angus, D. J., Schutter, D. J. L. G., Terburg, D., van Honk, J., & Harmon-Jones, E. (2016). A review of social neuroscience research on anger and aggression. In E. Harmon-Jones & M. Inzlicht (Eds.), *Frontiers of social psychology. Social neuroscience: Biological approaches to social psychology* (pp. 223–246). Routledge/Taylor & Francis Group. https://doi.org/10.4324/9781315628714-12

Beckerman, S., Erickson, P. I., Yost, J., Regalado, J., Jaramillo, L., Sparks, C., Iromenga, M., & Long, K. (2009). Life histories, blood revenge, and reproductive success among the Waorani of Ecuador. *Proceedings of the National Academy of Sciences of the United States of America*, *106*(20), 8134– 8139. https://doi.org/10.1073/pnas.0901431106

Bond, C. F., & Robinson, M. (1988). The evolution of deception. *Journal of Nonverbal Behavior*, *12*(4), 295–307. https://doi.org/10.1007/BF00987597

Booth, A., Shelley, G., Mazur, A., Tharp, G., & Kittok, R. (1989). Testosterone, and winning and losing in human competition. *Hormones and Behavior*, *23*(4), 556–571. https://doi.org/oi: 10.1016/0018–506X(89)90042-1

Bos, P. A., van Honk, J., Ramsey, N. F., Stein, D. J., & Hermans, E. J. (2013). Testosterone administration in women increases amygdala responses to fearful and happy faces. *Psychoneuroendocrinology*, *38*(6), 808–817. https://doi.org/10.1016.j.psyneuen.2012.09.005

Caspi, A., McClay, J., Moffitt, T. E., Mill, J., Martin, J., Craig, I. W., Taylor, A., & Poulton, R. (2002). Role of genotype in the cycle of violence in maltreated children. *Science, 297*(5582), 851–854. https://doi.org/10.1126/science.1072290

Chagnon, N. A. (1988). Life histories, blood revenge, and warfare in a tribal population. *Science, 239*, 985–992. https://doi.org/10.1126/science.239.4843.985

Chow, T. E., Westphal, A. J., & Rissman, J. (2018). Multi-voxel pattern classification differentiates personally experienced event memories from secondhand event knowledge. *NeuroImage, 176*, 110–123. https://doi.org/10.1016/j.neuroimage.2018.04.024

Dierick, H. A., & Greenspan, R. J. (2006) Molecular analysis of flies selected for aggressive behavior. *Nature Genetics, 38*(9), 1023–1031. https://doi.org/10.1038/ng1864

Dolinoy, D. C., Huang, D., & Jirtle, R. L. (2007). Maternal nutrient supplementation counteracts bisphenol A-induced DNA hypomethylation in early development. *Proceedings of the National Academy of Sciences, 104*(32), 13056–13061. https://doi.org/10.1073/pnas.0703739104

Ekman, P., & O'Sullivan, M. (1991). Who can catch a liar? *American Psychologist, 46*(9), 913–920. https://doi.org/10.1037//0003-066x.46.9.913

Greely, H. T., & Farahany, N. A. (2019). Neuroscience and the criminal justice system. *Annual Review of Criminology, 2*, 451–471. https://doi.org/10.1146/annurev-criminol-011518-024433

Kanwisher, N. (2009). The use of fMRI in lie detection: What has been shown and what has not. In E. Bizzi, S. E. Hyman, M. E. Raichle, N. Kanwisher, E. A. Phelps, S. J. Morse, W. Sinnott-Armstrong, J. S. Rakoff, & H. T. Greely (Eds.), *Using imaging to identify deceit* (pp. 7–13). Cambridge, MA: American Academy of Arts and Sciences.

Kleinmuntz, B., & Szucko, J. J. (1984). Lie detection in ancient and modern times: A call for contemporary scientific study. *American Psychologist, 39*(7), 766–776. https://doi.org/10.1037/0003-066X.39.7.766

Lagerspetz, K. M., & Lagerspetz, K. Y. (1971). Changes in the aggressiveness of mice resulting from selective breeding, learning and social isolation. *Scandinavian Journal of Psychology, 12*(4), 241–248. https://doi.org/10.1111/j.1467-9450.1971.tb00627.x

Langleben, D. D., Schroeder, L., Maldjian, J. A., Gur, R. C., McDonald, S., Ragland, J. D., O'Brien, C. P., & Childress, A. R. (2002). Brain activity during simulated deception: An event-related functional magnetic resonance study. *Neuroimage, 15*(3), 727–732. https://doi.org/10.1006/nimg.2001.1003

Lewis, M. (2015). The origins of lying and deception in everyday life. *American Scientist, 103*(2), 128. https://doi.org/10.1511/2015.113.128

Lin, L., Christidis, P., & Stamm, K. (2017, September). Datapoint: A look at psychologists' specialty areas: News from APA's Center for Workforce Studies. *American Psychological Association Monitor on Psychology, 48*, 15.

Ling, S., & Raine, A. (2018). The neuroscience of psychopathy and forensic implications. *Psychology, Crime, and Law, 24*(3), 296–312. https://doi.org/01.1080/1068316X.2017.1419243

Meehl, P. E. (1954). *Clinical vs. statistical prediction.* Minneapolis, MN: University of Minnesota Press.

Meynen, G. (2018). Forensic psychiatry and neurolaw: Description, development, and debates. *International Journal of Law and Psychiatry, 65*, 101345. https://doi.org/10.1016/j.ijlp.2018.04.005

Neal, T. M. S., Slobogin, C., Saks, M. J., Faigman, D. L., & Geisinger, K. F. (2019). Psychological assessments in legal contexts: Are courts keeping "junk science" out of the courtroom? *Psychological Science in the Public Interest, 20*(3), 135–164. https://doi.org/10.1177/1529100619888860

Poldrack, R. A., Monahan, J., Imrey, P. B., Reyna, V., Raichle, M. E., Faigman, D., & Buckholtz, J. W. (2018). Predicting violent behavior: What can neuroscience add? *Trends in Cognitive Sciences*, *22*(2), 111–123. https://doi.org/10.1016/j.tics.2017.11.003

Raichle, M. E. (2009). An introduction to functional brain imaging in the context of lie detection. In E. Bizzi, S. E. Hyman, M. E. Raichle, N. Kanwisher, E. A. Phelps, S. J. Morse, W. Sinnott-Armstrong, J. S. Rakoff, & H. T. Greely (Eds.), *Using imaging to identify deceit* (pp. 3–6). Cambridge, MA: American Academy of Arts and Sciences.

Raine, A. (1993). *The psychopathology of crime: Criminal behavior as a clinical disorder*. New York, NY: Academic Press. https://doi.org/10.1016/B978-0-08-057148-5.50005-8

Rakoff, J. S. (2009). Lie detection in the courts: The vain search for the magic bullet. In E. Bizzi, S. E. Hyman, M. E. Raichle, N. Kanwisher, E. A. Phelps, S. J. Morse, W. Sinnott-Armstrong, J. S. Rakoff, & H. T. Greely (Eds.), *Using imaging to identify deceit* (pp. 40–45). Cambridge, MA: American Academy of Arts and Sciences.

Reinisch, J. M. (1981). Prenatal exposure to synthetic progestins increases potential for aggression in humans. *Science*, *211*(4487), 1171–1173. https://doi.org/10.1126/science.7466388

Schindler, S., & Reinhard, M. A. (2015). Catching the liar as a matter of justice: Effects of belief in a just world on deception detection accuracy and the moderating role of mortality salience. *Personality and Individual Differences*, *73*, 105–109. https://doi.org/10.1016/j.paid.2014.09.034

Suchotzki, K., Verschuere, B., Van Bockstaele, B., Ben-Shakhar, G., & Crombez, G. (2017). Lying takes time: A meta-analysis on reaction time measures of deception. *Psychological Bulletin*, *143*(4), 428–453. https://doi.org/10.1037/bul0000087

ten Brinke, L., Vohs, K. D., & Carney, D. R. (2016). Can ordinary people detect deception after all? *Trends in Cognitive Science*, *20*, 579–588. https://doi.org/10.1016/j.tics.2016.05.012

Trivers, R. (2011). *Deceit and self-deception: Fooling yourself the better to fool others*. London: Allen Lane.

Vilares, I., Wesley, M. J., Ahn, W-Y., Bonnie, R. J., Hoffman, M., Jones, O. D., Morse, S. J., Yaffe, G., Lohrenz, T., & Montague, P. R. (2017). Predicting the knowledge—recklessness distinction in the human brain. *PNAS*, *114*(12), 3222–3227. https://doi.org/10.1073/pnas.1619385114

Weisberg, D. S., Keil, F. C., Goodstein, J., Rawson, E., & Gray, J. R. (2008). The seductive allure of neuroscience explanations. *Journal of Cognitive Neuroscience*, *20*(3), 470–477. https://doi.org/10.1162/jocn.2008.20040

Wrangham, R. W. (2017). Two types of aggression in human evolution. *Proceedings of the National Academy of Sciences*, *115*(2), 245–253. https://doi.org/10.1073/pnas.1713611115

Yoder, K. J., & Decety, J. (2018). The neuroscience of morality and social decision-making. *Psychology, Crime, and Law*, *24*(3), 279–295. https://doi.org/10.1080/1068316X.2017.1414817

Glossary

Aggression	The act of causing deliberate harm to another.
Forensic neuroscience	The application of neuroscience principles to the understanding and management of criminal behavior.
Forensic psychology	The application of psychological science and practice to resolve legal matters.

Polygraph measures	Measures of general arousal used in an attempt to detect deception.
Proactive aggression	Premeditated aggression, similar to hunting behavior.
Psychological assessment	A formal measure of a psychological construct, such as intelligence by an intelligence test.
Reactive aggression	Impulsive aggression triggered by environmental stimuli.

5 | Neuroeducation

LEARNING OBJECTIVES

After reading this chapter, you should be able to:

▶ 1. Define neuroeducation and identify the interdisciplinary fields that contribute to this domain.

▶ 2. Explain the contributions of neuroscience to our understanding of reading and mathematics.

▶ 3. Identify the contributions of neuroscience to our understanding of executive functions, including working memory, attention, and inhibitory control, and the role of these insights in education.

▶ 4. Evaluate the interventions designed to enhance executive function, including mindfulness, special school programs, nootropics, and brain stimulation.

▶ 5. Describe the controversies over the efficacy of brain training.

Educational Neuromyths

Educators have enough on their plates without cultivating an expertise in neuroscience. As a result, they can become reliant on so-called "middlemen," particularly the authors of popular press books and purveyors of commercial educational programs. These middlemen attempt to translate neuroscience research into educational practice, often with poor results. In 2002, the Brain and Learning Project of the Organization for Economic Cooperation and Development (OECD) coined the term "neuromyth" to describe

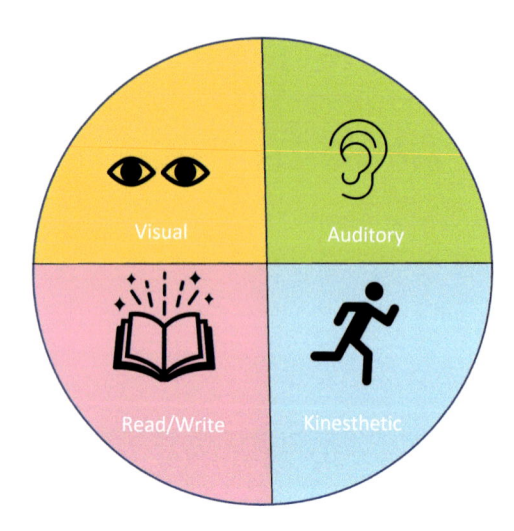

FIGURE 5.1 Many teachers continue to endorse discredited neuromyths, like the VARK (visual, auditory, read/write, kinesthetic) "Learning Styles" model.

Source: Author.

incorrect applications of brain science to education. Among the identified neuromyths are the following (OECD, 2002):

1. Plasticity is restricted to critical periods of development.
2. Enriched environments only have an effect within the first three years of life.
3. Teaching to one's preferred learning style improves learning.
4. We only use 10% of our brain.
5. Multiple languages compete for resources and a second should not be learned until the first is well established.
6. Left brain/right brain myths.

While some of these might seem obviously wrong to you (and we hope that #4 is high on that list), you might be thinking "but, but …" in response to some of the others. These neuromyths are widely believed in and out of educational settings. Just this morning, an Alexa belonging to your author made an apparent statement of fact about the left brain/right brain myth to explain successful people (leading to some sputtering of coffee on the part of the author).

One of the most pervasive neuromyths is number three on the OECD's list—the idea that teaching to a student's preferred "learning style" (visual, auditory, read/write or kinesthetic, abbreviated VARK—Figure 5.1) would improve learning. While it's true that these different sensory modalities have their own pathways and networks in the brain, they are also remarkably interconnected. It is also true that individuals might have a preferred way of learning, based on their subjective, and therefore potentially biased, observations of their own experience. In carefully controlled research, however, no benefits have been demonstrated when students are instructed in their preferred modality (Pashler et al., 2008). In fact, all learners seem to benefit similarly when information is presented in multiple modalities. Despite widely publicized articles critical of learning styles theory, a Google search of "learning styles" returns over 4 million results, with most of the entries on the first few pages being supportive of the concept.

Surveyed teachers believe about half of the neuromyths identified by the OECD and are especially likely to believe those associated with commercial educational programs (Dekker et al., 2012). Ironically, teachers who expressed the greatest enthusiasm for incorporating neuroscience in the classroom, read popular science magazines, and scored highest in tests of general knowledge were the same teachers who were most likely to endorse neuromyths. This suggests that better general knowledge of neuroscience is not necessarily protective against endorsement of neuromyths.

Why should we be concerned about neuromyths? What harm is done by presenting information in different sensory modalities? Any teacher can tell you that preparing lesson plans is a time-consuming process. Time spent deliberately trying to match student learning styles is time wasted, and teachers cannot afford to do that. Precious financial resources are tied up in learning centers and commercial programs offering assessments and remedies based on learning styles neuromyths. Even more concerning is the tendency of teachers who endorse learning styles to think of them as a fixed, unchangeable entity (Nancekivell et al., 2020). This belief can have the effect of limiting expectations about a particular child's abilities.

Believing that plasticity has a limited window and that enriched environments only help early in life can also lead to poor educational practices. As we will see later in this chapter, plasticity in most domains related to learning extends throughout the lifetime. Otherwise, we would not bother presenting rehabilitation programs to adults with cognitive disorders, stroke, or traumatic brain injuries. Enriched environments contribute to that plasticity, and older children and adults alike benefit from ongoing mental challenges.

Believing neuromyths about multiple language learning might lead to unfortunate policies. Children have an advantage over adults in learning to produce and distinguish speech sounds such that most people learning a second or subsequent language later in life will speak with a more pronounced accent. In many parts of the world, multiple languages are presented very early in the educational process, whereas in the United States, additional languages are often delayed until students are in middle or high school, possibly due in part to this prevailing neuromyth. As a result, students in the U.S. might not reach the level of proficiency in second or third languages that students do in many other nations. It is also common for educators to think of bilingual or multilingual children as lagging behind, as their vocabulary learning must be divided among their languages. In a longitudinal study of bilingual children in Quebec, the rate of vocabulary growth did not differ between monolingual and bilingual children in their main language (MacLeod et al., 2018). One might argue instead that the bilingual children were learning vocabulary at a faster rate than their monolingual peers, given their need to learn new words in more than one language.

The left brain/right brain neuromyth continues to haunt us and has the potential to encourage several negative outcomes in addition to its plain and simple inaccuracy. This neuromyth has spawned whole industries of self-help for everything from attention deficit hyperactivity disorder (ADHD) to art. People are spending time and money on these fraudulent resources that could be used on real evidence-based practices. In addition, these myths promote a fixed mindset, described by Carol Dweck (2016) as a belief that intellectual abilities are predetermined and unchanging. Using this mindset, you either have a talent, say for math or art, or you don't. As Dweck points out, using fixed mindset thinking makes individuals avoid intellectual risk for fear of looking stupid and reduce their efforts in the face of challenge. In contrast, maintaining a growth mindset, or a recognition that abilities can be improved, leads to sustained effort to overcome challenges and a willingness to make mistakes along the way to improved performance. Although mindset appears to have a weak impact on academic achievement overall, children with low socioeconomic status or otherwise at risk for academic problems seem to benefit from mindset interventions (Sisk et al., 2018).

How can neuroscientists help educators benefit from research findings without initiating neuromyths? In this chapter, we describe the many evidence-based ways that neuroscience can inform the educational process.

What Is Neuroeducation?

Neuroeducation, also known as Educational Neuroscience or Mind, Brain, and Education, is an interdisciplinary field that attempts to use neuroscience research to improve learning and instruction. Simultaneously, the study of the brain's processing of academic subjects like reading and mathematics, along with executive processing essential to school performance like working memory and metacognition, enriches the neuroscience literature. Neuroeducation attempts to understand the learning process of both typical learners and those with atypical learning.

The desire to meld the disciplines of neuroscience and education has spawned university programs and degrees as well as new journals. This desire grew out of advances in neuroscience technologies, such as brain imaging, and the popularization of neuroscience during the 1990s (designated "The Decade of the Brain" in the United States). It was nurtured by the existing collaborative nature of the neurosciences, which are essentially interdisciplinary at the core. Neuroscience already pulls together many fields, including biology, chemistry, physics, medicine, engineering, statistics, and psychology. Productive collaborations such as cognitive neuroscience and social neuroscience encourage others to propose further collaborations and applications such as neuroeducation.

The emergence of neuroeducation is not lacking critics. Bruer (1997) argues that connecting education and neuroscience is "a bridge too far." Bowers (2016) doesn't mince words either, stating that "there are no current examples of neuroscience motivating new and effective teaching methods, and ... neuroscience is unlikely to improve teaching in the future" (p. 1). Many critics believe that the field of psychology is sufficient for informing educational practice, with no further contributions to be gained from neuroscience. Considering this type of criticism, enthusiasm for neuroeducation seems to have tapered off. Nonetheless, advocates of neuroeducation continue to push forward (c.f., Ansari et al., 2012). Thomas et al. (2019) argue that neuroscience can not only make direct contributions to education, but also does so indirectly by further clarifying topics in psychology.

Challenges for Neuroeducation

Among the many challenges faced by neuroeducation are communication, misunderstandings about the biology of behavior, methods, and managing expectations (Ansari et al., 2012).

Communication

In any interdisciplinary endeavor, it is essential to speak the language of experts in the other disciplines and to be up to date with their methods and conclusions. Neuroscientists might be relatively unaware of contemporary educational research and classroom teaching methods while educational researchers might not be well-versed in neuroscience. The highly controlled research environment expected by neuroscientists might seem very foreign to educational researchers accustomed to working in more natural settings.

These differences might lead to the types of misunderstanding that culminate in the neuromyths described at the beginning of this chapter. A resolution is to make sure that both neuroscientists and educators are well trained in each other's disciplines. The educator does not need to know how to conduct an fMRI study but needs to know enough about it to think critically about published reports using fMRI. The neuroscientist needs to know enough about contemporary learners, teaching methods, and instruction to ask the right research questions.

Methodology

Neuroeducation faces some methodological roadblocks. Because children are considered a vulnerable group of research participants according to government research ethics regulations, gaining access to child participants is generally more difficult than recruiting adult participants.

Using neuroscience methods such as fMRI in neuroeducation features the methodological challenges described in Chapter 1 along with a few additional twists. As Seghier et al. (2019) point out, young children will find it difficult to stay still during an fMRI scan. The limits to the number of participants imposed by the cost of fMRI might make it difficult to capture the variability in children's learning, especially when comparing typically developing children to those with learning disabilities. Highly controlled neuroscience research methods do not necessarily translate well to the natural and ecological setting of the classroom. Many neuroeducation questions benefit from long-term, longitudinal assessment. Development in general is gradual, and the cross-sectional methods required in neuroscience might not capture cognitive changes associated with educational practices. Longitudinal assessment raises additional issues of cost and access to participants.

Seghier et al. (2019) propose that neuroeducation would be well served by engaging in current best practices in open science. For example, negative findings should be given space in journals so that educators do not waste time and resources on interventions that do not work. The cost issues associated with fMRI and other neuroscience technologies can be at least partially mitigated through the sharing of data and the development of large-scale data repositories.

Managing Expectations

As we mentioned in Chapter 1, people tend to put more weight on explanations that include biological explanations of behavior. Teacher training should be carefully designed to prevent this bias. A corollary of this bias is the idea of neuroscience as a "quick fix" for a variety of problems. Like other applications described in this book, applying neuroscience to education requires time and careful evidence-based practice approaches.

Neuroeducation Applied to Specific Subjects

Neuroeducation has attempted to understand how foundational skills like reading and mathematics are acquired by typically developing individuals and by those who experience a learning disability.

Reading

Reading is one of the most complex processes we ask our brains to do. Unlike the spoken languages on which it is based, learning to read requires formal instruction and laborious practice. A typically developing child exposed to spoken language will learn to use spoken language, but this is not at all the case with reading. Reading is also a foundational skill, along with mathematics, for success at all levels of education. Identifying and remediating problems with reading can open pathways to academic success that otherwise would be closed.

One of the most common criticisms of neuroeducation is the "we already knew that" defense. In other words, educators argue that behavioral measures are sufficient and that the addition of neuroscience adds little or no value. However, Hoeft et al. (2007) demonstrated that a combination of behavioral and neuroscience measures did a better job of predicting individual differences in reading than models using only one or the other.

A particularly productive area of collaboration between education and neuroscience is the study of **dyslexia**, defined as difficulty learning to read despite exposure to formal instruction and lack of other cognitive deficits such as intellectual disability. When college students underwent brain imaging while reading, students with dyslexia showed different patterns of activation than those who did not have dyslexia (Shaywitz et al., 2002). Instead of showing activation in pathways connecting visual and auditory processing, the individuals with dyslexia showed greater activation in frontal lobe areas associated with language production (e.g., Broca's area), as if they were reading out loud to themselves (see Figure 5.2). As anyone who has read a bedtime story to a child knows, reading out loud is slower than reading silently. As reading slows, working memory struggles to hold the initial part of a passage in memory long enough to process the whole, leading to the comprehension difficulties that are also common in cases of dyslexia.

These different patterns of activation seen in cases of dyslexia represent the reader's efforts to compensate for their condition. The evaluation of these compensations can lead to productive remediation. Children with dyslexia are notoriously poor at phonological awareness, or the ability to distinguish between phonemes or speech sounds. To help them compensate, the Lindamood Bell remediation program for dyslexia trains children to connect the movements of their vocal apparatus, rather than a phoneme as is typically done in phonics instruction, to the printed letter. As you make the "nnnn" and "mmm" sounds aloud, pay attention to how your mouth and tongue are doing different things while making sounds that are quite similar when heard. The Lindamood Bell approach predates the Shaywitz et al. (2002) observations but is still quite consistent with them. Using a motor pathway to compensate for reading difficulties characterizes both the fMRI observations and the remediation approach. But does it work? Not only

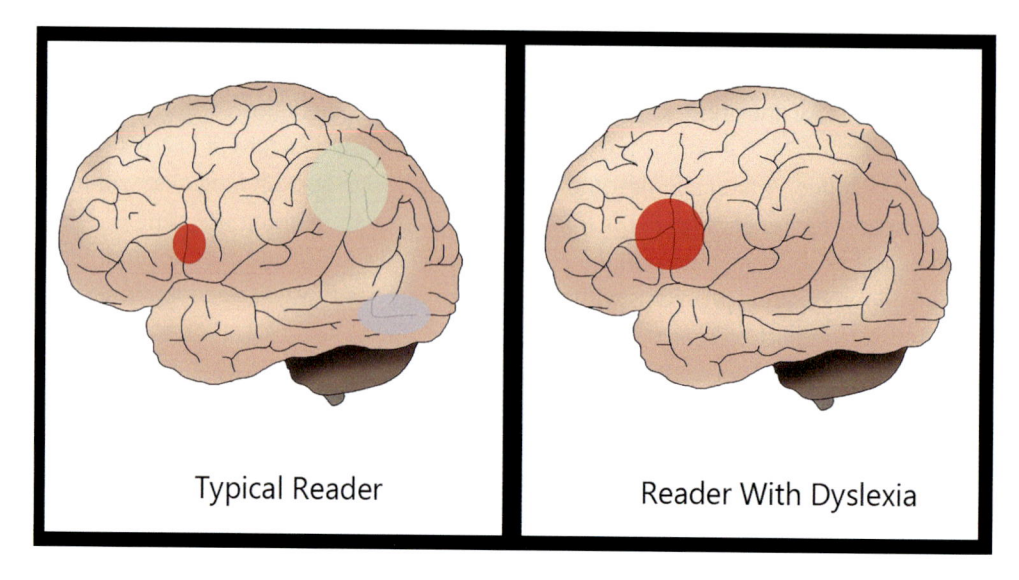

FIGURE 5.2 Brain imaging with fMRI during reading showed that typical readers and readers with dyslexia had different patterns of brain activity. Compared to typical readers, readers with dyslexia showed little activity in the occipito-temporal areas associated with processing word form (blue) or in the parieto-temporal areas that engage in word analysis (green). However, they show increased activity in Broca's area (red).
Source: Karla Freberg.

does the instruction produce improvements in reading when assessed by scientists not affiliated with the program, but it also "normalized" the activity of posterior pathways found to be underactive by Shaywitz and his colleagues (Meyler et al., 2008). Activation continued to normalize one year after remediation. These results highlight the important role that neuroscience can play in establishing and supporting evidence-based practice (see Chapter 1).

Dyslexia and other reading problems are often diagnosed as late as the third or fourth grade (ages 8–10) as the curriculum in the U.S. switches from acquisition of skills ("learning to read") to practice of skills ("reading to learn," as in using reading skills to learn information about social studies or science). Late identification means late remediation, and early remediation is usually associated with better outcomes. By the time most identifications occur, the child is well aware that schooling is more difficult than it appears to be for peers, which might lead to an overall dislike of school and a fixed mindset sense of being "bad at school." This can have devastating long-term consequences. Children who express enjoyment of school at age six outperform those who do not enjoy school as long as ten years later, even when intellectual ability and socioeconomic status are controlled (Morris et al., 2021). Neuroscience holds the promise of much earlier identification of children who will go on to develop reading problems. Language and reading problems at age eight have been predicted in infants using event-related potentials (ERP; see Chapter 1; Molfese, 2000).

Neuroscience might act as a correction to existing educational policy based on behavioral data. Classroom teachers struggle to track the progress of large groups of children, and neuroscience might make assessment more accurate and objective. Educators often make assumptions about when a particular ability, like associating letters and speech sounds as required in phonics, is fully developed and needs no further instruction. Neuroscience does not always support these truisms. For example, Froyen et al. (2009) demonstrated that associations between letters and speech sounds were still developing years after existing school policies dictated that they should be mature. Armed with the neuroscience data, educators can make needed adjustments to policy and curriculum.

Finally, consistent with our discussion of the reciprocal relationship between brain and behavior, it comes as no surprise to learn that learning to read changes the brain. In this case, the study of reading acquisition helps us further understand the underlying neuroscience. In comparisons of literate and illiterate adults, the ability to read was associated with different patterns of activity in areas associated with reading, but also in areas associated with the perception of speech and vision (Dehaene et al., 2010). For example, in readers, areas activated by the visual presentation of words spread to the temporal lobe areas usually associated with the recognition of faces. These changes in activation patterns were similar in adults who had learned to read in childhood or in adulthood, indicating a lack of critical period for these changes resulting from learning to read.

Mathematics

The U.S. educational system is far more forgiving of "being bad at math" than it is of "being bad at reading," although both skills are foundational for further education. As a result, research on mathematics learning often takes a back seat to research on reading. Compared to our understanding of reading acquisition, we know relatively little about the typical development of numerical literacy, let alone about the problems that occur in mathematical learning. Without much of a behavioral foundation from the educational standpoint, it has been difficult to establish neuroscience correlates of mathematical learning.

One area of mathematical learning that is relatively well understood is the judgment of magnitude, or the ability to say "which is more" when observing either numerals or objects (Figure 5.3). Classic observations by Jean Piaget identified the characteristic progression of thinking by young children when making these judgments, such as assuming that spreading objects out meant "more" relative to a line of the same number of objects placed close together. Children under the age of seven years typically struggle with this task, but older children do not.

Poirel et al. (2012) presented a computerized version of Piaget's number conservation task to children undergoing functional magnetic resonance imaging (fMRI; see Chapter 1).

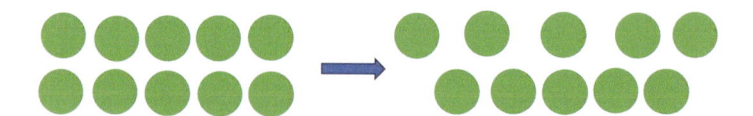

FIGURE 5.3 Which row has more balls in it? Jean Piaget observed that preschool children had difficulty with this question, but older children did not. Younger children could answer correctly when viewing the left half of this array ("They are the same"), but they were likely to answer that the upper line on the right had "more" because the line was longer. They confused the spatial orientation of the objects with their quantity. Older children correctly noted that both lines contained the same number of balls, demonstrating that they understood conservation of number (the number doesn't change because the objects look different).

Source: Author.

Results indicated that two processes were involved with successful strategies. First, the child needed to inhibit a misleading strategy: length = number, which probably is a useful heuristic in many types of situations. Second, the child needed to demonstrate the ability to reverse a cognitive operation. Piaget argued that to succeed in this conservation task, children needed to mentally reverse the transformation of the length of the line of objects from spread out to the original. Children who succeeded in the task, but not those who were unsuccessful, showed increased activity in the **left intraparietal sulcus (IPS**; see Figure 5.4), an area known to be involved with mathematical reasoning and the likely correlate of the mental transformation part of the task, as well as in areas of the right insula and inferior frontal gyrus known to be involved with inhibitory control. These latter areas are possibly involved in the inhibition of the length = number strategy.

Numerical magnitude judgments are made in surprisingly similar ways by human infants, human adults, and non-human animals. These results support the idea that a sense of number is not reliant on language and that it is very likely to be both ancient and innate (Lyons & Ansari, 2015). A chimpanzee named Sheba was taught to associate

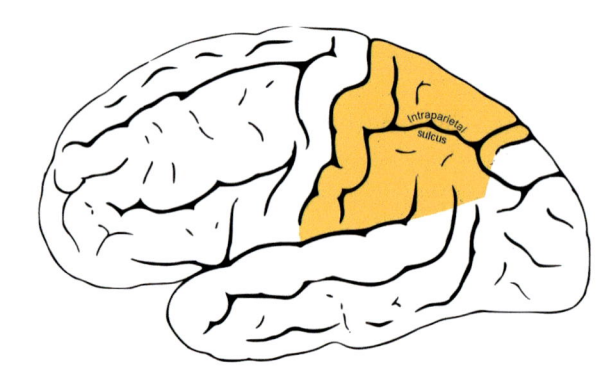

FIGURE 5.4 The intraparietal sulcus appears to be important for thinking about number.
Source: Author.

quantities with Arabic numerals, count, and judge magnitude (Boysen & Berntson, 1989). She actually performed better when using Arabic numerals than the M&Ms with which she was trained, as these appear to be a special, potentially distracting treat for chimpanzees. Human infants and non-human primates show the same effects of distance and ratio on magnitude judgments as adults (Brannon, 2006). Individuals make faster and more accurate judgments as numbers become farther apart (e.g., 6 versus 7 is more difficult than 2 versus 9). Infants make discriminations between larger numbers of elements (8 versus 16) but have more difficulty with smaller differences (12 versus 16). However, the abilities of human infants improve over time. A six-month-old infant requires a 1:2 ratio (or half, such as 4 versus 8) before discriminating a difference, whereas a nine-month-old infant can make a 2:3 ratio (or two-thirds, such as 6 versus 9) discrimination.

Neuroscience data from several different types of studies emphasize the importance of the IPS to this sense of number. Studies of individuals with brain damage have shown that the meaning of numbers is disrupted by damage to the parietal lobe, and the intraparietal sulcus (IPS) in particular. We mentioned the IPS earlier in the context of solving Piaget's conservation of number task. Damage to other parts of the brain can impact a person's memorized arithmetic facts (e.g., 2 x 12 = 24) while leaving the person's sense of number, including numerical magnitude, intact. These observations are corroborated by fMRI studies that show activation in the IPS in response to numerical stimuli, whether Arabic numeral (2) or word (two), or when presented visually or spoken (Brannon, 2006). Cells in the IPS and prefrontal cortex of rhesus monkeys are maximally responsive to a single number (e.g., three) and reduce their firing rate as the number of stimuli becomes more different from the target number (Nieder & Miller, 2004). The right IPS is activated when individuals judge both countable sizes (how many?) and continuous sizes like length (Sokolowski & Ansari, 2016).

The relationship between this innate, non-symbolic sense of numerical magnitude and a child's later acquisition of formal mathematics is unclear. Some researchers argue that symbolic abilities originate in their connections with the non-symbolic sense of number (e.g., Dehaene, 2008), but others (e.g., Lyons & Ansari, 2015) are not so sure. Both symbolic and non-symbolic performance contributed to overall math achievement, but symbolic performance was more strongly related to achievement (Fazio et al., 2014). Thus, symbolic performance is a more appropriate focus for educational intervention. It is possible that direct connections between non-symbolic and symbolic representations for the numbers 1 through 4 exist (Feigenson et al., 2004). The Munduruku people of Brazil do not have names for numbers greater than five in their language (Pica et al., 2004). These direct connections might serve as a basis for learning rules about larger numbers, but the processes by which this might occur have not been outlined.

Neuroscience has also begun to illuminate the effects of learning and development on the way the brain handles numbers, as in mental arithmetic, or the ability to perform computations in your head without writing anything down or using a calculator. The activity of the brain during mental arithmetic changes as a function of age (Rivera et al.,

2005). As children grow older, the left inferior parietal cortex appears to become more specialized for this type of processing. Younger children rely more on the frontal cortex and subcortical structures involved with memory, such as the hippocampus.

Researchers have used neuroscience to differentiate the use of strategies to solve arithmetic problems. Think about some of the numerical problems you might have solved recently, such as figuring out how much you could afford to spend on eating out until your next paycheck. Did you use a retrieval strategy (the number just popped into your head)? Or did you use a procedural strategy (you broke the problem into multiple steps)? With more experience with a specific type of problem, most people begin to rely more on retrieval strategies and less on procedural strategies (Siegler & Shrager, 1984). The use of retrieval strategies is associated with higher activation in the left angular gyrus, an area of the parietal lobe near the edge of the temporal lobe (Grabner et al., 2009). Understanding developmental changes in arithmetic strategies is helpful not only for the development of appropriate instruction, but also for the understanding of dyscalculia, which often is accompanied by poor use of strategies. Children with low mathematics achievement appear to rely on procedural strategies in cases where their higher-performing peers have switched to retrieval strategies (De Smedt et al., 2011).

Just as we learn about the correlates of typical reading by investigating dyslexia, we can also gain insights into typical mathematical processing by studying cases of **dyscalculia**, which affects between 1.3% and 10% of the population (Devine et al., 2013). Like dyslexia, dyscalculia is diagnosed in those with typical intelligence and exposure to typical instruction. Dyscalculia affects a person's knowledge of numbers and arithmetic, which in turn influences educational attainment and employment opportunities. Developmental dyscalculia (DD; as opposed to dyscalculia acquired due to brain injury) can take several forms. When it appears in a "pure" form, for example, without dyslexia, it is associated with problems in the intraparietal sulcus (IPS; Rubinsten & Henik, 2009).

Scientists debate whether dyscalculia has its roots in deficits in the ability to judge numerical magnitudes (c.f. Bugden & Ansari, 2016) or if it is a more purely numerical perceptual deficit (Bulthé et al., 2019). A clever study by Fooks et al. (2021) used psychometric methods to demonstrate that adults with dyscalculia showed obvious deficits in their sensitivity to size. However, these same individuals showed intact size constancy, or the ability to perceive objects at various distances as being the same size. In other words, we do not think that a human being in the distance is a miniature human being, but rather that the human being is a normal size but is just far away from us (see Figure 5.5). Apparently, individuals with dyscalculia can compensate for weaknesses in magnitude perception using implicit (unconscious) processes like size constancy. These compensations might account for some of the mixed findings in this area.

The neuroeducation field can provide an important service by stimulating and energizing further research into the developmental course of mathematical abilities, both in typically developing children and children with specific difficulties in processing numbers.

FIGURE 5.5 The perceptual process of size constancy allows us to perceive objects at various distances to be the same size. This assumes, however, that the objects are familiar to us, like people or dogs. If you are unaware that the photo on the left depicts the Gateway Arch in St. Louis, MO, you would have a tough time judging its size without other familiar cues, such as the buildings shown in the photo on the right.

Sources: https://pixabay.com/photos/monument-gateway-arch-st-louis-1126742/; https://commons.wikimedia.org/wiki/File:St_Louis_night_expblend_cropped.jpg

Executive Function

Executive function consists of top-down functions that manage behavior when more automatic processes like instincts are not appropriate (Diamond & Ling, 2019). Executive functions are effortful. Executive functions form a critical aspect of neuroeducation, as they predict school readiness in children even better than IQ or entry-level reading and math skills as well as school success from the earliest grades through university study (Diamond & Ling, 2019).

At the core of executive function are inhibitory control, working memory, and cognitive flexibility. From these core abilities emerge higher order executive functions, including reasoning, problem-solving, and planning (Diamond & Ling, 2019). These executive functions are dependent on networks connecting the prefrontal cortex to structures such as the anterior cingulate cortex, the parietal lobe, and subcortical structures such as the nucleus accumbens (see Chapter 2). As children mature, the networks supporting executive functions demonstrate increased connectivity (Zelazo & Carlson, 2020). Frontal lobe lesions, smaller volume of the prefrontal cortex, and lesser thickness in the prefrontal cortex are all associated with poor executive functioning (de Boer et al., 2021). The prefrontal cortex simultaneously acts to inhibit irrelevant processing while enhancing activity in goal-relevant networks.

Inhibitory control includes three sub-domains. Self-control, or behavioral inhibition, refers to control over one's behavior, impulses, and emotions. It includes the ability to delay gratification. A second aspect is control of attention. This includes selective attention, or the ability to focus while shutting out distractions. We also engage in cognitive inhibition, or the active suppression of unwanted thoughts and memories. Children and youth with poor inhibitory control are likely to experience an array of difficulties in the classroom, including disruptive behavior and lack of motivation to complete assignments. Completing school, which takes years of work, requires considerable delayed gratification. Children with poor impulse control are much less likely to finish high school, which can have major implications for both their own lives and the economic well-being of their communities (Moffitt et al., 2011).

Short-term memory works like a scratch pad for memory processing, holding information in place, and is quite limited in the amount of information that can be held and the duration of time for which information can be held. **Working memory** not only holds information in place but performs operations on it. We use working memory to follow instructions, plan next steps, or combine bits of information. Although very similar to one another, the two processes can be distinguished using separate tasks. Simple forward-span tasks ask the participant to recall items in the order they were presented and tap short-term memory alone. No operations on the items are required. In contrast, re-ordering span tasks that require the participant to re-order a list according to a criterion, like best to worst, require use of working memory. The two processes also show slightly different developmental trajectories, with short-term memory maturing earlier than working memory (Diamond, 1995). Short-term and working memory are processed by overlapping but separable neural networks. The dorsolateral prefrontal cortex (DLPC) often acts as an attention "switch" and is activated during working memory tasks but not short-term memory tasks (Eldreth et al., 2006).

We see pronounced individual differences in working memory capacities, which contribute to differences in IQ scores. People with large working memory capacity for verbal information differ from those with smaller capacities in the amount of activation observed in the anterior cingulate cortex (Osaka et al., 2003). In addition, people with smaller working memory capacities were more dependent on simple rehearsal strategies for maintaining information (repeating information over and over), while people with larger capacities used semantic strategies, such as making up stories to help them remember. Some learning disabilities, including dyslexia, tax working memory more than usual, contributing to difficulty comprehending things like multiple choice questions. By the time the student reaches the last option in a multiple choice question, her working memory might no longer hold the original question itself, making the selection of a correct option nearly impossible.

Cognitive flexibility, or updating, allows a person to change perspectives, whether that means a simple grouping of objects first by size and then by color or taking the perspective of other people (Miyake et al., 2000). People with good cognitive flexibility are less susceptible to functional fixedness, or thinking about something in a single way. Freedom from functional fixedness contributes to creativity. Cognitive flexibility allows us to "roll with the flow," successfully tackling change in the environment.

Behavioral neuroscience might help us understand one further influence on executive function—happiness. As you might have noticed in your own work, we experience better working memory and selective attention (focus) when we're feeling happy (Csikszentmihalyi et al., 2005). Happiness in turn is associated with activity in the brain's pleasure circuits, which influence the prefrontal areas of the brain that are so essential to executive function (Wang & Lupica, 2014). Activity in these pathways ensures that we stay on task and meet our goals, even if this requires long hours of work.

Given the importance of executive functions to educational outcomes, it should come as no surprise that many have attempted to intervene to improve them. Results regarding the efficacy of such efforts are mixed. The variety of methods makes them very difficult to evaluate. The Tools of the Mind curriculum presented to kindergarten students in Massachusetts improved executive functions, with the bonus of also improving reading, vocabulary, and math progress the following year (Blair & Raver, 2014). Mindfulness training with and without movement like yoga has demonstrated promising improvements on executive function, possibly due to reductions in stress (Diamond & Ling, 2019). However, meta-analyses have not provided support for the ability to intervene with executive function (Kassai et al., 2019). Observed transfer effects appear to be weak or absent altogether. What is missing so far is an evaluation of these same approaches using neuroscience tools. If stress reduction indeed moderates the success of mindfulness, neuroscience should help illuminate that.

Promising School Programs

Diamond and Ling (2019) review many different programs aimed to raise executive functions through school curricula. These programs do not appear to have been influenced much, if at all by neuroscience, but focus more on self-control and social competencies. A possible next step would be to conduct further evaluations of children in these programs using neuroscience measures. In addition, using our understanding of the neuroscience of executive function, we might develop novel approaches to interventions.

Non-invasive Brain Stimulation

In recent years, two types of non-invasive brain stimulation, repeated transcranial magnetic stimulation (rTMS) and transcranial electrical stimulation (tES; see Chapter 1) have been investigated as possible interventions for improving executive function.

In a large meta-analysis of brain stimulation directed at the prefrontal cortex, de Boer et al. (2021) found no significant effects of stimulation on working memory. A small but significant benefit was found for improving inhibition, but this was limited to reduced motor impulsivity. No improvement was found in inhibition tasks like the Stroop Task, which requires suppression of certain responses, or in tasks related to delayed gratification (see Figure 5.6). No effects were found in tasks related to cognitive flexibility or planning tasks. These results are consistent with a general role of the prefrontal cortex in inhibition, and the inhibition of movement in particular. It is likely that other types of executive function involve more extensive networks. Further research using brain imaging might help to pinpoint the effects of brain stimulation on executive functioning.

Transcranial electrical stimulation (tES) has the potential to influence brain plasticity and memory (Bréchet et al., 2021). This stimulation, by influencing particular cortical oscillations (wave forms detected using EEG; see Chapter 1), can mimic the brain's activity during the formation of a memory. Patients with Alzheimer's disease show memory deficits, of course, but also show reduced gamma wave activity. Gamma activity in the hippocampus plays an essential role in the formation of episodic memory, or memory for one's personal events. This is precisely the type of memory that fails first in Alzheimer's disease. The recent development of equipment that can administer this type of stimulation safely at home has spurred further investigations into brain stimulation as a possible intervention for Alzheimer's disease and other dementias. If these methods prove to be efficacious, it is likely that researchers will also investigate them with healthy individuals as well.

Pharmaceutical Interventions: Nootropics

Nootropics are substances, both natural and synthetic, that boost cognitive function and are often referred to as "smart drugs." But do they really work? Evidence for the efficacy and safety of most commercial, non-prescription nootropics is lacking, but this does not stop people from purchasing them.

FIGURE 5.6 Stimulation of the prefrontal cortex showed some improvement on motor inhibition, but not for the more complex inhibition required to succeed in the Stroop task. To correctly name the color of the ink, the participant must inhibit the strong impulse to simply read the word. Response times are faster in congruent than in incongruent trials.

Source: Adapted from https://commons.wikimedia.org/wiki/File:Trials_in_the_Stroop_Task.jpeg

Most psychological disorders involve some deficits in executive functioning but do so in diverse ways. Notable among psychological disorders for disrupted executive functioning is attention deficit hyperactivity disorder (ADHD), which is characterized by impulsivity and reduced sustained or on-task attention abilities. The most common treatment for ADHD is stimulant medication, which might initially seem counterintuitive given the hyperactivity that often accompanies this disorder. However, as we mentioned earlier, the prefrontal cortex is especially important to the inhibition of unwanted behavior. This function is dependent on the activity of dopamine (see Chapter 2), and there is some evidence that children with ADHD experience lower than normal dopamine activity. In turn, the stimulant medications typically prescribed for children with ADHD, such as methylphenidate (Ritalin) and Adderall, a collection of amphetamine salts, are potent dopamine agonists. This does not imply that medication for ADHD is a magic bullet. Children with ADHD who are medicated do not outperform children with ADHD who are not medicated (about half) in long-term outcomes such as high school graduation and college entrance (Loe & Feldman, 2007).

It is a common misunderstanding to think that children with ADHD respond differently to stimulant medications (becoming calmer) than children who do not have ADHD (Arnsten, 2006). Stimulant medications are not diagnostic for ADHD. If they were, all we would need to do to confirm a diagnosis would be to administer a stimulant and observe the outcome. The fact that everyone responds to these stimulants in similar ways is also supported by the high rates of ongoing abuse of stimulant drugs by college students wishing to benefit from better attention and longer on-task behavior. This does not mean that we are advocating for the use of stimulant medications for improved cognition, as these drugs have significant side effects.

Caffeine has long been consumed for its effects on alertness, mood, and concentration, but can it influence other aspects of executive function? Caffeine consumption is associated with lower rates of mild cognitive impairment and conversion to Alzheimer's disease (Haller et al., 2017). It is important to recognize that these studies are correlational. Although the impact of caffeine on cognitive function is dose-dependent (more caffeine, if intake is still moderate, provides more protection), we are not randomly assigning participants to caffeine and no caffeine groups. As a result, we can't say for certain that consuming caffeine *causes* a reduction in risk for cognitive decline. It is also quite possible that the physiology that can sustain caffeine consumption is also more resistant to cognitive decline. In other words, the same person who is jittery after one cup of coffee might be more susceptible to cognitive decline (see Figure 5.7).

Does this mean that we should be advocating for caffeine consumption to improve memory in schools? Realistically, many children are already exposed to significant amounts of caffeine through their consumption of soft drinks. Drug effects are always measured as a function of body weight, so a small child consuming a can of Coca Cola is experiencing a similar amount of caffeine as an adult having a cup of coffee. While the impact of this consumption is worthy of study, we actually don't know much about it. The ethical constraints on research with children make this type of research very difficult to perform. However, a modest dose of caffeine (200 mg; about the amount in 12 ounces of brewed coffee) produced faster text reading speed in healthy young adults (Franceschini et al., 2020). Caffeine also boosted performance on a global visual perception task that is often challenging for people with dyslexia. Caffeine has also been shown to improve creative problem-solving, one of the higher-order executive functions discussed in this section (Zabelina & Silvia, 2020).

It is very likely that while discovering preventive measures and treatments for Alzheimer's disease that additional effective nootropics will emerge. At that point, we will have some difficult decisions to consider, not unlike the issues facing sports authorities tasked with managing performance-enhancing drugs. Will there be equitable access to nootropics? What about side effects?

Brain Training

Computerized cognitive training (CCT), known more generally by its popular name of "brain training," refers to interventions presented through technology rather than people that are designed to improve many aspects of cognition.

Like many neuroeducation interventions, brain training is provided primarily by commercial entities. One market forecast predicts that the global cognitive assessment and training market will grow from $3.2 billion in 2020 to $11.4 billion by 2025 (MarketsAndMarkets, 2020). Among the influences pushing this boom are an increased gamification of cognitive assessment and COVID-19 effects on eLearning and testing

FIGURE 5.7 Many people are already consuming one nootropic—caffeine. As more research identifies treatments for cognitive decline, the use of nootropics by healthy individuals is likely to be the focus of intense debates.

Source: https://commons.wikimedia.org/wiki/File:Coffee_break_(3457656569).jpg

cognition at home. Concerns on the part of consumers about possible cognitive after-effects of COVID-19 might increase interest in both assessment and brain training programs they can explore on their own in the privacy of their own homes (see Figure 5.8).

Although any effective "training" by definition involves changes in the brain and its functioning, there is no need to understand the nervous system before evaluating many of the claims made on behalf of the cognitive interventions available today. The main connection between neuroscience and brain training is the foundational claim that neural plasticity makes brain training feasible throughout the lifespan. In other words, you can indeed teach an old dog new tricks. The discovery that the brain maintains some plasticity outside of previously assumed "critical windows" (please review Neuromyth #1 earlier in this chapter) has given hope to many older adults and individuals who have experienced brain injury. However, we need to know much more before we endorse commercial games as cure-alls for cognitive deficits or decline.

In addition to the contributions of neuroplasticity, there are other aspects of brain training that seem reasonable. Brain training is a form of mental activity. Many people believe that staying mentally active will help prevent mental decline, the so-called "use it or lose it" hypothesis (Salthouse, 2006). Most of the evidence for this hypothesis, however, remains correlational. We don't randomly assign adults to mental activity and no mental activity groups, so we are unable to say that staying mentally active *causes* lower risk for cognitive decline. It is likely that many confounding variables participate in this relationship, including cognitive ability and education. Nonetheless, it remains good advice to maintain a commitment to mental activity. We can't guarantee that playing

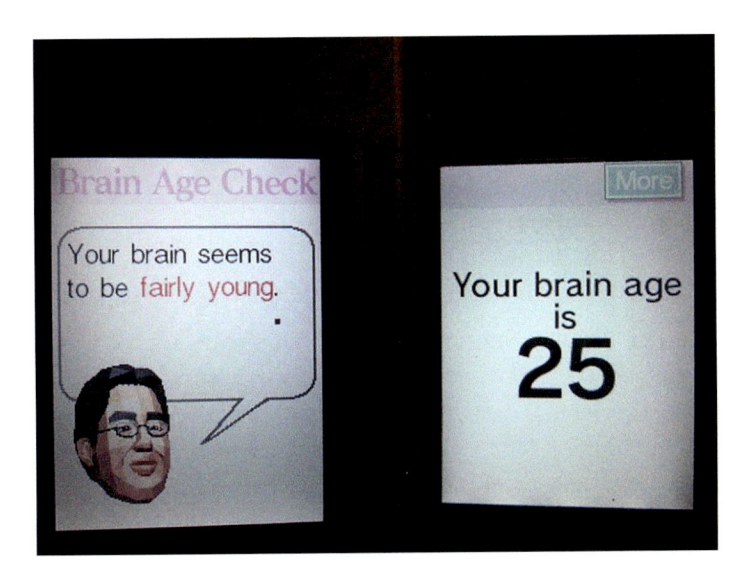

FIGURE 5.8 Can commercial brain training programs like Nintendo's Brain Training program really do what they claim to do? Only carefully conducted research can really tell.
Source: www.flickr.com/photos/wetwebwork/163811080

Sudoku daily will prevent cognitive decline, but continuing to engage with mentally stimulating activities you enjoy seems like a good idea.

We assume that "practice makes perfect." In other words, practicing a task is likely to result in improved performance, whether that is working on a tennis serve or using flashcards to master your neuroscience vocabulary terms. We also believe that practice on one skill can transfer to related activities. In fact, we could not in good conscience recommend that you invest in a college education unless significant **transfer** was known to occur. Some of the details of what you learn in college might be forgotten, but you are also learning strategies for memorization, time management, metacognition, information search, and critical thinking at the same time. These types of skills, we hope, will sustain your efforts as lifetime learners.

The efficacy of commercial brain training is the subject of an intense debate. Not only do these programs involve the transfer of skills, but they do so through technology and without human interaction, such as we typically expect in a teaching or rehabilitation situation. In 2014, more than 70 scientists signed a position statement arguing that brain training effects had been over-hyped by commercial providers and that there was little scientific support for brain training efficacy (Stanford Center for Longevity, 2014). This publication elicited an equally passionate response by a group of 111 scientists arguing in favor of brain training (Cognitive Training Data, 2014). A subsequent review by Simons et al. (2016) criticized the research cited in this latter supportive statement. While debate is always a healthy thing for science, this topic has generated an unusual amount of acrimony.

Despite their strong areas of disagreement, the two sides do agree on several issues (Harvey et al., 2018).

- Commercial claims of the benefits of brain training can be overstated and unsubstantiated.
- More research on brain training is needed.
- Brain training neither prevents nor cures Alzheimer's disease.
- Brain training does not work in a single "dose," but requires sustained effort.
- Physical exercise plays an important role in brain health.

Then where do these scientists disagree? As we mentioned earlier, an important premise of commercial brain training is that transfer of practice effects can occur. Although some traditional rehabilitation programs train specific skills, like driving a car or cooking dinner, most commercial brain training targets more general improvements in cognition, like attention or memory. Under what circumstances can we expect training on one task to benefit performance on an untrained but related task? Fortunately for our evaluation efforts, the topic of transfer of learning has an extensive history in psychological science, going back at least as far as psychology pioneers William James and Edward Thorndike, each of whom proposed theories regarding the circumstances necessary for transfer.

Central to the discussion of transfer today is the degree of similarity between the practiced and unpracticed task (Barnett & Ceci, 2002; Klahr & Chen, 2011). **Simple practice** means that you repeatedly perform the same task, and no transfer is necessary. If you practice parallel parking your car or your tennis serve, you should gradually improve. **Near transfer** refers to transfer effects on highly similar tasks, like performing better on a quiz made up of algebra problems after practicing similar types of algebra problems as homework. **Far transfer** refers to the more abstract and global effects of practice. For example, if you train on a computerized task that requires attention, is your attention while reading this textbook improved? Harvey et al. (2018) included a third level of transfer—**environmental transfer**. This means that a trained task would impact everyday functioning. Many a student has asked why it is necessary for everyday living to know how to compute the volume of a cylinder. As you can imagine, the lines between levels of transfer, particularly for near and far transfer, are often blurred and hard to establish. For some scholars, showing that a computerized training task improves performance on standardized neuropsychological tests is not transfer at all, whereas other scholars believe this to be an example of near transfer.

Another component of the controversy results from lumping all brain training programs together (Cognitivetrainingdata.org, 2021). As this statement argues, you would not study one "pill" and claim that "pills" either do or do not work. CCT or brain training programs come in many different forms, with some more closely aligned to neuroscience than others. Some programs target single domains, like working memory, while others target whole arrays of domains. Some programs are designed to be used by individuals working alone, while others involved a trained facilitator (Harvey et al., 2018). Most have been evaluated within the context of multifaceted treatment programs, as it would be ethically impossible to withhold standard treatment from patients with cognitive challenges. This introduces a level of variability in the research outcomes that clouds points of agreement.

One of the larger investigations of CCT in healthy older adults was the Advanced Cognitive Training for Independent and Vital Elderly (ACTIVE) study (Jobe et al,. 2001). Nearly 3000 adults over the age of 65 were divided into four groups: control (no treatment), memory strategy (instructor led; no computer), reasoning training (instructor led; no computer), or speed training (adaptive computerized training). Each of the three treatment groups had one hour of training twice a week for five weeks for a total of ten sessions. Each of the training groups experienced significant improvement in near transfer relative to the control group. Although the improvement decreased over time, it was still significant ten years later. The improvements did not show far transfer, as measured by performance on neuropsychology tests outside of the trained domains. However, the three treatment groups showed slower decline than the control group in measures of daily living, suggesting an improvement in environmental transfer from the cognitive training. The speed training group showed improvements in depressive symptoms, self-rated health, driving cessation, and real-world automobile crash incidence. Impressively, these long-term benefits resulted from only ten sessions of training.

ACTIVE used programs developed by the commercial CCT organization Posit Science, affiliated with leading neuroplasticity expert Michael Merzenich. Posit Science programs have been evaluated by independent research groups using EEG (Mishra et al., 2016; Berry et al., 2010; Anderson et al., 2013), fMRI (Scalf et al., 2007), PET (Shah et al., 2014), diffusion tensor imaging (Strenziok et al., 2014), and pupillometry (Burge et al., 2013). Patients with schizophrenia using Posit Science targeted cognitive training related to social cognition showed changes in activity in networks associated with facial emotion processing (Haut et al., 2019). Older adults with mild cognitive impairment showed long-term improvement in a variety of autonomic measures including heart rate variability as well as network connectivity assessed using fMRI after training with processing speed and attention programs (Lin et al., 2020). Posit Science continues to be supported by high-quality research (Shah et al., 2017).

It is likely that CCT will continue to generate debate and we must be cautious about over-extending claims made on its behalf. A 2015 report issued by the Institute of Medicine (now the National Academy of Medicine) outlined a set of evaluation criteria that CCT programs should be able to meet:

▶ Has the product demonstrated transfer of training to other laboratory tasks that measure the same cognitive construct as the training task (e.g., if some aspect of memory is being targeted in the product, is transfer demonstrated to other memory tasks)?

▶ Has the product demonstrated transfer of training to relevant real-world tasks?

▶ Has the product performance been evaluated using an active control group whose members have the same expectations of cognitive benefits as do members of the experimental group?

▶ How long are the trained skills retained?

▶ Have the purported benefits of the training product been replicated by research groups other than those selling the product? (pp. 189–190).

Much work remains on the part of neuroeducators to figure out the best evidence-based practices for preventing and treating cognitive decline. As a side benefit, however, while pursuing these preventive and remediation approaches, we might also discover ways to augment our existing cognitive skills. These methods certainly cause no harm, so further exploration can proceed without risk.

Neuroscience and the Evaluation of Cognitive Training

Neuroscience has an important role to play in the continuing evaluation of efforts to boost cognitive functioning through training (Kuchinsky & Haarmann, 2019). Evaluation of neural plasticity resulting from training, such as changes in brain structure and function, might help neuroeducators identify neural systems that both support important functions, such as working memory, and are modifiable through training.

Using non-invasive methods such as fMRI and EEG, researchers have been able to correlate improvements in working memory and attention following training with underlying circuits. For example, EEG allowed researchers to see that practice enhanced the detection of distracting information by the parietal lobe, activating the prefrontal cortex, which then in turn prevented the storage of further distracting information by the parietal lobe (Liesefeld et al., 2014). Blocking the distracting information reduced the demands on working memory.

Neuroscience might also help untangle the issues of transfer of training, persistence of training effects, and individual differences in responses to training. Transfer should occur when both trained and novel tasks overlap, or engage similar neural activity (Kuchinsky & Haarmann, 2019). Many existing studies do not examine the persistence of training effects, but this is a critical factor in designing evidence-based treatments. While fMRI is probably too costly to use repeatedly to track the persistence of training effects, EEG provides a useful, cost-effective alternative. Individual differences, especially those that are evident prior to training, can influence the benefits of training. More information about the impact of individual differences would allow neuroeducators to predict who is most likely to benefit from a certain type of training.

Using cost-effective methods like EEG, neuroscience can help validate and improve behavioral training by increasing our knowledge of the neural correlates of practice and transfer.

Chapter Summary

The marriage between neuroscience and education is a promising one, but like most marriages, there are some issues to work out. The honeymoon might be over, but if expectations for the collaboration remain realistic, much can be accomplished. Scholars in both fields must continue to find common language and points of agreement regarding goals and methods.

The benefits of continuing this collaboration are many. As our workplaces require increasing amounts of education for success, the waste in human capital from failure to educate children and youth effectively is something we cannot afford. Democracies depend on an educated public, especially in an era of social media and the spread of misinformation. Contributions of neuroscience to the assessment of educational practices and to the deeper understanding of how learning proceeds in the brain could help inform innovative educational practice. In a reciprocal fashion, the questions asked by educators, such as how children learn mathematics, can provide neuroscientists with new directions for their own research programs and opportunities to contribute to solutions to significant real-world problems.

Review Questions

1. Which of the following is the best definition of neuroeducation (LO 5.1)?
    a. The study of the neural correlates of early childhood acquisition of information.
    b. The use of neuroscience to improve and understand learning and instruction.
    c. The use of classroom data to inform the neuroscientific basis of learning.
    d. The use of neuroscience to understand disorders of learning, such as dyslexia.
2. Individuals with dyslexia show which of the following patterns of brain activity while reading (LO 5.2)?
    a. They use anterior (forward) parts of the brain while reading more than typical readers do.
    b. They use posterior (back) parts of the brain while reading more than typical readers do.
    c. There are no discernable differences in brain activity while reading between people with and without dyslexia.
    d. They show vastly reduced levels of brain activity during reading compared to typical readers.
3. Which of the following is an example of inhibitory control (LO 5.3)?
    a. Holding information in memory to plan next steps.
    b. Ability to avoid functional fixedness.
    c. Ability to focus on information and tune out distractions.
    d. Use information to follow instructions.
4. Which of the following is suspected of being a nootropic (LO 5.4)?
    a. Aspirin
    b. Antidepressants
    c. Antihistamines
    d. Caffeine

5. Which of the following is an example of far transfer (LO 5.5)?

    a. Jorge, an English major, is pursuing a career as a social media manager.
    b. Gina goes on Quizlet to find questions sets similar to the ones provided by her biochemistry professor to practice for an exam.
    c. Cyrus is recovering from a traumatic brain injury, and he is using a driving simulator to learn how to drive again.
    d. Malia is practicing several relatively easier pieces by Beethoven to help her master a difficult piece.

Thought Questions

1. What do you think the best strategies are for overcoming existing neuromyths and preventing new ones?
2. How would you investigate the relative contributions of genetics and environment to impulse control?

Answer Key for Review Questions

1. b
2. a
3. c
4. d
5. a

References

Anderson, S., White-Schwoch, T., Choi, H. J., & Kraus, N. (2013). Training changes processing of speech cues in older adults with hearing loss. *Frontiers in Systems Neuroscience, 7*(97), 1–9. https://doi.org/10.3389/fnsys.2013.00097

Ansari, D. (2010). Neurocognitive approaches to developmental disorders of numerical and mathematical cognition: The perils of neglecting the role of development. *Learning and Individual Differences, 20*(2), 123–129. https://doi.org/10.1016/j.lindif.2009.06.001

Ansari, D., De Smedt, B., & Grabner, R. H. (2012). Neuroeducation—A critical overview of an emerging field. *Neuroethics, 5*(2), 105–117. https://doi.org/10.1007/s12152-011-9119-3

Arnsten, A. F. (2006). Stimulants: Therapeutic actions in ADHD. *Neuropsychopharmacology, 31*(11), 2376–2383. https://doi.org/10.1038/sj.npp.1301164

Barnett, S.M., & Ceci, S.J. (2002). When and where do we apply what we learn? A taxonomy for far transfer. *Psychological Bulletin*, 128(4), 612–637. https://doi.org/10.1037/0033-2909.128.4.612

Berry, A. S., Zanto, T. P., Clapp, W. C., Hardy, J. L., Delahunt, P. B., Mahncke, H. W., & Gazzaley, A. (2010). The influence of perceptual training on working memory in older adults. *PLoS ONE*, 5(7), e11537. https://doi.org/10.1371/journal.pone.0011537

Blair, C., & Raver, C. (2014). Closing the achievement gap through modification of neurocognitive and neuroendocrine function: Results from a cluster randomized controlled trial of an innovative approach to the education of children in kindergarten. *PLOS One*, 9(11), e112393. https://doi.org/10.1371/journal.pone.0112393

Bowers, J. S. (2016). The practical and principled problems with educational neuroscience. *Psychological Review*, 123(5), 600–612. https://doi.org/10.1037/rev0000025

Boysen, S., & Berntson, G. (1989). Numerical competence in a chimpanzee (*Pan troglodytes*). *Journal of Comparative Psychology*, 103(1), 23–31. https://doi.org/10.1037/0735-7036.103.1.23

Brannon E. M. (2006). The representation of numerical magnitude. *Current Opinion in Neurobiology*, 16(2), 222–229. https://doi.org/10.1016/j.conb.2006.03.002

Bréchet, L., Yu, W., Biagi, M. C., Ruffini, G., Gagnon, M., Manor, B., & Pascual-Leone, A. (2021). Patient-tailored, home-based non-invasive brain stimulation for memory deficits in dementia due to Alzheimer's disease. *Frontiers in Neurology*. https://doi.org/10.3389/fneur.2021.598135

Bruer, J. T. (1997). Education and the brain: A bridge too far. *Educational Researcher*, 26(8), 4–16. https://doi.org/10.3102/0013189X026008004

Bugden, S., & Ansari, D. (2016). Probing the nature of deficits in the "approximate number system" in children with persistent developmental dyscalculia. *Developmental Science*, 19(5), 817–833. https://doi.org/10.1111/desc.12324

Bulthé, J., Prinsen, J., Vanderauwera, J., Duyck, S., Daniels, N., Gillebert, C. R., Mantini, D., Op de Beeck, H. P., & De Smedt, B. (2019). Multi-method brain imaging reveals impaired representations of number as well as altered connectivity in adults with dyscalculia. *NeuroImage*, 190, 289–302. https://doi.org/10.1016/j.neuroimage.2018.06.012

Burge, W. K., Ross, L. A., Amthor, F. R., Mitchell, W. G., Zotov, A., & Visscher, K. M. (2013). Processing speed training increases the efficiency of attentional resource allocation in young adults. *Frontiers in Human Neuroscience*, 7(684), 1–7. https://doi.org/10.3389/fnhum.2013.00684.

Cognitivetrainingdata.org. (2014). *Cognitive training data response letter*. www.cognitivetrainingdata.org/the-controversy-does-brain-training-work/response-letter/

Cognitivetrainingdata.org (2021). *The controversy*. www.cognitivetrainingdata.org/the-controversy-does-brain-training-work/

Csikszentmihalyi, M., Abuhamdeh, S., & Nakamura, J. (2005). Flow. In A. J. Elliot & C. S. Dweck (Eds.), *Handbook of competence and motivation* (pp. 598–608). New York, NY: Guilford Publications.

de Boer, N. S., Schluter, R. S., Daams, J. G., van der Werf, Y. D., Goudriaan, A. E., & van Holst, R. J. (2021). The effect of non-invasive brain stimulation on executive functioning in healthy controls: A systematic review and meta-analysis. *Neuroscience and Biobehavioral Reviews*, 125, 122–147. https://doi.org/10.1016/j.neubiorev.2021.01.013

Dehaene, S. (2008). Symbols and quantities in parietal cortex: Elements of a mathematical theory of number representation and manipulation. In P. Haggard & Y. Rossetti (Eds.), *Sensorimotor foundations of higher cognition (attention and performance)* (pp. 527–574). New York: Oxford University Press.

Dehaene, S., Pegado, F., Braga, L. W., Ventura, P., Nunes Filho, G., Jobert, A., Dehaene-Lambertz, G., Kolinsky, R., Morais, J., & Cohen, L. (2010). How learning to read changes the cortical networks for vision and language. *Science, 330*(6009), 1359–1364. https://doi.org/10.1126/science.1194140

Dekker, S., Lee, N., Howard-Jones, P., & Jolles, J. (2012). Neuromyths in education: Prevalence and predictors of misconceptions among teachers. *Frontiers in Psychology, 3*, 429. https://doi.org/10.3389/fpsyg.2012.00429

De Smedt, B., Holloway, I. D., & Ansari, D. (2011). Effects of problem size and arithmetic operation on brain activation during calculation in children with varying levels of arithmetical fluency. *Neuroimage, 57*(3), 771–781. https://doi.org/10.1016/j.neuroimage.2010.12.037

Devine, A., Soltész, F., Nobes, A., Goswami, U., & Szűcs, D. (2013). Gender differences in developmental dyscalculia depend on diagnostic criteria. *Learning and Instruction, 27*, 31–39. https://doi.org/10.1016/j.learninstruc.2013.02.004

Diamond, A. (1995). Evidence of robust recognition memory early in life even when assessed by reaching behavior. *Journal of Experimental Child Psychology, 59*, 419–456. https://doi.org/10.1006/jecp.1995.1020

Diamond, A., & Ling, D. S. (2019). Review of the evidence on, and fundamental questions about, efforts to improve executive functions, including working memory. In J. M. Novick, M. F. Bunting, M. R. Dougherty, & R. W. Engle (Eds.), *Cognitive and working memory training: Perspectives from psychology, neuroscience, and human development*. Oxford Scholarship Online. https://doi.org/10.1093/oso/9780199974467.003.0008

Dweck, C. S. (2016). *Mindset: The new psychology of success*. New York, NY: Penguin Random House.

Eldreth, D. A., Patterson, M. D., Porcelli, A. J., Biswal, B. B., Rebbechi, D., & Rypma, B. (2006). Evidence for multiple manipulation processes in prefrontal cortex. *Brain Research, 1123*(1), 145–156. https://doi.org/10.1016/j.brainres.2006.07.129

Fazio, L. K., Bailey, D. H., Thompson, C. A., & Siegler, R. S. (2014). Relations of different types of numerical magnitude representations to each other and to mathematics achievement. *Journal of Experimental Child Psychology, 123*, 53–72. https://doi.org/10.1016/j.jecp.2014.01.013

Feigenson, L., Dehaene, S., & Spelke, E. (2004). Core systems of number. *Trends in Cognitive Science, 8*(7), 307–314. https://doi.org/10.1016/j.tics.2004.05.002

Fooks, N., Hadad, B-S., & Rubinsten, O. (2021). Nonsymbolic-magnitude deficit in adults with developmental dyscalculia: Evidence of impaired size discrimination but intact size constancy. *Psychological Science, 32*(8), 1271–1284. https://doi.org/10.1177/0956797621995204

Franceschini, S., Lulli, M., Bertoni, S., Gori, S., Angrilli, A., Mancarella, M., Puciio, G., & Facoetti, A. (2020). Caffeine improves text reading and global perception. *Journal of Psychopharmacology, 34*(3), 315–325. https://doi.org/10.1177/0269881119878178

Froyen, D. J., Bonte, M. L., van Atteveldt, N., & Blomert, L. (2009). The long road to automation: Neurocognitive development of letter-speech sound processing. *Journal of Cognitive Neuroscience, 21*(3), 567–580. https://doi.org/10.1162/jocn.2009.21061

Grabner, R.H., Ansari, D., Koschutnig, K., Reishofer, G., Ebner, F., & Neuper, C. (2009). To retrieve or to calculate? Left angular gyrus mediates the retrieval of arithmetic facts during problem solving. *Neuropsychologia, 47*(2), 604–608. https://doi.org/10.1016/j.neuropsychologia.2008.10.013

Haller, S., Montandon, M-L., Rodriguez, C., Moser, D., Toma, S., Hofmeister, J., & Giannakopoulos, P. (2017). Caffeine impact on working memory-related network activation patterns in early stages of cognitive decline. *Functional Neuroradiology, 59*, 387–395. https://doi.org/10.1007/s00234-017-1803-5

Harvey, P. D., McGurk, S. R., Mahncke, H., & Wykes, T. (2018). Controversies in computerized cognitive training. *Biological Psychiatry: Cognitive Neuroscience and Neuroimaging, 3*, 907–915. https://doi.org/10.1016/j.bpsc.2018.06.008

Haut, K., Galindo, B., Lee, A., Lokey, S., Nahum, M., & Hooker, C. (2019). F158. Changes in emotion processing network following social cognitive training in individuals with schizophrenia. *Biological Psychiatry*, *85*(10), S274. https://doi.org/10.1016/j.biopsych.2019.03.695

Hoeft, F., Meyler, Hernandez, A., Juel, C., Taylor-Hill, H., Martindale, J. L., McMillon, G., Kolchugina, G., Black, J. M., Faizi, A., Deutsch, G. K., Siok, W. T., Reiss, A. L., Whitfield-Gabrieli, S., & Gabrieli, J. D. E. (2007). Functional and morphometric brain dissociation between dyslexia and reading ability. *Proceedings of the National Academy of Sciences of the United States of America*, *104*(10), 4234–4239. https://doi.org/10.1073/pnas.0609399104

Institute of Medicine. (2015). Committee on the Public Health Dimensions of Cognitive Aging; Board on Health Sciences Policy. In D. G. Blazer, K. Yaffe, and C. T. Liverman (Eds.), *Cognitive aging: Progress in understanding and opportunities for action*. Washington, DC: National Academies Press.

Jobe, J. B., Smith, D. M., Ball, K., Tennstedt, S. L., Marsiske, M., Willis, S. L., Rebok, G. W., Morris, J. N., Helmers, K. F., Leveck, M. D., & Kleinman, K. (2001). ACTIVE: A cognitive intervention trial to promote independence in older adults. *Controlled Clinical Trials*, *22*, 453–479. https://doi.org/10.1016/S0197-2456(01)00139-8

Kassai, R., Futó, J., Demetrovics, Z., & Takacs, Z. K. (2019). A meta-analysis of the experimental evidence on the near- and far-transfer effects among children's executive function skills. *Psychological Bulletin*, *145*, 165–188. https://doi.org/10.1037/bul0000180

Klahr, D., & Chen, Z. (2011). Finding one's place in transfer space. *Child Development Perspectives*, *5*(3), 196–204. https://doi.org/10.1111/j.1750-86-6.2011.00171.x

Kuchinsky, S. E., & Haarmann, H. J. (2019). Neuroscience perspectives on cognitive training. In J. M. Novick, M. F. Bunting, M. R. Dougherty, & R. W. Engle (Eds.), *Cognitive and working memory training: Perspectives from psychology, neuroscience, and human development*. Oxford Scholarship Online. https://doi.org/10.1093/oso/9780199974467.003.0008

Liesefeld, A. M., Liesefeld, H. R., & Zimmer, H. D. (2014). Intercommunication between prefrontal and posterior brain regions for protecting visual working memory from distractor interference. *Psychological Science*, *25*(2), 325–333. https://doi.org/10.1177/0956797613501170

Lin, F., Tao, Y., Chen, Q., Anthony, M., Zhang, Z., Duje Tadin, D., & Heffner, K. L. (2020). Processing speed and attention training modifies autonomic flexibility: A mechanistic intervention study. *NeuroImage*, *213*, 116730. https://doi.org/10.1016/j.neuroimage.2020.116730

Loe, I., & Feldman, H. (2007). Academic and educational outcome of children with ADHD. *Journal of Pediatric Psychology*, *32*(6), 643–654. https://doi.org/10.1016/j.ambp.2006.05.005

Lyons, I. M., & Ansari, D. (2015). Foundations of children's numerical and mathematical skills: The roles of symbolic and nonsymbolic representations of numerical magnitude. *Advances in Child Development and Behavior*, *48*, 93–116. https://doi.org/10.1016/bs.acdb.2014.11.003.

MarketsAndMarkets (2020). *Cognitive assessment and training market*. www.marketsandmarkets.com/Market-Reports/cognitive-assessment-market-1039.html

MacLeod, A., Castellanos-Ryan, N., Parent, S., Jacques, S., & Séguin, J. R. (2018). Modelling vocabulary development among multilingual children prior to and following the transition to school entry. *International Journal of Bilingual Education and Bilingualism*, 1–20. https://doi.org/10.1080/13670050.2016.1269718

Meyler, A., Keller, T. A., Cherkassky, V. L., Gabrieli, J. D. E., & Just, M. A. (2008). Modifying the brain activation of poor readers during sentence comprehension with extended remedial instruction: A longitudinal study of neuroplasticity. *Neuropsychologia*, *46*, 2580–2592. https://doi.org/10.1016/j.neuropsychologia.2008.03.012

Mishra, J., Sagar, R., Joseph, A. A., Gazzaley, A., & Merzenich, M. M. (2016). Training sensory signal-to-noise resolution in children with ADHD in a global mental health setting. *Translational Psychiatry*, *6*(4), e781. https://doi.org/10.1038/tp.2016.45

Miyake, A., Friedman, N. P., Emerson, M. J., Witzki, A. H., Howerter, A., & Wager, T. D. (2000). The unity and diversity of executive functions and their contributions to complex "frontal lobe" tasks: A latent variable analysis. *Cognitive Psychology*, *41*(1), 49–100. https://doi.org/10.1006/cogp.1999.0734

Moffitt, T. E., Arseneault, L., Belsky, D., Dickson, N., Hancox, R. J., Harrington, H., Houts, R., Poulton, R., Roberts, B. W., Ross, S., Sears, M. R., Thomson, W. M., & Caspi, A. (2011). A gradient of childhood self-control predicts health, wealth, and public safety. *Proceedings of the National Academy of Sciences of the United States of America*, *108*(7), 2693–2698. https://doi.org/10.1073/pnas.1010076108

Molfese, D. L. (2000). Predicting dyslexia at 8 years of age using neonatal brain responses. *Brain and Language*, *72*(3), 238–245. https://doi.org/10.1006/brln.2000.2287

Morris, T. T., Dorling, D., Davies, N. M., & Smith, G. D. (2021). Associations between school enjoyment at age 6 and later educational achievement: Evidence from a UK cohort study. *npj Science of Learning*, *6*, 18. https://doi.org/10.1038/s41539-021-00092-w

Nancekivell, S. E., Shah, P., & Gelman, S. A. (2020). Maybe they're born with it, or maybe it's experience: Toward a deeper understanding of the learning style myth. *Journal of Educational Psychology*, *112*(2), 221–235. http://dx.doi.org/10.1037/edu0000366

Nieder, A., & Miller, E. K. (2004). A parieto-frontal network for visual numerical information in the monkey. *Proceedings of the National Academy of Sciences of the United States of America*, *101*(19), 7457–7462. https://doi.org/10.1073/pnas.0402239101

OECD (2002). *Neuromyth 1*. www.oecd.org/education/ceri/neuromyth1.htm

Osaka, M., Osaka, N., Kondo, H., Morishita, M., Fukuyama, H., Aso, T., & Shibasaki, H. (2003). The neural basis of individual differences in working memory capacity: An fMRI study. *NeuroImage*, *18*(3), 789–797. https://doi.org/10.1016/S1053-8119(02)00032-0

Pashler, H., McDaniel, M., Rohrer, D., & Bjork, R. (2008). Learning styles: Concepts and evidence. *Psychological Science in the Public Interest*, *9*, 105–119. http://dx.doi.org/10.1111/j.1539-6053.2009.01038.x

Pica, P., Lemer, C., Izard, V., & Dehaene, S. (2004). Exact and approximate arithmetic in an Amazonian indigene group. *Science*, *306*(5695), 499–503. https://doi.org/10.1126/science.1102085

Poirel, N., Borst, G., Simon, G., Rossi, S., Cassotti, M., Pineau, A., & Houdé, O. (2012). Number conservation is related to children's prefrontal inhibitory control: An fMRI study of the Piagetian task. *PLoS One*, *7*(7), e40802. https://doi.org/10.1371/journal.pone.0040802

Rivera, S. M., Reiss, A. L., Eckert, M. A., & Menon, V. (2005). Developmental changes in mental arithmetic: Evidence for increased functional specialization in the left inferior parietal cortex. *Cerebral Cortex*, *15*(11), 1779–1790. https://doi.org/10.1093/cercor/bhi055

Rubinsten, O., & Henik, A. (2009). Developmental dyscalculia: Heterogeneity might not mean different mechanisms. *Trends in Cognitive Sciences*, *13*(2), 92–99. https://doi.org/10.1016/j.tics.2008.11.002

Salthouse, T. A. (2006). Mental exercise and mental aging: Evaluating the validity of the "use it or lose it" hypothesis. *Perspectives in Psychological Science*, *1*(1), 68–87. https://doi.org/10.1111/j.1745-6916.2006.00005.x

Scalf, P. E., Colcombe, S. J., McCarley, J. S., Erickson, K. I., Alvarado, M., Kim, J. S., Wadhwa, R. P., & Kramer, A. F. (2007). The neural correlates of an expanded functional field of view. *The*

Journals of Gerontology. Series B, Psychological Sciences and Social Sciences, 62(Special Issue 1), 32–44. https://doi.org/10.1093/geronb/62.special_issue_1.32

Seghier, M. L., Fahim, M. A., & Habak, C. (2019). Educational fMRI: From the lab to the classroom. *Frontiers in Psychology, 10*, 2769. https://doi.org/10.3389/fpsyg.2019.02769

Shah, T., Verdile, G., Sohrabi, H., Campbell, A., Putland, E., Cheetham, C., Dhaliwal, S., Weinborn, M., Maruff, P., Darby, D., & Martins, R. N. (2014). A combination of physical activity and computerized brain training improves verbal memory and increases cerebral glucose metabolism in the elderly. *Translational Psychiatry, 4*(12), e487. https://doi.org/10.1038/tp.2014.122

Shah, T. M., Weinborn, M., Verdile, G., Sohrabi, H. R., & Martins, R. N. (2017). Enhancing cognitive functioning in healthy older adults: A systematic review of the clinical significance of commercially available computerized cognitive training in preventing cognitive decline. *Neuropsychology Review, 27*(1), 62–80. https://doi.org/10.1007/s11065-016-9338-9.

Shaywitz, B. A., Shaywitz, S. E., Pugh, K. R., Mencl, W. E., Fulbright, R. K., Skudlarski, P., Constable, R. T., Marchione, K. E., Fletcher, J. M., Lyon, G. R., & Gore, J. C. (2002). Disruption of posterior brain systems for reading in children with developmental dyslexia. *Biological Psychiatry, 52*(2), 101–110. https://doi.org/10.1016/s0006-3223(02)01365-3

Siegler, R. S., & Shrager, J. (1984). Strategy choices in addition and subtraction: How do children know what to do? In C. Spophian (Ed.), *Origins of cognitive skills* (pp. 229—293). Hillsdale, NJ: Erlbaum.

Simons, D. J., Boot, W. R., Charness, N., Gathercole, S. E., Chabris, C. F., Hambrick, D. Z., & Stine-Morrow, E. A. L. (2016). Do "brain-training" programs work? *Psychological Science in the Public Interest, 17*(3), 103–186. https://doi.org/10. 1177/1529100616661983

Sisk, V. F., Burgoyne, A. P., Sun, J., Butler, J. L., & Macnamara, B. N. (2018). To what extent and under which circumstances are growth mind-sets important to academic achievement? Two meta-analyses. *Psychological Science, 29*(4), 549–571. https://doi.org/10.1177/0956797617739704

Sokolowski, H. M., & Ansari, D. (2016). Symbolic and nonsymbolic representation of number in the human parietal cortex: A review of the state-of-the-art, outstanding questions and future directions. In A. Henik (Ed.), *Continuous issues in numerical cognition: How many or how much* (pp. 326–353). Cambridge, MA: Academic Press.

Stanford Longevity Center (2014). *A consensus on the brain training industry from the scientific community.* https://longevity.stanford.edu/a-consensus-on-the-brain-training-industry-from-the-scientific-community-2/

Strenziok, M., Parasuraman, R., Clarke, E., Cisler, D. S., Thompson, J. C., & Greenwood, P. M. (2014). Neurocognitive enhancement in older adults: Comparison of three cognitive training tasks to test a hypothesis of training transfer in brain connectivity. *NeuroImage, 85*(3), 1027–1039. https://doi.org/10.1016/j.neuroimage.2013.07.069.

Thomas, M. S. C., Ansari, D., & Knowland, V. C. P. (2019). Annual research review: Educational neuroscience: Progress and prospects. *The Journal of Child Psychology and Psychiatry, 60*(4), 477–492. https://doi.org/10.1111/jcpp.12973

Wang, H., & Lupica, C. R. (2014). Release of endogenous cannabinoids from ventral tegmental area dopamine neurons and the modulation of synaptic processes. *Progress in Neuro-Psychopharmacology & Biological Psychiatry, 52*, 24–27. https://doi.org/10.1016/j.pnpbp.2014.01.019

Zabelina, D. L., & Silvia, P. J. (2020). Percolating ideas: The effects of caffeine on creative thinking and problem solving. *Consciousness and Cognition, 79*, 102899. https://doi.org/10.1016/j.concog.2020.102899

Zelazo, P. D., & Carlson, S. M. (2020). The neurodevelopment of executive function skills: Implications for academic achievement gaps. *Psychology & Neuroscience, 13*(3), 273–298. http://dx.doi.org/10.1037/pne0000208

Glossary

Cognitive flexibility	The ability to change perspectives. Also known as updating.
Computerized cognitive training (CCT)	Interventions presented through technology designed to improve cognition. Also known by the informal term "brain training."
Dyscalculia	A condition characterized by difficulties in learning mathematics despite normal cognitive ability and exposure to typical instruction.
Dyslexia	A condition characterized by difficulties in learning to read despite normal cognitive ability and exposure to typical instruction.
Environmental transfer	Practicing a skill that improves "real world" functioning.
Executive function	Higher level cognitive processes that manage behavior when more automatic processes, like instincts, are not appropriate.
Far transfer	Practicing a skill improves a more general area of skill, such as practicing an attention task and observing improved attention on diverse tasks relatively unrelated to the practice task.
Inhibitory control	An executive function that includes self-control, control of attention, and cognitive inhibition.
Left intraparietal sulcus (IPS)	An area known to be involved with mathematical reasoning.
Near transfer	Practicing a skill improves performance on very similar skills.
Neuroeducation	An interdisciplinary field combining education and neuroscience. Also known as educational neuroscience and mind, brain, and education.
Nootropics	Substances that boost cognitive function.
Short-term memory	A component of memory that holds small amounts of information for relatively short periods of time.
Simple practice	Repeating a skill to improve performance.
Transfer	The improvement on related skills following the practice of a skill.
Working memory	A component of memory related to short-term memory but providing the ability to operate on information as well as hold it.

6 Consumer Neuroscience

LEARNING OBJECTIVES

After reading this chapter, you should be able to:

▶ 1. Define consumer neuroscience and identify the interdisciplinary fields that contribute to this domain.

▶ 2. Describe the neuroscience methodologies that are most frequently used in consumer neuroscience.

▶ 3. Identify the challenges that face the application of neuroscience theories and methods to consumer behavior.

▶ 4. Discuss the advantages of using mixed methods in consumer neuroscience.

▶ 5. Identify the steps in the product development process that make use or could make use of neuroscience tools and methods, including consideration of the user experience (UX).

▶ 6. Evaluate the potential for neuroscience insights to be used to manipulate behavior.

Inside the Heads of Consumers

People have been trying to influence others to choose certain products for centuries. Ancient cultures such as Egypt, Greece, and Rome featured commercial messages written out on papyrus. With the advent of newspapers and magazines, however, modern advertising took a leap forward. Psychology's own John B. Watson (1878–1958) revolutionized the advertising industry after losing his academic position at Johns

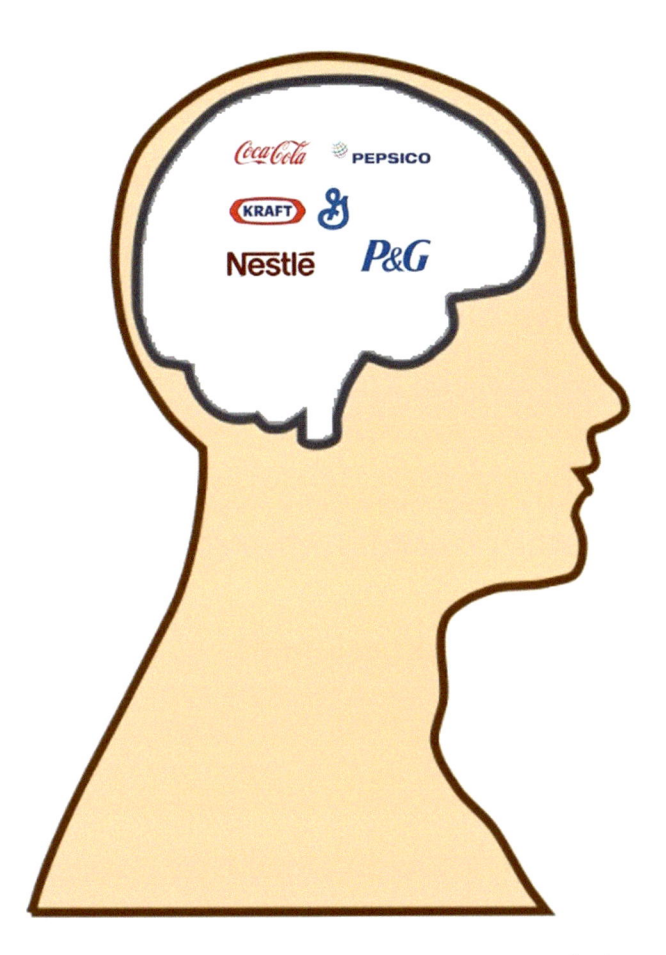

FIGURE 6.1 Consumer neuroscience attempts to use neuroscience methods to understand and manipulate consumer behavior.

Sources: Adapted by the author from https://freesvg.org/silhouette-of-a-brain-inside-a-human-vector-illustration and www.flickr.com/photos/x1brett/6969354214

Hopkins University for having an affair with a student. When Watson found that blindfolded smokers couldn't tell the difference between brands of cigarettes, he realized that the brands could be differentiated by pairing them with an appealing image. Advertising was never the same after that. Watson also understood the role of emotion in advertising. Emotions of fear, rage, and love played important roles in Watson's theories of child development. By appealing to the consumers' emotions, he hoped to make his advertisements persuasive.

In today's media-saturated environment, consumers might be exposed to many thousands of commercial messages every day. Yet many of these seem to fall on deaf ears. How many advertisements can you remember seeing over the past day or two?

Any? Even with the advent of carefully tailored ads based on your social media habits, many seem to fall flat. How can advertisers predict whether an advertisement will have the desired persuasive effect (see Figure 6.1)?

Consumer behavior analysts have relied on basic behavioral methods, such as consumer satisfaction surveys and focus groups, for years. However, it is possible that these direct methods, like many instances of self-report, might not be helpful or even accurate. Berns and Moore (2011) found that when teenagers rated unfamiliar songs on a scale of one to five, the results were not predictive of the songs' later sales. However, the teenagers' recorded brain responses were more predictive of the songs' later success (see Figure 6.2). This suggests that neuroscience methods have greater ability to assess consumer preferences than many of the traditional methods used previously. The results also imply that product preference can occur at an implicit, or relatively unconscious level of processing.

In this chapter, we will explore the use of neuroscience theory and methodology to understand, and in some cases manipulate consumer behavior.

What Is Consumer Neuroscience?

Consumer neuroscience is the application of neuroscience to the understanding and shaping of consumer decision-making and behavior (Alvino et al., 2020).

FIGURE 6.2 Ryan Tedder, lead singer of OneRepublic, wrote one of the songs, "Apologize," that Berns and Moore's fMRI data indicated would be a success when it was still an unknown recording on MySpace.

Source: www.flickr.com/photos/jenzbie/48915633313

Consumer neuroscience represents an interdisciplinary collaboration between marketing, psychology, and neuroscience. Its application crosses many domains, including the following:

- Advertising
- Branding
- Online/user experience (UX)
- Pricing
- Product development
- Product experience.

Consumer behavior has long been an area featuring applied psychology principles, including attitudes, emotion, cognition, and persuasion. Among the behavioral components still essential to understanding consumer behavior are observation, self-report, surveys, and reaction time experiments. Neuroscience is seen as a way to corroborate or expand the understanding gained through these traditional methods.

The field of consumer neuroscience has obviously been driven by and continues to adapt to the availability of tools and technologies. The application of technologies is often limited by expense. Entry-level magnetic resonance imaging machines can cost as little as $225,000, but a high-quality machine like you would find at most research institutions and medical facilities is likely to cost at least $1 million and probably more. That does not include the cost of constructing and maintaining a facility. A room housing MRI equipment must provide some sort of shielding on walls, floor, and ceiling, usually made of copper, to prevent both outside interference affecting data and interference from the scanner with outside technologies. Copper lined rooms are not cheap. Technologies also require significant training to use. As a result, many top marketing firms are beginning to hire neuroscientists to administer and oversee consumer neuroscience efforts. One of the challenges is that this work by private entities is not shared publicly in the way academic research is shared. Our ability to know exactly what these neuroscientists are doing is weak. As one critic noted, if any of the tech giants (Facebook, Twitter, Google, Amazon, etc.), who now employ armies of neuroscientists and social psychologists, provide you with an EEG recording device linked to their technology, you should be very, very worried.

A Role for Emotion

John Watson's message about the importance of emotion did not seem widely accepted in consumer behavior circles until relatively recently. Instead, advertisers initially concentrated on providing information to consumers that would appeal to reason. In other words, you should buy an Apple or PC because of the features that meet your needs, not because you have an emotional attachment to a brand. As you probably already know from your studies of persuasion in social psychology, affect (or emotion) is a critical component of an attitude. The other components, of course, are behaviors and cognitions, together with affect making "the ABCs" of an attitude. We are also very familiar with the affect heuristic, or that "gut feeling" that guides our decisions. So, it should come as no surprise to you (nor would it have to John Watson) that successful advertising features strong emotional appeals. The most successful advertisements, measured by metrics like influence on sales and market share, were very emotional but included little if any appeal to consumers' reason (Binet & Field, 2009).

Emotions have evolved over the millennia to inform rapid approach and avoidance behaviors of animals. In your psychology coursework, you have no doubt run across a whole host of theories about emotion, from the classic James-Lange and Cannon-Bard theories to Schachter and Singer's two-factor theories and so on. A complete discussion of these theories is beyond the scope of this textbook, but the key take-away is that emotions have two components, a physical response and a subjective, cognitive response. These components interact, with many theorists assuming that the physical response (feeling butterflies in the stomach) helps us identify our subjective, cognitive states (I'm scared).

Antonio Damasio and his colleagues (1991) proposed a **somatic marker** theory of emotion, in which physiological responses to emotional stimuli become associated with situations. When those or similar situations are encountered again, the somatic markers provide guidance for approach or withdrawal. Somatic markers and their influence on decision-making will be discussed in more detail in the upcoming chapter on Neuroeconomics. For now, our interest in somatic markers centers around the way the concept is used to justify practices in consumer neuroscience. Because Damasio and others have explored brain correlates of emotional responses, consumer neuroscientists strive to see how activity in these areas of the brain correlates with consumers' tendencies to approach, as opposed to ignore or avoid, their messages.

As we will also see in upcoming chapters on Neuroeconomics and Leadership, emotions do influence many types of decisions we make, not just those related to purchases. Daniel Kahneman, in his 2011 book *Thinking Fast and Slow*, proposes two cognitive systems. A slow, conscious system processes information consciously and rationally with effort, while a fast, less conscious system processes information in more automatic and emotional ways. Kahneman's depiction of cognition parallels the **Elaboration Likelihood Model (ELM)** proposed by Richard Petty and John Cacioppo (1981). The ELM proposes two "routes to persuasion," a central route similar to Kahneman's slow system and a peripheral route that is similar to Kahneman's fast system. Petty and Cacioppo maintain that we do not have sufficient resources to approach all persuasive messages using the central route. We reserve that route for issues of great personal importance. For example, if your college or university was proposing a steep increase in tuition that would impact your ability to continue your studies, it is likely that you would examine the messages about that issue very carefully. The logic of the arguments will take center stage and you will be hard to distract from consideration of any logical flaws. In contrast, when we are not paying much attention to a message, it can slip under the radar of our logical processors. When people use the peripheral route, they are much more susceptible to persuasion based on superficial factors, such as the attractiveness of a spokesperson or the emotional content of the message. When driving down a highway, our cognitive resources are taxed by the challenges of driving, so a billboard we pass might have more influence than if we saw the same message while sitting at our desks at home. This peripheral, "low attention" type of processing is the one deliberately targeted by advertisers because it produces the largest effects on consumer behavior. If we respond to an ad using the central route, with all of its logical reasoning, we might not buy that product we don't really need after all.

The psychology of persuasion offers a further word of caution to consumer behavior practitioners. Manipulating emotions can be tricky, particularly if the emotions aroused are negative. Human beings are predisposed to place more weight on negative stimuli than on positive stimuli, such as our vastly superior abilities to detect bitter tastes compared to sweet tastes. We can definitely be at risk from negative stimuli (most poisons are bitter) but less at risk if we miss out on positive stimuli. This makes negative appeals a very potent approach to persuasion and explains why we see so many negative stories in the news media and in political campaigns (Figure 6.3).

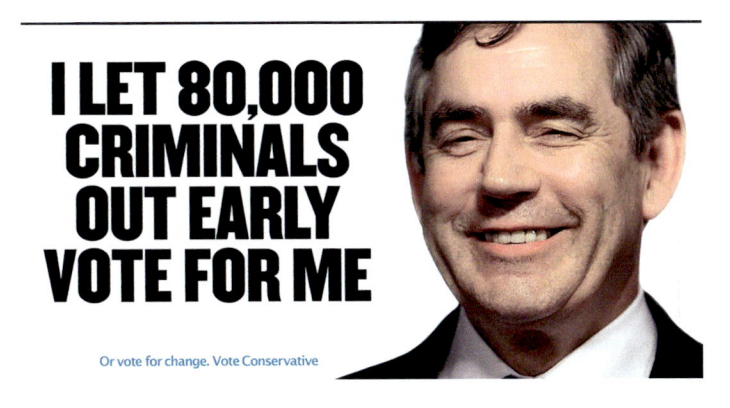

FIGURE 6.3 James Gordon Brown served as Prime Minister of the United Kingdom from 2007 to 2010. Like nearly all politicians, Brown was the subject of negative (withdrawal), emotional advertising by opponents, which seems to be more effective at persuading voters than advertising featuring the positive attributes of one's own candidate (approach).
Source: www.flickr.com/photos/conservatives/4469610650

One of the most influential ads of the 1970s was the famous "Crying Indian" ad for Keep America Beautiful. The ad featured Iron Eyes Cody tearing up when witnessing pollution. The facts that Iron Eyes Cody was actually an actor of Italian heritage rather than a Native American and that Keep America Beautiful was a conglomerate of beverage companies who were somewhat terrified of the budding environmental movement in the United States did not hamper the appeal of the ad. What made this ad successful is that it raised strong emotions, but also gave consumers a clear course of action for dealing with those emotions—stop littering. In contrast, persuasive messages that provoke strong emotions without giving consumers a clear action step tend to be ignored. Your author's community is home to one of the few remaining nuclear power plants in the United States, although it too, is slated for decommissioning soon (Figure 6.4). The power plant has been controversial throughout its decades of existence, with many doomsday messages from activists about its proximity to earthquake faults and the impact of stored radioactive materials and so on. The locals tend to ignore such messaging, however, as few believe they really have a say in whether the plant stays or goes. In other words, without clear action steps, an emotional appeal is likely to fail. Consumer marketers generally do not have a problem with providing action steps, in the form of purchasing their product, but the fact that emotional messages can be very difficult to handle remains.

Even more challenging is the finding that emotion does not have a linear relationship with consumer responses. It is very likely that the level of emotional intensity interacts in significant ways with the type of emotion elicited. For example, reactions to an environmental message were better when the message elicited low rather than high levels of guilt (Jimenez & Yang, 2008). Higher levels of guilt have been associated with increasing anger, leading consumers to feel manipulated by the advertisement (Cotte et al., 2005). It probably would take a more significant action step to reduce high guilt compared to low guilt.

If identifying the correct level of emotional response to achieve persuasion is so difficult, perhaps this is one area in which neuroscience can be helpful. Neuroscience, of course, has built up a large literature on emotion. The participation of subcortical pathways in our emotional experiences is consistent with observations of automatic and less conscious processing. One of the most dramatic examples of how emotional processes can run behind the desktop of conscious awareness was reported by Pegna et al. (2005). Their participant was completely blind due to damage to his visual cortex. However, when shown a photo of an angry face while undergoing fMRI, the man's amygdala responded appropriately to the threat the photo implied. The man himself couldn't tell you whether he was "looking at" a face, a dog, or a building, but his amygdala knew. Pathways connecting his eyes to the thalamus and then to the amygdala provided the necessary information for provoking an emotional response at a subconscious level.

A further complication, however, is the fact that emotion recruits numerous components of the nervous system, including the autonomic nervous system, the amygdala,

FIGURE 6.4 Negative, emotional messaging by activists regarding Diablo Canyon Nuclear Power Plant has not been very persuasive. Few local residents believe they have a say in whether the plant stays or goes (it is in the process of being retired from old age), so they tune out the messages. Effective emotional messages give audiences a clear action step that they can take to reduce their negative emotions.

Source: https://commons.m.wikimedia.org/wiki/File:Diablo_Canyon_Nuclear_Power_Plant.jpg

the insula, the cingulate cortex, the basal ganglia, and the cerebral cortex. We do not have "happy" or "sad" centers of the brain. Instead, the same structures and networks participate in many emotions, just in nuanced ways. For example, you might think that we could use methods of measuring activity in the autonomic nervous system to help identify a person's emotional state, but these measures do not show strong associations with particular emotions (Cacioppo et al., 2000). Autonomic measures do seem to correlate with either positive or negative emotions, with responses being more pronounced for negative emotions (Cacioppo et al., 2011). However, autonomic activity does not help us distinguish between two positive states (happy or hopeful) or two negative states (anger or fear). We often discuss the role of the amygdala in detecting threat, which elicits negative emotions like fear, but the amygdala also processes positive stimuli and even some stimuli that don't seem emotional at all (Blackford et al., 2010).

While neuroscientists can certainly correlate the response of the nervous system to a participant's emotional state and emotional intensity within the lab, there is still much to do to ensure that such measures are ecologically valid and predictive of a consumers' responses in the safety of their own homes or while they are shopping in person.

Do Implicit Attitudes Drive Behavior?

A larger initial question, of course, is whether attitudes of any type, explicit or implicit, drive behavior. The answer is that attitudes do not automatically lead to behavior. Attitudes are most likely to predict behavior when they are strong, stable, and specific. A person who has a real passion for using R instead of SPSS is more likely to use R than a student in a beginning statistics course who is relatively inexperienced with both platforms. Knowing someone's attitudes might be more helpful in predicting their general tendencies in the future (I enjoy salted caramel ice cream and plan to consume it at some point in the future) as opposed to predicting a single behavior, like a purchase decision (I'm going to buy some McConnell's salted caramel ice cream on my next trip to the supermarket).

One of the basic tenets of emotional advertising is that it elicits **implicit associations** with a brand. The consensus is that advertising that requires explicit, conscious processing can have a negative effect on the consumers' relationship with the brand. One wonders if advertisers have so little faith in the quality of their brands that they fear the use of the central route to persuasion on the part of consumers. If your product is that good, shouldn't it hold up to reason? That being said, an assumption that implicit associations underlie effective advertising requires more scrutiny.

You might already be familiar with the concept of implicit associations due to discussions of diversity, equity, and inclusion. The basic idea is that people can harbor implicit biases that impact their behavior without their conscious awareness, just as Pegna et al.'s participant showed a typical amygdalar response to threat without conscious awareness of having been exposed to an angry face. Implicit bias training has become very common in many organizations and usually includes a test of implicit bias as a stimulus for discussion.

The distinction between implicit and explicit awareness has long been an area of study in cognitive psychology, and in the study of memory in particular. Explicit, conscious memories require active search, and include memories for your personal experience (episodic memories) and memories for factual information (semantic memories). Implicit, unconscious memories are accessed automatically without effortful search. These include classically conditioned responses. If you have test anxiety, you don't "decide" to feel anxious when you enter a testing situation. The testing situation stimuli have acquired the ability to elicit your anxiety automatically. Once mastered, many procedures are retrieved implicitly. Learning to drive a standard transmission car can be difficult—clutch, gas, shift—but once learned, you just drive to school without thinking about how to carry out all the steps.

Social psychologists Anthony Greenwald and Mahzarin Banaji (1995) argued that implicit and explicit processes are relevant to social constructs as well as memories. If your memories of past unpleasant testing experiences can affect your current responses to a new testing situation without much conscious awareness, it becomes feasible that implicit processes can affect your attitudes and behavior as well. To demonstrate this point, Greenwald and his colleagues (1998) developed the computerized **Implicit Association Test (IAT)**. The IAT has been used widely to assess implicit bias that might otherwise be masked by problems with self-report instruments, such as the influence of social desirability. Even when assured of anonymity, participants are unlikely to admit to being racist, sexist, and so on.

The IAT assumes that reaction time represents the strength of an implicit association. There are many ways to present the IAT, but one will be described here as an example. Two categories are identified, such as spiders/flowers and good/bad. Crossed versions of these categories (e.g., spider or pleasant; flower or unpleasant) appear in the upper corners of the screen. A word, name, or image then appears on the screen and the participant must push one key if the stimulus fits either the spider or pleasant categories and another key if the stimulus fits either the flower or unpleasant categories (Figure 6.5). These are later reversed, and if reaction time is faster for spider–unpleasant than for spider–pleasant, this is interpreted as an implicit dislike of spiders. If you would like to try this for yourself, you can visit the Project Implicit website at Harvard University (https://implicit.harvard.edu/implicit/takeatest.html) and either participate in a real study or do a practice run.

Since its inception, the IAT has provoked controversy, which is largely beyond the scope of this book. In short, the IAT has been criticized because of both its validity and reliability. Research attempting to compare the ability of the IAT and explicit measures to predict actual behavior is mixed. Worse for the basic premise are findings that people can accurately predict their own results on the IAT (Hahn et al., 2014). If the IAT is accessing information of which we are unaware, how can we possibly know how we'll perform on it? The instrument's test–retest reliability is particularly weak, far below the standard typically accepted in psychology. These concerns have not hampered the

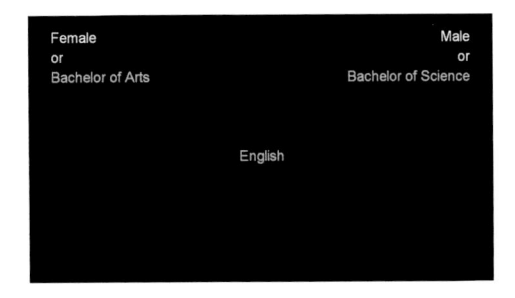

FIGURE 6.5 A sample screen from one version of the Implicit Association Test (IAT). If you react more quickly to the Female or BA categories than the Female or BS categories, the test assumes you have an implicit association between males and science and females and the arts.

Source: https://en.wikipedia.org/wiki/File:ImplicitAssociationTest.jpg

acceptance of the IAT and the concept of implicit bias by the popular press and the public at large.

The mixed findings regarding the relationships between attitudes, whether explicit or implicit, and behavior complicate the application of neuroscience to the prediction of consumer behavior. Self-report measures have their share of limitations, but implicit measures certainly do, too. If the relationship between an implicit association and related behavior is weak or variable, it doesn't do us much good to be able to identify an implicit association using the IAT or neuroscience tools. Without more clarity and agreement regarding basic concepts and assessments, how do we know what the neuroscience data are saying? These obstacles have not been sufficient to dissuade consumer neuroscientists from pursuing implicit associations, however.

The Tools of Consumer Neuroscience

Chapter 1 provided an overview of the neuroscience tools often used in applications, and many, if not all of those are staples in consumer neuroscience. In this chapter, we will focus on the application of these tools to consumer neuroscience, and you might want to refer to Chapter 1 for more of the technical details of these methods. No one tool is likely to provide information of interest. The use of multiple tools simultaneously provides the best insights.

Despite the controversies outlined in the previous section, consumer neuroscience has embraced variations on the IAT for evaluating associations with brands and products. Implicit measures are used to evaluate branding, messaging, and responses to packaging. While implicit measures are not directly related to neuroscience, they are theoretically supported by the idea that not all brain processes are available for conscious evaluation. Like the general field of implicit attitudes, this area of application to consumer behavior is sorely in need of additional objective research.

Facial coding uses cameras to evaluate spontaneous facial expressions as participants respond to messaging and other aspects of consumer behavior. Like implicit measures, facial coding does not rely on neuroscience methods, but the rationale is based on assumptions about the automaticity of authentic emotional expressions as described by Paul Ekman (e.g., Ekman et al., 1972) and David Matsumoto (e.g., Matsumoto, 2001). Psychologists hold differing opinions about the universality of facial expressions. It is likely that we begin with certain innate tendencies featuring specific movements of the brow, eye, cheek, and mouth areas of the face in infancy. Around the age of 12 to 14 weeks, human infants clearly demonstrate social smiling, regardless of whether they are sighted or visually impaired (Sullivan & Lewis, 2003). Although adults across the globe share about 70% of the facial expressions used to respond to situations and stimuli, cultural differences do emerge (Cowen et al., 2021). Thus, applying facial coding across cultural domains should be done with care.

Eye tracking using infrared cameras can pinpoint gaze and eye movements. Many applications involve participants' viewing material on a screen, but it is possible to capture more ecologically valid data with mobile, head-mounted equipment. As a consumer walks past a display, the data will indicate what caught that person's attention and for how long. Eye tracking is particularly helpful to user experience (UX) web designers, who need to know if their "sale" banner catches the appropriate attention (Figure 6.6). Once again, this methodology is not related to neuroscience directly, other than the fact that we have a fair understanding of eye movements and their significance in the study of sensation and perception. Further research is needed to correlate variations in eye movements in response to viewing consumer goods to underlying brain processing and subsequent behavior.

Measures of Autonomic Arousal

Consumer neuroscience has made use of several inexpensive, non-invasive methods to assess general arousal in response to stimuli related to brands, packaging, advertisements, and so on.

Pupillometry, or the analysis of pupil size, provides data related to the state of the autonomic nervous system. Under conditions of arousal, the sympathetic division of the autonomic nervous system dilates the pupils. Pupillometry is usually done in conjunction with eye tracking to pinpoint the stimulus that is associated with any change. A single arousal measure, like pupil size, is quite general. A person could be aroused in a positive or negative way, but pupil size does not provide further insight into the nature of the arousal. That must be inferred from the situation. Light levels, of course, further influence pupil size. Pupillometry in a laboratory, where lighting is controlled, is easier to assess than in an ecologically valid setting like a supermarket. Developmental factors also influence pupil size. Like any muscle, the muscles of the iris lose elasticity with age. Older adults often experience less change in pupil size and may even experience pinpoint pupils under most lighting conditions.

Heart rate and heart rate variability are also used as measures of arousal, often accompanied by measures of respiration. The sympathetic division of the autonomic nervous system acts to speed up the heart in response to arousing stimuli. Like pupil size, however, this effect is very general and gives little if any insight into the valence (positive or negative) features of the arousal. Just as light can interfere with arousal measures of pupil size, physical activity can influence heart rate and respiration, so care must be taken to standardize the conditions in which any measures are taken. Wearable technology, such as the Apple Watch or Fitbit, make collection of heart rate and heart rate variability data rather simple.

Skin conductance, also known as the Galvanic skin response, is an arousal measure based on recordings taken by surface electrodes on the palm of the hand or fingertips.

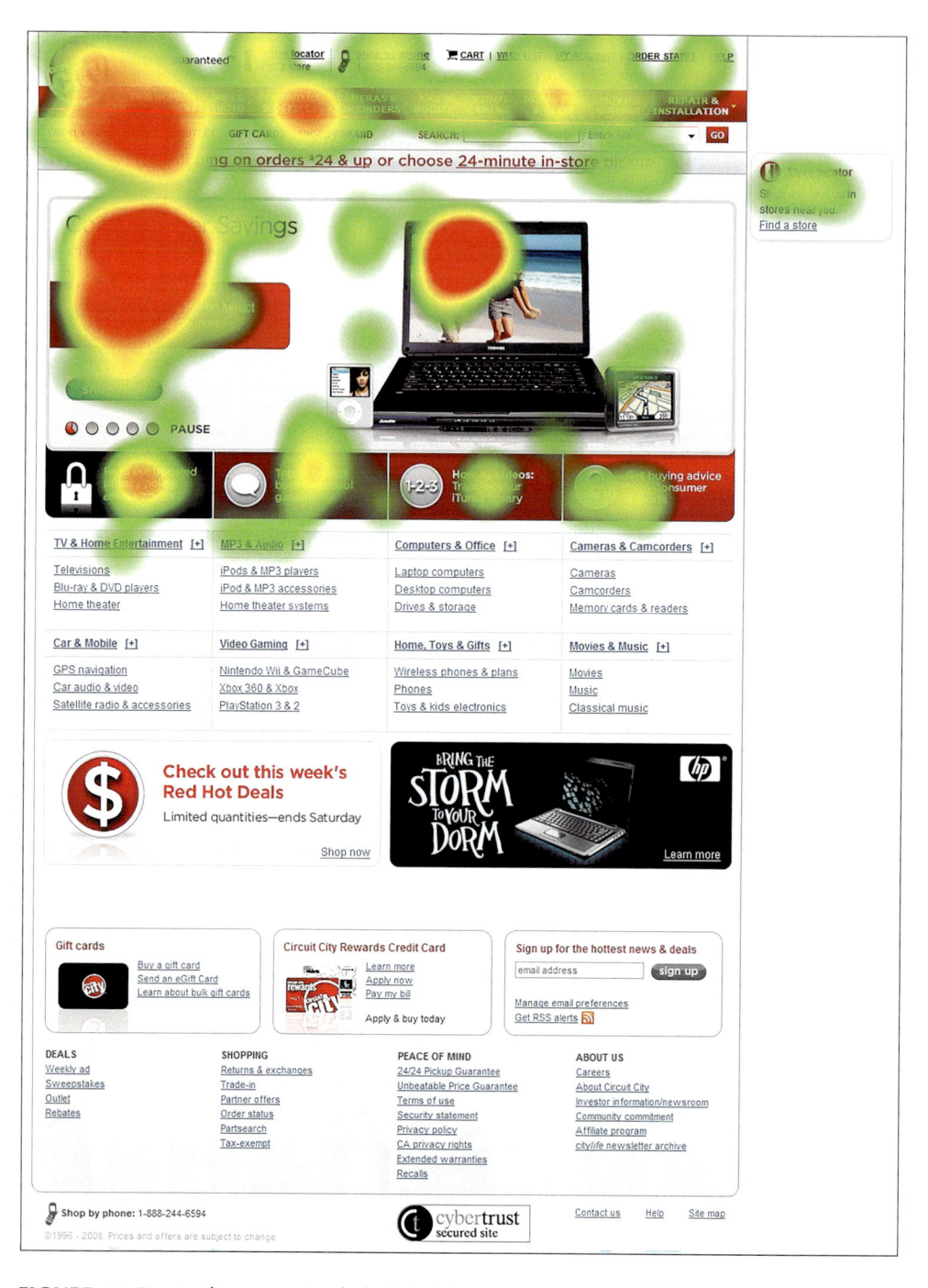

FIGURE 6.6 Eye tracking is particularly helpful to user experience (UX) designers who want to see what consumers attend to on a website. Apparently, these participants were not aware of "This week's Red Hot Deals."

Source: Author.

In a similar fashion to previously discussed measures of arousal, skin conductance is quite general. It tells you whether the participant is aroused, but not whether the arousal is due to a specific emotion or even a positive or negative reaction. Skin conductance is most useful when correlated with additional measures.

All measures of arousal based on autonomic activity, such as pupillometry, heart rate, respiration, and skin conductance, suffer from the same weaknesses we see in traditional polygraph applications (see Chapter 4). These same arousal measures have often been used to detect deception on the part of employees or suspected criminals. In the hands of a skilled examiner, traditional polygraph methods are accurate about 65% of the time (Kleinmuntz & Szucko, 1984). Although this is better than a chance hit rate of 50%, it is not good enough to put a person in prison, so it is rare to see traditional polygraph results admitted to courts of law. There are two basic problems with applied arousal measures. First, they tell us very little about WHY someone is aroused. People who flunk a polygraph test might very well be lying, but they might also be so upset by being accused that their arousal levels are quite high. In controlled studies, about one third of innocent individuals test as guilty as measured by traditional polygraph. Second, it is easy to cheat. Any B actor in Hollywood can imagine themselves as innocent and pass a polygraph test. At least one quarter of guilty people can pass this type of test. Although it's hard to imagine that a participant in a marketing study would want to fool an examiner, the fact that these autonomic functions do respond to cognitive control is a concerning bit of noise in the experimental procedure.

Measures of Brain Activity

Measures of brain activity have the potential to provide more detailed information about consumers' responses to stimuli. As mentioned previously, the application of these methods can involve expensive equipment and the need for high levels of training for those using the tool and interpreting the data.

In discussing the use of brain activity measures and consumer neuroscience, it becomes necessary to draw a line between academic consumer neuroscience, published in peer-reviewed journals, and consumer neuroscience as practiced by commercial agencies. Jonna Brenninkmeijer and her colleagues (2020) provide an interesting, in-depth case study of a commercial organization they refer to by the pseudonym Neuro-X. They outline a strategy common to many similar organizations:

1. Use a legitimate, respected scientist as the "face" of the organization.
2. An inside marketer, when presenting to the public and to clients, deflects questions by saying "I am not a scientist," and that she will ask the scientist what can be shared.

3. Once a customer agrees to participate, they interact directly with in-house researchers, who design an experiment.

4. Scans are conducted with 24 participants, and the data are analyzed by an in-house scientist. In contrast to academic studies, where analysis of a single scan can take up to 40 hours, data for all participants are analyzed within two days using a highly scripted method that produces automated results.

5. Reports provided to the client do not include any fMRI data. The report makes simplistic conclusions in the form of scores on positive and negative emotions. These emotion scores are interpreted in terms of the customer's question (e.g., Is this ad effective?) and compared to previous materials that were shown to be effective or ineffective.

The details of the organization's methods remain quite secret in contrast to the work of academic consumer neuroscientists. One professor interviewed by Brenninkmeijer et al. (2020), said Neuro-X was "a bit loose with their *p*-values. They dare to show results with a $p = 0.20$" (p. 77). As you might have learned in other coursework, one aspect of the replicability crisis in psychology is related to the misinterpretation of *p* values. Given the very small sample size of 24 used for each study by this agency, reporting high *p* values as significant becomes even more problematic.

Perhaps another measure of success would be client satisfaction with these services. Some case studies are available. Marketing giant Nielsen's Consumer Neuroscience division won a prestigious David Ogilvy Award for Excellence in Advertising Research with work for a pet rescue organization. They claimed that changes made to a public service announcement (PSA) after their neuroscience analysis led to more engagement, attention, and memory. They noted that after the PSA launched, traffic to the pet rescue organization's website increased 133%. Any psychology student having had a course in research methods would have many questions about this research design. Were the same participants used in the before and after evaluations of the PSA? What measure demonstrated "engagement" and how strong were the effects? Can we say that the increased web traffic was *caused* by the PSA? How do we know the edits mattered? Once again, the inaccessibility of these types of commercial reports to traditional peer review makes it very difficult to evaluate their worth.

Functional magnetic resonance imaging (fMRI)

Functional MRI (fMRI) is often viewed as the gold standard of contemporary neuroscience methods for its ability to pinpoint patterns of activity in the brain. At the same time, consumer neuroscientists face several obstacles when trying to use this tool to gauge participants' reactions to brands, advertisements, and packaging. In addition to the barriers of cost and training, fMRI requires immobility. Many participants find lying flat in a tube to be uncomfortable, and this might influence their responses. These factors limit the ecological validity of participant responses compared to a freely moving participant in a supermarket. Because the banging noise of the magnets is quite loud, it is difficult to present sound stimuli, even when using earphones. Because of the variability in participants' responses and the high rate of unusable data, large numbers of participants are needed to draw valid conclusions, and this is time-consuming and expensive.

Although some consumer neuroscientists make claims about using fMRI to vet movie trailers and advertisements, there are several challenges to this approach. First, although fMRI provides excellent information about structure (spatial resolution), its temporal resolution is poor. Several seconds might separate the presentation of a stimulus and a measurable response as seen in the fMRI. This makes correlating a stimulus, like a particular scene in a movie trailer, with a response quite tricky. Second, consumer neuroscientists need to know what response to evaluate. As mentioned earlier in the chapter, the brain does not have "emotion centers." Patterns of activity do correlate with certain emotions, but as we discussed previously, translating emotional responses to actual subsequent behaviors, like deciding to attend a movie, is not simple.

A final difficulty is the **reverse inference** problem that is discussed frequently in this book. It is one thing to know that a stimulus evokes a pattern of activity in the brain. It is an entirely different matter to say that when you see that pattern again, you "know" what the person is thinking. Reverse inference is not necessarily wrong, but it can be performed carelessly (Hutzler, 2014). A prominent group of neuroscientists exemplified carelessness in reverse inference in a 2007 opinion piece in the *New York Times* (Iacoboni et al., 2007). Based on 20 undecided voters in fMRI research that was never peer-reviewed, the authors made sweeping generalizations about their resulting data. They stated that activity in the anterior cingulate cortex as participants viewed a photo of Hillary Clinton meant that "they were battling unacknowledged impulses to like Mrs. Clinton." Perhaps being accustomed to the rather dry writing needed for journal articles did not prepare these researchers well for writing for the public, leading them to make conclusions that they would never include in a peer-reviewed piece.

Is there any potential, then, for the use of fMRI in commercial consumer neuroscience? It is difficult to assess these applications, as they are rarely subjected to peer review. There appears to be some evidence that fMRI is superior to focus groups. A British game show, Quizmania, was absolutely hated by focus groups, but after testing involving fMRI, the studio proceeded with the show, which became a huge hit. Drew and John Dowdle, directors of *The Poughkeepsie Tapes*, participated in a demonstration by consumer neuroscience firm MindSigns (Kotler, 2010). After seeing the response of participants to a short clip from the film using fMRI, the brothers made an edit by removing a green filter used during a scary scene. The onset of the green filter coincided with a drop in the viewer's brain activity, which the MindSigns personnel interpreted as "loss of interest." Again, the temporal resolution for fMRI is unlikely to allow researchers to pinpoint responses to stimuli. No mention is made of further testing of the re-edited scene after the green filter was removed, and without peer review, we have no idea how significant the change in activity might have been.

Electroencephalography (EEG)

Because of its relatively low cost and ease of use, EEG has been broadly applied by consumer neuroscientists, both academic and commercial. Unlike fMRI, EEG enjoys very precise temporal resolution, so responses can be correlated more exactly to stimuli. At the same time, as noted in Chapter 1, EEG provides a very surface level analysis of brain activity, as activity in deeper structures cannot be assessed with this method. Magnetoencephalography (MEG) overcomes this problem, but like fMRI, it is very expensive and difficult to administer. While it is becoming more popular as a method among academic consumer neuroscientists (e.g., Vecchiato et al., 2011), it is unlikely to find much use in commercial organizations unless the technology is adapted to make it easier to use. The potential of mobile scanning, discussed in Chapter 1, might stimulate research in this direction, as mobility would provide enormous advantages.

One common use of EEG data by consumer neuroscientists is to assess attention. As we mentioned in Chapter 2, the waking brain usually alternates between focused and unfocused thought, spending about 50% of the waking day in each state. These states are usually correlated with faster, less synchronous beta waves in the former and slower, more synchronous alpha waves in the latter. Periodically, in response to a notable change in the stimulus environment, such as a loud noise, the EEG will show very fast gamma wave activity. Changes in EEG waveforms, therefore, can provide insights regarding the amount of focus a participant might be experiencing when viewing advertising or other marketing materials. The traditional analysis of frequency bands such as alpha and beta, however, is very broad, making their significance difficult to interpret (Tognoli et al., 2021).

Chapter 1 introduced a variation on this standard EEG approach that resulted in the measurement of event-related potentials (ERPs). Briefly, this means that a participant's responses to many presentations of a stimulus are averaged so that much of the "noise" is filtered out. The science of ERP analysis is advancing rapidly, and researchers can now isolate discrete brain microstates lasting mere microseconds (a microsecond is one millionth of a second; see Figure 6.7). In one initial demonstration, Stephanie Cacioppo and her colleagues (2016) were able to view participants' microstate progression as they viewed a simple checkerboard stimulus and then waited for the appearance of the next. Currently freely available to academic researchers, this approach might catch on with commercial agencies if neuroscientists they hire are familiar with the method and necessary statistical analyses.

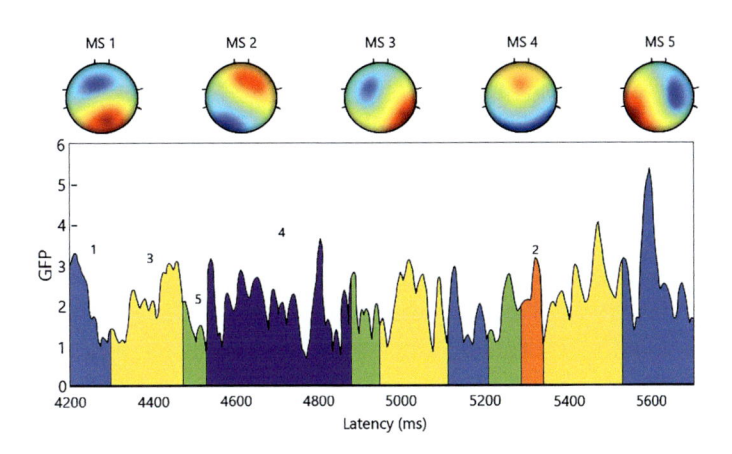

FIGURE 6.7 Using high-definition EEG, researchers can identify brain microstates as participants process stimuli. Microstates have been nicknamed the "atoms of thought."
Source: Adapted from Poulsen et al. (2018) by Karla Freberg.

A second major commercial application of EEG technology is the assessment of emotion. One of the well-established connections between EEG recordings and emotion is the asymmetry of recorded alpha activity in the right and left frontal cortices during both rest and task performance. Positive emotions are associated with more left hemisphere frontal lobe activity compared to right hemisphere frontal lobe activity. Negative emotions are associated with more right hemisphere frontal lobe activity than left hemisphere frontal lobe activity. This model is referred to as the valence model of frontal asymmetry (Gable et al., 2021). More recently, the model has been modified to associate asymmetry with motivational states rather than simple emotional valence. According to this view, greater left hemisphere activity is associated with approach, while greater right hemisphere activity is associated with withdrawal. This modification clarifies situations in which emotion and motivation are incongruent. For example, it is possible to identify two positive emotional states that show equal positive valence yet differ in approach motivation, with one being high in approach motivation and the other being low. In these cases, frontal asymmetry is more predictive of approach motivation than the degree of positive emotion.

One cautionary note about using asymmetry as a metric for emotion is the individual variation seen in hemisphere laterality, or differences in the functions of the right and left hemispheres. Hemisphere laterality is related to handedness. Over 90% of human beings are right-handed, and about 96% of right-handers demonstrate "typical laterality," which usually means that they process language primarily in the left hemisphere and are likely to show the pattern of asymmetry described above. However, the remaining 4% of right-handers as well as people who are left-handed or somewhat ambidextrous can demonstrate atypical laterality in which language processing either occurs in the right hemisphere or fairly equally in both hemispheres. For this reason, non-right-handers are typically excluded from small fMRI studies due to the "noise" their atypical laterality introduces to the data. Consumer neuroscientists probably want to sell their product to left-handers, too, so are well-advised to include them in their samples. However, data should be analyzed with their laterality in mind.

Although EEG is a relatively simple technology compared to fMRI, assessment and analysis of results should be done with some care. Machine learning models perform better than human observers when carrying out artifact cleaning (Smith et al., 2017). Researchers must also carefully consider their experimental design. Is EEG viewed as a simple correlate or indicator of an emotional state? The result of a stimulus? The cause of an outcome? Smith et al. (2017) recommend assessing the participants' emotional state before and after the EEG recording occurs to control for any unintended manipulations of emotion. Interpretation of the data is also complex. Individual differences in frontal asymmetry are larger during an emotional task than during rest, which is an important cautionary point for consumer neuroscientists who use this approach. Asymmetry is influenced by individual differences in cognitive ability and the personal relevance of stimuli (Reznik & Allen, 2017). These last two points speak to the need for appropriate numbers of participants. In other words, performing an EEG study of emotion is relatively easy. Doing it well is less easy.

Consumer neuroscientists also make an argument for EEG as a predictor of memory, both formation and retrieval. In particular, increases in theta and gamma frequencies are correlated with encoding and retrieval (Osipova et al., 2006). Subsequently recalled television ads are associated with these increases during encoding (Vecchiato et al., 2010). Combining EEG measures of attention, emotion, and memory predicted later TV population-wide viewership and relevant Twitter activity (Shestyuk et al., 2019).

Studying individuals in isolation might not be the best strategy. Dmochowski et al. (2014) found that the degree of similarity of EEG responding across a small group of participants watching television shows together was more predictive of the show's eventual success than any of their data taken individually. These researchers suggest that stimuli that are viewed as favorable might be those that elicit a stereotypical response from the brain that is typical of peers.

Mixed Methods

As in most types of research, the use of more than one method often provides more accurate insights. If all methods used point in the same direction, our confidence in a result is increased.

Marketing giant Nielsen chronicles its use of multiple methods to refine a 30-second PSA entitled "Cheerleader," produced for the Ad Council's "Fatherhood Involvement" campaign (Smith & Marci, 2016). You can view the PSA here: www.youtube.com/watch?v=hTIzjVxvV2U. The ad features a father helping his daughter with her cheerleading routine. Nielsen collected EEG, skin conductance, heart rate, eye tracking, facial coding, and self-report data from a group of fathers as they watched the ad. Each of the methods provided its own set of insights, such as the identification of clutter in the closing sequence caused by divided attention between the actors and the contact phone number. Time-sensitive EEG recordings provided guidance for making scene-level changes. These data allow the creative staff to make necessary adjustments. Taken together, the methods provide a more complete picture than any one method could contribute.

Contributions to Marketing Processes

Although neuroscience tools can augment our understanding of consumer behavior in general, we can also highlight the specific areas of marketing in which the tools are especially helpful.

Introducing a new product can be very expensive, and mistakes can be equally disastrous. The marketing literature is full of accounts of catastrophes resulting from a misjudging of the appeal of new products. A classic case study revolves around the introduction of New Coke, released by Coca Cola in 1985 in response to lagging sales. In blind taste tests, New Coke seemed like it was substantially preferred to the original Coca Cola formulation and to rival Pepsi. Despite an investment of $4 million in development costs, the product did not do well and was discontinued in 2002. Coca Cola reintroduced the original formula as "Coca Cola Classic," and enjoyed a boost in sales. This case study is often cited as an example of the dangers of underestimating consumers' emotional attachment to a brand. After the introduction of the new formula, a woman in Georgia swung her umbrella at a man stocking the new product, yelling "it tastes like sh*t." Phone calls to Coca Cola headquarters went from 400 to 1500 calls per day, mostly complaints about the new product. This emotional outburst was not necessarily based on real preferences. One of the key protestors against the new formulation, Gay Mullins, became a media darling. Unfortunately, he was unable to tell the difference between New Coke and Coke Classic in a blind taste test. We obviously have no way of knowing whether neuroscience could have predicted this failure, but it is possible that methods such as the analysis of frontal asymmetry could have picked up on any negative emotional reactions to New Coke (Figure 6.8).

As shown by the New Coke case, a final physical product is evaluated by consumers not just for its objective features, like taste, but also according to its cultural relevance and cost. As we will see in an upcoming chapter on Neuroeconomics, neuroscience has made important contributions to our understanding of decision-making based on cost and the desirability of products. It is likely that these insights will prove to be very valuable to marketers. Neuroscience might also illuminate individual differences in

FIGURE 6.8 Could neuroscience have prevented the New Coke debacle?
Source: Karla Freberg.

consumer responses to a product based on their goals and objectives. Not all products lend themselves to this type of analysis given current tools. You can certainly conduct a taste test during an fMRI, but it is not feasible to compare the driving experience of a Mercedes versus a BMW. However, consumer responses to packaging and promotion for products can certainly be assessed with neuroscience tools. Capturing these ecologically valid experiences is currently outside the typical realm of neuroscience applications, but it is possible that in conjunction with virtual reality technologies, such an analysis is not that far away.

Consumer neuroscientists are using neuroscience tools to adjust the context in which a purchase decision is made. Context can translate into large differences in sales. The next time you shop for groceries, pay attention to the product placement you see on shelves. Leading brands are more likely to be found at eye level. Note that products targeting children are placed somewhat lower (sitting in cart level or walking level) than those targeting adults. Few consumers stoop down to the lowest shelves to retrieve an item. The "facings," or number of product units that appear horizontally on a shelf is positively correlated with sales. Researchers know the approximate speed at which a consumer moves down an aisle and the more horizontal space a product has, the more likely it is to be noticed. Savvy retailers do not leave music choices to their Gen Z staff. Instead, they make sure the music is somewhat slower, which slows down the consumers' rate of walking, again resulting in more time to see each facing. Impulse items are located around the cash register, courtesy of John Watson. Are you feeling manipulated yet?

Marketers did not need neuroscience to develop these practices, but they are certainly using neuroscience to refine them. Retail outlets and websites are evaluated for disruptions, or any distractions that interfere with the customer experience. Choice of display of the product is designed to maximize sales.

Finally, marketers are interested in the consumer's post-purchase experience. Traditional methods, such as asking consumers to produce diary-style reports of when and how they use a product and their corresponding responses to the experience, leave a bit to be desired. Think about the experience you might have had, say with an iPhone. **User experience (UX)** experts oversee the entire process, from the design and testing to purchase to troubleshooting. UX experts focus on pleasure, efficiency, and fun. The goal is to meet each individual user's needs with the context of where and how the product is used. UX seems like a natural place for neuroscience applications, but current descriptions of neuroscience in UX are mostly limited to applications related to sensation, perception, and cognition principles that do not require neuroscience tools. Eye tracking, however, has proved useful to UX specialists concentrating on web design.

A nagging problem in UX related to online shopping is the abandonment of shopping carts. Rates of abandonment usually are at least 50% and can be much higher for clothing and some other products. People abandon items in their shopping carts for several reasons, such as window shopping without intent to buy, price comparison shopping, unwillingness to pay shipping and handling fees that seem too high and so on. Psychologists have pursued these aspects of the shopping experience, but much work remains to be done (Bell et al., 2020). The motivational, cognitive, and emotional aspects of the online shopping experience is an area in which neuroscience tools might become particularly helpful.

Changing Minds

Marketing is not just about evaluating consumer behavior. Marketing also aims to change consumer behavior. Does consumer neuroscience have a role in changing minds? This might sound remarkably unethical, but marketing already influences consumer behavior in other ways.

Consumers can be segmented, or divided into groups that are more or less likely to respond to certain products and messaging. This is typically accomplished by looking at demographic variables, such as age or gender, or by psychographic variables, such as attitudes and lifestyle. At some future date, it might be possible to segment audiences according to differences in neuroscience measures between buyers and non-buyers of a product. Evaluation of consumer self-control, for example, could illuminate the likelihood of impulse purchases. The neuroscience contributions to our understanding of decision-making will be explored in more detail in the following chapter on neuroeconomics.

Chapter Summary

Neuroscience is already widely used to understand consumer behavior, and it is likely that this type of application will grow in frequency and scope in the future. In many cases, practitioners appear to be "coloring within the lines," or not asking more of the neuroscience tools than they are able to deliver. However, the lack of transparency that characterizes any commercial venture makes a full picture of how well the data are used and interpreted difficult to assess. We applaud those organizations that have been willing to submit their practices to peer review and hope more will do so in the future.

Review Questions

1. Which of the following fields are combined in consumer neuroscience (LO 6.1)?
    a. Marketing, psychology, and neuroscience.
    b. Psychology, neuroscience, and economics.
    c. Neuroscience, medicine, and organizational science.
    d. Neuroscience, education, and marketing.
2. Which of the following is NOT typically used in consumer neuroscience research (LO 6.2)?
    a. Facial coding
    b. Eye tracking
    c. Single cell recording
    d. Functional MRI (fMRI)
3. Which of the following is a common challenge faced by consumer neuroscientists (LO 6.3)?
    a. Lack of access to neuroscience tools.

b. Ethical requirements imposed by federal guidelines.

c. The need to share proprietary research in peer-reviewed journals.

d. The lack of a linear relationship between emotion and consumer responses to stimuli.

4. Which of the following is the best example of using mixed methods in consumer neuroscience research (LO 6.4)?

   a. Comparing consumer reactions to two tastes while undergoing fMRI.
   b. Combining EEG and eye-tracking to assess reactions to a commercial.
   c. Using several different statistical analyses until you obtain significant effects.
   d. Using different methods to assess each of several different groups of participants as they watch a commercial.

5. Which of the following is the best example of the use of consumer neuroscience in UX (LO 6.5)?

   a. Using online surveys to evaluate a purchase experience.
   b. Using diaries to track the purchase experience.
   c. Using interviews to discover why people leave items in online shopping carts.
   d. Using eye tracking to assess consumer responses to web design.

6. Which of the following efforts to change consumers' minds is most likely to use neuroscience methods in the future (LO 6.6)?

   a. Segmentation of groups that are more or less likely to respond to products and messaging.
   b. Influencing implicit attitudes.
   c. Identifying specific areas of the brain associated with positive or negative emotions elicited by a product.
   d. Identifying specific areas of the brain involved with a particular attitude.

Thought Questions

1. Imagine that you were tasked to produce government policies regulating the ethical uses of consumer neuroscience by private organizations like Apple or Facebook. What elements would you include?

2. Which do you think has a greater influence on your own consumer choices—implicit or explicit attitudes? Why?

Answer Key for Review Questions

1. a
2. c
3. d
4. b
5. d
6. a

References

Alvino, L., Luigi, P., Abhishta, A., & Henry, R. (2020). Picking your brains: Where and how neuroscience tools can enhance marketing research. *Frontiers in Neuroscience, 14*, 1221, https://doi.org/10.3389/fnins.2020.577666

Bell, L., McCloy, R., Butler, L., & Vogt, J. (2020). Motivational and affective factors underlying consumer dropout and transactional success in ecommerce: An overview. *Frontiers in Psychology, 11*, 1546. https://doi.org/10.3389/fpsyg.2020.01546

Berns, G. S., & Moore, S. E. (2011). A neural predictor of cultural popularity. *Journal of Consumer Psychology, 22*(1), 154–160. https://doi.org/10.1016/j.jcps.2011.05.001

Binet, L., & Field, P. (2009). Empirical generalizations about advertising campaign success. *Journal of Advertising Research, 49*(2), 130–133. https://doi.org/10.2501/S0021849909090163

Blackford, J. U., Buckholtz, J. W., Avery, S. N., & Zald, D. H. (2010). A unique role for the human amygdala in novelty detection. *NeuroImage, 50*(3), 1188–1193. https://doi.org/10.1016/j.neuroimage.2009.12.083

Brenninkmeijer, J., Schneider, T., & Woolgar, S. (2020). Witness and silence in neuromarketing: Managing the gap between science and its application. *Science, Technology, and Human Values, 45*(1), 62–86. https://doi.org/10.1177/0162243919829222

Cacioppo, J. T., Berntson, G. G., Larsen, J. T., Poehlmann, K. M., & Ito, T. A. (2000). The psychophysiology of emotion. In M. Lewis & J. M. Haviland-Jones (Eds.), *Handbook of emotions* (pp. 173–191). New York: Guilford Press.

Cacioppo, J. T., Berntson, G. G., Norris, C., & Gollan, J. (2011). The evaluative space model. In P. A. M. Van Lange, A. W. Kruglanski, & E. T. Higgins (Eds.), *Handbook of theories of social psychology: Volume 1* (pp. 50–72). Thousand Oaks, CA: Sage. https://doi.org/10.4135/9781445249215.n4

Cacioppo, S., Weiss, R. M., & Cacioppo, J. T. (2016). Dynamic spatiotemporal brain analyses of the visual checkerboard task: Similarities and differences between passive and active viewing conditions. *Psychophysiology, 53*(10), 1496–1506. https://doi.org/10.1111/psyp.12723

Cotte, J., Coulter, R., & Moore, M. (2005). Enhancing or disrupting guilt: The role of credibility and perceived manipulative intent. *Journal of Business Research, 58*, 361–368. https://doi.org/10.1016/S0148-2963(03)00102-4

Cowen, A. S., Keltner, D., Schroff, F., Jou, B., Adam, H., & Gautam, P. (2021). Sixteen facial expressions occur in similar contexts worldwide. *Nature, 589*, 251–259. https://doi.org/10.1038/s41586-020-3037-7

Damasio, A. R., Tranel, D., & Damasio, H. C. (1991). Somatic markers and the guidance of behaviour: Theory and preliminary testing. In H. S. Eisenberg, H. M. Benton, and A. Lester (Eds.), *Frontal lobe function and dysfunction* (pp. 217–229). Oxford University Press.

Dmochowski, J. P., Bezdek, M. A., Abelson, B. P., Johnson, J. S., Schumacher, E. H., & Parra, L. C. (2014). Audience preferences are predicted by temporal reliability of neural processing. *Nature Communications, 5*(1), 1–9. https://doi.org/10.1038.ncomms5567

Ekman, P., Friesen, W. V., & Ellsworth, P. (1972). *Emotion in the human face: Guidelines for research and an integration of findings*. London: Pergamon Press.

Gable, P. A., Paul, K., Pourtois, G., & Burgdorf, J. (2021). Utilizing electroencephalography (EEG) to investigate positive affect. *Current Opinion in Behavioral Sciences, 39*, 190–195. https://doi.org/10.1016/j.cobeha.2021.03.018

Greenwald, A. G., & Banaji, M. R. (1995). Implicit social cognition: Attitudes, self-esteem, and stereotypes. *Psychological Review, 102*(1), 4–27. https://doi.org/10.1037/0033-294x.102.1.4

Greenwald, A. G., McGee, D. E., Schwartz, J. L. K. (1998). Measuring individual differences in implicit cognition: The Implicit Association Test. *Journal of Personality and Social Psychology, 74*(6), 1468–1480. https://doi.org/10.1037/0022-3514.74.6.1464

Hahn, A., Judd, C. M., Kirsch, H. K., & Blair, I. V. (2014). Awareness of implicit attitudes. *Journal of Experimental Psychology: General, 143*(3), 1369–1392. https://doi.org/10.1037/a0035028

Hutzler, F. (2014). Reverse inference is not a fallacy per se: Cognitive processes can be inferred from functional imaging data. *NeuroImage, 84*, 1061–1069. https://doi.org/10.1016/j.neuroimage.2012.12.075

Iacoboni, M., Freedman, J., Kaplan, J., Jamieson, K. H., Freedman, T., Knapp, B., & Fitzgerald, K. (2007). *This is your brain on politics*. The New York Times. www.nytimes.com/2007/11/11/opinion/11freedman.html?smid=url-share

Jimenez, M., & Yang, K. C. (2008). How guilt level affects green advertising effectiveness. *Journal of Creative Communications, 3*, 87–88. https://doi.org/10.1177/097325861000300301

Kahneman, D. (2011). *Thinking fast and slow*. New York, NY: Farrar, Straus, & Giroux.

Kleinmuntz, B., & Szucko, J. J. (1984). A field study of the fallibility of polygraph lie detection. *Nature, 308*, 449–450. https://doi.org/10.1038/308449a0

Kotler, S. (2010). *Hollywood science: Reading your mind to make horror movies ever scarier*. Popular Science. www.popsci.com/science/article/2010-05/hollywood-science-how-your-brain-reacts-horror-movies/

Matsumoto, D. (2001). Culture and emotion. In D. Matsumoto (Ed.), *The handbook of culture and psychology* (pp. 171–194). New York, NY: Oxford University Press.

Osipova, D., Takashima, A., Oostenveld, R., Fernández, G., Maris, E., & Jensen, O. (2006). Theta and gamma oscillations predict encoding and retrieval of declarative memory. *Journal of Neuroscience, 26*(28), 7523–7531. https://doi.org/10.1523/JNEUROSCI.1948-06.2006

Pegna, A. J., Khateb, A., Lazeyras, F., & Seghier, M. L. (2005). Discriminating emotional faces without primary visual cortices involves the right amygdala. *Nature Neuroscience, 8*(1), 24–25. https://doi.org/10.1038/nn1364

Petty, R. E., & Cacioppo, J. T. (1981). *Attitudes and persuasion: Classic and contemporary approaches*. Dubuque, IA: Wm. C. Brown.

Poulsen, A. T., Pedroni, A., Langer, N., & Hansen, L. K. (2018). Microstate EEGlab toolbox: An introductory guide. *bioRxiv*. https://doi.org/10.1101/289850

Reznik, S. J., & Allen, J. J. B. (2018). Frontal asymmetry as a mediator and moderator of emotion: An updated review. *Psychophysiology, 55*, e12965. https://doi.org/10.1111/psyp.12965

Shestyuk, A., Kasinathan, K., Karapoondinott, V., Knight, R. T., & Gurumoorthy, R. (2019). Individual EEG measures of attention, memory, and motivation predict population level TV viewership and Twitter engagement. *PLOS ONE*. https://doi.org/10.1371/journal.pone.0214507

Smith, E. E., Reznik, S. J., Stewart, J. L., & Allen, J. J. B. (2017). Assessing and conceptualizing frontal EEG asymmetry: An updated primer on recording, processing, analyzing, and interpreting frontal alpha asymmetry. *International Journal of Psychophysiology*, *111*, 98–114. https://doi.org/10.1016/j.inpsycho.2016.11.005

Smith, M. E., & Marci, C. (2016). From theory to common practice: Consumer neuroscience goes mainstream. *Nielsen Journal of Measurement*, *1*(2), 3–11.

Sullivan, M. W., & Lewis, M. (2003). Emotional expressions of young infants and children: A practitioner's primer. *Infants & Young Children*, *16*(2), 120–142.

Tognoli, E., Benites, D., & Kelso, A. S. (2021). A blueprint for the study of the brain's spatiotemporal patterns. arXiv:2016.00637 [q-bio.NC].

Vecchiato, G., Astolfi, L., De Vico Fallani, F., Toppi, J., Aloise, F., Bez, F., Wei, D., Kong, W., Dai, J., Cincotti, F., Mattia, D., & Babiloni, F. (2011). On the use of EEG or MEG brain imaging tools in neuromarketing research. *Computational Intelligence and Neuroscience*, *2011*, 643489. https://doi.org/10.1155/2011/643489

Vecchiato, G., Astolfi, L., Fallani, F. D. V., Cincotti, F., Mattia, D., Salinari, S., Soranzo, R., & Babiloni, F. (2010). Changes in brain activity during the observation of TV commercials by using EEG, GSR and HR measurements. *Brain Topography*, *23*(2), 165–179. https://doi.org/10.1007/s10548-009-0127-0

Glossary

Consumer neuroscience	The application of neuroscience to the understanding of consumer decision-making and behavior.
Elaboration Likelihood Model (ELM)	A model of persuasion that postulates a central route, focused on logic, and a peripheral route, susceptible to influence by surface characteristics of an argument.
Eye tracking	The use of infrared cameras to record gaze and eye movements.
Facial coding	The evaluation of spontaneous facial expressions.
Implicit association	An unconscious connection between a stimulus and an attitude.
Implicit Association Test (IAT)	A controversial test of implicit associations.
Pupillometry	The evaluation of pupil diameter as a measure of arousal.
Reverse inference	A logical argument that assumes you can use observed brain activity to infer a cognitive state.

Somatic marker   A theoretical physical trace based on an association between an experience and the emotions it elicited.

User experience (UX) A professional field that evaluates all interactions with a brand or product from the point-of-view of the user.

7 Neuroeconomics

LEARNING OBJECTIVES

After reading this chapter, you should be able to:

▶ 1. Define neuroeconomics.
▶ 2. Describe the reciprocal contributions of economics and neuroscience to our understanding of decision-making.
▶ 3. Explain the neural correlates of value and choice behaviors.
▶ 4. Discuss the implications of emotion and social behavior for decision-making.
▶ 5. Identify the neural mechanisms for implementing a choice.

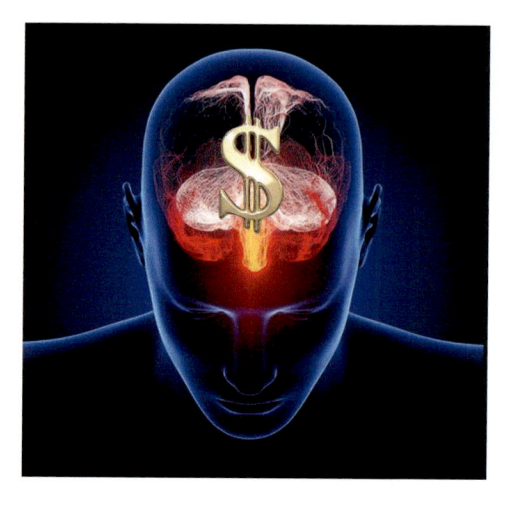

FIGURE 7.1 Neuroeconomics is the study of the biological correlates of choice and decision-making.

Sources: www.flickr.com/photos/arselectronica/13994747444; www.maxpixel.net/Dollar-Sign-Currency-3558407

How Well Do You Make Decisions?

This chapter is all about choices and decision-making (Figure 7.1). Thinking back on your life so far, you can probably identify choices that qualify as the good, the bad, and the ugly. We all make mistakes, but overall, it would be counterproductive for people to make consistently bad choices. If a person's pattern of decision-making is regularly self-destructive, it is possible that some sort of pathology is present. Animals depend on making appropriate approach and withdrawal decisions to survive, so given the forces of evolution and the learning from consequences described by B. F. Skinner, we will assume that all of us have the potential to make good choices when it counts.

However, just like we might fall prey to false information or fake news, there are circumstances that inhibit good decision-making. As we will see in this chapter, good decision-making requires significant cognitive resources. When we're tired, distracted, rushed into a decision, or taking short cuts, the outcomes might not be as good. Decision-making probably should be as rational as possible but is often quite impulsive. We are susceptible to confirmation bias, or the selection of information that conforms to our values and world views. This can lead to our rejection of reasonable solutions in favor of decisions that are "obviously right." Conformity, and our basic desire for social connection, can lead us to be influenced by what others think rather than coming to our own conclusions. There are situations where "tried and true" actually works, but relying on the methods we've always used rather than being open to novel approaches limits our decision-making capabilities. Finally, selecting a simple choice instead of a more complex one because you understand the simple one better is a short cut that often backfires.

What skills promote good decision-making? You probably won't like the first answer very much—good problem solving requires a strong mastery of probability. If your education has been like mine, you have answered countless exam questions about decks of cards and coin flips and rolling dice. These topics might be useful for professional gamblers, but how are the rest of us benefiting from this knowledge? Well, a decision (I think I'll attend community college to save some money or I'll work a year before going to grad school) is essentially a bet on the future. You are gambling that your choice will give you an optimum or at least an acceptable outcome. Individual differences in decision-making are heavily influenced by variations in people's understanding of probability (Cokely et al., 2018). At the same time, education is not a guarantee that a person has a good grasp of numbers and probability. Physicians tend to be much brighter than the average person and they surely have many years of education under their belts, but nearly half were unable to answer this simple question correctly: If Patient A has a 1% risk of getting a disease in the next ten years, and Patient B's risk is double that of Patient A's, what is Patient B's risk? This is not a trick question! The answer is 2% (2 x.01 =.02). You might have seen the famous lily pad problem that is also likely to fool smart, educated people. If lily pads double in area every day and completely cover a pond after 30 days, how long does it take for the lake to be half covered? The answer is 29 days, not 15, but many people struggle to reach that conclusion (Figure 7.2).

In addition to paying more attention when our professors are explaining probability, what else can we do to become better decision-makers? Consider the social norms that might be influencing your decisions. How important is it for you to do what others would do or recommend? Seek out dissenting opinions, despite our typical aversion to this. We love to talk with people who are equally convinced that our decisions are brilliant. We tend to give them only those bits of information that support the decision we want to make, seeking reassurance for our choices instead of honest opinions. Meta-cognition, or knowing what we do (and do not) know, is best for familiar topics. Therefore, if your decision rests upon information with which you are less familiar, do your homework first. Try to avoid over-confidence, but at the same time, don't fall prey to unwarranted under-confidence either. If you have the luxury to take time to make a decision, don't rush. It's tempting to rush, because facing an important choice can be unpleasant and we like to get it over with. Give yourself time to take breaks to do less cognitively demanding tasks, perhaps by taking a walk and enjoying the nature around you. Then return refreshed to the choice at hand.

Discovering additional insights about making better decisions is one of the goals of this chapter. While neuroeconomics has the potential to influence large systems of behavior, from corporations to nations, it also can improve our everyday experiences.

FIGURE 7.2 Even intelligent, well-educated people might lack the numerical and probability skills needed to make good decisions. The famous lily pad problem catches many unaware.

Source: Karla Freberg.

What Is Neuroeconomics?

Neuroeconomics is a hybrid discipline combining economics, cognitive psychology, and neuroscience (Glimcher, 2008). The goal of the field is to better understand human choice and decision-making.

Compared to many of the other topics covered in this book, neuroeconomics remains more closely aligned with academic research than with concrete applications. We met some of the more concrete applications of these concepts in our earlier chapter on Consumer Neuroscience. However, even if a large proportion of the scientists pursuing this field conduct basic research on decision-making, the potential applications of their findings are many and diverse. Human decision-making occurs across many domains, from daily problem-solving to making purchases to pursuing romantic relationships or selecting a restaurant for your dinner. Fractured decision-making abilities characterize a wide range of psychological disorders, including hoarding behavior and substance abuse. A better understanding of these processes offers remarkable potential to make people's lives better. At the same time, attempting to answer the questions of the economist drives the neuroscientist to perfect methods and gain a greater understanding of how the brain works.

Economists seek to predict the choices made by human beings. Beginning with Adam Smith's 1776 *The Wealth of Nations*, economics has maintained an on-again/off-again love affair with psychological phenomena. The classic economists, including Smith and John Maynard Keynes, relied heavily on psychological concepts, such as Keynes' "propensity to consume" and "animal spirits" that influenced investment decisions. In the 1930s, economics pivoted to embrace mathematical models. This trend pushed the field farther away from psychology for many years. According to this approach, you don't need to know why people choose an apple over an orange as long as their choices conform to axioms, or established propositions like "if a person chooses an apple over an orange once, then they should always do so." The mathematical, "neoclassic" economists built up a rich literature over the subsequent decades.

In the 1950s and 1960s, economists began to discover and publish "paradoxes," or patterns of choice that clearly violated important axioms. While neoclassicists scrambled to incorporate these contradictory observations into their existing theories, Israeli psychologists Daniel Kahneman and Amos Tversky demonstrated, using the experimental methods of their field, that the paradoxes were far from a fluke, and that the problems facing classic theories were quite extensive. For example, the fact that people would accept a riskier solution if a situation were framed in terms of loss (number of people who "die" rather than number of people who are "saved"), conflicted with some of the most general axioms supporting theories of choice (Tversky & Kahneman, 1987). Like-minded scholars, both economists and psychologists, began referring to themselves as behavioral economists, moving economics back into alignment with psychological principles yet again. **Behavioral economics** is truly an interdisciplinary approach, using theories and methods associated with economics and psychology.

Behavioral economists began to extend their areas of study to explore phenomena like **heuristics**, or the mental shortcuts we take while reasoning. Emotional and social contexts were found to shape decision-making in significant ways. For example, following the terrorist attacks of 9/11, so many people feared airline travel (miniscule risk) that they opted to travel by car (much higher risk) to destinations they would otherwise use air travel to reach (Figure 7.3). This resulted in a significant increase in traffic fatalities, estimated at 2300 excess driving deaths (Blalock et al., 2009).

While the behavioral economists were hard at work, similar trends were influencing the developing fields of cognitive psychology and neuroscience. Just as the behavioral economists were frustrated by the unwillingness of neoclassical economists to consider the "black box" of the mind, so were the cognitive psychologists debating with the strict behaviorists along similar lines. Strict behaviorists, like B. F. Skinner, did not dispute the idea that important activity took place as the mind processed inputs and planned

FIGURE 7.3 Economists assume human beings make rational decisions, but this is not always the case. Following the terrorist attacks of 9/11, traffic fatalities increased as fearful individuals chose much riskier auto travel over much safer air travel.

Source: https://ndla.no/subject:1:06270029-7aa7-4a7a-b383-128b275ff150/topic:2:184990/resource:1:99791

outputs. They just didn't think it was possible to observe these processes scientifically. They also believed that the processes of the mind followed the same rules as easily observable, outward behaviors, so there was no need to come up with special sets of rules to describe how these processes took place. Cognitive scientists disagreed and searched for methods that would provide more insight into the brain's processing of information. At the same time, neuroscientists, still limited by ethical constraints, inched forward using animal models and analyses of lesions in clinical cases.

In these limited circumstances, early cognitive neuroscientists began to focus on the nervous system correlates of sensation and perception, as these were readily assessed by existing methods. An approach that turned out to be particularly productive for the eventual development of neuroeconomics was the use of **signal detection theory**, which requires an observer to make a simple yes/no choice about whether a stimulus is detected. In the language of signal detection, four outcomes are possible (see Table 7.1). We explored an application of this approach in Chapter 4's discussion of polygraph accuracy. The correct detection of a stimulus is a "hit." A "miss" consists of failing to detect a stimulus. Stating a stimulus is present when it is not is a "false alarm," and correctly stating that no stimulus is present is a "correct rejection." Signal detection provides powerful insights into choice behavior in response to ambiguous stimuli, whether we're evaluating radiologists' abilities to detect tumors in mammograms or the likelihood that police officers might shoot an unarmed citizen. Faced with an ambiguous situation (does that person have a weapon or not?), the police officer must weigh the risks of a false alarm (shooting an unarmed person) against the risks of a miss (not shooting an armed person and likely being killed or injured yourself). The radiologist must choose between putting a woman through further testing and stress for a false alarm versus missing a tumor that is present.

In one of the first demonstrations of the ability to correlate brain activity with choice behavior, researchers used signal detection to evaluate the responses of monkeys to ambiguous visual stimuli (Newsome et al., 1989). While recording from single neurons in anesthetized but alert monkeys, the monkeys were asked to indicate the direction of motion in a dot display in which some of the dots moved coherently and others at random. These displays look similar to the static on a television when a channel isn't coming in clearly. The researchers were recording from area MT in the middle temporal

TABLE 7.1 Possible outcomes in signal detection

	Answer "Yes"	Answer "No"
Stimulus Present	Hit	Miss
Stimulus Absent	False Alarm	Correct Rejection

lobe, which is known to process information about visual movement. Most of the neurons in area MT demonstrate a preference for a particular speed and direction of movement. The monkey indicated its choice (yes, movement or no, no movement) by looking in a particular direction at the end of each trial while the responses of the area MT cells were observed. This study stimulated further efforts to identify the neural underpinnings of choice.

The development of brain imaging technologies in the 1980s and 1990s was a significant game-changer for neuroeconomics. Suddenly, the black box seemed to be open for viewing. This resulted in a burst of activity surrounding the question of what neural processes supported decision-making. In other words, this approach to neuroeconomics was simply an extension of behavioral economics made possible by the addition of information from the neurosciences. Ross (2005) labeled this approach to neuroeconomics as "behavioral economics in the scanner."

A second approach to neuroeconomics, labeled "neurocellular economics" by Ross (2005, 2008) was to take economic theories and use them to explain neural mechanisms. According to this approach, classic economic models can be applied to neural networks as well as to individuals. For example, classic utility theory states that decisions can be described in terms of the value, or utility, placed on them by individuals. Instead of considering individual humans making decisions based on utility, what if single neurons or networks did the same? These two approaches are in the process of converging into what Serra (2021) calls a "neural-and-behavioral economics" program. This merger would use what we know about the biological limits on decision-making to better understand and predict choice behaviors.

The development of neuroeconomics has not been completely smooth. As we observed in our chapter on neuroeducation, interdisciplinary efforts require a common language and strong communication. Just as some educators believe neuroscience has nothing to offer them, some economists feel similarly. Gul and Pesendorfer (2008) published a chapter "The Case for Mindless Economics," and argued that the reductionism of neuroscience was unlikely to impact economic theory. Reductionism refers to the breaking down of complex constructs into their component parts. This approach, of course, runs the risk of losing information provided by a "big picture" or more holistic, Gestalt perspective. These are growing pains typical of many novel endeavors. As concrete improvements emerge from the collaboration, like those reviewed in our chapter on consumer neuroscience, confidence in the benefits of neuroeconomics should continue to grow.

From its early beginnings, neuroeconomics has expanded to become the subject of numerous degree programs, specialized journals, and a professional society (Society for Neuroeconomics). The number of papers featuring neuroeconomics continues to grow, with a Google Scholar search for "neuroeconomics" since 2020 returning 3,430 results for papers and books (see also Figure 7.4).

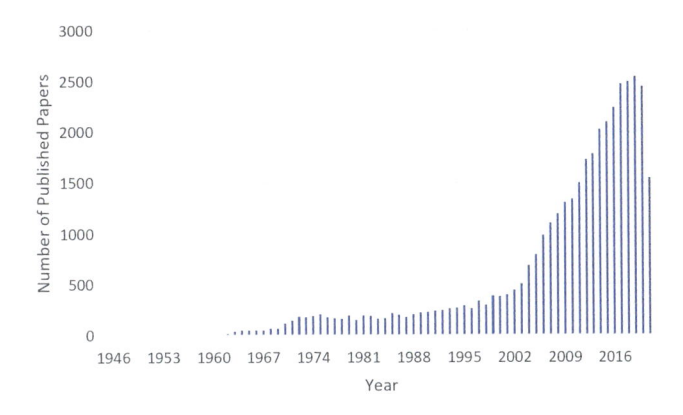

FIGURE 7.4 Publications if the PubMed database that includes the words "decision-making" and "brain" by year.

Source: Author.

What is Value?

Apple versus PC? Mercedes versus BMW? Apples and oranges? How do we decide which items to choose? These are known as simple choices, but like most of our topics, things are not quite as simple as they might seem outwardly. To make these choices requires several parallel processes in the brain. First, the brain must assign a **value** to each option. Next, those values must be compared to each other. Finally, a movement must be made to implement the choice, such as reaching for an apple instead of for an orange. Neuroeconomists believe that an understanding of simple choice can help us understand a wide range of human behaviors (Rangel & Clithero, 2014).

Decisions can be classified as perceptual or value-based choices. Perceptual choices involve reactions to stimulus inputs. We met one example of this type of choice earlier in the chapter when describing the work of Newsome and his colleagues (1989). In their classic study, monkeys needed to indicate the direction of movement of a display of dots. These choices are similar to many we make every day. Is it safe to make a left turn? Or is that oncoming car moving too quickly? In contrast, the examples at the beginning of this section (PC versus Apple) are known as value-based decisions.

While both perceptual and value-based decisions involve choices, the type of processing involved in each is distinct. Of the two, value-based decisions are more subjective, whereas perceptual choices adhere to the signal detection theory described earlier. Value-based decisions form the bulk of what neuroeconomists attempt to explain. These decisions require the brain to compute values for each option using a common scale (Padoa-Schioppa, 2011). This is similar to currency. The price of an apple and an orange at the store provides us one way to compare their relative value. In reality, the valuation of choices is much more complicated. What if you are allergic to citrus? Then it really doesn't matter how much an orange costs. In general, the way we value an option is based on prior associations between the option and its outcomes. If eating oranges has made you happy in the past, you assign a positive value to oranges. If eating oranges has made you ill, you will apply a negative value to this choice. In other words, the value of a choice is not absolute and unchanging, but rather established by learning, updated regularly, and supported by context.

A major breakthrough in the understanding of value-based decisions has been the more sophisticated understanding of the role of learning, and reinforcement learning in particular. You might recall from your study of B. F. Skinner and operant conditioning that behaviors followed by reinforcement subsequently become more frequent while those followed by punishment drop in frequency. This rather reflexive view of the roles of reinforcement and punishment has been updated to consider factors such as an animal's ability to predict a reward. From a neuroscience perspective, the prediction and seeking of reward is tightly linked to systems using the neurochemical dopamine.

You might have read or heard about dopamine as being essential to the reward systems in the brain. This is true in the sense that pathways such as the mesolimbic system, connecting the midbrain to anterior structures in the limbic system, support the experiences of pleasure and reward. Activity in these pathways and their relationship to frontal lobe executive areas is clearly distorted in cases of addiction, and substances that directly promote excess dopamine activity, such as methamphetamine and cocaine, are among the most addictive on the planet. Children with attention deficit/hyperactivity disorder (ADHD) are suspected of having lower than typical levels of dopamine activity, which in turn might account for their need for more frequent reinforcement to remain on track.

Later observations of dopamine activity showed that activity in dopamine pathways did not occur in all cases of reward, but rather in cases of rewards that were unexpected. If frontal areas of the brain have already indicated that a reward is expected, the dopaminergic neurons do not respond. So rather than reacting to any old reward, dopaminergic neurons compare predictions of reward to what actually occurs. When an expected reward is delayed or fails to appear, these neurons decrease their activity. Any differences between an expected and perceived reward, or a **reward prediction error**, stimulates a learning process in which the value of a stimulus is updated (Montague, 2007).

This updating process helps us understand how rewards are viewed not as separate entities, but in context. Classic research by Walter Mischel and his colleagues (1988) showed how children varied in their abilities to resist eating a marshmallow when promised a second one if they waited for a researcher to return (Figure 7.5). This can be viewed as a modern take on the folk saying, "a bird in the hand is worth two in the bush." Under what circumstances will we trade the certainty of the marshmallow or bird at hand for the future, riskier promise of two? The children who waited, or showed good delay of gratification skills, experienced superior outcomes across many domains

FIGURE 7.5 Classic research by Walter Mischel and his colleagues demonstrated the importance of delayed gratification in decision-making.
Source: Karla Freberg.

later in life. Later research, however, illuminated more nuanced conclusions (e.g., Watts et al., 2018). Trust in the researcher, for example, played a large role in the decision. If you don't trust the researcher, taking the marshmallow right in front of you now would seem to be a reasonable decision.

As shown in Table 7.2, neuroscience research with both animals and humans has identified several structures involved with the assignment of value to a stimulus, such as a marshmallow on a plate in front of you. Damage to any one of these structures can interfere with good decision-making.

Overall, the human brain places a higher priority on avoiding danger than on obtaining reward. We are many times more sensitive to bitter tastes than to sweet tastes. If you fail to detect a bitter taste, often associated with toxins, you might die. The worst thing that happens if you fail to detect a sweet taste is that you miss out on a source of calories that is likely to be pleasant. We generally do not die from that. Not surprisingly then, people are remarkably loss averse, choosing to avoid the risk of loss even if this choice might result in a larger gain. Loss aversion involves activity in the amygdala. Two patients with rare damage to the amygdala showed typical preference for large gains and small losses in a gambling game, but compared to control participants, they were much more likely to take large gambles (De Martino et al., 2010). Their inability to experience the fear of loss resulted in less risk aversion. Activity in the insula is associated with disgust and some types of punishment (Serra, 2021). The hypothalamus participates in the valuation of food, whereas the posterior cingulate cortex participates in the valuation of money (Levy & Glimcher, 2011). These findings suggest that different networks might encode the value of different types of reward. The posterior cingulate cortex also participates in the evaluation of delayed options.

TABLE 7.2 Brain structures involved with assigning value to a choice

Structure	Role in Decision-Making
Orbitofrontal Cortex (OFC)	Assigns value of many different types of rewards in the short term
Nucleus Accumbens	Assigns value of many different types of rewards
Dorsolateral Prefrontal Cortex (DLPC)	Assigns value over longer period of time; involved in social and self-control aspects of decision-making
Amygdala	Loss aversion and emotion regulation in face of risky choices
Anterior Insula	Disgust and response to possible punishment
Anterior cingulate cortex	Conflict resolution, such as between contradictory choices and cost/benefit differences
Posterior cingulate cortex	Assigns value to risky or delayed options
Hypothalamus	Participates in loss aversion for primary rewards, such as food (not secondary, like money)
Hippocampus	Working memory during a choice task
Striatum	Constructs subjective value from input
Ventromedial Prefrontal Cortex	Constructs subjective value from input

In addition to the structures already identified, the orbitofrontal cortex provides general value information about rewards. Eslinger and Damasio (1985) chronicle the challenges faced by Patient EVR after his orbitofrontal cortex was damaged during surgery to remove a tumor. Following his surgery, Patient EVR began to make a series of uncharacteristically poor decisions, leading to the loss of his job and marriage. The anterior cingulate cortex provides a rough cost–benefit analysis, helping us decide whether a particular reward is worthy of the effort needed to obtain it. Rats with damage to their anterior cingulate cortex will no longer climb over a barrier to obtain a larger reward, which they normally would do (Salamone et al., 1994). The dorsolateral prefrontal cortex processes value over time, particularly in cases requiring self-control.

The outputs of these networks converge at central comparison points, the **ventromedial prefrontal cortex** and possibly the striatum, a part of the basal ganglia containing the nucleus accumbens (see Chapter 2; Glimcher, 2014). Levels of activity in these two areas not only represent the value assigned to a choice, but also the effects of delay and social factors, discussed in a later section.

Once the options have been assigned a value, we still need to compare them. Neuroeconomists offer two solutions to how this might happen. One model, the "winner takes all," is essentially the same as the standard economic **utility model**—line up all the options according to their assigned value and pick the best one. A second type of model, a "**drift-diffusion**" model, proposed that we have a threshold for a satisfactory expected reward. We review one option after the other and as soon as an option passes the threshold, we pick it without necessarily considering the remaining options.

Which model do people use? It is possible that both processes occur depending on the complexity of the decision and the speed with which a decision must be made. Herbert Simon (1957) distinguished between "maximizing," or reaching the best outcome, and "satisficing," or reaching an acceptable outcome. The winner takes all model leads to maximizing, but it takes time. The drift-diffusion model might work better if time is short. There is also some evidence that people tend toward one type of decision style over the other. Maximizers are perfectionists who need time to make decisions. They look at more profiles on online dating sites than satisficers do, and even after they enter committed relationships, they continue to compare their partner to other possible partners (French & Meltzer, 2019).

Emotion Versus Reason?

From the time of Aristotle and Plato, reason and emotion have been viewed as separate, often competing parts of the mind. Fans of *Star Trek* see regular examples of this distinction in the emotionally suppressed, yet highly logical Vulcans. You might recall a decision or two made at the height of an emotion that in retrospect, do not seem to be very reasonable choices. But do emotions usually interfere with good decision-making? Do they deserve their bad reputation?

Beginning with a Darwinian approach, it seems unlikely that emotions survived the cauldron of evolution if they consistently led us in the wrong directions. After all, one of the benefits of emotion is the provision of a quick, automatic approach or avoidance impulse. If you run across a rattlesnake in your path, you don't want to take time to reason about its true identity (rattlesnake or something that looks like a rattlesnake) or its potential danger to you (maybe it won't notice you). You should just get out of there quickly. At the same time, most of us have experienced situations in which our emotions lead us in the wrong direction.

These observations have led psychologists, beginning with William James (1890), to propose a dual system approach featuring a quick, emotional pathway and a slower, reasoned pathway to decision-making. This dual system framework has been adopted by

NEUROECONOMICS

behavioral economists in frameworks like Kahneman's *Thinking Fast and Slow* (2011). Type 1 decisions are characterized by low-effort, automatic processing while Type 2 decisions are effortful and analytic.

Neuroscience enters the arena in efforts to find the neural correlates of these two modes of processing, typically in situations involving people's assessment of risk and the potential for gains and losses. Antonio Damasio and his colleagues (Bechara et al., 1994) used the Iowa gambling task to observe risky decisions. After all, as we've pointed out previously, decision-making and gambling have much in common. When you make a decision in uncertain circumstances, you are gambling on the future. The Iowa Gambling Task requires participants to choose cards from four decks of cards (Figure 7.6). Two of the decks were "safe," which means that choosing them consistently over the course of a session would result in winnings. The other two decks featured winning cards with better payoffs than the winning cards in the safe decks, but the losing cards were also more impactful. Repeatedly choosing from these two decks was generally catastrophic.

What would you do? You have no idea what rules govern the decks—you must figure this out. If you're like most of Bechara et al.'s participants, you will initially stay with the risky decks due to the occasional large payoffs. Over time, however, you will shift to the safer decks. Bechara et al. found one group of participants, however, who were unable to make this shift. They studied patients who had experienced damage to the orbitofrontal cortex (see Chapter 2). This area of the frontal lobes, lying right behind the bony orbits protecting the eyes, has been associated with the mind's sensitivity to

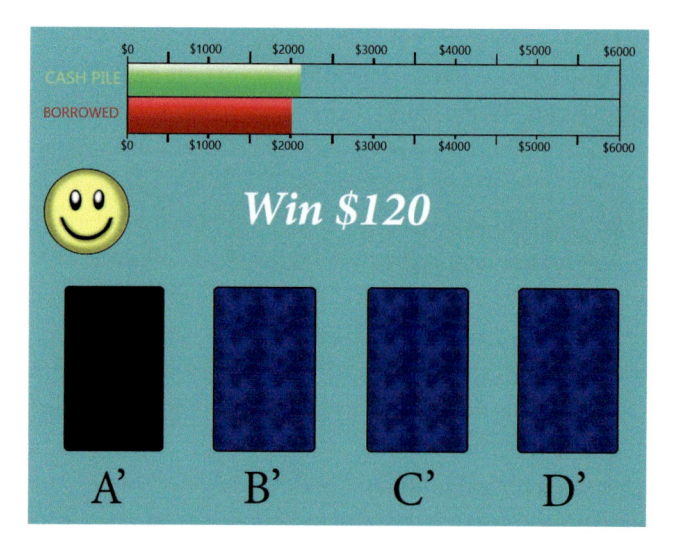

FIGURE 7.6 Participants performing the Iowa Gambling Task must select a card from one of four decks. Most people manage to figure out that choosing two of the four decks gives a better overall return.

Source: Karla Freberg.

reward and punishment in a given situation. This type of damage does not affect reason. Patients with orbitofrontal damage can learn and state rules of conduct, but just have difficulty following them. These patients persevere in choosing the risky decks. As early as ten trials into the task, healthy participants begin to show stress when considering the risky decks, as measured by skin conductance, but patients with damage to the orbitofrontal cortex show no such signs.

These results support a positive role for emotions in decision-making. Fear of loss can make you select a safer, more positive choice. Does this mean that emotions always help us make good choices? Very few things about human behavior are that simple. Damasio followed up the original study (Shiv et al., 2005) with a variation in which the risky choices now produced the best outcomes. How did the healthy participants and patients do this time? The healthy participants continued to be risk-averse, and as a result, they didn't do very well. In contrast, the patients with orbitofrontal damage were not emotionally deterred by losses and continued to follow their initial risky strategies, which means they performed better this time than the healthy participants.

The answer to a question of whether emotion helps or hurts decision-making, therefore, looks like so many others in psychology: it depends. But if emotion helps in one context while hurting in another, doesn't this mean the effects cancel out and we should just stick with reason? Not necessarily. Gambling games in laboratories are highly controlled situations with minimal ecological validity. In real-world situations, it might be the case that the types of contexts that benefit from emotional processing are more common than those that don't. This would support the evolutionary conservation of emotional decision-making in the most rational animals on the planet.

Efforts to correlate specific brain activity to emotional and rational decisions use the **framing effects** outlined by Tversky and Kahneman (1981). In a classic example they call the "Asian Disease Problem," participants are told that 400 out of a group of 600 people will die, but as you will see, this is framed in two different ways. Participants must choose between a safe and a risky course of action to recommend to the President. When the problem is framed in a negative way (400 people will die), only 22% of the participants chose the safe option. When the problem was framed in a positive way (200 will be saved), 72% preferred the safe option. Apparently, if you have already "saved" people, you don't want to make that worse.

This experiment has obvious parallels to the way people react to news about the COVID-19 pandemic. As of September 24, 2021, John Elflein, writing for the website Statista, stated that 231,412,404 cases of COVID had occurred worldwide, with 4,742,994 deaths. In other words, about 98% survive infection and about 2% of those who are infected die. In Tversky and Kahneman's terms, negative frames talking about the deaths of 2% of those infected will lead to riskier decisions (lockdowns, vaccine mandates, etc.) than positive frames that focus on the 98% who survive infection. To be clear, your author is both vaccinated and in favor of vaccinations in general.

TABLE 7.3 Choices from the classic "Asian Disease Problem" posed by Tversky and Kahneman (1981). Which would you choose from each row?

	Safe Option	Risky Option
Positive Frame	Save 200 (out of 600) lives	One-third chance of saving all the lives and a two-thirds chance of saving no lives
Negative Frame	400 will die	One-third chance that no one will die and a two-thirds chance that all will die

Framing in neuroeconomics is usually investigated in terms of gains and losses. When financial results are framed as losses, people make riskier choices than when equivalent outcomes are framed as gains. You don't want to lose what you have just gained. Choices made by participants can be described as frame-consistent (risky choice in response to loss; safe choice in response to gain) or frame-inconsistent (safe choice in response to loss; risky choice in response to gain). During observation using fMRI, increased activity has been observed in the amygdala during frame-consistent choices and in the anterior cingulate cortex during frame-inconsistent choices (De Martino et al., 2006, Roiser et al., 2009, Xu et al., 2013). These results were interpreted using the dual system approach. The fear and anxiety associated with the amygdala represents a quick, emotional response to gains and losses. The more executive functions of the anterior cingulate cortex might represent a more reasoned choice. The oddities of the overall framing effects described by Tversky and Kahneman, therefore, might result from an emotional intrusion into what should be a reasoned process.

Early writing by Herbert Simon (1955) suggested another interpretation. He emphasized "limits on computational capacity" as a major factor in human decision-making. This is consistent with the view in cognitive psychology of heuristics as mental shortcuts. Cognitive psychologists have identified several heuristics, which are beyond the scope of this book. Kahneman and Tversky delighted in showing us where our heuristics can fail. This does not mean that heuristics always fail, or even fail most of the time to give us a satisfactory solution (Gigerenzer, 2008).

Using a heuristic could result in faulty decisions if you need to consider ALL relevant information to reach a good decision. At the same time, we rarely have time and energy to do that, so using a heuristic might be better than not making a timely decision. As U.S. General George S. Patton stated, "A good plan, violently executed now, is better than a perfect plan next week" (generalpatton.com, n.d.). Ill-formed problems, like choosing a spouse, defy logic and reason, making the use of heuristics a reasonable alternative. While it is true that you are more likely to be killed by a cow than by a shark (contrary to the availability heuristic), it is also likely, given the way memory works, that the things that come to mind easily are truly significant and important to consider when making a decision. Evolution is unlikely to result in thinking processes that are counterproductive most of the time.

It is interesting to note that emotion is not prominently featured in research on heuristics. This opens the possibility that the types of frame-based choices used to support a dual model of emotion versus reason are really the result of restricted cognitive effort instead (Li et al., 2017). These researchers confirmed that frame-consistent choices involved the amygdala, but more generally, were associated with activity in the default mode network (DMN). Activity in this network is associated with mind wandering and a general lack of focused thought. Further, the brain activity during frame-inconsistent choices was consistent with networks supporting focused thought. According to this approach, Kahneman's Type 1 and Type 2 decisions do not necessarily represent a dichotomy of emotion versus reason, but rather a reflection of their position on a continuum between disengaged and engaged thinking.

Social Decision-making

In line with our general emphasis on the importance of context in making decisions, we cannot neglect one of the most significant influences on human choice—the social environment. Human beings are a remarkably social species. In fact, one of the prevailing theories of why the human brain grew so fast so quickly is the advantages of a big brain in navigating complex social environments. The rigors of calculus and organic chemistry pale in comparison to the difficulties we face when interpreting an ambiguous text message. As a species, we are dependent on cooperation for our survival, but are also quite capable of deciding to act in selfish, self-serving ways.

The field of **social neuroscience** pioneered by John Cacioppo and his colleagues (e.g., Cacioppo & Berntson, 1992; Cacioppo et al., 2006) is yet another powerful interdisciplinary approach that this time seeks to correlate nervous system function with the social self. Several aspects of the social brain that influence decision-making include theory of mind, mirror systems, and empathy. Together, these systems are activated when people face social dilemmas and opportunities to cooperate or bargain.

Theory of mind (Premack & Woodruff, 1978) refers to the recognition that others have a point of view and knowledge that is different from one's own. This capacity emerges around the age of four years and is believed to be delayed or impaired in cases of autism spectrum disorder. The accidental discovery of mirror neurons in monkeys, or neurons that fire in response to observing an action without reference to the individual performing the action (Di Pellegrino et al., 1992; Gallese et al., 1996; Rizzolatti et al., 1996) led to investigations of mirror systems in humans. Because we do not typically perform single cell recordings in humans, unless they are about to undergo surgery, we speak of systems rather than individual neurons. A mirror system allows you to understand the goals and actions of others by simply observing their movement. This recognition happens very quickly and automatically. Finally, empathy emerges from activity in areas of the brain associated with motivation and emotion. It operates separately from the other systems that provide the ability to take another's perspective. The distinction is exemplified in the case of the psychopath, who feels neither remorse nor empathy. Psychopaths manipulate others, often quite successfully, and could not do so without an excellent understanding of the beliefs and intentions of their targets. What is lacking from their behavior is any sense of inflicted harm. These social processes and their neural correlates are important for understanding why and when human beings abandon self-interest to act in the interest of others or the general good.

When you think about the important decisions you've made recently, how many of them involve others? Economists have tried to model some of these types of social decisions by using game theory and investigating the best strategies for social interactions. Game theory attempts to identify strategies that emerge as decision-makers try to maximize their own outcomes (Lee, 2008). The games take several forms. For example, in the ultimatum game, one player offers some of their money to the other player. If the other player rejects the offer, neither gets any money. How much would you offer in this scenario? At what point would you reject an offer? The average offer in the ultimatum game is 40%, and about half of the players reject offers of 20% or less. In many cases, social decision-making does not conform to what is in the sole best interest of the decision-maker. Instead, people frequently show evidence of a sense of fairness and concern for others (Lee, 2008). How do we make these decisions?

Studies with nonhuman primates support an evolutionary trend in the altruism and cooperation shown by human decision-makers. Non-human primates, along with several other species, show a basic sense of fair play. In a famous series of studies with capuchin monkeys, Sarah Brosnan and Frans de Waal (2003) showed that a capuchin monkey would work happily to earn a slice of cucumber. That is, she is happy with her paycheck until she sees her neighbor perform the same task and get rewarded with a much more valuable grape, at which time the first monkey throws a bit of a fit (along with her cucumber slice) and refuses to work anymore. Humans, however, are in a class by themselves when it comes to fairness (Lee, 2008). Even though other primates will cooperate and show altruism (self-sacrifice on behalf of another), they are more likely than humans to favor options that promote their own self-interests (Figure 7.7).

Studies of brain activity during social games share many of the features described earlier in the valuation section of this chapter. We see activity in many familiar locations, such as the insula, orbitofrontal cortex, and striatum, whether we are watching a person engage in an individual task or a social task. However, differences do occur.

FIGURE 7.7 A basic sense of fairness, demonstrated by capuchin monkeys and other non-human primates, might have contributed to the human ability to cooperate.
Source: www.maxpixel.net/White-headed-Capuchin-Monkeys-Mammal-Primate-3285054

People respond differently when they know they're playing with another human being rather than a computer (Serra, 2021). The striatum appears to be especially important in social decision-making (Lee, 2008). In the classic prisoner's dilemma game, in which players can choose to cooperate or not, cooperation produces an increase of activity in the striatum while failure to reciprocate on the part of the other player reduces activity in the striatum.

Altruistic punishment contributes to cooperation. In the ultimatum game, rejecting an offer means you get no money, but the cheap proposer gets none as well. If allowed to play more than once, it is likely that the cheap proposer will increase the offer. Low offers in the ultimatum game are correlated with activity in the anterior insula of the recipient of the offer, which is associated with disgust. The activity is stronger when the unfair offer is rejected than when it is accepted. Administering punishment to others has both positive and negative effects. In some cases, punishing someone who really deserves it activates the caudate nucleus, another part of the basal ganglia that participates in reward. This reinforcing aspect of punishment is one of the reasons psychologists object to the physical punishment of children. Once an adult experiences a sense of reward for administering punishment, Skinner would predict that punishment would be used more and more frequently, possibly leading to abuse.

As you might have noticed from your personal experience, people are not uniformly cooperative and altruistic. Significant individual differences emerge during social decision-making, probably due to some extent to genetic variations. Of particular interest are genes related to dopamine and serotonin receptors and functioning. Hormones might also play a role in observed differences. High testosterone predicts a rejection of low offers in the ultimatum game (Burnham, 2007) while oxytocin is related to greater trust in social games (Kosfeld et al., 2005).

Implementing the Decision

Much of this chapter has focused on the processes leading to the choice of one option over another. Less is known about what happens once that choice has been made. How does the choice lead to action?

Researchers have attempted to answer this question using a very simple perceptual choice, such as looking at a red or green light (Platt & Glimcher, 1999). Information about possible actions and a choice of action involve the parietal lobe, and the **lateral intraparietal area (area LIP)** in particular (Glimcher, 2014). It is likely that similar processes are involved with more abstract and complex decisions, such as whether you enroll in an inexpensive community college to save money or take on student loans to attend an Ivy League school, but further research will be needed to illuminate these mechanisms.

Chapter Summary

Neuroeconomics in many respects has provided a model interdisciplinary effort, with many papers developed by authors representing multiple fields, including cognitive neuroscience, economics, and psychology. These collaborations are bearing fruit for each of the disciplines, as the neuroscience of decision-making continues to inform economics and psychology, while economics and psychology provide further questions for the cognitive neuroscientist. We would hope to see other applied fields emulate this level of cooperation.

As mentioned in the introduction to this chapter, neuroeconomics remains very close to the academic world as opposed to the "real world," but its potential for impacting real world applications is immense. Decision-making is something that we do many times each day, often with significant outcomes. A better understanding of how these decisions are made can help us develop interventions to help those whose decision-making is leading them in self-destructive directions. We should be able to better identify the flaws in our reasoning and develop checks and balances against making bad decisions, both on personal and larger organizational levels. It is hard to imagine a more useful application of neuroscience.

Review Questions

1. Which of the following fields contribute to neuroeconomics (LO 7.1)?
   a. Economics, cognitive psychology, and neuroscience.
   b. Economics, developmental psychology, and neuroscience.
   c. Economics, social psychology, and neuroscience.
   d. Economics, behavioral psychology, and neuroscience.

2. Which of the following represents an effort to use economic theories to advance neuroscience (LO 7.2)?
   a. Using fMRI to observe decision-making in a gambling task.
   b. The use of economic utility theory to understand the operation of neural networks.
   c. The use of single cell recordings to understand perceptual choice.
   d. The understanding of the importance of reward prediction errors in decision-making.

3. Which of the following structures is likely to serve as a central comparison point for computing the value of two stimuli (LO 7.3)?
   a. The amygdala
   b. The dorsolateral prefrontal cortex
   c. The ventromedial prefrontal cortex
   d. The posterior insula

4. Which of the following most accurately describes the role of emotion in decision-making (LO 7.4)?
   a. Positive emotions promote good decision-making, but negative emotions promote poor decision-making.
   b. Positive emotions promote poor decision-making, but negative emotions promote good decision-making.
   c. All emotions tend to promote poor decision-making.
   d. All emotions tend to promote good decision-making.

5. Which of the following structures is important in implementing perceptual choices (LO 7.5)?
   a. The ventromedial prefrontal cortex
   b. The orbitofrontal cortex
   c. The lateral intraparietal area (area LIP)
   d. The anterior insula

Thought Questions

1. Heuristics are often presented in psychology as "mistakes." Under what circumstances, however, might using heuristics be positive?

2. Imagine that you are a participant in an ultimatum game. What would be your offer? At what point would you refuse an offer from another participant? How do you think this correlates with other decisions you have made?

Answer Key for Review Questions

1. a
2. b
3. c
4. d
5. c

References

Bechara, A., Damasio, A. R., Damasio, H., & Anderson, S. W. (1994). Insensitivity to future consequences following damage to human prefrontal cortex. *Cognition, 50,* 7–15. https://doi.org/10.1016/0010-0277(94)90018-3

Blalock, G., Kadiyali, V., & Simon, D. H. (2009). Driving fatalities after 9/11: A hidden cost of terrorism. *Applied Economics, 41*(14), 1717–1729. https://doi.org/10.1080/00036840601069757

Brosnan, S., & de Waal, F. (2003). Monkeys reject unequal pay. *Nature, 425,* 297–299. https://doi.org/10.1038/nature0196

Burnham, T. C. (2007). High-testosterone men reject low ultimatum game offers. *Proceedings of the Royal Society B: Biological Sciences, 274*(1623), 2327–2330. https://doi.org/10.1098.rspb.2007.0546

Cacioppo, J. T., & Berntson, G. G. (1992). Social psychological contributions to the decade of the brain: Doctrine of multilevel analysis. *American Psychologist, 47*(8), 1019–1028. https://doi.org/10.1037//0003-066x.47.8.1019

Cacioppo, J. T., Visser, P. S., & Pickett, C. L. (Eds.). (2006). *Social neuroscience: People thinking about thinking people.* Cambridge, MA: MIT Press.

Cokely, E., Feltz, A., Ghazal, S., Allan, J. N., Petrova, D., & Garcia-Retamero, R. (2018). Decision making skill : From intelligence to numeracy and expertise. In K. Ericsson, R. Hoffman, A. Kozbelt, & A. Williams (Eds.), *The Cambridge handbook of expertise and expert performance* (pp. 467–505). Cambridge: Cambridge University Press. https://doi.org/10.1017/9781316480748.026

De Martino, B., Camerer, C. F., & Adolphs, R. (2010). Amygdala damage eliminates monetary loss aversion. *Proceedings of the National Academy of Sciences of the Unites States of America, 107*(8), 3788–3792. https://doi.org/10.1073/pnas.0910230107

De Martino, B., Kumaran, D., Seymour, B., & Dolan, R. J. (2006). Frames, biases, and rational decision-making in the human brain. *Science, 313*(5787), 684–687. https://doi.org/10.1126/science.1128356

di Pellegrino, G., Fadiga, L., Fogassi, L., Gallese, V., & Rizzolatti, G. (1992). Understanding motor events: A neurophysiological study. *Experimental Brain Research*, 91(1), 176–180. https://doi.org/10.1007/bf00230027

Elflein, J. (2021, September 24). *Number of coronavirus (COVID-19) cases, recoveries, and deaths worldwide as of September 24, 2021.* Statista. Retrieved on September 25, 2021, from www.statista.com/statistics/1087466/covid19-cases-recoveries-deaths-worldwide/

Eslinger, P. J., & Damasio, A. R. (1985) Severe disturbance of higher cognition after bilateral frontal lobe ablation: Patient EVR. *Neurology, 35*(12), 1731–1741. https://doi.org/10.1212/wnl.35.12.1731

French, J. E., & Meltzer, A. L. (2019). Maximizing tendencies in marriage: Accentuating the implications of readily observable partner characteristics for intimates' satisfaction. *Personality and Social Psychology Bulletin, 45*(10), 1468–1481. https://doi.org/10.1177/0146167219832337

Gallese, V., Fadiga, L., Fogassi, L., & Rizzolatti, G. (1996). Action recognition in the premotor cortex. *Brain, 119*(2), 593–609. https://doi.org/10.1093/brain/119.2.593

generalpatton.com (n.d.). *Quotes.* Generalpatton.com/quotes/

Gigerenzer, G. (2008). Why heuristics work. *Perspectives on Psychological Science, 3*(1), 20–29. https://doi.org/10/1111/j.1745-6916.2008.00058.x

Glimcher, P. W. (2008). Neuroeconomics. *Scholarpedia, 3*(10). 1759. https://doi.org/10.4249/scholarpedia.1759

Glimcher, P.W. (2014). Value-based decision making. In P.W. Glimcher & E. Fehr (Eds.), *Neuroeconomics: Decision making and the brain* (2nd ed.) (pp. 373–391). Amsterdam: Elsevier.

Gul, F., & Pesendorfer, W. (2008) The case for mindless economics. In A. Caplin & A. Schotter (Eds.), *The foundations of positive and normative economics: A handbook* (pp. 3–42). New York: Oxford University Press.

James, W. (1890). *The principles of psychology*. New York, NY: Holt.

Kahneman, D. (2011). *Thinking, fast and slow*. New York, NY: Farrar, Straus, & Giroux.

Kosfeld, M., Heinrichs, M., Zak, P. J., Fischbacher, U., & Fehr, E. (2005). Oxytocin increases trust in humans. *Nature, 435,* 673–676. https://doi.org/10.1038/nature03701

Lee, D. (2008). Game theory and neural basis of social decision making. *Nature Neuroscience, 11*(4), 404–409. https://doi.org/10.1038/nn2065.

Levy, D. J., & Glimcher, P. W. (2012). The root of all value: A neural common currency for choice. *Current Opinion in Neurobiology, 22*(6), 1027–1038. https://doi.org/10.1016/j.conb.2012.06.001

Li, R., Smith, D. V., Clithero, J. A., Venkatraman, V., Carter, R. M., & Huettel, S. A. (2017). Reason's enemy is not emotion: Engagement of cognitive control networks explains biases in gain/loss framing. *Journal of Neuroscience, 37*(13), 3588–3598. https://doi.org/10.1523/JNEUROSCI.3488-16.2017

Mischel, W., Shoda, Y., & Peake, P. K. (1988). The nature of adolescent competencies predicted by preschool delay of gratification. *Journal of Personality and Social Psychology, 54,* 687–696. https://doi.org/10.1037//0022-3514.54.4.687

Montague, P. R. (2007). Neuroeconomics: A view from neuroscience. *Functional Neurology, 22*(4), 219–234.

Newsome, W. T., Britten, K. H., & Movshon, J. A. (1989). Neuronal correlates of a perceptual decision. *Nature, 341*(6237), 52–54. https://doi.org/10.1038/341052a0

Padoa-Schioppa, C. (2011). Neurobiology of economic choice: A good-based model. *Annual Review of Neuroscience, 34*, 333–359. https://doi.org/10.1146/annurev-neuro-061010-113648

Platt, M. L., & Glimcher, P. W. (1999). Neural correlates of decision variables in parietal cortex. *Nature, 400*(6741), 233–238. https://doi.org/10.1038/22268

Premack, D., & Woodruff, G. (1978). Does the chimpanzee have a theory of mind?. *Behavioral and Brain Sciences, 1*(4), 515–526. https://doi.org/10.1017/S0141525X00076512

Rangel, A., & Clithero, J. A. (2014). The computation of stimulus values in simple choice. In P. W. Glimcher & E. Fehr (Eds.), *Neuroeconomics: Decision making and the brain* (2nd ed., pp. 125–148). Oxford: Elsevier.

Rizzolatti, G., Fadiga, L., Gallese, V., & Fogassi, L. (1996). Premotor cortex and the recognition of motor actions. *Cognitive Brain Research, 3*(2), 131–141. https://doi.org/10.1016/0926-6410(95)00038-0

Roiser, J. P., De Martino, B., Tan, G. C., Kumaran, D., Seymour, B., Wood, N. W., & Dolan, R. J. (2009). A genetically mediated bias in decision making driven by failure of amygdala control. *Journal of Neuroscience, 29*(18), 5985–5991. https://doi.org/10.1523/JNEUROSCI.0407-09.2009

Ross, D. (2005). *Economic theory and cognitive science: Microexplanation.* Cambridge, MA: MIT Press.

Ross, D. (2008). Two styles of neuroeconomics. *Economics and Philosophy, 24*(3), 473–483. https://doi.org/10.1017/S0266267108002095

Salamone, J. D., Cousins, M. S., & Bucher, S. (1994). Anhedonia or anergia? Effects of haloperidol and nucleus accumbens dopamine depletion on instrumental response selection in a T-maze cost/benefit procedure. *Behavioral Brain Research, 65*(2), 221–229. https://doi.org/10.1016/0166-4328(94)90108-2

Serra, D. (2021). Decision-making: From neuroscience to neuroeconomics—An overview. *Theory and Decision, 91*, 1–80. https://doi.org/10.1007/s11238-012-09830-3

Shiv, B., Loewenstein, G., Bechara, A., Damasio, H., & Damasio, A. R. (2005). Investment behavior and the negative side of emotion. *Psychological Science, 16*, 435—439. https://doi.org/10.1111/j.0956-7976.2005.01553.x

Simon, H. A. (1955). A behavioral model of rational choice. *The Quarterly Journal of Economics, 69*(1), 99–118. https://doi.org/10.2307/1884852

Simon, H. A. (1957). *Models of man: Social and rational; Mathematical essays on rational human behavior in society setting.* New York, NY: Wiley.

Smith, A. (1776). *An inquiry into the nature and causes of the wealth of nations.* London: W. Strahan.

Tversky, A., & Kahneman, D. (1981). The framing of decisions and the psychology of choice. *Science, 211*(4481), 453–458. https://doi.org/10.1126/science.7455683

Tversky, A., & Kahneman, D. (1987). Rational choice and the framing of decisions. In R. M. Hogarth & M. W. Reder (Eds.), *Rational choice: The contrast between economics and psychology* (pp. 67–94). Chicago, IL: University of Chicago Press.

Watts, T. W., Duncan, G. J., & Quan, H. (2018). Revisiting the Marshmallow Test: A conceptual replication investigating links between early delay of gratification and later outcomes. *Psychological Science, 29*(7), 1159–1177. https://doi.org/10.1177/0956797618761661

Xu, P., Gu, R., Broster, L. S., Wu, R., Van Dam, N. T., Jiang, Y., Fan, J., & Luo, Y. J. (2013). Neural basis of emotional decision making in trait anxiety. *Journal of Neuroscience, 33*(47), 18641–18653. https://doi.org/10.1523/JNEUROSCI.1253-13.2013

Glossary

Behavioral economics	A subfield of economics combining economics and psychology.
Drift-diffusion model	A theory of choice in which we have a threshold for a good enough reward and pick the first option that passes that threshold.
Framing effect	The effect on decision-making of presenting information in either positive or negative ways.
Heuristic	A mental short-cut, or rule of thumb, used to reach a conclusion.
Lateral intraparietal area (area LIP)	An area of the brain believed to participate in implementing a choice.
Neuroeconomics	An interdisciplinary field combining economics, cognitive psychology, and neuroscience.
Reward prediction error	A discrepancy between the reward that was expected and the reward that was received.
Signal detection theory	An explanation of the behavior of people asked to indicate whether an ambiguous stimulus appeared or not.
Social neuroscience	The study of the correlations between neuroscience and social behaviors.
Theory of mind	The knowledge that others have mental processes and content different from one's own.
Utility model	A classic economic model suggesting that we make choices by assigning values and probabilities to choices and then choosing the best one.
Value	A worth assigned to a stimulus.
Ventromedial prefrontal cortex	An area in the frontal lobe associated with value judgments.

8 Leadership

LEARNING OBJECTIVES

After reading this chapter, you should be able to:

▶ 1. Define leadership.

▶ 2. Describe the relationships between leadership studies and organizational neuroscience.

▶ 3. Compare the pros and cons of neuroscience methods in organizational neuroscience.

▶ 4. Summarize results from neuroscience approaches to leader behavior.

▶ 5. Identify ways that neuroscience can inform leadership training.

What Makes a Leader?

Leadership refers to a process of social influence that maximizes the efforts of others toward the achievement of a goal (Kruse, 2013). The pages of history are bookmarked by the exploits of groups of people under the direction of leaders. Single human beings cannot do all that much, but groups of people cooperating on a shared mission are formidable. Human beings, however, are often as difficult to "herd" as the infamous cat, and it takes special individuals to influence their movement in a particular direction.

Who comes to mind when you hear the word "leader?" Often, we think of great military minds, such as Alexander the Great, Genghis Khan, Tokugawa Ieyasu, Julius Caesar, or Napoleon Bonaparte (Figure 8.1). We might consider change agents like Jesus, Mahatma Gandhi, Nelson Mandela, or Dr. Martin Luther King or influential political leaders like Winston Churchill, Simon Bolivar, Lee Kuan Yew, or Abraham Lincoln.

LEADERSHIP

FIGURE 8.1 Leaders influence their followers in a shared direction. Among the remarkable leaders in history was Genghis Khan (1158—1227), who killed so many people that he temporarily reversed global warming.
Source: https://commons.wikimedia.org/wiki/File:Genghis_Khan_The_Exhibition_(5465078899).jpg

Other leaders emerge from the corporate world, such as Elon Musk or Jeff Bezos. Leaders do not always influence their followers in a prosocial direction. The carnage that was the 20th century featured the work of a number of larger-than-life leaders, including Adolph Hitler (more than 6 million Jews killed in the Holocaust plus the casualties of WWII), Josef Stalin (direct execution of at least 1 million of his own people, and responsibility for the deaths of tens of millions more due to resulting starvation and imprisonment), and Mao Zedong (at least 1 million directly killed and many tens of millions killed as a result of policies and political purges; Mao estimated that he would need to kill 50 million of his people to achieve his goals). In the 13th century, Genghis Khan killed so many people that he actually reversed global warming. The fields formerly farmed by the dead returned to forest, cooling the planet measurably.

What, if anything, do these people have in common? Can we use neuroscience to gain a better understanding of what leadership means? Can we predict who will or will not be an effective leader? Can we distinguish between leaders with different leadership styles?

Leadership and Organizational Neuroscience

The use of neuroscience methods and theories to understand leadership falls under the umbrella of **organizational neuroscience**. Organizational neuroscience "explores the implications of brain science for workplace behavior" (Becker et al., 2011, p. 933). While leadership certainly takes place outside the workplace, the neuroscience of leadership has found a home within this interdisciplinary field.

Prior to the advent of brain imaging technologies, organizational behavior scholars had already embraced several biological premises. Organizational behavior is often described in evolutionary terms, as leadership and reputation management are framed as evolved capacities that developed to aid survival in a social species. Behavioral genetics provides another biological frame for organizational behavior, often leading to a more "nature" than "nurture" approach to topics such as leadership. As implied by the evolutionary approach, leadership abilities might be heritable rather than acquired or learned. Twin studies provide evidence that genetics play a role in the attainment of leadership roles (Zhang et al., 2009). Finally, a variety of non-invasive physiological measures, particularly those related to stress, are featured in numerous organizational studies. As a result, it has been a relatively small step for organizational scholars to embrace newer neuroscience technologies, including brain imaging (Jack et al., 2019). As a result, neuroscience features more prominently each year among scholars interested in leadership. A Google Scholar search requiring both "neuroscience" and "leadership" returned about 325,000 results.

As we have seen in most of our chapters, the scholars in the "home" discipline, organizational behavior in this case, have mixed feelings about whether adding neuroscience to their existing work will prove beneficial. Some are wildly enthusiastic, while others express concerns that neuroscience will provide a false credibility to research findings or contribute nothing at all of value. Like each of our interdisciplinary fields, it is essential for researchers to become as informed as possible about the "other" side, even if that means simply mastering a common vocabulary or knowing enough to say whether data have been interpreted and explained correctly based on theory. Clear communication and shared teams are also essential for moving the field forward.

Methods in Organizational Neuroscience

Scholars in organizational neuroscience have embraced a wide range of neuroscience methods, but tend to stay away from research with nonhuman animals, such as single-cell recordings and lesions. These methods are used often in neuroeconomics, but as we mentioned in Chapter 7, neuroeconomics is aligned more closely than many of the fields outlined in this book with academic research. Otherwise, you will see many familiar approaches used in this field.

Analysis of Neurochemicals

Researchers have attempted to identify the neurochemical correlates of leadership. Early research focused on testosterone, with higher testosterone associated with leadership and lower testosterone associated with followership (Newman et al., 2005). As we observed earlier in Chapter 4, however, testosterone is complicated. Levels fluctuate frequently in response to competition and other situational stimuli. Testosterone also interacts with cortisol, which is released in higher quantities at times of stress. Testosterone is typically negatively correlated with cortisol. In youth, aggression is associated with higher testosterone only when this is combined with low cortisol. It is interesting that this same pattern of high testosterone coupled with low cortisol also characterizes powerful and socially dominant individuals.

The literature on testosterone, cortisol, and leadership is mixed. Sherman et al. (2016) reported that real executives' testosterone levels predicted the number of their subordinates, but only for low-testosterone males. Van der Meij et al. (2016) were unable to find any significant relationships between testosterone and leadership style or with the likelihood of having a leadership position. Moe et al. (2021) did not observe support for a role for high testosterone coupled with low cortisol in negotiation, individual problem-solving, or group problem-solving.

Oxytocin, like most neurohormones, is a multi-tasker, participating in functions from uterine contractions during and after giving birth to the milk let-down reflex of nursing mammals. More relevant to the current discussion is oxytocin's role in social bonding. Oxytocin is released in response to a simple hug from a partner in women (Light et al., 2005) and during orgasm for both men and women. Higher than average oxytocin levels predict more physical intimacy and higher levels of support in couples (Gouin et al., 2010). Oxytocin levels during pregnancy predict the responsiveness of the new mother to her infant. Oxytocin and its counterpart, vasopressin, have also been connected to trust, cooperation, memory for social information, recognition of emotions, and resilience during stress (Meyer-Lindenberg et al., 2011).

Logically, then, we might see oxytocin as the subject of research in leadership, especially in the more interpersonal aspects of the role. One of the advantages of oxytocin for research purposes is that it is easily manipulated by administration as a nasal spray. Kosfeld et al. (2005) created quite a stir (and stimulated a large amount of research) by showing that nasally administered oxytocin made participants more trusting in a computer game of trust (see Chapter 7). Gordon and Berson (2018) trained a confederate (a "fake" participant working for the researchers) to exhibit charisma. Charisma refers to the "charm" and interpersonal attractiveness that attracts our attention in others, including leaders. Oxytocin nasal spray was administered to a group of participants in a double-blind, placebo controlled design. In other words, neither the participants nor their observers knew which participants received oxytocin or placebo. Oxytocin administration influenced the participants' reactions to both the charismatic leader and to each other. The relationship between naturally occurring oxytocin levels and leader/follower behaviors has yet to be explored in depth.

In Chapter 4, we investigated the participation of serotonin in aggressive behavior. Generally, serotonin is central to neural systems of mood, appetite, sleep, and dominance. Serotonin's contribution to dominance is most likely due to its role in suppressing impulsive aggression. As such, it might contribute to the social competence of an individual. Among primates with strong social hierarchies, such as rhesus monkeys, serotonin levels are positively correlated with an individual male's position on the hierarchy. Higher-ranking monkeys exhibit less aggression than their subordinates, supporting the idea that serotonin inhibits aggressive impulses. Serotonin might also reduce aggression by enhancing empathy. Youth with callous-unemotional forms of psychopathy do not demonstrate normal serotonin function (Blair, 2013).

Does this mean that people wanting to become dominant leaders should try to enhance their serotonin levels? Probably not. While it is likely that individual predispositions, probably genetic in origin, influence serotonin levels, serotonin, like testosterone, can fluctuate due to circumstances. It is quite possible that being in a leadership position could also influence one's serotonin levels. Dominance in zebrafish develops gradually over days when two fish of the same sex are housed together (Sundvik et al., 2021; Figure 8.2). Dominance and submissiveness were correlated with subsequent serotonin levels. This suggests that experience in social hierarchies could stimulate changes in gene expression (Qu et al., 2017). Surprisingly, given the importance of social dominance in leadership, the literature on a role for serotonin, apart from consideration of its role in stress and depression, is quite sparse.

Dopamine, which is associated with planning, reward, and movement (see Chapter 2) might also play a role in the management of social hierarchies. Most of the relevant research involves animals, although studies in humans support a correlation between dopamine receptor density and dominance (Martinez et al., 2010). As is the case with all the neurochemicals described here, much further research is needed before we understand the connections between dopamine, dominance, and leadership.

Simple measures of hormone function are unlikely to be adequate for capturing complex aspects of leader behavior. The scientific literature on testosterone and leadership stands in stark contrast to popular press headlines, such as "Your Brain on Hormones: How Neuroscience Can Make You a Better Leader," "How to Boost Testosterone and Reduce Cortisol Levels to Lead Better," or "Boost These Hormones to Succeed as a Leader at Work."

Observing the Brain

Like many applications of neuroscience, organizational neuroscience makes frequent use of methods that assess brain activity, such as fMRI, EEG, and fNIRS (see Chapter 1).

Of particular interest, however, is the simultaneous scanning of two or more individuals involved in a social interaction, or "**hyperscanning**" (Jack et al., 2019). After all, leadership does not occur in a vacuum, so assessing the behavior of leadership in context is crucial. Hyperscanning assesses the degree of synchrony of activity between

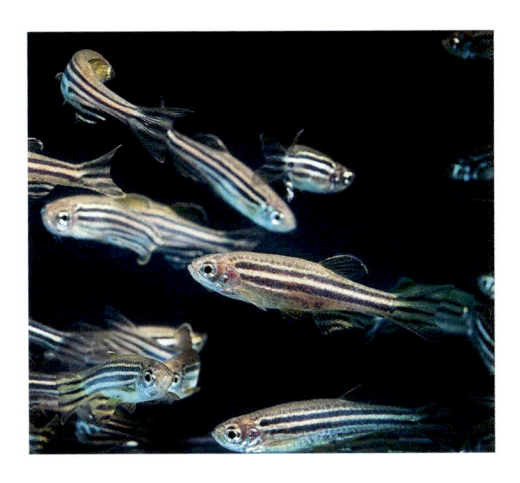

FIGURE 8.2 Research with zebrafish demonstrates that dominance emerges with experience and is reflected in changes to systems using the neurochemical serotonin.
Source: https://commons.wikimedia.org/wiki/File:Zebrafish_(26436913602).jpg

two or more brains, and can be done using fMRI, EEG, or fNIRS. As we observed in Chapter 1, fNIRS has limitations in spatial and temporal resolution, but is also resistant to artifacts from the movement of the participants. This makes it possible to assess brain synchrony in more realistic situations, which makes it an ideal approach for organizational neuroscience. It has even been adapted to evaluate the synchrony between parents and babies during parent–child interactions (Figure 8.3). Hyperscanning has been used to evaluate behavioral synchronization and leadership when individuals are engaged in simple tasks (e.g., Dumas et al., 2010, 2012). Balconi et al. (2019) used EEG and autonomic hyperscanning during a performance review and were able to detect different levels of interpersonal synchrony related to two different leadership styles. Waldman et al. (2015) used EEG to track the engagement of a whole group during a 45-minute team problem-solving task. While it is possible to assess engagement at the end of this type of task using surveys, the fluid nature of engagement over time would be lost. You could also observe the group, but people are rather good at hiding how they are thinking. Hyperscanning won't completely replace traditional methods, but it has significant potential for increasing our understanding of group dynamics and the leader–follower dyad (Waldman et al., 2019).

Observation of brain activity, especially in cases in which fMRI is used, is often aimed at determining localization of function. If participants engage in a task, what parts of the brain become more active? According to Jack et al. (2019), localization of function research is important for organizational neuroscientists to understand, but it is not a primary approach of the field. Instead, organizational neuroscience makes considerable use of **forward inference**, illustrated in Figure 8.4. In forward inference, a psychological state is induced and the resulting pattern of brain activity is assessed. Studies of forward inference have been used to ask whether different patterns of activity can be used to

FIGURE 8.3 Hyperscanning, which can be done with EEG, fMRI, or fNIRS, evaluates the synchrony of two brains. One application is to look at parent–child interactions.
Source: Karla Freberg.

distinguish between competing theories. For example, Yoon et al. (2006) used fMRI to ask whether the same or different patterns of brain activity occur while participants consider brand personalities and human personalities. People spontaneously seem to apply human attributes to inanimate objects, including products, so one hypothesis suggests that brain patterns would not differentiate between human and object stimuli. At the same time, as a social species, we have significant numbers of behaviors that seem uniquely applied to other humans or animals. Can you predict what the researchers found? If you predicted that different patterns of brain activity were observed during the judging of humans and objects, you are correct! Are there other ways this research question could be answered? Undoubtedly, but the addition of neuroscience to the organizational behavior toolkit offers an additional layer of understanding.

Organizational neuroscience also makes use of reverse inference, also illustrated in Figure 8.4 As we've seen previously in this book, reverse inference, while not impossible, is very difficult to do well, and its application in organizational neuroscience shares many of the same promises and challenges as are found in other fields. As we have noted before, reverse inference is the assumption that if activity in an area of the brain is observed during a particular task, it can also be assumed that when activity in that area is seen again, the area is engaged in that same task. In plain English, this means that if we see activity in the anterior cingulate cortex (ACC) when a person is experiencing cognitive conflict, we assume that the next time we see the same pattern of ACC activity, it's likely the person is experiencing cognitive conflict. This may be true, but we can't always know for certain. What we don't want to do is interpret reverse inferences in a sloppy way, such as saying that when we see activity in the amygdala, we know for certain that a person is frightened.

The major obstacle to the appropriate use of reverse inference is the incredible networking found in the brain. Particular areas of the brain rarely have single functions. Instead, they participate in multiple overlapping networks that are engaged by a wide

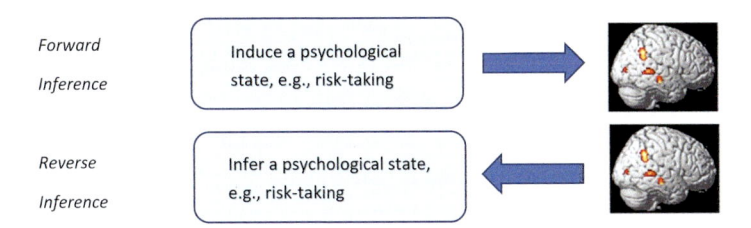

FIGURE 8.4 Forward and reverse inference. In forward inference, we assume that a psychological state produces a pattern of activity in the brain. In reverse inference, we assume that if we see a particular pattern of activity in the brain, we know something about the person's psychological state.

Photo source: www.flickr.com/photos/nihgov/30079903896

variety of tasks. Instead of saying with confidence, "the amygdala is responsible for detecting threat," it is more accurate to say that "the amygdala participates in networks that organize an animal's response to threat." Just as geneticists reject the idea that we have "a gene for" certain conditions, like a "gene for ADHD" or "a gene for alcoholism," neuroscientists do not want to say we have "a structure for" any particular function. Brain structures and their functions do not enjoy a one-to-one correspondence or anything even close to that. Even when an area of the brain has a relatively clear connection with a process, like the amygdala with fear or the hypothalamus with hunger, it remains highly unlikely that these are the structures' *only* connections to important processes. It is also highly unlikely that the *only* place functions as important as fear and hunger are managed are these two structures.

Despite strong warnings about the use of reverse inference (e.g., Poldrack, 2006), this approach is essential for organizational neuroscience (Jack et al., 2019). Organizational neuroscience tackles some of the most sophisticated cognitive tasks people face: social behavior and decision-making. The use of reverse inference to illuminate these behaviors is, in the words of Jack et al., "inevitable" (2019, p. 435). The key, then, is to do reverse inference well. This requires strong, predictive hypotheses of the type encouraged by open science practices. Pre-registering hypotheses, preferably in public repositories, discourages researchers from the type of after-the-fact or post hoc searches for "anything significant" that has caused so much disruption across many scientific disciplines. Nor do we want to make careless inferences across multiple studies. For example, if we find different levels of activity in a brain area in effective leaders compared to ineffective leaders, then look at other studies that say the brain area is involved with empathy, we can't jump to the conclusion that effective leaders are more empathic. These types of misinterpretation can be very seductive, but they have helped give reverse inference an often deservedly bad reputation.

Instead of relying on a small set of studies showing us "what a particular part of the brain does," we can instead make use of a growing number of large, public repositories of data. For example, a tool called Neurosynth (Yarkoni et al., 2011), uses a meta-analytic approach that allows scientists to check purported functions associated with an area of the brain with a large swath of the published literature (see Figure 8.5). While definitely a step forward, any meta-analytic tool is only as good as the literature on which it is based, and neuroscientists notoriously disagree when assigning functions to parts of the brain. A paper published by Lieberman and Eisenberger (2015), actually using data from Neurosynth, generated so much controversy that the dispute garnered its own hashtag: #cingulategate.

Influencing the Brain

Naturally occurring lesions, or brain damage, can illuminate the functions of brain structures and networks. The downside of course, is the small number of relevant participants available. However, neuroscientists have made several important conclusions based on observations of Patient S.M., a woman who has a rare condition that destroyed her amygdalas in both hemispheres (e.g., Feinstein et al., 2011). While unlikely to be a frontline method in organizational neuroscience, an evaluation of case studies of patients with lesions can further support observations made using other methods.

As we mentioned in Chapter 1, repeated transcranial magnetic stimulation (rTMS) has the potential to disrupt the function of relatively shallow areas of cerebral cortex lying immediately below the point of magnetic stimulation. In many ways, this can produce an effect similar to a temporary lesion. This method was used by Krause et al. (2012) to investigate facial emotion recognition in people with high or low empathy.

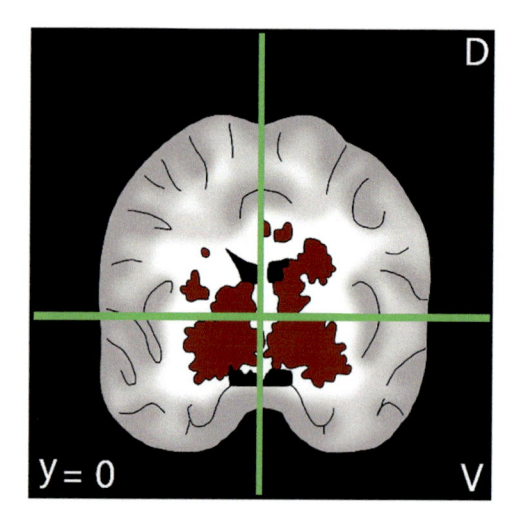

FIGURE 8.5 Neurosynth automatically generates images like this one, which represents a meta-analysis of 922 studies of reward.
Source: Karla Freberg.

They found that disruption in the vicinity of the medial prefrontal cortex reduced the accuracy of facial emotion recognition in people with high empathy, but actually improved accuracy in people with low empathy. As empathy is regularly featured in organizational science, this approach has the potential to assist investigators in their understanding of its impact on a wide variety of behaviors. Repeated TMS has the advantage of being used with healthy volunteers, whereas traditional clinical lesion studies are often conducted with people whose brain damage is only one of many challenges to their wellbeing.

Transcranial direct current stimulation (tDCS), also discussed in Chapter 1, is beginning to show up in the organizational neuroscience literature. It has the advantage of being non-invasive, but the use of electricity rather than magnetism reduces its precision of application relative to rTMS. Magnetism moves right through the skull bones, but electrical signals are dampened significantly by the skull.

Multiple Methods

As we have seen in many other instances, the safest approach to understanding brain correlates of behaviors and mental processes of interest is to integrate data from multiple sources, ideally those that are applied simultaneously. If we use two or more methods at the same time, such as EEG and fMRI, many of the limitations of each technology can be offset by the other, such as temporal and spatial resolution.

Design Considerations

Organizational neuroscience is no different from any other science in its need for the use of appropriate research designs. Jack et al. (2019) make several recommendations in this regard. First, they suggest that organizational researchers make use of the existing neuroscience literature to generate hypotheses related to organizational questions. From this thorough literature search should emerge neuroscience data relative to unanswered questions in organizational behavior. These nexus points can serve as the stimulus for new studies.

A second recommendation suggests sticking with simple research designs when possible. Neuroscience is rarely simple, but in interdisciplinary research, it is often wise to take baby steps. Jack et al. (2019) cite as an example of complexity a study by Molenberghs et al. (2017) that attempted to associate patterns of brain activity in a 2 x 2 x 2 design investigating type of message from a leader (inspirational or not), the in-group or out-group status of the person delivering the message, and whether the statements were oriented personally or collectively. While the resulting data are undoubtedly useful, Jack et al. (2019) recommended instead that the authors could have more effectively addressed one chunk, such as the in-group or out-group status of the leader.

A third recommendation calls for maintaining a "broader" view of the brain and cognition. The phenomena of interest to organizational scholars are quite complex and can usually be broken down into multiple components. Jack et al. (2019) provide the example of transformational leadership, which is characteristic of leaders who inspire followers to exceed their perceived capabilities. Hopefully, you have known a person who brought out these unexpected qualities in your own behavior, perhaps as a teacher or coach. The organizational literature has identified many qualities that contribute to transformational leadership, including emotion recognition, perspective taking, envisioning, and emotion regulation. Balthazard et al. (2012, as cited by Jack et al., 2019) were able to distinguish transformational leaders from nontransformational leaders using EEG analyzed by a computer algorithm, but Jack et al. (2019) criticize the study on the basis of its lack of connection to the existing organizational behavior literature. They argue instead that the researchers could have identified the specific neural signatures that differentiated the two types of leaders while correlating these with other measures of leadership attributes.

Finally, Jack et al. (2019) list a number of tailored designs useful to organizational neuroscience. For example, they suggest careful studies of the neural effects of behavioral interventions. Neural responses to an intervention, such as leadership training, could then be correlated to actual behavior change.

Leader Behavior

Organizational behavior scholars have identified several models of leadership behavior, referring to either the individual leader or to the interaction between a leader and set of followers. We have already discussed transformational leadership (Bass & Avolio, 1990), but this is just one of many approaches. A complete review of leadership models is beyond the scope of this textbook, but we will highlight some of the approaches that are most amenable to evaluation using neuroscience methods and theory.

Traditionally, the evaluation of leader behavior has relied heavily on survey measures. Respondents, both the leaders themselves and followers, share perceptions of leader behavior. This is not all that different from what you do when you complete student evaluations of your professors, as your professors are essentially "leaders" in the classroom setting. You might be asked how well-prepared, well-organized, engaging, or inspiring your professors are. These types of assessments, whether we're talking about leaders or professors, have some significant flaws. For example, they are notoriously subject to bias. Female professors are typically given lower evaluations than male professors. Physically attractive professors garner higher evaluations than their less attractive colleagues. For a time, the popular RateMyProfessors.com even allowed students to apply a "chili pepper" rating system to note how attractive their professors were. Survey evaluations are also unrelated to actual outcomes. Students who find their professor's humor engaging might not actually be learning very much at all (Esarey & Valdes, 2020). Similarly, even important leadership variables like transformational leadership account for less than 10% of organizational outcomes (Waldman & Balthazard, 2015).

Neuroscience, used judiciously and interpreted with care, might provide some needed insights into topics previously addressed using the survey method. Just as student evaluations should be viewed within a more global context of peer review and independent evaluators rather than used in isolation, neuroscience can add an additional layer to our ability to evaluate a leader.

Leader Characteristics

Returning to our initial question of what makes a leader, we see that organizational researchers have focused on personality traits. This implies a static, fixed approach to leadership as opposed to framing leadership as something you can learn to do. The basic consensus in organizational behavior is that some people take to leadership more readily than others, but everyone can learn to be a better leader than they were previously.

Efforts to identify the traits that distinguish leaders from others has an extensive history. Researchers distinguish between **foundational traits** and **leadership capacities** (Zaccaro et al., 2018). The former category includes factors such as genetic predisposition, personality, cognitive ability, motives, and values. Leadership capacities include cognitive skills, social capacity, knowledge, and expertise. These interact with more situational factors to produce outcomes, such as the reaction of followers and effectiveness.

Big 5 personality traits such as conscientiousness, extroversion, and openness not only predict the behavior of a leader in a leadership role, but also the leader's predisposition for seeking leadership roles. Although the measures of Big 5 traits are among the most valid and reliable in psychology, they are still largely self-reported. A person evaluated for leadership potential would not have too much difficulty figuring out how to answer the questions. Can neuroscience provide another method for evaluating these traits?

Because Big 5 traits are moderately heritable, we can assume that some individual differences between leaders and non-leaders are genetic. However, efforts to identify structural and functional differences in the brain that correlate with levels of a personality trait have not been particularly fruitful. Instead, researchers are making progress by zooming out a bit to consider functional connectivity, or the relative behavior of networks. These analyses often employ the seed method, in which you define a starting point in the brain (the seed region) and then evaluate the connectivity originating from the seed. These searches are most productive when guided by theory and the type of careful understanding of structures and their functions provided by methods like Neurosynth. One example of this approach has been the analysis of the functional connectivity of the amygdala with regard to neuroticism and extroversion. Different patterns of connectivity correlate with scores on these two traits (Markett et al., 2018). Even more nuanced results emerge when connectivity is observed in the presence of a relevant stimulus. Trait anxiety was found to reliably correlate with connectivity in a cluster of limbic structures that changed in response to the presentation of emotional facial stimuli (Cao et al., 2016). To be most useful, Markett et al. (2018) argue that connectivity analyses of personality should be evaluated within the context of the effects of genetics and environmental influences in general on connectivity. As is true of all personality assessment, an eventual goal of the neuroscientific assessment of personality is to link observations of brain structure and function to actual behaviors, not just scores on a test. These are the types of initiatives in neuroscience that might prove to be particularly useful in leadership studies.

Leadership capacities, more so than the foundational traits, develop with experience. At the same time, the likelihood that a leader develops these capacities is influenced by foundational traits. For example, decision-making and problem-solving capacities are likely to be developed differently by leaders with higher cognitive ability. Foundational traits might tilt a leader in the direction of a particular style of leadership, whether that is transformational leadership or servant leadership (a style in which the leader *serves* the people instead of people serving the leader).

Foundational traits and capacities interact in complex ways. It is unlikely that neuroscience will supply easy answers, but it has potential for testing one model against another.

Dark Leadership

You might be wondering at this point about what happened to some of those leaders we mentioned at the outset of the chapter, people like Hitler, Stalin, and Mao. Where do they fit in with our characterization of leadership traits? The answer, in short, is that they don't, at least not very well. Furtner et al. (2017) pointed out that the leadership literature has been dominated by a "heroic" model of a leader, but that is definitely not the whole story. As these researchers explain, selfish and impulsive leaders are quite capable of being as effective as prosocial leaders. A full understanding of leadership requires us to explore both light and dark (see Figure 8.6).

The term "**dark triad of personality**" combines narcissism, Machiavellianism, and psychopathy (Paulhus & Williams, 2002). Narcissists have an inflated view of their own worth and require excessive amounts of attention and admiration. They show little empathy for others. This combination makes them vulnerable to a whole host of relationship problems, yet they manage to thrive in some organizational settings. Narcissism falls on a continuum, and only at very high, self-defeating levels is it diagnosed as narcissistic personality disorder (American Psychiatric Association (APA), 2013). Psychopathy, a lack of remorse and empathy, is not technically a diagnosable condition. The closest category in the *Diagnostic and Statistical Manual of Mental Disorders* (DSM-5, APA, 2013) is antisocial personality disorder (ASPD). However, ASPD conflates many of the characteristics of psychopathy with criminal behavior. The vast majority of psychopaths are not, in fact, criminals, nor do the majority of criminals meet criteria for psychopathy (see Chapter 4). Finally, Machiavellianism is named after the infamous political advisor to the 1500s Medici family, Niccolò Machiavelli. Machiavellianism is a cold, cunning, manipulative, means-to-an-end approach to gaining power. The three dark triad traits feature considerable overlap. All three share selfishness, coldness, deception, and manipulation, leading to speculation that they share a common "dark core." One way to characterize a possible dark core is to consider social dominance. This underlying motivation might make the person with dark triad traits seek out leadership opportunities.

How well do people with dark triad personalities do? Objectively, nice people do not always finish first. Narcissists had higher salaries, and people with Machiavellian traits inhabited higher leadership roles and expressed greater career satisfaction. Psychopathy, however, was negatively correlated with objective career outcomes (Furtner et al., 2017). While it might seem counterintuitive, people working for narcissists enjoy more success and rate their jobs as more satisfying. It is possible that the narcissistic leader takes good care of followers to maintain their admiration.

Maccoby (2000) argued that most dominant leaders across military, religious, political, and economic domains have a narcissistic personality. People with narcissistic

FIGURE 8.6 The character of Darth Vader from Star Wars reminds us that people do not just follow prosocial leaders.
Source: Karla Freberg.

personalities often spontaneously emerge as group leaders, which you might have noticed during a group project or club meeting or two. The most highly regarded military leaders can be viewed as examples of "bright" narcissism, which features egotism and high self-esteem minus manipulativeness and strong impression management (Paunonen et al., 2006).

According to Simonton (1986), the most Machiavellian presidents of the first 39 (Washington through Reagan) were Richard Nixon, Lyndon Johnson, Martin van Buren, and James Polk. These presidents had the greatest success moving their legislative agendas, possibly due to their willingness to be forceful. They were also the most likely to demonstrate intellectual brilliance.

Even though psychopathy is often viewed as the most pathological of the dark triad traits, psychopaths do reach senior leadership positions using their excellent impression management and communication skills. They also manage to divide followers into camps of supporters and "enemies," and typically reach success by outflanking the latter. Followers are required to be highly conforming and dependable. Although the psychopathic leader might attain important positions, their leadership might be short-lived due to poor organizational outcomes. Employees working for a psychopathic leader show less creativity and commitment.

What can neuroscience contribute to our understanding of dark triad traits? Twin studies have demonstrated that all three traits show evidence of heritability, but Machiavellianism shows the lowest heritability of the three (Furnham et al., 2013). This in turn suggests some adaptive advantages for these traits over the course of evolution. Such a suggestion is consistent with research noting "light" sides to the dark triad traits.

While not specific to leadership, neuroscientists have provided some insights into dark triad traits that might be useful to understanding how these traits impact interpersonal relationships. Gordon and Platek (2009) ran a very small study that evaluated neural responses with fMRI to the photographs of real people who had taken assessments of dark triad traits and trustworthiness. Of the three dark triad traits, psychopathy provoked the largest discernible response, not surprisingly in the amygdala. This might reflect subtle recognition of danger related to dealing with a person who appears to have high psychopathy. The fact that psychopathy is apparent in a person's facial appearance is interesting in itself. Faces were masked using software that removed hair, ears, and neck to leave only the face on a black background. The small size of this study calls for caution, of course, but follow-up research could be interesting.

More recently, Nummenmaa et al. (2021) observed reactions to violent videos by criminal psychopaths and non-criminals with high psychopathy scores. The brain activity, structural features, and connectivity in both sets of participants were quite similar and distinct from healthy controls without strong psychopathic tendencies. Both criminals and non-criminals with psychopathic traits showed cortical atrophy in frontal and insular areas relative to controls. They experienced greater activity in emotional circuits while viewing violent videos. This leaves the question of why some of these individuals engage in criminal behavior while others do not to be answered by future research.

Paul Babiak and Robert Hare (2019) argue that psychopaths are very prevalent in the workplace and are often difficult to distinguish from non-psychopaths. It is highly unlikely that Human Resources departments will suddenly start investing in brain imaging like that used by Nummenmaa et al. (2021) to identify job candidates with psychopathic tendencies, but the use of brain imaging might find more acceptance among scholars interested in dark triad leadership.

Leadership Style

As mentioned previously, organizational science has identified a vast array of different approaches to understanding and categorizing leading, whether that is transactional versus transformational, leader–member exchange, autocratic versus authoritarian, participative or democratic, laissez-faire, paternalistic, servant leadership, or task-oriented versus relationship-oriented. Organizational neuroscience has just begun to scratch the surface in the attempt to correlate biological processes with these different leader constructs.

The distinction of **task-oriented** versus **relationship-oriented** leading is a classic dichotomy in the leadership literature, reaching back at least as far as Bales (1958). Bales diverged from his contemporaries by suggesting that groups needed not one, but two leaders. One would manage the tasks set for the group, while the other would tend to the emotional needs of the group. Thinking back to your own organizational experiences, whether these are work-related, school group projects, or clubs and teams, you can probably recall instances where different people seemed to assume these roles for your groups.

In the research that followed, organizational scholars argued that effective leaders needed to develop both types of capacities. However, in the real world, this combined skill has been elusive. One sample described by Bass and Bass (2008) contained 46% highly task-oriented managers, 19% highly relationship-oriented managers, 29% who were low in both task- and relationship-orientation, and only 6% who were balanced between the two roles. Although it's possible that from among those 6% will emerge very senior leaders, it is a bit discouraging that the ability to bridge both styles is so rare.

Organizational neuroscientists have proposed a biological rationale for why we shouldn't expect most people to incorporate both task- and relationship-oriented styles. Boyatzis et al. (2014) make an interesting analogy between task-orientation/relationship-orientation and the operation of brain networks managing focused and unfocused thought. As described in Chapter 2, unfocused thought, which can include daydreaming or mind-wandering, is associated with activity in a default mode network (DMN; Figure 8.7). This network is distinct from task-related networks that engage when we concentrate on something. These networks are to some extent mutually inhibitory, which means when one is engaged, the other is relatively quiet. It doesn't make sense to say that you are focused and unfocused at the same time. Under normal conditions, we spend approximately equal amounts of waking time in both focused and unfocused thought, shifting seamlessly from one to the other throughout the day.

Boyatzis et al. (2014) suggest that task orientation is an example of focused thought, whereas relationship-orientation has more in common with the types of thought managed by the DMN. The content of thought during DMN activation can be described as self-management. We think about where we have been, where we are, and where we are going. These processes require hard work. The energy used during DMN activation is only about 10% less than when the brain is engaged in problem-solving or other focused thought. Boyatzis et al. (2014) argue that it is reasonable to extend these self-processes to an assumption that they are also connected with a person's ability to manage social relationships.

One of the basic problems with this approach is that we are possibly looking at stable tendencies when we talk about task-oriented or relationship-oriented leaders. To support this connection between these leadership styles and the activity of brain networks, we would need to identify individual differences in the operation of the task-related networks and DMN that correlate with this difference in style. That's a bit of a jump. Do people who excel in task-oriented versus relationship-oriented leadership really experience regular and large differences in the operation of these key networks? To find out, Boyatzis et al. (2014) recommend true experiments, in which one network

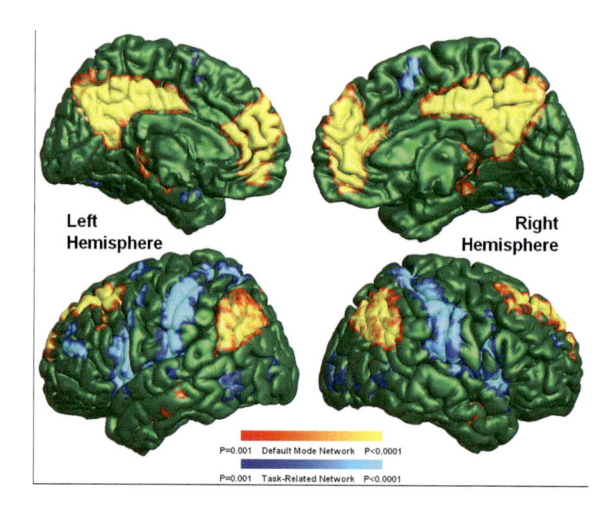

FIGURE 8.7 Can the distinction between a task-related (focused) brain network and the default mode network (DMN) help us understand task and relational approaches to leadership?

Source: https://commons.wikimedia.org/wiki/File:Default_mode_and_task-related_maps_for_healthy_subjects.jpg

or the other would be manipulated, or a person's ability to switch between them would be influenced, followed by observations of naturalistic leadership behavior. Manipulating these networks, however, is no easy thing. Various suggestions for using oxytocin or meditation (enhancing DMN activity) or methylphenidate (Ritalin; enhancing attention and focus) are still very speculative.

Another logical obstacle to this approach is the outward–inward characterization of the focused and DMN networks. Activity in the DMN is generally assumed to correlate with inward types of mentalization. How can a person who is unfocused and looking inward do a better job of taking care of others? The mirror systems, for example, which allow us to understand and anticipate the behavior of others, are generally grouped with task-related networks rather than the DMN. To be fair, the science related to our understanding of the DMN has advanced significantly since 2014 to incorporate analyses of connectivity within the DMN among many other features. Many conditions, including major depressive disorder and Alzheimer's disease, are correlated with patterns of disruption of the connectivity in the DMN. While the approach proposed by Boyatzis et al. (2014) is probably far too simplistic, it is possible that individual variations in task-related and DMN connectivity might be interesting to pursue. In one provocative study, Waldman et al. (2015, as cited in Waldman et al., 2019) argued that observations of individual activity in the DMN did a better job of predicting ethical leadership than traditional surveys.

Another example of efforts to link leadership styles with neural correlates was presented by Molenberghs et al. (2017). These researchers used fMRI to distinguish between brain activity associated with an in-group or out-group political leader delivering inspirational, collective-oriented messages or noninspirational, personal-oriented statements. Inspirational leaders emphasize the role of the followers in future collective success, demonstrate their own sacrifices for the group, and frequently use collective words like "we" and "us." In contrast, personal-oriented leaders focus on their own role in future success, appear to be more self-aggrandizing, aggressive, and arrogant, and use personal pronouns like "I" and "me" more often. The authors framed the different patterns of response they observed within hypotheses related to transformational leadership. This research was novel in that it looked for biological correlates within the recipients of leader behavior, whereas most of the existing literature focuses on the leaders instead.

Leadership Development

So far in this chapter, we have focused primarily on the factors that distinguish leaders from non-leaders. While many people believe that leaders are born, not made, organizational science recognizes that much can be done to enhance an individual's leadership skills. Can neuroscience play a role in this process?

Leadership development is a multibillion dollar business. Despite that, the efficacy of many contemporary training methods is in doubt. Beer et al. (2016) outline some of the pitfalls. In many cases, managers rate the training positively, but over time revert to their previous behavior. Individuals do not always have the power to implement the changes they learn about in their training. If existing systems are not consistent with new patterns of leadership, all the training in the world is not going to help. As we said previously, leadership does not take place in a vacuum.

As we saw in Chapter 5, one of the premises supporting the application of neuroscience to stimulate change (in education in Chapter 5 and in leadership behavior here) is the plasticity of the human brain. While some people might gravitate to leadership naturally, the idea of brain plasticity suggests that learning to be a leader is possible. But how do we do that? Waldman et al. (2011) propose neurofeedback as one possibility. If we can identify patterns of brain activity, say with EEG, perhaps it is possible to train a person to sustain those levels of activity. **Neurofeedback** is a subtype of biofeedback, where individuals are taught to control behaviors that otherwise run on autopilot. For example, you can learn to control "white coat hypertension," or a jump in blood pressure when a health professional is about to measure it, by learning to visualize a relaxing situation, like a day at the beach. Neurofeedback is a vibrant area of research, with methods ranging from fMRI to fNIRS to EEG. However, its efficacy has yet to pass the standards required for most insurers to cover it for conditions like attention deficit hyperactivity disorder or traumatic brain injury. Even more work would need to be done to demonstrate a role for neurofeedback in leadership training.

Virtual reality (VR), while not technically a neuroscience approach, offers potential for the assessment and training of leaders in ecologically valid ways (Alcañiz et al., 2018). Most of the neuroscience tools discussed in this chapter require a stationary, laboratory setting, which makes realistic scenarios difficult to present. In contrast, virtual reality provides a means for presenting realistic scenarios while still maintaining a high level of control (Figure 8.8). In addition, contemporary VR tools can measure the movement of the participant, including non-verbal cues like body language. Goggles can measure eye movement and gaze. Wearables can measure external variables like skin conductance and heart rate simultaneously. The end result is a rich, multi-method snapshot of behavior within a fairly realistic setting.

VR is already used for training in many domains, including healthcare, education, and industry. However, it remains relatively rare in leadership training. Alcañiz et al. (2018) propose that situations could be constructed to elicit participant behaviors, such as empathy. The participant's decision (help or not), the amount of time taken to make the decision, and the participant's gaze metrics could provide important feedback that could then be used to identify weak points in need of training.

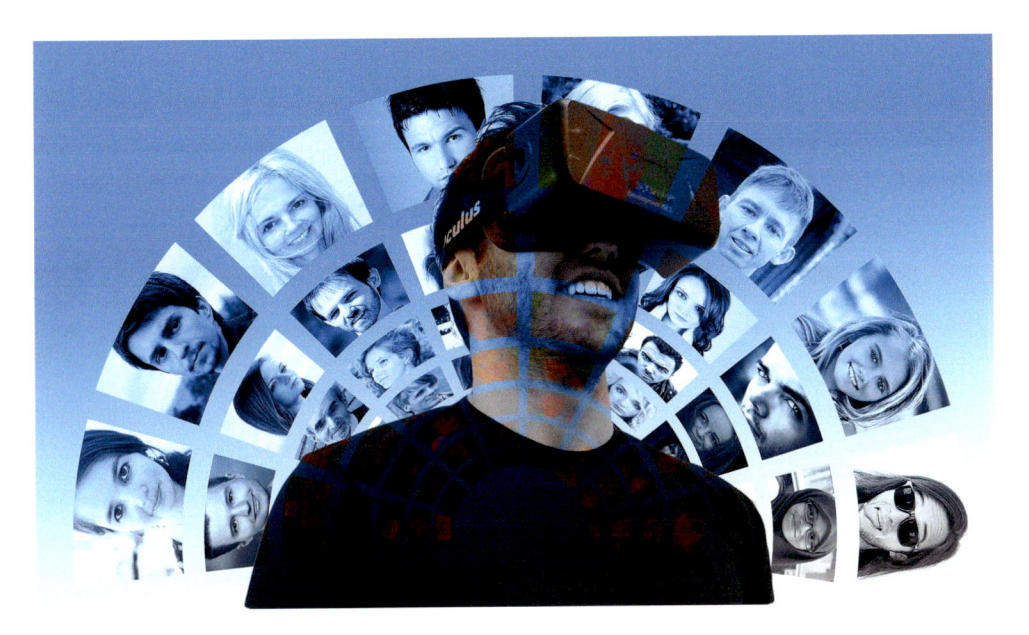

FIGURE 8.8 Virtual reality has the potential to move leadership assessment and training forward.
Source: https://upload.wikimedia.org/wikipedia/commons/7/79/Virtual-reality-2229924_1920.jpg

Chapter Summary

A neuroscientific approach to leadership falls under the heading of organizational neuroscience, or the use of neuroscience to understand and improve group and organizational functioning. Neuroscience methods add another layer of analysis to the traditional survey-based methodologies used traditionally to assess leader behaviors. Organizational neuroscientists have begun to use neuroscience approaches to test their existing hypotheses about leader characteristics, leadership styles, and leader development. An exciting addition to the organizational toolkit is hyperscanning, or the ability to analyze synchrony in the responses of members of a group. Finally, organizational neuroscience might help to correct some of the problems with the efficacy of leader training.

Review Questions

1. Which of the following is the best definition of leadership (LO 8.1)?
    a. The ability to control the behavior of other people.
    b. The ability to complete tasks required of a group.

c. The ability to maximize the efforts of others in reaching a goal.

d. The ability to communicate inspiring messages to influence others.

2. How would you characterize the relationship between leadership neuroscience and organizational neuroscience (LO 8.2)?

   a. Leadership neuroscience is a subfield of organizational neuroscience.

   b. Organizational neuroscience is a subfield of leadership neuroscience.

   c. Organizational neuroscience and leadership neuroscience are separate, parallel fields.

   d. Organizational neuroscience and leadership neuroscience overlap, but rarely cooperate in departments, professional societies, and journal publications.

3. What conclusions have emerged from studies of testosterone and leadership (LO 8.3)?

   a. High testosterone is strongly, positively correlated with leadership.

   b. High testosterone is strongly, negatively correlated with leadership.

   c. High testosterone is positively correlated with leadership, but not problem-solving and negotiation.

   d. No clear relationship between testosterone and leadership has been demonstrated.

4. Of the "dark triad" characteristics, which has the most negative impact on leader behavior (LO 8.4)?

   a. Narcissism

   b. Machiavellianism

   c. Psychopathy

   d. All three dark triad traits have approximately equal negative impacts on leader behavior.

5. Which of the following best summarizes research in contemporary leadership development (LO 8.5)?

   a. Leadership development programs regularly incorporate multiple neuroscience measures.

   b. Neurofeedback has been shown to be efficacious in helping leaders develop their skills.

   c. Leadership development efforts are quite primitive, as very little money can be made by offering programs.

   d. Leadership training is not very effective as trained individuals quickly revert back to previous ways of behaving.

Thought Questions

1. Thinking about a leader you found particularly inspirational, what traits outlined in this chapter did this person seem to have? How would you use neuroscience methods to understand this type of leadership more thoroughly?
2. Why do you think people follow dark triad leaders? What could neuroscience learn about followership that would help us avoid following the wrong people?

Answer Key for Review Questions

1. c
2. a
3. d
4. c
5. d

References

Alcañiz, M., Parra, E., & Giglioli, I. A. C., (2018). Virtual reality as an emerging methodology for leadership assessment and training. *Frontiers in Psychology, 9*, 1658. https://doi.org/10.3389/fpsyg.2018.01658

American Psychiatric Association (APA; 2013). *Diagnostic and statistical manual of mental disorders* (5th ed.). Washington, DC: Author.

Babiak, P., & Hare, R. D. (2019). *Snakes in suits: Understanding and surviving the psychopaths in your office* (revised edition). New York, NY: HarperCollins.

Balconi, M., Cassioli, F., Fronda, G., & Vanutelli, M. E. (2019). Cooperative leadership in hyperscanning: Brain and body synchrony during manager–employee interactions. *Neuropsychological Trends, 26*, 23–44. https://doi.org/10.7358/neur-2019-026-bal2

Bales, R. F. (1958). Task roles and social roles in problem-solving groups. In E. Maccoby, T. Newcomb, & E. Hartley (Eds.), *Readings in social psychology* (pp. 437–447). New York, NY: Rinehart & Winston.

Bass, B. M., & Avolio, B. J. (1990). Developing transformational leadership: 1992 and beyond. *Journal of European Industrial Training, 14*(5), 21–27. https://doi.org/10.1108/03090599010135122

Bass, B. M., & Bass, R. (2008). *The Bass handbook of leadership: Theory, research, and managerial applications*. New York, NY: Simon & Schuster.

Becker, W. J., Cropanzano, R., & Sanfey, A. G. (2011). Organizational neuroscience: Taking organizational theory inside the neural black box. *Journal of Management, 37*(4), 933–961. https://doi.org/10.1177/0149206311398955

Beer, J., Finnström, M., & Schrader, D. (2016). Why leadership training fails—and what to do about it. *Harvard Business Review*. https://hbr.org/2016/10/why-leadership-training-fails-and-what-to-do-about-it

Blair, R. J. R. (2013). The neurobiology of psychopathic traits in youths. *Nature Reviews Neuroscience*, 14(11), 786–799. https://doi.org/10.1038/nm3577

Boyatzis, R. E., Rochford, K., & Jack, A. I. (2014). Antagonistic neural networks underlying differentiated leadership roles. *Frontiers in Human Neuroscience*, 8, 114. https://doi.org/10.3389/fnhum.2014.00114.

Cao, H., Bertolino, A., Walter, H., Schneider, M., Schäfer, A., Taurisano, P., Blasi, G., Haddad, L., Grimm, O., Otto, K., Dixson, L., Erk, S., Mohnke, S., Heinz, A., Romanczuk-Seiferth, N., Mühleisen, T. W., Mattheisen, M., Witt, S. H., Cichon, S.H., … Meyer-Lindenberg, A. (2016). Altered functional subnetwork during emotional face processing: A potential intermediate phenotype for schizophrenia. *JAMA Psychiatry*, 73(6), 598–605. https://doi.org/10.1001/jamapsychiatry.2016.0161.

Dumas, G., Chavez, M., Nadel, J., & Martinerie, J. (2012). Anatomical connectivity influences both intra-and inter-brain synchronizations. *PLOS One*, 7(5), e36414. https://doi.org/10.1371/journal.pone.0036414

Dumas, G., Nadel, J., Soussignan, R., Martinerie, J., & Garnero, L. (2010). Inter-brain synchronization during social interaction. *PLOS One*, 5(8), e12166. https://doi.org/10.1371/journal.pone.0012166

Esarey, J., & Valdes, N. (2020). Unbiased, reliable, and valid student evaluations can still be unfair. *Assessment & Evaluation in Higher Education*, 45(8), 1106–1120. https://doi.org/10.1080/02602938.2020.1724875

Feinstein, J. S., Adolphs, R., Damasio, A. R., & Tranel, D. (2011). The human amygdala and the induction and experience of fear. *Current Biology*, 21(1), 34–38. https://doi.org/10.1016/j.cub.2010.11.042

Furnham, A., Richards, S. C., & Paulhus, D. L. (2013). The dark triad of personality: A 10 year review. *Social and Personality Psychology Compass*, 7(3), 199–216. https://doi.org/10.1111/spc3.12018

Furtner, M. R., Maran, T., & Rauthmann, J. F. (2017). Dark leadership: The role of leaders' dark triad personality traits. In M. G. Clark, & C. W. Gruber (Eds.), *Leader development deconstructed* (pp. 75–100). Cham, Switzerland: Springer.

Gordon, D. S., & Platek, S. M. (2009). Trustworthy? The brain knows: Implicit neural responses to faces that vary in dark triad personality characteristics and trustworthiness. *Journal of Social, Evolutionary, and Cultural Psychology*, 3(3), 182–200. https://doi.org/10.1037/h0099323

Gordon, I., & Berson, Y. (2018). Oxytocin modulates charismatic influence in groups. *Journal of Experimental Psychology: General*, 147(1), 132–136. https://doi.org/10.1037/xge0000375

Gouin, J.-P., Carter, C. S., Pournajafi-Nazarloo, H., Glaser, R., Malarkey, W. B., Loving, T. J., Stowell, J., & Kiecolt-Glaser, J. K. (2010). Marital behavior, oxytocin, vasopressin, and wound healing. *Psychoneuroendocrinology*, 35(7), 1082–1090. https://doi.org/10.1016/j.psyneuen.2010.01.009

Jack, A. I., Rochford, K. C., Friedman, J. P., Passarelli, A. M., & Boyatzis, R. E. (2019). Pitfalls in organizational neuroscience: A critical review and suggestions for future research. *Organizational Research Methods*, 22(1), 421–458. https://doi.org/10.1177/1094428117708857

Kosfeld, M., Heinrichs, M., Zak, P. J., Fischbacher, U., & Fehr, E. (2005). Oxytocin increases trust in humans. *Nature*, 435(7042), 673–676. https://doi.org/10.1038/nature03701

Krause, L., Enticott, P. G., Zangen, A., & Fitzgerald, P. B. (2012). The role of medial prefrontal cortex in theory of mind: A deep rTMS study. *Behavioural Brain Research*, *228*(1), 87–90. https://doi.org/10.1016/j.bbr.2011.11.037

Kruse, K. (2013). *What is leadership?* Forbes. www.forbes.com/sites/kevinkruse/2013/04/09/what-is-leadership/?sh=3aece1d5b90c

Lieberman, M. D., & Eisenberger, N. I. (2015). The dorsal anterior cingulate cortex is selective for pain: Results from large-scale reverse inference. *Proceedings of the National Academy of Sciences of the United States of America*, *112*(49), 15250–15255. https://doi.org/10.1073/pnas.1515083112

Light, K. C., Grewen, K. M., & Amico, J. A. (2005). More frequent partner hugs and higher oxytocin levels are linked to lower blood pressure and heart rate in premenopausal women. *Biological Psychology*, *69*(1), 5–21. https://doi.org/10.1016/j.biopsycho.2004.11.002

Maccoby, M. (2000). Narcissistic leaders: The incredible pros, the inevitable cons. *Harvard Business Review*, *78*, 68–77.

Markett, S., Montag, C., & Reuter, M. (2018). Network neuroscience and personality. *Personality Neuroscience*, *1*, E14. https://doi.org/10.1017/pen.2018.12

Martinez, D., Orlowska, D., Narendran, R., Slifstein, M., Liu, F., Kumar, D., Broft, A., Van Heertum, R., & Kleber, H. D. (2010). Dopamine type 2/3 receptor availability in the striatum and social status in human volunteers. *Biological Psychiatry*, *67*(3), 275–278. https://doi.org/10.1016/j.biopsych.2009.07.037

Meyer-Lindenberg, A., Domes, G., Kirsch, P., & Heinrichs, M. (2011). Oxytocin and vasopressin in the human brain: Social neuropeptides for translational medicine. *Nature Reviews Neuroscience*, *12*(9), 524–538. https://doi.org/10.1038/nrn3044

Moe, H. T., Strand, M. F., Karp, T., & Norbom, H. M. (2021). Cortisol and testosterone in leadership practice. *Psych*, *3*, 153–162. https://doi.org/10.3390/psych3020013

Molenberghs, P., Prochilo, G., Steffens, N. K., Zacher, H., & Haslam, S. A. (2017). The neuroscience of inspirational leadership: The importance of collective-oriented language and shared group membership. *Journal of Management*, *43*(7), 2168–2194. https://doi.org/10.1177/0149206314565242

Newman, M. L., Sellers, J. G., & Josephs, R. A. (2005). Testosterone, cognition, and social status. *Hormones and Behavior*, *47*, 205–211. https://doi.org/10.1016/j.yhbeh.2004.09.008

Nummenmaa, L., Lukkarinen, L., Sun, L., Putkinen, V., Seppälä, K., Karjalainen, T., Karlsson, H. K., Hudson, M., Venetjoki, N., Salomaa, M., Rautio, P., Hirvonen, J., Lauerma, H., & Tiihonen, J. (2021). Brain basis of psychopathy in criminal offenders and general population, *Cerebral Cortex*, *31*(9), 4104–4114. https://doi.org/10.1093/cercor/bhab072

Paulhus, D. L., & Williams, K. M. (2002). The Dark Triad of personality: Narcissism, Machiavellianism, and psychopathy. *Journal of Research in Personality*, *36*, 556–563. https://doi.org/10.1016/S0092-6566(02)00505-6

Paunonen, S. V., Lönnqvist, J.-E., Verkasalo, M., Leikas, S., & Nissinen, V. (2006). Narcissism and emergent leadership in military cadets. *The Leadership Quarterly*, *17*, 475–486. https://doi.org/10.1016/j.leaqua.2006.06.003

Poldrack, R. A. (2006). Can cognitive processes be inferred from neuroimaging data? *Trends in Cognitive Science*, *10*(2), 59–63. https://doi.org/10.1016/j.tics.2005.12.004

Qu, C., Ligneul, R., van der Henst, J-B., & Dreher, J-C. (2017). An integrative interdisciplinary perspective on social dominance hierarchies. *Trends in Cognitive Sciences*, *21*(11), 893–908. https://doi.org/10.1016/j.tics.2017.08.004

Sherman, G. D., Lerner, J. S., Josephs, R. A., Renshon, J., & Gross, J. J. (2016). The interaction of testosterone and cortisol is associated with attained status in male executives. *Journal of Personality and Social Psychology, 110*(6), 921–929. https://doi.org/10.1037/pspp0000063

Simonton, D. K. (1986). Presidential personality: Biographical use of the Gough Adjective Check List. *Journal of Personality and Social Psychology, 51*(1), 149–160. https://doi.org/10.1037/0022-3514.51.1.149

Sundvik, M., Puttonen, H., Semenova, S., & Panula, P. (2021). The bullies are the leaders of the next generation: Inherited aminergic neurotransmitter system changes in socially dominant zebrafish, *Danio rerio. Behavioural Brain Research, 409*, 113309. https://doi.org/10.1016/j.bbr.2021.113309

Van der Meij, L., Schaveling, J., & van Vugt, M. (2016) Basal testosterone, leadership and dominance: A field study and meta-analysis. *Psychoneuroendocrinology, 72*, 72–79. https://doi.org/10.1016/j.psyneuen.2016.06.005

Waldman, D. A., & Balthazard, P. A. (2015). Neuroscience of leadership. *Monographs in Leadership and Management, 7*, 189–211. https://doi.org/10.1108/S1479-357120150000007007

Waldman, D. A., Balthazard, P. A., & Peterson, S. J. (2011). Leadership and neuroscience: Can we revolutionize the way that inspirational leaders are identified and developed? *Academy of Management Perspectives, 25*(1), 60–74. https://doi.org/10.5465/amp.25.1.60

Waldman, D. A., Wang, D., & Fenters, V. (2019). The added value of neuroscience methods in organizational research. *Organizational Research Methods, 22*(1), 223–249. https://doi.org/10.1177/1094428116642013

Waldman, D. A., Wang, D., Stikic, M., Berka, C., & Korszen, S. (2015). Neuroscience and team processes. In D. A. Waldman & P. A. Balthazard (Eds.), *Organizational neuroscience* (pp. 277–294). London: Emerald Books.

Yarkoni, T., Poldrack, R. A., Nichols, T. E., Van Essen, D. C., & Wager, T. D. (2011). Large-scale automated synthesis of human functional neuroimaging data. *Nature Methods, 8*(8), 665–670. https://doi.org/10.1038/nmeth.1635

Yoon, C., Gutchess, A. H., Feinberg, F., & Polk, T. A. (2006). A functional magnetic resonance imaging study of neural dissociations between brand and person judgments. *Journal of Consumer Research, 33*(1), 31–40. https://doi.org/10.1086/594132

Zaccaro, S. J., Green, J. P., Dubrow, S., & Kolze, M. J. (2018). Leader individual differences, situational parameters, and leadership outcomes: A comprehensive review and integration. *Leadership Quarterly, 29*, 2–43. https://doi.org/10.1016/j.leaqua.2017.10.003

Zhang, Z., Ilies, R., & Arvey, R. D. (2009). Beyond genetic explanations for leadership: The moderating role of the social environment. *Organizational Behavior and Human Decision Processes, 110*, 118–128. https://doi.org/10.1016/j.obhdp.2009.06.004

Glossary

Big 5 personality traits	A leading approach to personality that postulates five key traits: openness to experience, conscientiousness, extroversion/introversion, agreeableness, and neuroticism.
Dark triad of personality	A personality combining psychopathy, narcissism, and Machiavellianism.

Forward inference	A logical interpretation of brain imaging or recording studies that associates an induced psychological state with a pattern of activity.
Foundational traits	Relatively static factors affecting leadership, such as genetics, personality, cognitive ability, motives, and values.
Hyperscanning	Simultaneous evaluation of the brain activity of two or more participants using technologies such as EEG, fNIRS, and fMRI.
Leadership	A process of social influence that maximizes the efforts of others toward the achievement of a goal.
Leadership capacities	Fluid attributes that contribute to leadership ability, including cognitive skills, social capacity, knowledge, and expertise.
Neurofeedback	A variation of biofeedback in which a person attempts to maintain a state using information from neural technologies.
Organizational neuroscience	An interdisciplinary field that investigates the neural correlates of workplace behavior.
Oxytocin	A neurohormone associated with many functions, including social bonding.
Relationship-oriented leadership	Leadership focused on the emotional well-being of followers.
Task-oriented leadership	Leadership focused on completing the tasks facing a group.

9 Health Neuroscience

LEARNING OBJECTIVES

After reading this chapter, you should be able to:

▶ 1. Distinguish between the philosophies of monism and dualism.
▶ 2. Define health neuroscience and describe its scope and methodologies.
▶ 3. Discuss the methodologies used in health neuroscience and the challenges faced by researchers in this field.
▶ 4. Describe the contributions of health neuroscience to our understanding of stress, the neurological outcomes of COVID-19, loneliness, and health behaviors.

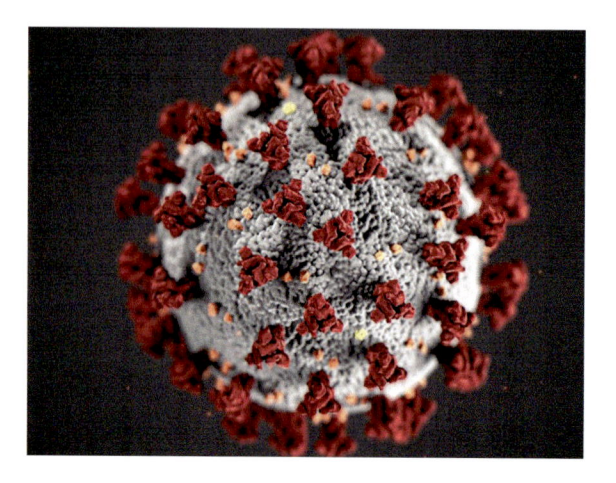

FIGURE 9.1 The COVID-19 pandemic has reminded us how important the interaction between mind and health can be.
Source: https://pxhere.com/en/photo/1608796

Mind and Body

In Chapter 1, we reviewed the **dualistic** philosophy of René Descartes, who believed that the mind and body were quite separate and followed very different rules. Contemporary neuroscientists, of course, do not share these views. Instead, neuroscientists are **monists** who believe that the mind is the result of the actions of the nervous system.

Although this monistic view of the mind influences all the chapters in this book, its influence on this chapter on health neuroscience is particularly central and profound. Physical illness can certainly impact the way our mind works. Just as certainly, however, the way we think and process information can have significant effects on our health (Figure 9.1).

A dramatic example of the influence of thinking on health was described by Cole et al. (2015). These researchers demonstrated that our perceptions of social connectivity could impact the performance of our immune systems. If you're like me, you might have assumed that your immune system was sort of like a computer's antivirus software—something that runs in the background without much awareness or influence on your part. Instead, your immune system is highly dependent on the signals it receives from the brain. Note, too, that we are not talking about the absolute reality of a person's social connections, but rather their *perceptions*. Some people feel lonely even though they have hundreds of friends and acquaintances while others feel socially connected if their dog greets them after a day at work or school.

Cole et al. (2015) argued that when people felt socially connected with others, this begins a series of messages that tell the immune system to gear up to deal with viruses. After all, as we now understand all too well from the COVID-19 pandemic, viruses like close social contact. To protect ourselves from COVID-19, we are advised to maintain social distancing. Somehow, our immune systems can tell when we feel socially connected, which raises the likelihood that we are in close contact with others. In contrast, when we are feeling lonely or disconnected from others, the message that goes to the immune system is a set of directions for gearing up to fight bacteria. Why would lonely people need to fight bacteria instead of viruses? This process emerges from our experience over the millennia, mostly spent as hunter–gatherers (Cacioppo & Cacioppo, 2018a). Over the majority of our species' history, people who were socially excluded from their group were at terrible risk, not from viruses anymore because they're not in close contact, but from predators and possibly other humans. Their biggest challenge is now the bacteria that love to gain entrance to the body through cuts and scrapes that could result from fighting, and the immune system knows that. Even though most of us have very different lifestyles today, this same process is wired into our brains.

The great irony of COVID-19 is that at the very time when we need our immune systems to robustly attack viruses, we are engaging in practices like lockdowns, stay-at-home, and social distancing that might threaten the ability of our immune systems to protect us. If COVID-19 precautions make a person lonely, then the immune system will dial down its preparation for dealing with viruses. We are still too close to the pandemic to fully understand the implications of our practices on mental health, which in turn, has direct consequences for our physical health, but we predict that those implications are enormous.

What Is Health Neuroscience?

Health is often defined as the absence of disease, pain, or discomfort. Others, however, view health as something more. It is a state of well-being as opposed to a simple absence of disease. The World Health Organization defines health as "a state of complete physical, mental, and social well-being and not merely the absence of disease or infirmity" (World Health Organization [WHO], 2003, para. 1). To reflect this broader definition, medicine now embraces a biopsychosocial model of health. This model combines biological factors (genetics, infection, injury), psychological factors (lifestyle, stress, health beliefs), and social factors (culture, family, and social support).

Health neuroscience has been defined as "an emerging field focused on understanding how the brain *affects* and is *affected by* physical health (Erickson et al., 2014, p. 446). More recently, health neuroscience has been described as a merger between health psychology and cognitive and social–affective neuroscience (Stillman & Erickson, 2018). This field spans the biopsychosocial model. We have already seen one example of how social support and perception can have remarkable biological effects. Health neuroscience is housed within the general domain of health psychology, while using the methods and theories of neuroscience. The goal is to gain further understanding of the relationships between the brain and health that will provide insights into health-related vulnerability and resilience across the lifespan. This understanding in turn should inform health policies and promote healthier development and aging (Erickson et al., 2014).

The model illustrated in Figure 9.2 shows the relationship of the brain with its influences and the processes it influences in turn that result in a state of relative health or well-being. Top-down influences on the right side of the figure represent the actions of the brain, such as the effects of the brain's determination of social connectivity on the immune system. Bottom-up influences include factors affecting the brain, such as smoking or inflammation. These processes take place within a context of social, cultural, and other environmental factors and are influenced by individual differences in genetics, epigenetics, and lifestyle factors.

Extending from this model, research in health neuroscience could use measures of brain structure and function as either independent or dependent variables. We could ask what types of brains are most likely to make different choices regarding COVID-19 precautions, like getting vaccinated or wearing a mask. Or we could ask whether the

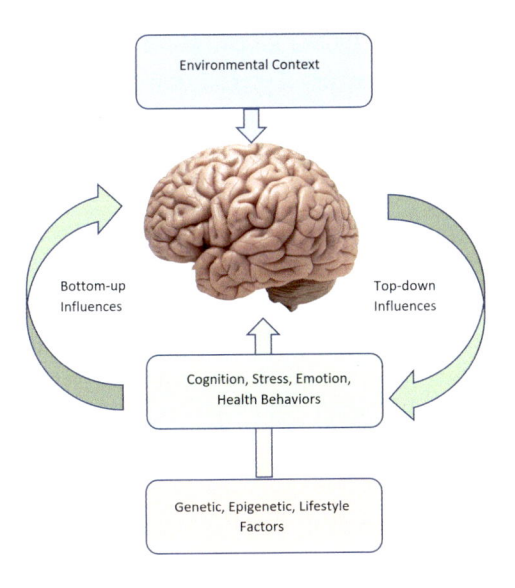

FIGURE 9.2 A model of health neuroscience.
Source: adapted from Figure 1 of Erickson et al. (2014).

stress or anxiety a person experiences regarding COVID-19 affects the performance of the brain in certain tasks.

You might be wondering where psychological health fits in this model. Erikson et al. (2014) suggest that mental and physical health are often intertwined, and where they interact, they become good research questions for health neuroscience. For example, smoking is much more common among people with psychosis, such as in schizophrenia, than it is in the general population (King et al., 2020). A health neuroscientist might want to know what there is about the brain of a person with schizophrenia that predisposes that person to heavier smoking. Conversely, a health neuroscientist might also ask what exposure to nicotine might do to the brains of people who do and do not experience psychosis.

This approach might seem so reasonable that you are wondering why we need a special field to emphasize it. Surprisingly, however, the influence of the brain in physical health has been neglected by many major models of health (Inagaki, 2020). This has led to a lag in our understanding of the brain's role in physical health compared to our understanding of its role in mental health. The relative neglect of the brain's role in physical health is also reflected in the rather recent (2015) inclusion of a new Psychological, Social, and Biological Foundations of Behavior subtest in the Medical College Admission Test (MCAT) used to screen potential medical students in the United States. Up until this time, people responsible for the preparation of the next generation of physicians saw no need to assess this knowledge. The addition of this section is meant to encourage premedical students to gain an understanding of the science of behavior in recognition of the fact that about half of all causes of mortality in the United States are linked to behavioral and social factors. Even so, few medical schools require even an introductory psychology course, let alone behavioral neuroscience coursework. The behavioral questions on the MCAT (your author has actually written a few of these) are not terribly complex and could be answered easily by students following an introductory psychology course or even self-study. Not only is health neuroscience playing catch-up in its understanding of physical health, but it also faces hurdles in communicating the importance of its findings.

Health neuroscience will have little impact unless it partners with public health as well as with the medical community. Health neuroscience has an important role to play in shaping policies aimed at improving health. For example, health neuroscience can contribute to initiatives like the Adverse Childhood Experiences (ACE) Study (Felitti et al., 1998), run by a large collaborative group of researchers affiliated with the Centers for Disease Control and Prevention (CDC; see Figure 9.3). Since the original study, this ongoing research initiative has worked to identify gaps in our understanding of how adverse childhood experiences, such as poverty, abuse, and neglect, lead to social, emotional, and cognitive impairment, which in turn can lead to risky health behaviors, disease, disability, social problems, and early death. Health neuroscience can help close some of those gaps. For example, research on the effects of air pollution associated with poverty on later cognitive function can help bridge gaps between poverty and cognition. This type of detailed finding can lead to real policy changes.

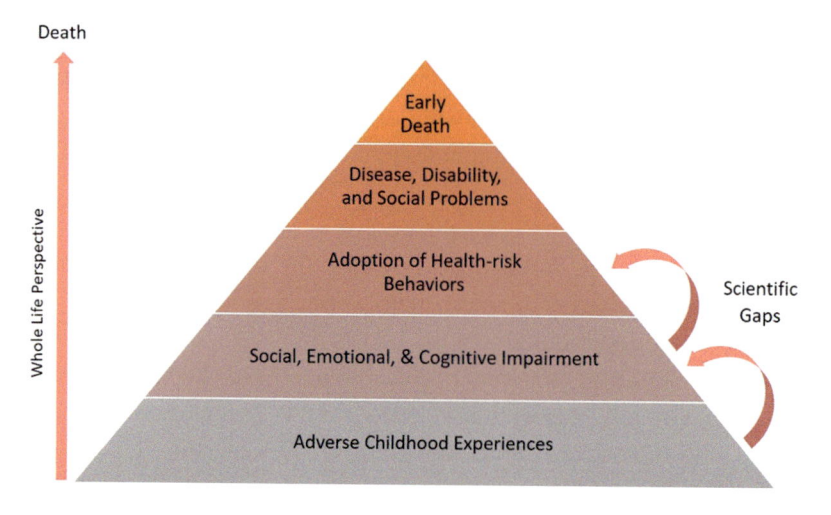

FIGURE 9.3 The ACE pyramid outlines research gaps that need to be filled to understand and prevent the impact of adverse child experiences. What do you think health neuroscience can contribute to filling those gaps?

Source: Author.

The Methods of Health Neuroscience

One of the key goals of health neuroscience is to establish brain biomarkers for physical health. **Biomarkers** are any biological indication that helps to distinguish between typical and unhealthy processes or conditions. Biomarkers can also lead to predictions of how individuals will respond to a particular treatment.

To meet this overarching goal, health neuroscience makes use of the same types of methodologies we have seen elsewhere in this book, particularly brain imaging, but on a scale not typical of other areas of the neurosciences. Health psychology research typically involves hundreds of participants, and as we have noted previously, assessing large samples can be time-consuming and expensive in studies using brain imaging. Collaborations among teams from multiple laboratories should help with this issue.

An additional challenge is the computation required to analyze the resulting data from large numbers of participants in studies with complex hypotheses. In Chapter 8, we saw how the repository Neurosynth was helping researchers evaluate their findings in light of the larger literature. Machine learning and big data methods are beginning to come to the rescue, allowing researchers to revisit and extend classic findings conducted with smaller samples (Inagaki, 2020).

To illustrate the potential of these new approaches, the ENIGMA Consortium (Enhancing NeuroImaging Genetics through Meta Analysis) brings together more than 1400 scientists from 43 countries to study the human brain (Thompson et al., 2020). This consortium also ensures that the participants being studied are more diverse and representative of the global population than is typically seen in published research. The pooled data quickly overcome the common problem of sample size in brain imaging studies, as the consortium has data on over 50,000 participants. Access to larger samples is critical to the ability to detect small effects, which are common in these types of studies.

ENIGMA was originally developed to merge two "big data" sources, brain imaging and genetics, with the goal of identifying the impact of genetics on the brain. Further, ENIGMA sought to connect this information to psychological disorders and to identify imaging biomarkers for diagnosis and response to treatment. The result is not simply the ability to conduct meta-analyses, but also what the researchers are calling "mega-analyses."

Although ENIGMA's focus is on psychological disorders, such as schizophrenia and depression, the group has already produced interesting insights into addiction, epilepsy, brain injury, Parkinson's disease, HIV, ataxia, and stroke recovery, which overlap with health neuroscience. Their recent creation of cross-disorder working groups brings together working groups within the consortium who are tackling similar issues. For example, one working group is investigating suicidal ideation and action. The model provided by ENIGMA, if adopted more widely to physical disease in additional to psychological disorder, could provide a treasure trove of insights that would be nearly impossible for researchers to produce working individually or on smaller teams.

Stress

A classic area of health psychology that involved neuroscience theories and measures at very early stages is the study of stress. **Stress** refers to an unpleasant emotional state that results from the perception of danger (Cacioppo et al., 2022).

Classic Models of Stress

As early as 1929, Walter Cannon was observing the way that the sympathetic nervous system (see Chapter 2) could be activated by a variety of challenges, such as extreme cold, lack of oxygen, or certain emotional experiences such as fear. These sources of stress are referred to as **stressors**. Perceiving stressors would initiate what Cannon referred to as a "fight or flight" reaction, consisting of increased heart rate, blood pressure, and respiration.

In an effort spanning decades, Hans Selye (1975) sought to expand Cannon's initial findings by exposing rats to stressors and observing how long they would swim before giving up (at which point, they are of course rescued) (Figure 9.4). Forced swimming, by contemporary standards, is not an ideal model of stress (Smith, 2012). Rats are excellent swimmers. After all, New World rats are primarily the descendants of the European *Rattus norvegicus*, which made their way to ships by swimming out to them in harbors and climbing ropes from anchors. As a result, the "stressiness" of swimming for rodents has been disputed. In metabolic terms, swimming also represents an anabolic process, in which muscle is built up, as opposed to the catabolic process of stress, which involves the breaking down of larger molecules. Gender differences exist, with females being much stronger and more willing swimmers than males. Smith (2012) notes that male rats "hold their breath and sit at the bottom of the pool for as long as they can before jumping/swimming up for a breath of air, rather than exercising the whole time." Alternatives to forced swimming include restraint and tilt of the cage. Individual differences in sensitivity to stress are measured by time spent in the open field. In the real world, that is generally where my cat is hanging out, so rodents who venture more often into the open field are less sensitive to perceived danger than those who hug the dark sides of a container.

Methods aside, Selye's (1946) resulting theory, the **general adaptation syndrome (GAS),** influenced our understanding of stress responses for many years. The GAS posits three stages: alarm, resistance, and exhaustion. In today's methodology, we might view the alarm phase as acute stress, or quick-onset, short-lasting stress. You've experienced this type of stress during close calls while driving. The fight-or-flight response is initiated, helping us deal with these immediate emergencies.

Selye's resistance stage is more akin to today's conceptualization of chronic stress. In modern living, most of us experience a rather steady state of ongoing stress. The stressors themselves might change, such as the introduction of COVID-19, but we always seem

FIGURE 9.4 A rat is stressed by the forced swim test. When it gives up, it is rescued.
Source: Karla Freberg.

to have something ongoing that we perceive as danger, whether that is a tough final exam or a dispute with a romantic partner or a problem at work or a shortage of money. Chronic stress, as we will see shortly, has the potential to produce negative impacts on overall health.

Selye's final stage, exhaustion, is most similar to a diagnosis of major depressive disorder. Not surprisingly, stress generally figures prominently in discussions of the causes of depression. In exhaustion, energy levels drop and death can even follow.

The HPA Axis and SAM

The perception of a stressor, whether that is an upcoming final exam or seeing a lion right in front of you, initiates programmed responses honed over the millennia to keep you alive. One system, the **sympathetic adrenal-medullary system** (**SAM**), is a neural response to the perception of threat while the other system, the **hypothalamic-pituitary-adrenal axis** (**HPA axis**), is primarily hormonal (Figure 9.5). Of course, the HPA remains "neural" in the sense that signals from the hypothalamus initiate the response.

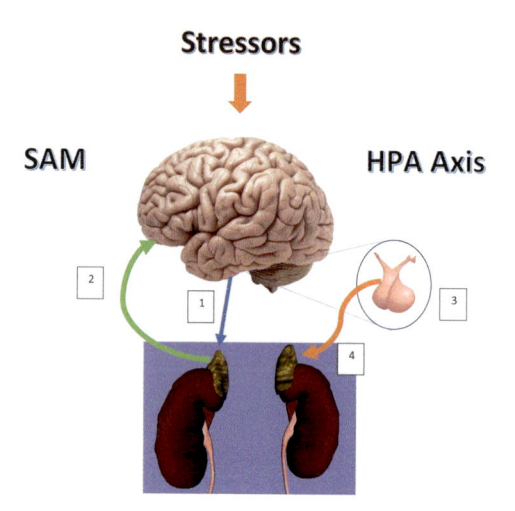

FIGURE 9.5 The perception of a stressor initiates the fast SAM and slower HPA axis responses. Activation of SAM (1) signals the adrenal glands to release epinephrine (adrenalin) and norepinephrine into the blood supply, which in turn prepares the body and brain for "fight or flight" (2). Activation of the HPA axis results when the hypothalamus signals the pituitary gland (3) to release hormones into the circulation. These in turn tell the adrenal glands to release cortisol into the circulation (4).

Activation of SAM results in a quick burst of norepinephrine and epinephrine release, leading to the classic fight-or-flight response.

The HPA axis is slower acting and more complex. Not only does it respond to neural signals indicating threat, but it also responds to the presence of inflammation, signaled by cytokines. The outcome of HPA activation is an increased release of **cortisol**. Cortisol, too, is complicated. Its release is circadian, or affected by time of day. Cortisol levels are typically quite high in the morning, dropping off gradually as the day progresses. This is possibly one of the reasons that a jolt of stress near bedtime, perhaps from viewing a scary movie, can delay the onset of sleep. Cortisol's main function is metabolic—it helps manage the supply of glucose that keeps the brain going.

These systems are costly in terms of the energy they need and the potential overactivation has for harming other systems. As a result, they are tightly regulated. Long-term exposure to circulating cortisol has wide-ranging negative effects, including the death of neurons. Patients with Cushing's disease, which produces abnormally high cortisol levels, experience reduced hippocampal volume. To prevent damage, the hippocampus contains a rich component of cortisol receptors. When they are filled, the hippocampus can signal the hypothalamus to reduce the release of cortisol from the adrenal glands. The system, however, is not foolproof. In the face of constant high levels of cortisol, the ability of the hippocampus to regulate the system can fail. Psychologically, this can result in depressed mood. Many patients with Cushing's disease or those who are treated with cortisol for other medical conditions experience profound depression. Ultimately, chronic severe stress can damage the hippocampus.

Epigenetics and Stress

In keeping with the goals of health psychology to understand health across the lifetime, neuroscience has already provided considerable insight into the effects of childhood experience on stress. This type of research can help fill the gaps identified by the ACE model mentioned earlier in the chapter.

Epigenetics refers to changes in the way genes behave that are not accompanied by changes in their underlying DNA. Genes can be turned on and off throughout the lifespan, which helps us understand why identical twins, with their identical DNA, can have very different outcomes. Our diet, whether we smoke or drink, the amount of stress we experience, and many other factors can produce epigenetic effects.

Michael Meaney and his colleagues (c.f. Francis et al., 1999; Meany, 2010) have demonstrated the epigenetic effects of maternal nurture on later resilience in the face of stress. Rodent moms engage in "lick and groom" behavior toward their pups. Some mothers are more nurturant than others. Offspring of highly nurturant moms experienced higher expression of genes related to cortisol receptors in the hippocampus. They were also more likely than the offspring of less nurturant moms to spend time in the open field. This situation is a reminder that stress, although unpleasant, has a purpose. While being resistant to stress sounds like a good thing, being stressed can also save your life.

Why would having more cortisol receptors make you more resilient to stress? The number of cortisol receptors in the brain is designed to provide an adequate response to stress, no more and no less. Genetically modified mice that underexpress receptors act depressed, whereas mice that overexpress receptors are not sensitive enough to stress (Gass, 2007). If you have large numbers of receptors, a "normal" amount of cortisol might not be enough of a signal to provoke an appropriate response. You might stay out in the open when that is not a great idea.

We are still in the process of sorting out the epigenetic influences on human resilience to stress. Human children who are kindly nurtured are also more resilient in the face of stress later in life. In particular, the first 1000 days following conception, until about the age of 2 years, seem to be important for predicting later chronic disease and life expectancy. Health neuroscientists are seeking biomarkers for the presence of unusual stress early in life. The first 280 of these days occurs between conception and birth, and low birth weight can be an indicator of prenatal stress. A biomarker for excessive stress in this early period of life is having an asymmetrical lower face, as indicated by misalignment of the upper and lower front teeth (Hujoel et al., 2017; Figure 9.6). A better understanding of what leads to these biomarkers will inform preventive efforts.

HEALTH NEUROSCIENCE

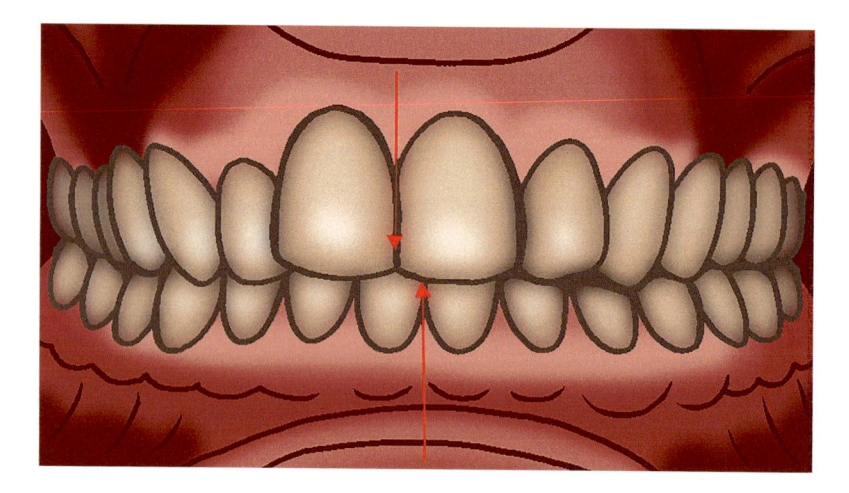

FIGURE 9.6 A biomarker for stress in the first 1000 days of life is a misalignment of the front teeth, as indicated by the arrows in this illustration.
Source: Karla Freberg

Health Impacts of Chronic Stress

Short-term bursts of stress are often beneficial. Not only does the stress response help you manage an emergency, but you can actually experience an improved immune system (Dhabhar, 2009). This is what happens when we push ourselves at the gym.

Over time, however, when acute stress turns into chronic stress, the immune system doesn't fare so well. You have probably noticed that at times of unusual stress, you might have been more vulnerable to illness. In the case of the COVID-19 pandemic, part of good prevention is to practice effective stress management strategies. Stressed patients with HIV progress to AIDS more quickly than less stressed patients (Harper et al., 2006). The basis for the stress–illness connection lies in the ability of cortisol to directly suppress white blood cells, or lymphocytes, the frontline defenders in the immune system. Excess activation of the HPA axis can produce this outcome. Unfortunately, this puts an added psychological burden on individuals with serious illnesses, who might blame themselves for not doing a better job of managing their stress.

Cortisol can have indirect effects on health as well. Because of its circadian role mentioned earlier, excess cortisol can have a negative impact on sleep quality (Van Cauter et al., 2000). Poor sleep quality, in turn, can initiate a cascade of effects that compromise many aspects of health.

Coping with Stress

By now, you might be despairing about your own stress levels and wondering what you should be doing to mitigate them. Most of the coping mechanisms we suggest are cognitive and behavioral rather than biological. However, given the reciprocal nature of behavior and the brain discussed at the outset of this chapter, we will argue that at some level, cognitive and behavioral coping works because it restores balance to neural and hormonal systems disrupted by chronic stress. For example, social connectivity is one of the best approaches to managing stress. If we reach out to others, we feel enormous relief. As we'll see in the next section, the effects of social connectivity have important neuroscience correlates.

Neurological Outcomes of COVID-19

Although we are still too close to the COVID-19 pandemic to fully appreciate its characteristics and impacts, health neuroscientists are busy tackling some of the troubling after-effects of COVID infection. Troubling reports of loss of smell and "brain fog," even in people who had only mild symptoms otherwise, have attracted the attention of researchers interested in the neurological correlates of COVID infection.

Neurological disorders, ranging from headaches and dizziness to strokes and seizures were found in as many as 83% of hospitalized patients (Liotta et al., 2020). The low oxygen levels and low blood pressure associated with COVID-19 can produce encephalopathy, or alterations in consciousness such as confusion. This was the most frequent type of neurological disorder found to affect 13.5% of over 4000 hospitalized patients (Frontera et al., 2021). Strokes were nearly eight times more likely following COVID infection than usually seen in cases of influenza.

Researchers are also hard at work trying to understand "**long COVID**," or lingering symptoms like fatigue and confusion that last much longer than the disease itself. The active infection might last a week or two, but many patients are reporting not feeling well weeks and months after they recover. Recovered COVID patients might also be experiencing higher levels of anxiety and depression, post-traumatic stress disorder, and cognitive dysfunction.

The idea that the COVID-19 virus can access the brain directly remains controversial. Inflammation can damage the blood–brain barrier, reducing the protection the brain enjoys otherwise from circulating toxins and pathogens. Virus particles could cross the blood–brain barrier at normally weak points, such as areas associated with assessing blood glucose levels. Virus particles could also enter the brain from the olfactory bulbs using retrograde transport, a system cells normally use to return molecules from axon terminals back to the cell body.

Normally, however, a direct invasion would produce cases of meningitis (inflammation of the meninges, or the membranes covering the brain) or encephalitis (more general brain inflammation), and these were not observed in the large-scale study by Frontera et al. (2021). Observed cognitive symptoms are more likely to be secondary, caused by the low oxygen levels or sepsis (over-response by the immune system) that characterize severe cases of COVID-19. Another mechanism for possible brain damage in COVID-19 is microvascular damage. This refers to the tendency for very small blood vessels to become damaged and leaky. This leads to small areas of hemorrhage, which in the brain can have serious results.

A group of researchers at the University of Oxford is using MRI to study brain outcomes of COVID-19 infections (University of Oxford, 2020). The group is focusing on the brainstem in particular. Other versions of coronaviruses have been found to be attracted to the brainstem, specifically the medulla (see Chapter 1). The viruses can access the medulla by entering the nasal mucosa and then making their way to the olfactory bulbs, which in turn provide access to the medulla.

A large group of researchers from 30 countries has received funding to track the long-term effects of COVID-19 on dementia (de Erausquin et al., 2021). Data collected will include blood samples, MRI images, and clinical data. Other viruses have been suspected of playing a role in dementia, and inflammation is an established risk factor.

In addition to the basic medical implications of these investigations, health neuroscience can provide additional insights into the cognitive, behavioral, social, and emotional correlates of COVID-19 outcomes.

Loneliness

At the beginning of this chapter, we discussed a study by Cole et al. (2015) that demonstrated a connection between feeling socially connected or not and the behavior of your immune system. These results might have come as a surprise to you, especially if your thinking is closer to Descartes regarding the relationship between mind and body.

In a letter to the prestigious British medical journal *The Lancet* in 2018, John and Stephanie Cacioppo asked readers to "imagine a condition that makes a person irritable, depressed, and self-centered, and is associated with a 26% increase in the risk of premature mortality" (2018b, p. 426). The answer, of course, is **loneliness**. Other researchers have argued that social isolation produces a risk of death comparable to smoking and alcohol use and a greater risk than obesity and lack of exercise (Holt-Lunstad et al., 2010). Not everyone accepts this approach. McLennan and Ulijaszek (2018) responded to the Cacioppos by objecting to the "medicalization" of loneliness. They did not dispute the dangers. In fact, they cited the same Holt-Lunstad et al. article mentioned here. Their concern was that viewing loneliness from a medical perspective might discourage efforts to make the public see public health problems as requiring integrated and holistic approaches. They argue that medical framing of obesity, discussed in the next section, has not been successful. This debate highlights an overall issue for health neuroscience. It is important to view health neuroscience as a helpful addition, not a replacement, for other views of health.

How might the perception of social isolation affect health? John and Stephanie Cacioppo (2018a) proposed an evolutionary theory of loneliness (ETL) to help explain these processes. As an evolutionary model, it epitomizes health neuroscience. The fact that humans are not alone in their ability to experience loneliness suggests that we share neural structures and functions with other animals that manage this process.

Before we get too much farther, let's stop and clarify what loneliness is and what it is not. Loneliness is not some objective fact, but rather a perception of social isolation. There is no magic number of friends that you need to be safe from loneliness. In fact, loneliness works in a rather homeostatic way. You have a setpoint, which is primarily genetic in origin, for the amount of social connectivity you need to feel well (Boomsma et al., 2005). Deficits from that setpoint will be perceived as loneliness, and several cognitive, behavioral, and physical outcomes will result.

Using the information in Table 9.1, how would you rate your own current levels of loneliness? Do the think the scale captures how you feel right now? Why or why not? Results usually indicate that in developed countries, between 25% and 50% feel lonely some of the time, and 5–10% feel lonely frequently or always. College students, and young people in general, typically report higher rates of loneliness than older adults. Although loneliness prevalence experiences an uptick after the age of 80, the ageist stereotype of the old, lonely person feeding pigeons in the park is not an accurate portrayal of the loneliness data.

Evolutionary Aspects of Loneliness

Why would we evolve the ability to experience something as negative as loneliness? Loneliness is not the only negative experience to evolve. Physical pain is very unpleasant, to say the least, but it provides important information to an organism. Rare individuals born without a sense of pain must be monitored very carefully, as they can injure themselves severely without any conscious awareness. Loneliness, like pain, probably

TABLE 9.1 This brief version of the UCLA Loneliness Scale was revised for use with large population surveys (Hughes et al., 2004). Sum your scores, with higher scores indicating more loneliness. A score of 10 or more is considered indicative of a person who is dealing with loneliness on a regular basis.

Statement	Never	Rarely	Sometimes	Often
1. How often do you feel that you lack companionship?	1	2	3	4
2. How often do you feel left out?	1	2	3	4
3. How often do you feel isolated from others?	1	2	3	4

evolved as a warning system, too. As we mentioned previously, a solitary human hunter–gatherer is not likely to last long if socially isolated. The feelings we perceive as loneliness act as a signal that our social connectivity is at risk.

We might expect people to respond to this signal by quickly working to repair the frayed connections they have with others, but this is not exactly what happens. Yes, when we're lonely, we do feel motivated to reconnect with others, but another competing set of behaviors is also triggered by loneliness—self-preservation. If you perceive that you are at risk, it is natural to go into self-preservation mode, and the behaviors we exhibit in this state are not particularly attractive (Cacioppo & Cacioppo, 2018a; Figure 9.7). We become hyper-vigilant to social threats. We see others having more fun, so we begin to think in confirmatory and biased ways (nobody likes me). This elicits a spiral of increasingly off-putting behavior that pushes individuals even farther from others. Lonely people are less likely to offer help to others, and they expect less help in return.

Health Neuroscience and Loneliness

Health neuroscience has provided substantial support for these observations. Using high definition EEG (see Chapter 1) to identify brain microstates, Cacioppo et al. (2016) showed participants photographs containing social and nonsocial threats. Participants identified as lonely using a screening instrument demonstrated brain microstates that indicated they were differentiating the social threats from the nonsocial threats much faster than non-lonely participants. Researchers are also beginning to trace the networks and pathways responsible for loneliness (Cacioppo & Cacioppo, 2018a). Not surprisingly,

FIGURE 9.7 John Cacioppo often compared being lonely to being "on the outside of the fish ball." Schooling fish will form massive, swirling fish balls when predators approach. Obviously, the fish on the outer surface of the ball are in more danger than the fish on the inside. When we're lonely, we perceive ourselves as outside of the social center where we are at risk.

Source: https://commons.wikimedia.org/wiki/File:Large_fish_school.png

these pathways converge on the SAM and HPA axis, resulting in a high state of chronic vigilance.

From our discussion of stress, you might guess that loneliness, through its activation of the HPA axis in particular, will have detrimental effects on the immune system. This might account for some of the mortality risk associated with loneliness. Other outcomes also threaten health. Sleep quality and quantity are disturbed, and inflammation increases. Although loneliness is distinct from depression, it can lead to depression. By doing so, the risks of depression for health are added to the existing load.

An interesting factor that does NOT appear to result from loneliness is an impact on other health behaviors, such as seeking medical services. If anything, lonely people are more rather than less likely to seek medical attention. When seeking medical care, you are interacting with other humans who are trained to act in caring ways, which is better for some lonely people than staying at home by themselves. In the United Kingdom, government initiatives provide medical practitioners with the ability to make "loneliness referrals." If a healthcare provider identifies a patient as lonely, the provider can refer the patient to agencies that will identify needs and provide solutions. Some people might need a person to walk their dog, while others want partners for a card game. Overall, the reduced load on the national healthcare system from these initiatives has been on the order of millions of dollars saved (Campaign to End Loneliness, 2021).

Remedies for Loneliness

If your scores on our loneliness instrument were high, do not despair. We have several suggestions for you to try out that should help reduce loneliness. While many of these are behavioral and cognitive, further health neuroscience should be able to explain their efficacy and contribute additional remedies.

Understanding loneliness as a natural process, rather than a pathology, is an important first step. There is nothing unnatural about feeling lonely. That fact, in itself, is often very reassuring. Once we understand how the self-preservation aspects of loneliness can interfere with our reconnecting with others, we can cognitively override those impulses.

We often think of loneliness in terms of very close relationships, and much of the loneliness of teens and young adults emerges in the form of wanting a romantic partner and not having one. While romantic relationships are important, it might be comforting to know that several small interactions during the day (weak ties) have as beneficial effect of staving off loneliness as having several close, important relationships (strong ties). If you take a moment to ask your baristas how their days are going, volunteer with a group on a beach cleanup, or stop by your professor's office hour for some advice on career plans, these little human interactions keep us from feeling lonely.

Health Behaviors

A 2009 survey by *Consumer Reports* asked 1000 Americans about how often they performed everyday prevention behaviors. We're happy to report that 91% read the warnings that come with prescription drugs and 87% report NOT drinking beer while using a power tool or mower. On the other hand, 58% never wear a bike helmet, 24% do not use seat belts in cars, and 27% do not use sunscreen when out of doors for extended periods of time. Then there are those 13% who DO apparently drink beer while using a power tool or mower. The data are only now coming in regarding the number of people choosing to be vaccinated for COVID-19 or wear a mask. As of October 2021, 56.8% of U.S. adults are fully vaccinated (Our World in Data, 2021). Worldwide, 47.5% of the adult population has received at least one dose with 35% fully vaccinated. Mask wearing has been up and down, depending on timing (pre- or post-availability of vaccination) and local government policies. Health psychologists and neuroscientists will be working to unravel some of these phenomena for years to come.

Health psychologists and health neuroscientists are particularly interested in the following common health behaviors: smoking, nutrition, alcohol use, and exercise. Together, these variables have very large impacts on well-being and longevity. Ford et al. (2009) found that people could reduce their risk for chronic disease (e.g., heart disease, cancer, and diabetes) by a whopping 78% simply by adopting four health habits: never smoke, exercise at least 30 minutes each day, maintain a nonobese weight, and eat a healthy diet that includes fruits and vegetables. That sounds easy! Unfortunately, in a sample of over 20,000 adults between the ages of 35 and 65 years, the researchers found only 9.1% did all four health behaviors. The mode (most frequent value) was the 35.4% who engaged in two of the health behaviors; 4% did none of them and 23.7% did only one. Again, the point here is not to "blame the victim," but rather to emphasize the enormity of the task ahead of public health policy-makers to translate scientific knowledge into evidence-based practice.

Smoking

Tobacco use is the leading preventable cause of death, with over 8 million people dying from tobacco use each year (WHO, 2020). Smoking generally reduces life expectancy by about 13 to 14 years. Although global rates of smoking continue to drop, the impact of e-cigarette use complicates the statistics. Many e-cigarette users do smoke traditional cigarettes, but others do not. While the inhalation of burnt tobacco brings its own share of health risks, **nicotine** alone is also risky. Recent scares related to serious lung disease might have slowed the growth in vaping, but between 8 and 10 million Americans vape regularly (CDC, 2020a). The likelihood of smoking is sensitive to a host of demographic variables, including gender, race, ethnicity, education, mental health, and income.

Two aspects of smoking are of particular interest to health neuroscientists. First, most smokers begin smoking in childhood or early adolescence. While there are many social components to this fact, the underlying features of the developing brain contribute as well. Second, tobacco use has a strong relationship with psychological disorders, some of which have important biological correlates. Whether tobacco proves to be a causal factor in these disorders or simply shares a common initiating factor with them, health neuroscience can play an important role in untangling these connections.

Developmental Course of Tobacco Use

Nicotine has established epigenetic capabilities. In particular, it initiates changes in the brain that make it easier to become addicted to other substances, such as cocaine (Ren & Lotfipour, 2019). Coupled with this epigenetic capacity of tobacco, the relative plasticity of the teen brain might account for the special vulnerability to addiction and long-term use among those who begin smoking at an early age.

The teen years have a well-deserved reputation for risky behavior. The adolescent brain features immature connections between the limbic system, the prefrontal cortex, and the amygdala. At the same time, relatively lower levels of serotonin and dopamine activity can lead to mood swings, sensation seeking, and difficulties with emotion regulation. Lower dopamine levels might produce different responses to the rewarding aspects of nicotine than would occur in an older person. Teens are not at all blind to the risks associated with behaviors such as texting while driving, but they respond differently to perceived risks than adults do. They are more likely to make emotional than rational decisions, especially in instances of high arousal. Teens are also far more susceptible to fear of social exclusion than adults, so are likely to be swayed more by social pressure to smoke.

Nicotine and Psychopathology

About 41% of adults with any type of diagnosed psychological disorder smoke tobacco, a percentage that is nearly three times higher than the rate of smoking in the general population (about 14%; Jamal et al., 2016). They are also heavy smokers, consuming nearly one third of all cigarettes sold in the U.S., despite making up about 20% of the population (CDC, 2019). Among people diagnosed with schizophrenia and other severe psychological disorders, the number of smokers is an astonishing 88% (Lucatch et al., 2018).

As discussed early in this chapter, health psychologists are interested in the roles played by the brain in these types of situations. Does smoking produce psychological disorder? Some researchers believe that to be the case, particularly for teens and depression (Martini et al., 2002). Others believe that people with schizophrenia and other severe disorders are smoking to self-medicate, or reduce unpleasant symptoms. Still others suggest that some third factor, possibly genetic, leads people to be both more likely to smoke and to develop severe psychological disorders. These possibilities continue to be hotly debated. They have profound implications for public health policy and the urgency to continue to reduce rates of smoking.

Nutrition

The foods we eat ultimately determine the structure of the body, including the brain. Nutrition, therefore, is a natural part of health neuroscience. Nutrition probably accounts for many of the psychological and health outcomes that vary as a function of socioeconomic status (SES; Rosales et al., 2009). Identifying the optimum intake of nutrients for brain health sounds like a job for a dietician, but that dietician is going to need some assistance from neuroscience.

Epigenetics

Many of the foods we eat have epigenetic capabilities, or the ability to turn genes on or off. Garlic, broccoli, and dietary fiber turn on anticancer genes. The prenatal epigenetic effects of diet are particularly important. As we saw in Chapter 3, pregnant mice fed food laced with bisphenol A (BPA) give birth to offspring that have unusually yellow fur and are obese. The BPA can activate the agouti gene at an inappropriate stage of development. However, if the mother mouse is also given food rich in folate and choline, her pups will have normal weight and brown fur. Prenatal epigenetic effects typically affect offspring for their entire lifetimes. Adults can experience epigenetic changes due to diet, but these are generally reversible.

Disordered Eating

Hunger is a tightly regulated function of the brain, but our eating behaviors are the result of complex combinations of physical and psychological mechanisms. In response to food insecurity, many cultures adopt social norms specifying a "clean plate." It becomes offensive to leave food on your plate. Children raised in such circumstances are likely to learn to ignore their internal signals of hunger, and instead be reliant on external cues (what is on my plate) to decide what and how much to eat.

The end result is that it is surprisingly difficult to "get it right." On one hand, the world has experienced an epidemic of **obesity**. In the United States, obesity in adults increased from 12% of the population in 1991 to 42% by 2018 (CDC, 2020b). Many poor countries face a "double burden" of disease due to the co-occurrence of malnourishment and obesity in low-income families. Malnourishment prenatally and early in development can often lead to obesity when the person is exposed to high-calorie, nutrient-poor foods later on (Haemer et al., 2009).

On the other hand, people experience other types of disordered eating, including anorexia nervosa, bulimia nervosa, and binge-eating disorder (APA, 2013). **Anorexia nervosa** is diagnosed in individuals who combine distorted body image (thinking they are obese when really quite thin) with a body weight below the lower limits considered to be healthy. **Bulimia nervosa** combines bingeing, or consumption of excess calories at one sitting, with guilt and efforts to purge the consumed calories through vomiting, laxatives, and other means. **Binge-eating disorder** overlaps with bulimia nervosa, but without the compensatory purging behaviors.

Disordered eating might have broad genetic vulnerabilities, but most health psychologists view the origin of these conditions to be social, cognitive, and emotional rather than directly biological. However, once they are in place, neural processes often work to keep them there. For example, Frank et al. (2021) used fMRI during a taste reward task with 197 women with a variety of eating disorders and 120 women who did not have an eating disorder. They observed reward prediction errors (see Chapter 8), a dopamine-mediated system that basically indicates how surprised you are about the appearance of a reward. Individuals with restricted types of eating disorders, like anorexia, had higher prediction errors, while individuals with bulimia and binge-eating disorders had lower prediction errors compared to controls. These neural signals might help explain how people manage hunger cues overall. Further neuroscience understanding of the processes supporting disordered eating can lead to better treatments and prevention.

Nutrition and Healthy Brain Aging

One of the most active areas of health neuroscience is the evaluation of healthy brain aging. Dementia takes a terrible toll on the individuals it strikes as well as their families and communities. Many factors, including genetics, contribute to a person's risk for dementia. We discussed some of the cognitive interventions in Chapter 5. Other promising interventions involve nutrition.

Morris et al. (2015) combined aspects of Mediterranean diets and the blood-pressure lowering DASH diet to produce what they called a MIND diet. They found that the **MIND diet** predicted a slower decline in cognition. Comparing the upper third of MIND diet scores (higher adherence to the diet) to the lowest third, the difference in cognitive performance was the equivalent of being 7.5 years younger in age. At this point, you might be anxious to know what is in this diet! The MIND diet contains green leafy vegetables, other vegetables, nuts, berries, beans, whole grains, seafood, poultry, olive oil, and wine, while avoiding red meats, butter and stick margarine, cheese, pastries and sweets, and fried/fast food. How are you doing so far?

Note that Morris et al. conducted a quasi-experimental study. They are not randomly assigning people to diet groups, which is an obvious next step in determining whether the diet actually *causes* the improved cognitive functioning. While their data are compelling, we still don't know to what extent the self-selection of diet influences the results. It is possible that the brains that choose a healthy diet are also those that are less susceptible to cognitive decline. Although the statistics used by Morris et al. and similar studies do a good job of controlling for extraneous effects, nothing works as well as random assignment to groups with placebo control to determine causality. What that placebo control would look like in this case is certainly subject to debate.

Alcohol

Alcohol has such a mixed reputation in health. We just finished reading that wine is a component of the MIND diet, which aims to preserve cognitive functioning in aging. At the same time, excess alcohol consumption leads to nearly 100,000 deaths each year in the U.S., and alcohol-impaired driving adds to this toll by accounting for nearly one-third of driving fatalities (NIAAA, 2020).

Similar to our earlier discussion of smoking, alcohol use and abuse results from complex interactions of biological and social factors. Genetic differences in liver enzymes are predictive of different risk for alcohol abuse across races and ethnicities. One of the health neuroscience contributions in this area has been the examination of the **P300 waveform** and the heritability of alcohol use disorder. The P300 waveform is a standard response seen in event-related potential (ERP) recordings (see Chapter 1) in response to both auditory and visual stimuli. Pre-adolescent sons of individuals with alcohol use disorder who have not yet experienced alcohol show reductions in the amplitude of the P300 wave (Hamidovic & Wang, 2019; Figure 9.8). The existence of the P300 wave was discovered more than 50 years ago, and it is believed to relate to attention. Not only might this neuroscience measure serve as a biomarker for individuals at risk for alcohol use disorder, but it might also help us understand the processes in the brain associated with the risk.

Exercise

Stillman and Erickson (2018) presented the question of **physical activity (PA)** as a model subject to illustrate the efficacy of health neuroscience, so we are providing a bit more space to this topic to work through their rationale. Relative to PA, the brain could be viewed as producing the physical activity, changing due to the physical activity, or mediating the effects of physical activity on other behaviors. When the brain serves the mediator role, PA could produce changes in brain structure or function that could then be translated into different behaviors, such as cognition.

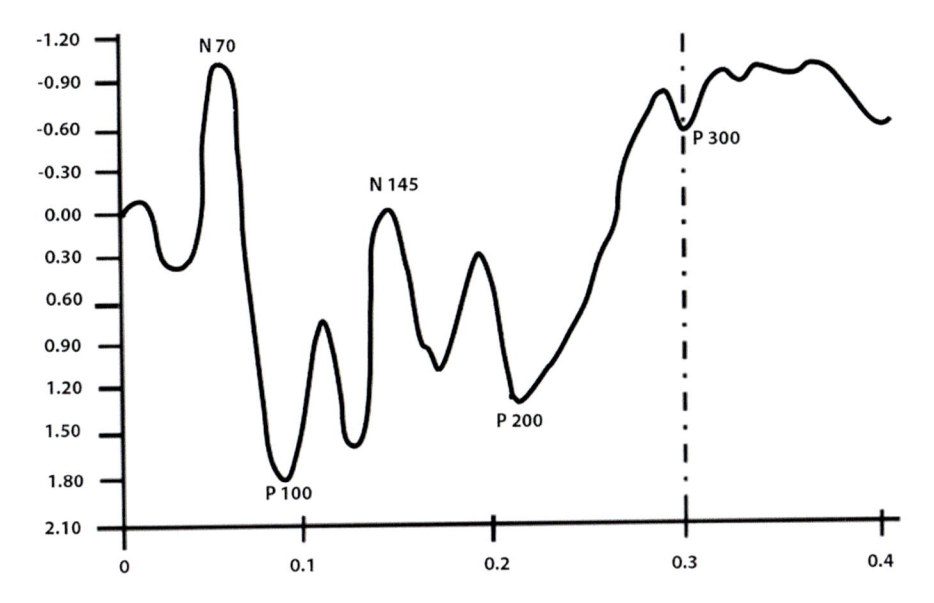

FIGURE 9.8 The height, or amplitude (as shown on the y-axis) of the P300 wave in response to visual and auditory stimuli is lower in the young children of adults with alcohol use disorder. The x-axis here is time.

Source: Author.

The Brain as an Outcome or Mediator

According to these authors, most of the PA literature treats the brain as an outcome variable or mediator. For example, many studies correlate cardiovascular fitness or other measures of PA with performance on cognitive tasks. In particular, executive function and memory appear to be positively correlated with these measures. But as we all know, we cannot infer causality from correlational results. The number of third variables that could influence both PA and cognitive performance are nearly endless, such as educational attainment, socioeconomic status, and so on.

To establish a causal relationship between PA and cognitive performance requires an experiment, and as noted by Stillman and Erickson (2018), a number of these have been done. In most of these cases, inactive adults are randomly assigned to exercise and control groups. In some cases, the control group is in a waitlist situation, where in other designs, the control group engages in another type of activity requiring the same time and commitment, such as toning and stretching.

Erickson et al. (2011, as cited by Stillman & Erickson, 2018) found that their 12-month walking group showed greater volume in the hippocampus compared to a control group that engaged in stretching and toning. This experimental group also showed superior performance on a spatial memory task. Research with mice has shown that the effects on the brain of exercise-induced proteins, such as irisin, might be responsible for the positive effects of PA on cognitive function (Islam et al., 2021).

These findings, interesting as they are, suggest but do not establish a role for the brain as a **mediator**. In other words, without further analysis, we don't know if the structural changes in the brain due to PA are *causing* the improved performance on the spatial memory task. Fortunately, statistical methods can test mediational models. These tests require large sample sizes, so they are not common. The mediation studies that do exist point toward a mediation role for the structural changes in the brain in the PA groups, but most of these have been cross-sectional in design (Erickson et al., 2014, as cited by Stillman & Erickson, 2018).

A **cross-sectional design** evaluates all participants at a given point in time and is subject to several confounds, including age, period, and cohort. **Age effects** involve the processes related to physical and social aging that are not related to the time period or the birth cohort (e.g., Gen Z) to which participants belong. **Period effects** result from events, such as the COVID-19 pandemic, that can occur in the middle of your experiment. **Cohort effects** are factors that describe the effects of being born at a certain time. It is very different to be 20 in 2022 than in 1972. Epidemiologists, who are scientists attempting to discover the causes of various diseases, face these problems all the time, and there are statistical ways to manage these effects. However, it is also desirable to use **longitudinal designs**, where you follow one group of people over a very long period of time. This approach is obviously expensive and time-consuming. A compromise is the **mixed-longitudinal design**, where you take people of different ages and follow them for a shorter period, perhaps five years or so. Engaging in more longitudinal studies should help health neuroscientists explore the brain mediation effects of PA (or any other relevant variable) with more confidence.

The Brain as a Predictor

The general approach to evaluating the brain as a predictor for outcomes is as follows. You supply a stimulus, watch the brain respond, and then assess subsequent health-related behaviors.

For example, both weight gain and success in quitting smoking can be predicted by watching the brain respond to relevant cues, such as high calorie food stimuli in the case of weight gain and the odor of tobacco in the case of smoking cessation. These are examples of how health neuroscience can help identify people who are more or less likely to respond to a particular treatment. These findings can be useful in constructing improved interventions. You can literally test your novel intervention to see how the brain responds.

The success of this type of endeavor, of course, is predicated on a very specific knowledge of what to look for in the brain. We also must consider our old friend reverse inference yet again. Just because we see a pattern of activity in response to high calorie food stimuli does not mean that those areas of the brain *cause* our responses to high calorie food stimuli.

How can we use the brain as predictor model to understand more about the effects of PA on cognition? Think about your own motivation to work out. You know it's good for you. But relatively few of us actually do the recommended amount of PA on a regular basis. Social-cognitive and social-affective psychologists know a great deal about individual differences in motivation to engage in PA. These can include factors such as exercise self-efficacy, or the belief that one can perform a given activity. For example, a physician might tell older, sedentary patients to walk at least 8000 steps per day, but if those patients do not believe that meeting this goal is possible, it is unlikely that they will even try. Other psychological models point to perceptions of health and fitness, social support, and a belief that PA will lead to positive outcomes as crucial predictors of PA engagement and continuity. Health neuroscience will not replace these important observations, but rather enrich them, much like we observed in the chapter on leadership. As Stillman and Erickson (2018) point out, well-established and important social, affective, and cognitive factors still do not explain most of the variability in people's engagement with PA, and the addition of a health neuroscience perspective might help to identify factors responsible for some of this further variance.

Moderators

Our goal here is not to give you a mini-course in research design, but certain concepts, such as moderation, become important to knowing how to evaluate published research in a field and how to address gaps in the research. **Moderating variables** increase or decrease the effects of your independent variable (PA in this case) on outcome variables, such as cognitive performance and brain health. These variables help scientists understand individual differences in response to an independent variable. If you have taken research methods previously, you might have thought of these individual differences as "noise" that should be controlled using random assignment to groups. In other cases, though, we can gain important insights from a further analysis of these factors. Stillman and Erickson (2018) suggest that depressive symptoms might play a role in the relationships between PA, brain structure and function, and cognitive functioning. Statistical methods allow researchers to identify modifiers and assess the extent of their impact on other variables.

Conclusions Based on the Model Research Question

Stillman and Erickson (2018) conclude their description of PA as a model line of research for health neuroscience by encouraging an expansion into the brain as predictor approach. In particular, they argue in favor of using neuroimaging to augment traditional survey methods.

Chapter Summary

In this chapter, we provided a rationale for using neuroscience to better inform areas of health psychology. As technologies in the neurosciences continue to improve, this application of neuroscience is positioned to add important depth to our understanding of topics such as stress, loneliness, and health behaviors by inserting the brain into research designs as a critical variable.

Review Questions

1. Which of the following is representative of a monistic approach to health (LO 9.1)?
   a. A sense of social isolation can weaken responses to COVID-19 infection.
   b. A person's cognitions are unlikely to affect the actions of the immune system.
   c. The immune system is best left to health professionals, as psychologists have little information about this type of basic system.
   d. Studying the activity of the nervous system does not tell us much about a person's health.

2. Which of the following is the best definition of health (LO 9.2)?
   a. The absence of disease, pain, or discomfort.
   b. The absence of disease and psychological disorder.
   c. A state of physical and psychological well-being.
   d. A state of physical well-being.

3. Which of the following is a correct statement about health neuroscience (LO 9.3)?
   a. Health neuroscience research generally requires fewer participants than other types of neuroscience research.
   b. Health neuroscience does not attempt to isolate biomarkers for diseases.
   c. Health neuroscience does not use brain imaging.
   d. Health neuroscience research requires more participants than other types of neuroscience research.

4. Which of the following best describes a person's response to feeling lonely (LO 9.4)?
   a. Lonely people work hard to be nicer to those around them.

b. Lonely people become defensive and selfish.

c. Loneliness is basically the same thing as depression, and causes the same behaviors.

d. The impact of loneliness on people's behavior has yet to be investigated scientifically.

Thought Questions

1. Why do you think humans and other animals evolved the ability to experience stress?
2. The US FDA recently approved e-cigarette products produced by RJ Reynolds because their benefits to people trying to quit smoking surpassed, in the opinion of the committee, the risk of addiction to young users. How would you use a health neuroscience approach to evaluate the outcomes of this decision?

Answer Key for Review Questions

1. a
2. c
3. d
4. b

References

American Psychiatric Association (APA; 2013). *Diagnostic and statistical manual of mental disorders* (5th ed.). Washington, DC: Author.

Boomsma, D. I., Willemsen, G., Dolan, C. V., Hawkley, L. C., & Cacioppo, J. T. (2005). Genetic and environmental contributions to loneliness in adults: The Netherlands Twin Register Study. *Behavior Genetics, 35*(6), 745–752. https://doi.org/10.1007/s10519-005-6040-8

Cacioppo, J. T., & Cacioppo, S. (2018a). Loneliness in the modern age: An evolutionary theory of loneliness (ETL). In J. M. Olson (Ed.), *Advances in experimental social psychology* (Vol. 58, pp. 127–197). New York, NY: Academic Press.

Cacioppo, J. T., & Cacioppo, S. (2018b). The growing problem of loneliness. *Lancet, 391*(10119), 426. https://doi.org/10.1016/S0140-6736(18)30142-9

Cacioppo, J. T., Freberg, L. A., & Cacioppo, S. J. (2022). *Discovering psychology: The science of mind* (4th ed.). Boston, MA: Cengage.

Cacioppo, S., Bangee, M., Balogh, S., Cardenas-Iniguez, C., Qualter, P., & Cacioppo, J. T. (2016). Loneliness and implicit attention to social threat: A high-performance electrical neuroimaging study. *Cognitive Neuroscience, 7*(1–4), 138–159. https://doi.org/10.1080/17588928.2015.1070136

Campaign to End Loneliness (2021). *About*. www.campaigntoendloneliness.org/about-the-campaign/

Cannon, W. B. (1929). *Bodily changes in pain, hunger, fear and rage* (2nd ed.). New York, NY: Harper & Row.

Centers for Disease Control and Prevention (CDC; 2019). *Current cigarette smoking among adults in the United States*. www.cdc.gov/tobacco/data_statistics/fact_sheets/adult_data/cig_smoking/index.htm

Centers for Disease Control and Prevention (CDC; 2020a). *About e-cigarettes*. www.cdc.gov/tobacco/basic_information/e-cigarettes/about-e-cigarettes.html

Centers for Disease Control and Prevention (CDC; 2020b). *Adult obesity facts*. www.cdc.gov/obesity/data/adult.html

Cole, S. W., Capitanio, J. P., Chun, K., Arevalo, J. M., Ma, J., & Cacioppo, J. T. (2015). Myeloid differentiation architecture of leukocyte transcriptome dynamics in perceived social isolation. *Proceedings of the National Academy of Sciences of the United States of America, 112*(49), 15142–15147. https://doi.org/10.1073/pnas.1514249112

Consumer Reports. (2009). *Risky business*. www.consumerreports.org/health/healthy-living/health-safety/risk-taking/overview/risk-taking-ov.htm

de Erausquin, G. A., Snyder, H., Carrillo, M., Hosseini, A. A., Brugha, T. S., Seshadri, S., & the CNS SARS-CoV-2 Consortium (2021). The chronic neuropsychiatric sequelae of COVID-19: The need for a prospective study of viral impact on brain functioning. *Alzheimer's & Dementia, 17*(6), 1056–1065. https://doi.org/10.1002/alz.12255

Dhabhar, F. S. (2009). Enhancing versus suppressive effects of stress on immune function: Implications for immunoprotection and immunopathology. *Neuroimmunomodulation, 16*(5), 300–317. https://doi.org/10.1159/000216188

Erickson, K. I., Creswell, J. D., Verstynen, T. D., & Gianaros, P. J. (2014). Health neuroscience: Defining a new field. *Current Directions in Psychological Science, 23*(6), 446–453. https://doi.org/10.1177/0963721414549350.

Felitti, V. J., Anda, R. F., Nordenberg, D., Williamson, D. F., Spitz, A. M., Edwards, V., Koss, M. P., & Marks, J. S. (1998). Relationship of childhood abuse and household dysfunction to many of the leading causes of death in adults. *American Journal of Preventive Medicine, 14*(4), 245–258. https://doi.org/10.1016/S0749-3797(98)00017-8

Ford, E. S., Bergmann, M. M., Kröger, J., Schienkiewitz, A., Weikert, C., & Boeing, H. (2009). Healthy living is the best revenge: Findings from the European Prospective Investigation into Cancer and Nutrition-Potsdam study. *Archives of Internal Medicine, 169*(15), 1355–1362. https://doi.org/10.1001/archinternmed.2009.237.

Francis, D., Diorio, J., Liu, D., & Meaney, M. J. (1999). Nongenomic transmission across generations of maternal behavior and stress responses in the rat. *Science, 286*(5442), 1155–1158. https://doi.org/10.1126/science.286.5442.1155

Frank, G. K. W., Shott, M. E., Stoddard, J., Swindle, S., & Pryor, T. (2021). Association of brain reward response with body mass index and ventral striatal-hypothalamic circuitry among young women with eating disorders. *JAMA Psychiatry, 78*(10), 112–1133. https://doi.org/10.1001/jamapsychiatry.2021.1580

Frontera, J. A., Sabadia, S., Lalchan, R., Fang, T., Flusty, B., Millar-Vernetti, P., Snyder, T., Berger, S., Yang, D., Granger, A., Morgan, N., Patel, P., Gutman, J., Melmed, K., Agarwal, S., Bokhari, M., Andino, A., Valdes, E., Omari, M., … Galetta, S. (2021). A prospective study of neurologic disorders in hospitalized patients with COVID-19 in New York City. *Neurology, 96*(4), e575–e586. https://doi.org/10.1212/WNL.0000000000010979

Gass, P. (2007). Glucocorticoid receptor mutant mice as models for stress-induced affective disorders. In G. Fink (Ed.), *Encyclopedia of stress* (2nd ed., pp. 176–182). New York, NY: Academic Press. https://doi.org/10.1016/B978-012373947-6.00678-4

Haemer, M. A., Huang, T. T., & Daniels, S. R. (2009). The effect of neurohormonal factors, epigenetic factors, and gut microbiota on risk of obesity. *Preventing Chronic Disease*, 6(3), A96.

Hamidovic, A., & Wang, Y. (2019). The P300 in alcohol use disorder: A meta-analysis and meta-regression. *Progress in Neuro-Psychopharmacology and Biological Psychiatry*, 95, 109716. https://doi.org/10.1016/j.pnpbp.2019.109716

Harper, F. K., Schmidt, J. E., Beacham, A. O., Salsman, J. M., Averill, A. J., Graves, K. D., & Andrykowski, M. A. (2006). The role of social cognitive processing theory and optimism in positive psychosocial and physical behavior change after cancer diagnosis and treatment. *Psychooncology*, 16, 79–91. https://doi.org/10.1002/pon.1068

Holt-Lunstad, J., Smith, T. B., & Layton, J. B. (2010). Social relationships and mortality risk: A meta-analytic review. *PLOS Medicine*, 7(7), 31000316. https://doi.org/10.1371/journal.pmed.1000316

Hughes, M. E., Waite, L. J., Hawkley, L. C., & Cacioppo, J. T. (2004). A short scale for measuring loneliness in large surveys: Results from two population-based studies. *Research on Aging*, 26(6), 655–672. https://doi.org/10.1177/0164027504268574

Hujoel, P. P., Masterson, E. E., & Bollen, A-M. (2017). Lower face asymmetry as a marker for developmental instability. *American Journal of Human Biology*, 29(5), e23005. https://doi.org/10.1002/ajhb.23005

Inagaki, T. K. (2020). Health neuroscience 2.0: Integration with social, cognitive, and affective neuroscience. *Social Cognitive and Affective Neuroscience*, 15(10), 1017–1023. https://doi.org/10.1093/scan/nsaa123

Islam, M. R., Valaris, S., Young, M. F., Haley, E. B., Luo, R., Bond, S. F., Mazuera, S., Kitchen, R. R., Caldarone, B. J., Bettio, L. E. B., Christie, B. R., Schmider, A. B., Soberman, R. J., Besnard, A., Jedrychowski, M. P., Kim, H., Tu, H., Kim, E. Choi, S. H., … Wrann, C. D. (2021). Exercise hormone irisin is a critical regulator of cognitive function. *Nature Metabolism*, 3(8), 1058–1070. https://doi.org/10.1038/s42255-021-00438-z

Jamal, A., King, B. A., Neff, L. J., Whitmill, J., Babb, S. D., & Graffunder, C. M. (2016). Current cigarette smoking among adults—United States, 2005–2015. *Morbidity and Mortality Weekly Report*, 65(44), 1205–1211. https://doi.org/10.15585/mmwr.mm6544a2

King, M., Jones, R., Petersen, I., Hamilton, F., & Nazareth, I. (2020). Cigarette smoking as a risk factor for schizophrenia or all non-affective psychoses. *Psychological Medicine*, 51(8), 1373–1381. https://doi.org/10.1017/S0033291720000136

Liotta, E. M., Batra, A., Clark, J. R., Shlobin, N. A., Hoffman, S. C., Orban, Z. S., & Koralnik, I. J. (2020). Frequent neurologic manifestations and encephalopathy-associated morbidity in Covid-19 patients. *Annals of Clinical and Translational Neurology*, 7(11), 2221–2230. https://doi.org/10.1002/acn3.51210

Lucatch, A. M., Lowe, D. J. E., Clark, R. C., Kozak, K., & George, T. P. (2018). Neurobiological determinants of tobacco smoking in schizophrenia. *Frontiers in Psychiatry*, 9, 672. https://doi.org/10.3389/fpsyt.2018.00672

Martini, S., Wagner, F. A., & Anthony, J. C. (2002). The association of tobacco smoking and depression in adolescence: Evidence from the United States. *Substance Use & Misuse*, 37(14), 1853–1867. https://doi.org/10.1081/JA-120014087

McLennan, A. K., & Ulijaszek, S. J. (2018). Beware the medicalization of loneliness. *Lancet*, 391(10129), 1480. https://doi.org/10.1016/S014-6736(18)30577-4

Meaney, M. J. (2010). Epigenetics and the biological definition of gene x environment interactions. *Child Development, 81*(1), 41–79. https://doi.org/10.1111/j.1467-8624.2009.01381.x

Morris, M. C., Tangney, C. C., Wang, Y., Sacks, F. M., Barnes, L. L., Bennett, D. A., & Aggarwal, N. T. (2015). MIND diet slows cognitive decline with aging. *Alzheimer's & Dementia, 11*(9), 1015–1022. https://doi.org/10.1016/j.jalz.2015.4.011

National Institute on Alcohol Abuse and Alcoholism (NIAAA). (2020). *Alcohol facts and statistics.* www.niaaa.nih.gov/publications/brochures-and-fact-sheets/alcohol-facts-and-statistics

Our World in Data (2021, October). *Coronavirus (COVID-19) vaccinations.* https://ourworldindata.org/covid-vaccinations?country=OWID_WRL

Ren, M., & Lotfipour, S. (2019). Nicotine gateway effects on adolescent substance abuse. *Western Journal of Emergency Medicine, 20*(5), 696–709. https://doi.org/10.5811/westjem2019.7.41661

Rosales, F., Reznick, J. S., & Zeisel, S. (2009). Understanding the role of nutrition in the brain and behavioral development of toddlers and preschool children: Identifying and addressing methodological barriers. *Nutritional Neuroscience, 12*(5), 190–202. https://doi.org/10.1179/147683009x423454

Selye, H. (1946). The general adaptation syndrome and the diseases of adaptation. *The Journal of Clinical Endocrinology & Metabolism, 6*(2), 117–230. https://doi.org/10.1210/jcem-6-2-117

Selye, H. (1975). Confusion and controversy in the stress field. *Journal of Human Stress, 1*(2), 37–44. https://doi.org/10.1080/0097840X.1975.9940406

Smith, C. (2012). Using rodent models to simulate stress of physiologically relevant severity: When, why and how. In X. Qian (Ed.), *Glucocorticoids: New recognition of our familiar friend.* www.intechopen.com/chapters/41175

Stillman, C. M., & Erickson, K. I. (2018). Physical activity as a model for health neuroscience. *Annals of the New York Academy of Sciences, 1428*(1), 103–111. https://doi.org/10.1111/nyas.13669

Thompson, P. M., Jahanshad, N., Ching, C. R. K., Salminen, L. E., Thomopoulos, S. I., Bright, J., Shatokhina, N., Tilot, A. K., Dennis, E. L., McMahon, A. B., Nir, T. M., Pizzagalli, F., Shiroishi, M. S., Villalon-Reina, J. E., Bauen, B. T., Dannlowski, U., Opel, N., Hahn, T., Bertolín, S., … Zelman, V. (2020). ENIGMA and global neuroscience: A decade of large-scale studies of the brain in health and disease across more than 40 countries. *Translational Psychiatry, 10*, 100. https://doi.org/10.1038/s41398-020-0705-1

University of Oxford (2020, May 1). *Using MRI to investigate the effect of COVID-19 on the brain.* www.ndcn.ox.ac.uk/news/using-mri-to-investigate-the-effect-of-covid-19-on-the-brain

Van Cauter, E., Leproult, R., & Plat, L. (2000). Age-related changes in slow wave sleep and REM sleep and relationship with growth hormone and cortisol levels in healthy men. *JAMA, 284*(7), 861–868. https://doi.org/10.1001/jama.284.7.861

World Health Organization (WHO). (2003). *WHO definition of health.* www.who.int/about/definition/en/print.html

World Health Organization (WHO). (2020). *Tobacco.* www.who.int/news-room/fact-sheets/detail/tobacco

Glossary

Age effects	Effects of aging on a characteristic.
Alcohol	Beverages containing ethyl alcohol as an intoxicant.

Anorexia nervosa	An eating disorder characterized by lower-than-healthy body weight and a distorted body image.
Biomarkers	Any biological indication distinguishing between typical and unhealthy processes and conditions.
Binge-eating disorder	An eating disorder characterized by overeating and guilt, but lacking compensatory purging behavior.
Bulimia nervosa	An eating disorder characterized by guilt, overeating, and purging efforts to compensate for overeating.
Cohort effects	Effects of being born at a particular point in history; generational effects.
Cortisol	A glucocorticoid neurohormone released in response to activity in the HPA axis; involved in glucose metabolism.
Cross-sectional design	A study conducted at one point in time with participants of different ages.
Dualism	A philosophy of mind and body that sees them as separate entities.
General adaptation syndrome (GAS)	A classic theory of stress made up of three stages: alarm, resistance, and exhaustion.
Health	A state of complete physical, mental, and social well-being and not merely the absence of disease or infirmity.
Health neuroscience	An interdisciplinary field focused on understanding how the brain affects and is affected by physical health.
Hypothalamic-pituitary-adrenal axis (HPA axis)	A primarily hormonal response to perceived threat resulting in the release of cortisol into the bloodstream.
Loneliness	A perceived state of social isolation.
Long COVID	A set of symptoms following infection with COVID-19 that outlasts the disease itself.
Longitudinal design	A study that follows a group of participants over a long period of time.
Mediator	A variable linking an independent variable and a dependent variable that explains the relationship between the two variables.
MIND diet	A diet featuring fruits, vegetables, nuts, berries, beans, whole grains, seafood, poultry, olive oil and wine believed to reduce the risk of cognitive decline.

Mixed-longitudinal design	A compromise between a cross-sectional and longitudinal design in which participants of different ages are followed for a limited period of time.
Moderating variable	A factor that increases or decreases the effects of an independent variable on a dependent variable.
Monism	A philosophy of mind and body that sees the mind as the outcome of activity in the brain.
Nicotine	The major psychoactive substance found in tobacco products.
Obesity	Medically defined as a body mass index (BMI) of 30 or higher.
P300 waveform	A feature observed in event-related potentials that might distinguish between people based on their risk for alcohol use disorder.
Period effects	Effects of current events on a measured variable.
Physical activity (PA)	Exercise.
Stress	An unpleasant emotional state resulting from the perception of danger.
Stressors	Sources of stress.
Sympathetic adrenal-medullary system (SAM)	A fast neural response to the perception of threat resulting in a burst of norepinephrine and epinephrine release.

10 | Robotics and Artificial Intelligence

LEARNING OBJECTIVES

After reading this chapter, you should be able to:

▶ 1. Describe the methods used to assess different types of consciousness and relate the current state of artificial intelligence (AI) to these benchmarks.

▶ 2. Trace the symbiotic relationship over time between computer science, cognitive science, and neuroscience.

▶ 3. Describe how studies of model organisms, including invertebrates, vertebrates, and primates, have contributed to the development of robotics.

▶ 4. Summarize the types of neural interfaces currently in use and potentially available in the future, with an emphasis on their ethical implications.

▶ 5. Evaluate the state of human–robot relations, including issues related to social robots and the use of robotics in war.

Can a Robot Be Conscious?

What does it mean to be **conscious**? It is easy to describe the opposite, unconsciousness, as lack of awareness. But consciousness itself has many different meanings. We can be conscious of ongoing events, both internally and externally. We can feel self-conscious, or sensitive to how we appear to others. We can be more or less conscious as we focus on our homework, daydream, or sleep. Sigmund Freud, who rarely makes an appearance in a neuroscience text, framed the conscious mind as a place in which ideas could be voluntarily accessed.

As if that question were not difficult enough, we can ask who or what is conscious? Most of us would agree that bacteria and viruses are incapable of consciousness, but that humans are, so that somewhere during evolution, consciousness became possible. But where? Further, is consciousness limited to individuals, or is there something like a collective consciousness? Army ants (*Eciton*) are not impressive as individuals, but together, show remarkable abilities to coordinate their actions, often building nests of nearly one million individuals.

What would it mean for a machine to become conscious? Hollywood certainly has some answers for us, and while some are benign ("Number Five" in the 1986 film *Short Circuit*), others are much less so (the memorable Arnold Schwarzenegger role in the original 1984 *Terminator*). In artificial intelligence (AI), **"weak" AI** refers to the ability to demonstrate intelligent behavior, while **"strong" AI** refers to full human cognition, including consciousness (Searle, 1980). Currently, many robots possess weak AI, and we seem to be getting closer to producing machines with strong AI.

The classic **Turing test**, developed by Alan Turing to assess strong AI in 1950, suggested that if you held a conversation with another human and a machine without being able to tell who was who, the machine passed the test. As far as we know, nobody has built such a machine, but efforts are coming closer and closer. A program that impersonated a 13-year-old Ukrainian, the Eugene Goostman program, convinced ten of 30 judges that "he" was really human. In 2018, Google Duplex, an AI voice technology, called a hairdresser to make an appointment without the hairdresser recognizing the AI as not being human. Google Duplex paused before responding and used "ummm" and "uhh." The 7000 people in the audience for this demonstration were suitably astonished, but experts are still debating whether Duplex truly passed the Turing Test.

Not only are robots becoming more cognitively similar to humans, but they are behaviorally so as well. Hanson Robotics produces "Sophia," whose cameras allow her to make eye contact and recognize people (Figure 10.1). Like Alexa and Siri, she features outstanding voice recognition and can chat with you. Hiroshi Ishiguro of Osaka University is on a mission to produce the most human-like robots possible, as he believes that this will make it easier for us to get along with robots. Ishiguro has even produced a robot that looks like himself! His robots are so lifelike that people have mistaken them for real people. We seem a few short steps away from *Star Trek*'s famous android Mr. Data.

But will these highly realistic robots become capable of true consciousness? In addition to the Turing Test, psychologists discuss the use of the mirror or **rouge test** as an indication of the self-awareness aspect of consciousness. Developmental psychologists find that human children generally recognize themselves in a mirror (as opposed to thinking that the image represents another child) at around the age of 18 months (Lewis & Brooks-Gunn, 1979). If you place a dot of color, perhaps rouge or lipstick, on children's foreheads at this age, they will touch their forehead. Prior to 18 months, they are more likely to reach out to touch the spot on the "baby in the mirror." Comparative psychologists have tested a wide range of animals to see who does or does not pass the mirror test. You might have observed that your cat most definitely does not recognize itself in a mirror.

ROBOTICS AND ARTIFICIAL INTELLIGENCE

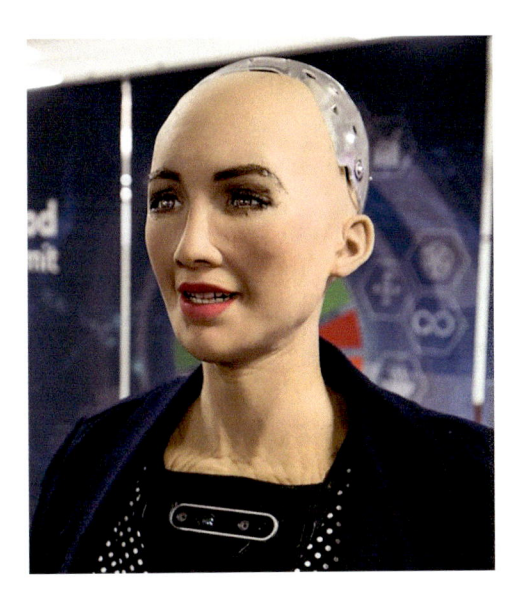

FIGURE 10.1 Hanson Robotics' Sophia can make eye contact and have a nice chat with you.
Source: https://commons.wikimedia.org/wiki/File:Sophia_at_the_AI_for_Good_Global_Summit_2018_(27254369347)_(cropped).jpg

FIGURE 10.2 The Nao robot might have demonstrated self-awareness.
Source: https://commons.wikimedia.org/wiki/File:NAO_waving.JPG

SoftBank Robotics' NAO robot is promoted as a tool to "welcome, inform, and entertain visitors" (SoftBank Robotics, n.d.). NAO[6], launched in 2018, can recognize shapes, objects, and people. It has touch sensors, sonars, and an inertial unit that allows the robot to locate itself in space. Not only has NAO passed the mirror test, but researchers claim other evidence of self-awareness (Bringsjord et al., 2015; Figure 10.2). Researchers told three of the NAO robots that two of them were given a pill that prevented them from speaking, while one was given a placebo. Two were simply muted. When the robots were asked who had received the active pills, one answered "I don't know." After a short pause, the robot said "Sorry, I know now. I was able to prove that I was not given a dumbing pill." What do you think? Did this robot demonstrate self-awareness?

A Long and Positive Collaboration

Cognitive psychology, which today includes human experimental psychology on topics such as memory and attention, computer analogies, and cognitive neuroscience, has had a long and fruitful relationship with computer science (Figure 10.3). In addition to a general dissatisfaction with the strict behaviorism of the first half of the 20th century, cognitive psychology was spurred forward by innovations in computer science. Like the human mind, computers must process input, store it, and then produce some sort of output. This model, overly simple by today's standards, nonetheless provided a starting point for modeling information processing.

FIGURE 10.3 Computer pioneer Grace Hopper demonstrates the first commercial computer, UNIVAC, around 1960.

Source: https://commons.wikimedia.org/wiki/File:Grace_Hopper_and_UNIVAC.jpg

Simultaneously, computer scientists were intrigued by the possibility of building machines that could perform human tasks, such as recognizing handwriting or the spoken word. Mathematician Norbert Wiener published his book *Cybernetics* in 1948, which stimulated further work on artificial intelligence. Wiener compared the actions of early computers to his mathematical analysis of brain waves. The actual term "artificial intelligence" is credited to John McCarthy, who use the term for a conference proposal in 1956 (Moor, 2006). Early efforts, however, were limited by the primitive state of the computer and its prohibitive expense. Renting a computer for a month in 1950 would cost the equivalent of over $2 million in today's dollars. Even fMRI technology is not that bad!

The field advanced over the next two decades as computers themselves improved, but experienced a big jump forward in the 1980s. "Deep learning" techniques and artificial neural networks allowed computers to learn from experience. Expert systems were developed to copy the decision-making of an expert human.

The 21st century saw two of the major barriers to AI removed—memory capacity and speed. Just ask one of your older professors about the speed and capacity of an early Apple IIe computer (which cost far more than today's much fancier models). The solution of these physical problems launched the current era of "big data." Huge amounts of data can be collected and processed. You chat with AI online or on the phone before you get to speak with a human representative. Your patterns of online activity are carefully analyzed for use in ad targeting. Driverless cars are on the road, and it is likely that the "universal translator" in *Star Trek* will be part of our phones soon. A long-term goal of AI is general intelligence, a machine that surpasses human cognition of all types. This, in turn, raises significant ethical considerations.

At the same time AI was benefitting from cognitive science, cognitive neuroscience is benefitting from AI. Specifically, **computational neuroscience**, or the use of mathematical tools and theories to understand brain function, uses AI for insights in how computation works in the brain.

Particularly important to both AI and neuroscience is the concept of the artificial neural network. An **artificial neural network** contains layers of "nodes," which operate like neurons (Figure 10.4). Just like early behaviorist views of the mind as a "black box" between stimuli and responses, artificial networks feature an input layer that connects to a "hidden layer," which then connects to an output layer. Connections between the layers feature mathematical weightings and operate like synapses. The system is "trained" by feeding it data, comparing output to ideal output, and using the difference between the original and ideal output to adjust the mathematical weightings. **Deep neural networks**, like the computer that beat a champion human player in the game Go in 2015, feature many hidden layers and extensive training.

How does this work? Imagine the facial recognition that allows you to tag a social media photo or access your phone. Input could be arrays of numbers that describe

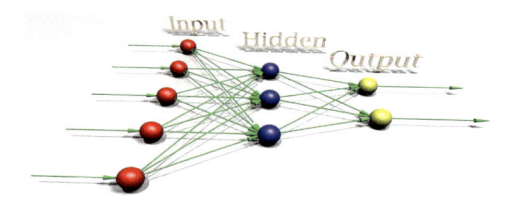

FIGURE 10.4 In a simple artificial neural network, the nodes (colored balls) play the role of neurons while the mathematical weights assigned to the connections (green arrows) represent synapses.
Source: www.flickr.com/photos/fdecomite/3237967443

each pixel in an image of a face. The hidden layer weightings assign their mathematical weights to these inputs and bingo, the photo is identified.

Understanding how the network functions can lead to further insights about how networks in the brain operate. Daniel Yamins and his colleagues (2014) constructed neural networks that could learn to recognize objects. Their network was modeled after the way the brain processes vision. The network received input from thousands of images of 64 objects that varied in size or position. After all, this is what we do every day. My coffee cup is still recognized as my coffee cup when it is upside down in the dishwasher, positioned in my Keurig, and sitting on my desk. My vantage point relative to the coffee cup and the lighting in my house do not interfere with my ability to recognize my trusty friend. The network constructed by Yamins et al. produced different patterns of activity as it learned about the objects. The researchers compared these patterns to real recordings taken from monkeys performing similar tasks. The networks that did the best job of recognizing objects had patterns of activity that were most like those recorded from the monkeys.

Neuroscientists already have quite a bit of knowledge about how the visual system operates. Other brain processes, however, are still obscure. The development of an artificial neural network at least provides a starting place for the neuroscientist. If the machine can perform a task this way, maybe the brain does something similar.

AI also offers workarounds for ethical considerations, at least for now! Neuroscientists, beginning with Karl Lashley (1929), have used deliberate brain damage in the form of lesions or larger ablations to identify components of the brain that are necessary to carry out a function. These destructive methods raise substantial ethical concerns in animal research and are impossible in human research. Animals, while like humans in many ways, still are not human, requiring us to generalize more than is comfortable in some instances. Humans also engage in behaviors of interest, such as language, that are either absent or far different in other animals, depending on your point of view. Using AI allows researchers to selectively deactivate neural components modeled after human brains to see what happens next.

AI and cognitive neuroscientists continue to collaborate on questions of interest. For example, the type of machine learning we have been discussing is known as **"supervised" learning**. Images are supplied as input and labeled regarding their content, such as bird or dog. While humans are fully capable of learning this way, babies learn to recognize many objects without somebody labeling them every time. Even pigeons, which are much smarter than their "bird brained" reputation implies, can learn to extract concepts from images such as "fish" or "people." When they are reinforced for pecking at images containing the target object, they can perform correctly when shown new images of the concept (Herrnstein, 1979; Herrnstein & de Villiers, 1980). We don't know much about how this type of **unsupervised learning** takes place. AI researchers, such as Yamins, are attempting to model this behavior by teaching the computer to be curious and to explore. The AI models can then help generate testable hypotheses for neuroscientists to use.

AI also has more practical attributes to share with cognitive neuroscience, or neuroscience in general. We have seen on several occasions in this textbook that the type of data used in neuroscience, such as fMRI data, is massive and complex. In the large collaborations we need, like ENIGMA as described in Chapter 9, patterns might be difficult for human beings to detect. This is where AI steps in, taking the form of machine learning which can sort through huge datasets and identify subtle patterns.

Models for Robots

It is interesting to note that the first autonomous robot was built in the early 1950s, not by an engineer, but by a neuroscientist, William Grey Walter. Walter wanted to demonstrate that neuron-like electronic devices could bridge sensory input and action. Thirty years later, another neuroscientist by the name of Valentino Braitenberg speculated on the possibilities of vehicles having sensors and networks inspired by the brain. Braitenberg argued that such machines could teach us about how the nervous system operates.

These pioneers shared a commitment to building machines to interact with environments, rather than machines processing information in isolation. Floreano et al. (2014) argue that just as nervous systems require an understanding of the body, AI systems benefit when they have the capability to "behave." Robots, therefore, have been modeled after a whole host of living animals, from invertebrates to humans, to capture aspects of behavior that each type does best. In turn, lessons learned from trying to model living creatures has provided new insights to neuroscientists.

Invertebrates

The simplicity of invertebrate systems, such as the famous sea slug *Aplysia californica*, has provided neuroscientists with many useful insights. Robotics shares this approach.

Many robots are modeled after insects. Insects typically respond with approach or avoidance to sensory input. A well-known example is the ability of crickets to discriminate among songs of male crickets and then locate the male. Webb and Scutt (2000) constructed a model that could reproduce this behavior. Further, their work was able to lend support to one of two competing hypotheses. Their results were consistent with a single neural system capable of both discrimination and localization rather than a hypothesis proposing two separate systems for these functions. Other researchers have been able to model invertebrate responses to odor, such as the ability of lobsters to detect and move toward odors in turbulent water.

Of great interest is the ability of insects, with their compound eyes, to navigate in complex environments. **Compound eyes** are characterized by poor spatial resolution (fine detail), fixed focus (causing blurriness near and far), and nearly complete lack of depth perception. Nonetheless, these eyes serve insects very well. Work with insect-based robots suggests that the insects take advantage of optic flow. If you haven't yet had a course in sensation and perception, **optic flow** refers to the amplitude of image motion (how fast the scene is changing) as you move through an environment. When traveling in a straight line, optic flow correlates with the distance of objects, but not when you turn. House flies will never look the same to you. Flies travel in straight lines interrupted by fast turns as they make their way across your room. These discoveries have not only informed neuroscience but have led to the development of robot drones that can avoid obstacles while flying near the ground or in cluttered environment (Floreano et al., 2014).

Invertebrate models have also been used to learn about output, or in this case, movement. Izquierdo and Beer (2013) outlined the necessary features of a nervous system capable of generating the movements of a worm. Robot models of insects with legs are used to study the generation of rhythm and coordinated gait, either by reflexes or **central pattern generators**. Central pattern generators are circuits that manage rhythmic movement without input carrying timing information. Imagine for a moment what it would be like to work in a laboratory filled with robot cockroaches, lobsters, insects, and crabs.

Robots have also been used to obtain insights into higher cognitive functions of insects, such as their ability to navigate over large distances over long periods of time. How does the honeybee find its way back to the hive? Robots have allowed researchers to test several competing theories, most of which involve brief visual snapshots of the target location and comparisons between those images and what is currently seen.

Webb (2020) points out that insects face many of the same challenges faced by vertebrates, and manage to survive with much simpler nervous systems. The fruit fly brain contains about 135,000 neurons, a minute amount compared to mice (70 million) or humans (86 billion). Techniques such as optogenetics, in which single cells in freely moving animals can literally be turned on by the application of light, have allowed neuroscientists to gain detailed knowledge of brain circuits. This foundation can then be modeled using computers, followed by testing the models in robot bodies in real environments. Webb (2020) describes how this process has led to robots that can mimic the active pursuit of dragonflies and the orienting of praying mantises. Further examination of the central complex of insect brains and mushroom bodies, which participate in learning about odor, are likely to lead to even more effective robots.

British startup, Opteran Technologies (2021), uses the honeybee brain, with its approximately 1 million neurons, as a model for its range of commercial robots. In contrast to the autonomous robots built for research, the insect-based robots do not require expensive and time-consuming deep machine learning or extensive data sets as input. Opteran engineers designed a robotic dog that can navigate through mazes using a single computer chip and two cameras. This results in a very lightweight (30 grams) design that requires only 3 watts of energy. Most other robots must be recharged after one half hour at most.

Vertebrates

Despite their more complicated nervous systems, vertebrates also engage in movement and sensory behaviors that lend themselves to modeling with robots.

The lamprey, a very primitive, eel-like animal, has a very well-understood nervous system. As a result, the lamprey has served as a model for many swimming robots (Figure 10.5). While these are primarily of interest to researchers, they also have practical uses, such as underwater inspection and maintenance or cleaning up microplastics in oceans. Robots can use similar mechanisms to mimic the four-legged gait of cats and dogs, and in one case, even camels.

FIGURE 10.5 Robots can mimic the movement of the lamprey, a primitive vertebrate.
Source: Karla Freberg.

While vision in vertebrates is obviously important, considerable effort has gone into replications of touch. We will discuss touch in more detail in a later section on prostheses. For now, robot models of whiskers have provided insight into the tactile systems of mammals. Many animals are dependent on whiskers, often more than on vision, for navigating through a space. Whiskers allow animals to assess the position, shape, and texture of objects they encounter, much like humans do when engaging in "active touch," or exploring an object you can't see by feeling it.

Robots can also mimic the navigation of rats through a space. This process, involving place cells in the hippocampus, is relatively well understood from a neuroscience perspective. Place cells respond to visual input and change their rate of firing depending on the rat's location. Robots modeling these place cell networks can return to goals, even when their starting points are changed.

Primates

Primate behavior is almost impossibly complex, but that has not deterred scientists anxious to model these behaviors.

Probably the best understood aspects of primate behavior is movement. Even that is remarkably complicated. Based on the development of a series of robots, designers concluded that we need some sort of internal representation of our bodies to move. A previously popular, competing hypothesis suggested that all you needed to do was program the muscle lengths needed to attain a position. This latter hypothesis simply did not fit observations from robots, so has been largely discarded.

We don't just move, but we also plan to move, which adds a further layer of complexity to the tasks of the robotics scientist. Fortunately, the situation is simplified somewhat by the fact that animals often use somewhat stereotypical ways to move. One approach to understanding the planning of movement is to identify movement "**primitives**" or specific actions like walking or a golf swing. Not only have movement primitives proved useful to robot designers, but they also help the neuroscientist understand **mirror neurons**. These neurons are activated when observing movement primitives, such as "reaching for food," regardless of who is doing the movement (self or other). This suggests that movement primitives enjoy a very specific representation in the brain.

Joint work on movement by neuroscientists and robotics scientists based on primates largely consists of reach and grasp movements. Primate walking incorporates the whole body and requires recording from the spinal cord, which is difficult to accomplish (Floreano et al., 2014). Humanoid robots can certainly walk, and often quite realistically, but their movements are not closely connected to the neuroscience of walking. Engineers have simply built the best walking machines they can, without trying to model human walking. Further research will be necessary to bring robotics and neuroscience closer together in this area of study.

Neural Interfaces and Prosthetics

Elon Musk's Neuralink project, which has the long-term goal of linking human brains and AI, along with Facebook's initiatives in wearable neural interface tech, brought increased awareness of the potential of neural interfaces, both in patients with neural conditions and in healthy individuals.

Neural interfaces are devices that interact with the nervous system. The devices can be implanted in the brain itself or worn outside, and can stimulate activity, record activity, or both. Efforts to use neural interfaces are surprisingly ancient. Ancient Egyptians treated arthritis with electric catfish and Romans use electric rays to treat their headaches. Neural interfaces are currently in use in applications such as deep brain stimulation for Parkinson's disease and depression, electric foot stimulators to aid in stroke recovery, cochlear implants for people with inner ear-related hearing loss, EEG headsets for gamers, and transcranial electrical and magnetic stimulation for a variety of purposes (Figure 10.6).

Virtual-reality gaming has pushed the development of wearable interfaces. Vestibular stimulation alters a user's sense of balance and direction. The vestibular system shares the inner ear with mechanisms for detecting sound, and it coordinates our response to the tilting of the head and linear acceleration, such as pulling away from a stop sign in your car. The interface works by applying electrical stimulation through electrodes positioned over the mastoid bones behind each ear. It is often used in conjunction with car racing games. If the user is standing or walking, the stimulation can produce turning or swaying.

FIGURE 10.6 Commercially available Necomimi cat ears change their position in response to basic EEG recordings taken through a headband.

Source: https://www.flickr.com/photos/37996583811@N01/8252497448/

In 2005, Matt Nagle, a patient with quadriplegia, became the first person to control an artificial hand using a brain–computer interface. Nagle had a chip implanted in his brain just under the skull. A computer interpreted the recorded energy and translated it to movement on a screen, allowing Nagle to play the early video game *Pong*, simply by thinking. Subsequently, the same approach was used to allow Nagle to operate a prosthetic hand (Figure 10.7). In 2012, an advanced version of BrainGate allowed a woman who had lost the use of her limbs following a stroke to control a robotic arm to obtain a sip of coffee from a cup.

2013 saw the development of the Argus retinal implant. An electronic stimulator was implanted in the eye, which allowed the patient to see flashing lights and distinctions between light and dark, like the border between the wall and the door. While it doesn't restore normal vision, the emotional benefits were significant. Retinal implants were subsequently approved by the U.S. Food and Drug Administration.

In 2018, researchers at the University of California, Berkeley, developed "neural dust," a tiny wireless nerve monitor and stimulator that can be implanted in many systems (Seo et al., 2016). Initially, neural dust might help people control prosthetics by thought in a much less cumbersome way than BrainGate. If successful, this type of technology might also be used to regulate seizures in patients with epilepsy or even modulate the immune system for those with autoimmune disorders.

Epidural stimulation, or electrical stimulation in the vicinity of the spinal cord through implanted electrodes, allowed patients with spinal injury to move (Harkema

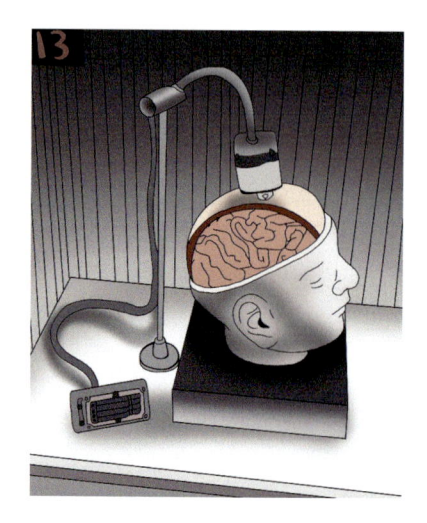

FIGURE 10.7 This Cyberkinetic BrainGate interface allowed Matt Nagle to operate a prosthetic hand with his thoughts.

Source: Karla Freberg.

et al., 2011). By 2018, researchers successfully implanted wireless devices near the spinal cord of patients with spinal injury, allowing them to walk again (Wagner et al., 2018). The current goal is to develop ways to administer this stimulation through external devices without the need for surgery.

In 2019, CTRL-Labs developed devices worn on the wrist that control a mouse on a computer. The device senses signals indicating the intent to move. This literally allows the person to "type" without touching anything. Potentially, nearly any technology could be controlled by such a device, whether that means turning on your oven or typing a paper.

Researchers continue to search for ways to install neural interfaces without invasive surgery. In 2020, two patients with amyotrophic lateral sclerosis (ALS; Lou Gehrig's disease) received wireless implants through their blood vessels rather than brain surgery (Oxley et al., 2021). These implants provided improvement in the ability of the patients to carry out daily living tasks.

Based on discoveries that recordings taken directly from the surface of the brain could distinguish between spoken and imagined vowels and consonants, researchers began to explore the possibility of brain-to-brain communication using imagined sounds. Grau et al. (2014) used non-invasive technology that allowed two people to communicate over distance. Their system was quite complicated. The "speaker" engaged in conscious motor imagery while recorded by surface wireless EEG. These signals were used to translate series of zeros and ones into words. This output was processed by a computer, sent over the internet, and translated into transcranial magnetic stimulation that caused the receiver to see a particular light, or phosphene. Phosphenes are the type of visual stimuli that you might "see" when you are sleepy and rub your eyes. They represent the output of retinal cells. The incoming information contained patterns analogous to words originally encoded by the zeros and ones. While not exactly a substitute for a cellphone call, this was a remarkable feat.

Several researchers have attempted a different approach to interfaces. Instead of inserting technology near the nervous system, they are growing neurons on silicon chips, forming neurochips. Eventually, such neurochips might be implanted to control prostheses and regulate brain functions.

The most pressing current ethical concerns stem from the invasive nature of most neural interfaces. Despite advances in non-invasive technologies, most applications involve surgery. While the patients seem to benefit significantly, the costs and benefits must be weighed carefully. Public opinion on neural interfaces divides when considering medical and non-medical uses. Most people are quite open to the idea of providing mobility and more normalcy to patients who have experienced sensory or mobility handicaps. However, there seems to be less support for augmentation of healthy participants.

Human–Robot Relations

Any *Star Wars* fan can repeat the robot C3PO's common opening line, "I am C-3PO, human/cyborg relations. And you are?" Technically, and by now you know we like to be technical in neuroscience, a cyborg is not the same thing as a robot. A cyborg has organic elements that have been enhanced with artificial components, so C-3PO doesn't seem to fit this description (Figure 10.8). But who are we to complain about *Star Wars*?

The main point here is how are robots and humans going to get along as the former become more commonplace? Much depends on the type of robot we're discussing. I don't have a close relationship with my Roomba, although I feel some level of guilt and sympathy for its having to clean up after my two very furry Australian shepherds. I'm sorry to say that my husband delights in asking all the latest "stump Alexa" questions that come across his social media feeds. So far, I'm not in the kind of occupation where I must be worried about being replaced by a robot. I'm a little bit wary of reports about robot-assisted surgery, but I am excited about the prospect of driverless cars. I fret when smart people like Elon Musk suggest we should be worried about a *Terminator* robot in the future, but I find the fact that he's now building his own robot reassuring. So overall, I suspect my emotional response to a future of living side-by-side with robots tilts to the positive side.

FIGURE 10.8 *Star Wars'* favorite C-3PO introduces himself as an expert in "human/cyborg relations," but we are still not sure exactly how humans and real robots are going to get along.
Source: www.flickr.com/photos/edwicks_toybox/31622763550

Social Robots

Possibly the most interesting challenge will be our interaction with **social robots**, or robots that interact with humans naturally. We already met Sophia and NAO[6], who fall in this category, but there are many new entries each year. Paro is a seal-like robot designed as a "pet" for people in long-term care (Figure 10.9). Aibo is Sony's playful robotic dog. Social robots have potential for providing emotional support and for building social skills. For example, social robots are being investigated for a possible treatment role for children with autism spectrum disorder (Cabibihan et al., 2013). Others are destined for work-related roles as academic tutors, receptionists, and help desk personnel.

Probably the most controversial of the social robots is the sex robot. I'm pretty sure this might be the last thing you expected to read about in a book on applied behavioral neuroscience. Nonetheless, sex robots are on their way, although they're currently far from being realistic. The sex toy industry globally is worth billions of dollars, so the money required to develop realistic sex robots is not a huge obstacle. However, Hollywood's depiction of Joaquin Phoenix's character falling in love with AI voiced by Scarlett Johansson in the 2013 film *Her* is not likely to be happening soon. Early efforts are still rather basic. Abyss Creations in California has been making RealDoll sex dolls for 20 years, but has recently developed a robotic head named "Harmony" that can be attached to the RealDoll silicon body. Harmony can tilt her head, blink, move her lips, make facial expressions, and hold short conversations. Using a mobile app, users can give Harmony levels of 18 personality traits, from intellectual and kind to jealous and adventurous. Harmony's mood shifts as a function of the way "she" is treated. The head

FIGURE 10.9 Paro, a robotic seal-like animal, provides emotional support to people who are unable to own a living pet, such as individuals in long-term care.

Source: www.flickr.com/photos/fondazionesantalucia/45908701391

alone costs between $8000 and $10,000, and the RealDoll body, which doesn't move on its own, costs another $6000 or more.

One of the interesting outcomes of Harmony's development is an observation by her creators that they don't want her to be *too* lifelike. This is in response to the "**uncanny valley**" hypothesis that states that people become generally more favorable toward robots as they become more human-like, just until they become really human-like (Figure 10.10). This hypothesis was first proposed by robotics expert Masahito Mori (1970/2012), and although it has been widely accepted, relatively little empirical research has been done on the existence of the uncanny valley.

The research on the uncanny valley has been inconsistent, likely due to some of the vagueness of Mori's initial model (Kätsyri et al., 2015). What exactly constitutes "humanness" when we are judging a stimulus? What emotional response are we measuring? One of the more promising explanations of the uncanny valley is a perceptual mismatch hypothesis. According to this view, inconsistencies between different levels of human-likeness from different aspects of the stimulus could be the cause of negative reactions. For example, seeing artificial eyes in a human face or vice versa would be potentially upsetting. A variation on this hypothesis suggests that we become increasingly sensitive to deviations from norms as stimuli become more realistic. Faces that are quite average are usually judged as more attractive, and we are sensitive to exaggerations, such as very large eyes. People do not find large eyes off-putting in a cartoon character, but some people find the rather outlandish proportions of a Barbie doll or GI Joe doll upsetting. This same process might explain the uncanny valley. In a meta-analysis of

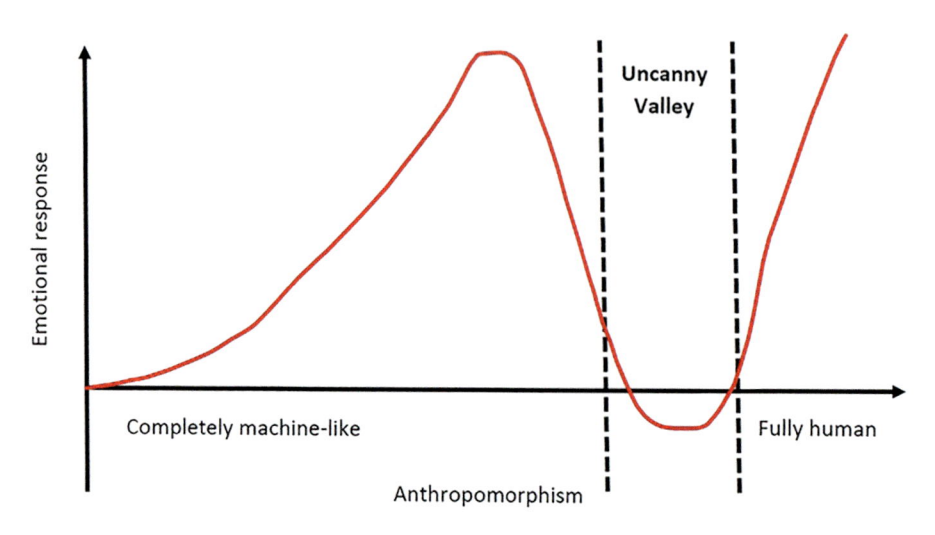

FIGURE 10.10 Mori's "uncanny valley" hypothesis states that comfort increases as robots become more human-like, but then dips (the valley) as they become more fully human.

Source: Author.

the existing research, Kätsyri et al. (2015) found the most support for this perceptual mismatch hypothesis.

The further development of more realistic sex robots raises legal and ethical concerns. If robots ever developed consciousness, this would engage a whole host of issues regarding their rights, including that of consent. While conscious robots are not likely in the near or possibly distant future, ethicists worry about how behavior toward the robot (no consent, possession) could spill over into a person's real-life interactions. Researchers are split between thinking realistic sex robots could reduce problems like sex trafficking or make them worse. More research is definitely needed in this area.

Robots and War

Unmanned drones have participated in the battlefield for decades, but the advent of more sophisticated autonomous robots raises new ethical challenges (Figure 10.11).

Currently, there no specific laws or treaties that prohibit **autonomous weapons**. Some weapons, like cluster bombs, are subject to these specific bans. Existing laws of war still do apply to autonomous weapons, but many people believe that is insufficient. The Campaign to Stop Killer Robots (n.d.) is a coalition of organizations seeking to ban

FIGURE 10.11 Robots, like this Talon, are already a regular part of military operations. The Talon finds and destroys IEDs to keep roads clear.
Source: https://commons.wikimedia.org/wiki/File:Talon_Readies_for_Deployment.jpg

fully autonomous weapons. In contrast, Russia and the U.S. blocked United Nations talks about a pre-emptive ban. China has a program for recruiting an elite group of "patriotic" children to help develop AI weapons. China is expected to develop intelligent and autonomous unmanned systems quickly.

One of the challenges is where to draw the line. Intelligent systems already are part of today's military, and more growth is expected. Robots participate in route clearance, or scanning roads for IEDs. Unmanned drones like the Reaper can kill a target thousands of miles away from the person controlling the drone. Hand-held drones perform surveillance. Current efforts include throwable robots for use in buildings, aerial drones that detect enemy drones, and robotic mules that carry supplies. Most people can agree that a *Terminator*-style robot is a really bad idea, but there are many AI applications in the greyer areas short of that model.

Ghostrobotics (2021) and SWORD International have developed a Special Purpose Unmanned Rifle, or SPUR, which is essentially a SWORD rifle mounted on one of Ghostrobotics' robot dogs. SPUR can be instructed to chamber a first round from an unloaded state as well as clear the chamber and safe the gun. SPUR's aim is accurate to nearly 4000 feet. Although SPUR currently needs a human operator, it is also possible to equip this type of robot with existing sighting systems that detect and "lock onto" potential threats. While the fire command still needs a human, it doesn't take too much imagination to guess that engineers are working on that issue.

In the past, inventors believed that their new technology would reduce the carnage of war. Dr. Gatling, inventor of the machine gun, hoped that his new invention would reduce the number of people needed at Civil War battles, but we all know how that turned out. It is likely that we are currently in the midst of yet another arms race, as Russia's Vladimir Putin has stated that the nation that leads in AI "will be the ruler of the world" (Meyer, 2017). *Star Trek*'s 1967 episode "A Taste of Armageddon," explored what might happen when war was conducted by machine. Like the moral of the episode, policy experts fear that replacing real soldiers with robots would make it easier to decide to go to war. Autonomous weapons are going to make mistakes, just like the humans who program them, and will decide who lives and dies without the morality and compassion of their makers. This might sound more like science fiction than reality, but this technology is on our doorstep today.

Chapter Summary

Computer scientists, cognitive psychologists, and neuroscientists have enjoyed a lengthy, symbiotic relationship in which advances in one field seed further advances in others. We anticipate that this friendly relationship will continue in the future. In the meantime, AI and robotics applications continue to rely on information from the neurosciences to advance their applications. During this process, discoveries and new hypotheses emerge that move neuroscience forward.

Ethical challenges will continue to be a major part of the advancement of AI and robotics, as human minds struggle with profound questions of what it means to be human, what it means to be conscious, and how we should relate to artificial intelligence.

Review Questions

1. Which of the following is the best example of the self-awareness type of consciousness (LO 10.1)?
   a. Experiencing variations in awareness, such as sleep, waking, anesthesia, and coma.
   b. Recognizing one's self in the mirror.
   c. Being aware of ongoing internal and external sensations.
   d. Being aware of the difference between you and others.

2. Which of the following correctly summarizes the relationship between computer science, psychology, and neuroscience (LO 10.2)?
   a. These fields have collaborated closely for decades.
   b. These fields were largely separate for decades, but have begun to collaborate in recent years.
   c. These fields remain quite separate.
   d. Computer science and psychology cooperate, but have yet to include neuroscience in their collaborations.

3. Which of the following robotic processes is LEAST likely to be modeled after real living systems (LO 10.3)?
   a. Insect vision
   b. Central pattern generators
   c. Navigation
   d. Bipedal walking

4. Which of the following would NOT be considered to be a neural interface (LO 10.4)?
   a. A wrist device that functions as a mouse controller
   b. Nootropics
   c. Wireless implants inserted in the blood supply
   d. Neural dust

5. What is the "uncanny valley" (LO 10.5)?

    a. The attitude gap between countries considering the development of autonomous weapons.

    b. The difference of opinion among robotics experts about whether a robot will ever be conscious.

    c. The dislike of robots with characteristics that are very close to human characteristics,

    d. The differences of opinion between cognitive neuroscientists and computer scientists about the development of neural interfaces for healthy people.

Thought Questions

1. Imagine that a new neural interface technology for enhancing memory and cognitive ability was invented. What policies would you recommend for equitable access to this technology?

2. Assume for a moment that a robot could achieve consciousness. What are the ethical guidelines and policies you would recommend for dealing with this situation?

3. What policies would you recommend for the development of autonomous weapons?

Answer Key for Review Questions

1. b
2. a
3. d
4. b
5. c

References

Bringsjord, S., Licato, J., Govindarajulu, N., Ghosh, R., & Sen, A. (2015). Real robots that pass tests of self-consciousness. *Proceedings of the 24th IEEE International Symposium on Robot and Human Interactive Communication (RO-MAN 2015*, pp. 498–504). New York, NY: IEEE. https://doi.org/10.1109/ROMAN.2015.7333698

Cabibihan, J-J., Javed, H., Ang, J., Jr., & Aljunied, S. M. (2013). Why robots? A survey on the roles and benefits of social robots in the therapy of children with autism. *International Journal of Social Robotics, 5*, 593–618. https://doi.org/10.1007/x12369-013-0202-2

Campaign to Stop Killer Robots (n.d.). *About us*. www.stopkillerrobots.org/about/

Floreano, D., Ijspeert, A. J., & Schaal, S. (2014). Robotics and neuroscience. *Current Biology, 24,* R910–R920. https://doi.org/10.1016/j.cub.2014.07.058

Ghostrobotics (2021). *Robots that feel the world*. www.ghostrobotics.io/about

Grau, C., Ginhoux, R., Riera, A., Nguyen, T. L., Chauvat, H., Berg, M., Amengual, J. L., Pascual-Leone, A., & Ruffini, G. (2014) Conscious brain-to-brain communication in humans using non-invasive technologies. *PLOS One, 9*(8), e105225. https://doi.org/10.1371/journal.pone.0105225

Harkema, S., Gerasimenko, Y., Hodes, J., Burdick, J., Angeli, C., Chen, Y., Ferreira, C., Willhite, A., Rejc, E., Grossman, R. G., & Edgerton, V. R. (2011). Effect of epidural stimulation of the lumbosacral spinal cord on voluntary movement, standing, and assisted stepping after motor complete paraplegia: A case study. *The Lancet, 377*(9781), 1938–1947. https://doi.org/10.1016/S0140-6736(11)60547-3

Herrnstein, R. J. (1979). Acquisition, generalization, and discrimination reversal of a natural concept. *Journal of Experimental Psychology: Animal Behavior Processes, 5*(2), 116–129. https://doi.org/10.1037/0097-7403.5.2.116

Herrnstein, R. J., & de Villiers, P. A. (1980). Fish as a natural category for people and pigeons. In G. H. Bower (Ed.), *The psychology of learning and motivation* (Vol. 14, pp. 59–95). New York, NY: Academic Press.

Izquierdo, E. J., & Beer, R. D. (2013). Connecting a connectome to behavior: An ensemble of neuroanatomical models of *C. elegans* klinotaxis. *PLOS Computational Biology*. https://doi.org/10.1371/journal.pcbi.1002890

Kätsyri, J., Förger, K., Mäkäräinen, M., & Takala, T. (2015). A review of empirical evidence on different uncanny valley hypotheses: Support for perceptual mismatch as one road to the valley of eeriness. *Frontiers in Psychology, 6,* 390. https://doi.org/10.3389/fpsyg.2015.00390

Lashley, K. S. (1929). *Brain mechanisms and intelligence: A quantitative study of injuries to the brain*. Chicago, IL: University of Chicago Press.

Lewis, M., & Brooks-Gunn, J. (1979). *Social cognition and the acquisition of self*. Boston, MA: Springer. https://doi.org/10.1007/978-1-4684-3566-5_8

Meyer, D. (2017, September 4). *Vladimir Putin says whoever leads in artificial intelligence will rule the world*. Fortune. https://fortune.com/2017/09/04/ai-artificial-intelligence-putin-rule-world/

Moor, J. (2006). The Dartmouth College Artificial Intelligence Conference: The next fifty years. *AI Magazine, 27*(4), 87–91.

Mori, M. (1970/2012; translated by K. F. MacDorman & N. Kageki). The uncanny valley. *IEEE Spectrum*. https://spectrum.ieee.org/the-uncanny-valley

Opteran Technologies (2021). *Intelligence is natural*. https://opteran.com/

Oxley, T. J., Yoo, P. E., Rind, G. S., Ronayne, S. M., Lee, C. M. S., Bird, C., Hampshire, V., Sharma, R. P. Morokoff, A., Williams, D. L., MacIsaac, C., Howard, M. E., Irving, L., Vrljic, I., Williams, C., John, S. E., Weissenborn, F., Dazenko, M., Balabanski, A. H., ... Opie, N. L. (2021). Motor neuroprosthesis implanted with neurointerventional surgery improves capacity for activities of daily living tasks in severe paralysis. First in-human experience. *Journal of NeuroInterventional Surgery, 13,* 102–108. https://doi.org/10.1136/neurintsurge-2020-016862

Searle, J. R. (1980). Minds, brains, and programs. *Behavioral and Brain Sciences, 3*(3), 417–457. https://doi.org/10.1017/S0141525X00005756

Seo, D., Neely, R. M., Shen, K., Singhal, U., Alon, E., Rabaey, J. M., Carmena, J. M., & Maharbiz, M. M. (2016). Wireless recording in the peripheral nervous system with ultrasonic neural dust. *Neuron, 91*(3), 529–539. https://doi.org/10.1016/j.neuron.2016.06.034

SoftBank Robotics (n.d.) *NAO[6]*. www.softbankrobotics.com/emea/en/nao

Wagner, F. B., Mignardot, J B., Le Goff-Mignardot, C. G., Demesmaeker, R., Komi, S., Capogrosso, M., Rowald, A., Seáñez, I., Caban, M., Pirondini, E., Vat, M., McCracken, L. A., Heimgartner, R., Fodor, I., Watrin, A., Sequin, P., Paoles, E., Van Den Keybus, K., Eberle, G., ... Courtine, G. (2018). Targeted neurotechnology restores walking in humans with spinal cord injury. *Nature, 563,* 65–71. https://doi.org/10.1038/s41586-018-0649-2

Webb, B. (2020). Robots with insect brains. *Science, 368*(6488), 244–245. https://doi.org/10.1126/science.aaz6869

Webb, B., & Scutt, T. (2000). A simple latency-dependent spiking-neuron model of cricket phonotaxis. *Biological Cybernetics, 82*(3), 247–269. https://doi.org/10.1007/s004220050024

Wiener, N. (1948). *Cybernetics: Or control and communication in the animal and the machine.* Cambridge, MA: MIT Press.

Yamins, D. L. K., Hong, H., Cadieu, C. F., Solomon, E. A., Seibert, D., & DiCarlo, J. J. (2014). Performance-optimized hierarchical models predict neural responses in higher visual cortex. *Proceedings of the National Academy of Sciences of the United States of America, 111*(23), 8619–8624. https://doi.org/10.1073/pnas.1403112111

Glossary

Artificial neural network	A trainable computer network containing layers of nodes that processes input and produces output.
Autonomous weapon	A weapon that independently decides to attack a target.
Central pattern generator	Neural circuit that manages rhythmic movement without input carrying timing information.
Compound eye	Eyes composed of many small eyes, such as those possessed by insects, featuring poor spatial resolution, fixed focus, and little depth perception.
Computational neuroscience	The use of mathematical tools and theories to understand brain function.
Conscious	To be aware.
Deep neural network	Artificial neural network featuring many hidden layers and extensive training.
Mirror neurons	Neurons that are activated when observing a movement regardless of the agent (self or other) carrying out the movement.
Neural interface	Device that interacts directly with the nervous system.
Optic flow	The amplitude of visual image motion as you move through an environment.

Primitives	Specific actions, such as walking or a golf swing.
Rouge test	A test of self-awareness indicated by the ability to recognize one's self in a mirror; also known as a mirror test.
Social robot	A robot designed to interact naturally with humans.
Strong AI	The ability of an artificial system to demonstrate full human cognition, including consciousness.
Supervised learning	Machine learning in which input is supplied to the system with accompanying labels.
Turing test	A definition of a conscious machine as one that could not be distinguished from a human during a conversation.
Uncanny valley	A hypothesis suggesting that humans are more favorable toward robots as they become more human-like up until the point where they become "too" human-like.
Unsupervised learning	Learning in which concepts are extracted from data.
Weak AI	The ability of an artificial system to demonstrate intelligent behavior.

Index

Note: **Bold** page numbers refer to tables; *italic* page numbers refer to figures.

Abyss Creations 255
acetylcholine 37, 45, **46**, 48
action potential 40–41
actuarial approach to violent behavior prediction 92
Adderall 117
adenosine 45, **46**
adrenalin *see* epinephrine
ad targeting 245
Advanced Cognitive Training for Independent and Vital Elderly (ACTIVE) study 121–122
adverse childhood experiences 214, *214*
advertising 132–134; and implicit associations 140; role of emotions in 133, 135–136, 137–138
affect heuristic 136
age effects 232
aggression 84–91; and brain structure 87–89; definition of 84; and genetics/culture 85–87; individual differences in 90–91; and neurochemicals 88–89, 187; proactive/premeditated 85, 86, 88, 89, 91; reactive/impulsive 85, 87–88, *88*, 89;

selective breeding and *86*; within-species 85
agonists 48
Aharoni, E. 92
Aibo (robot) 255
Alcañiz, M. 202
alcohol use 32, 48, 88, 230, *231*
alpha waves 17, 18, 148
altruism 176, 177
Alzheimer's disease 38, 116, 117, 201
Amen, Daniel 53–54, *54*
American Psychiatric Association 55
American Psychological Association 65
amino acids 47
amphetamines 61
amygdala 34, 65, 68, 90, 138, 139, **170**, 196; and aggression 87–88; and decision-making 174; and loss aversion 170; of psychopaths 91
amyotrophic lateral sclerosis (ALS) 253
androgens (prenatal exposure), and aggression 89
anorexia nervosa 229

antagonists 48
anterior cingulate cortex (ACC) 20, 33, 92, 114, 147, 170, **170**, 174, 190
anterior insula **170**, 177
antidepressants 47, 68
antihistamines 47, 61
antisocial personality disorder (ASPD) 197
Aplysia californica 247
applied neuroscience 1
applied research 3, 11
Argus retinal implant 252
arithmetic problems 111–112
arousal 15, 16, 30; autonomic arousal measures 143, 145; and norepinephrine 45; polygraph measures 93, 94
artificial intelligence (AI) 242, 245–247; *see also* robots
artificial neural networks 245, 246, *246*
Asian Disease Problem 173, **174**
astrocytes 39
attention 123, 148; control of 114; selective 114, 115
attention deficit hyperactivity disorder (ADHD) 58, 117, 168; diagnosis of 56–57;

INDEX

inattentive subtype of 56; prevalence rates of 56, 57, *57*; treatment of 61
attitude: affect and 136; and behavior 140–142
autism spectrum disorder 58, 59, 72, 175, 255
autonomic nervous system (ANS) 13–16, 30–31, 35, 36, 139, 143
autonomous weapons 257–258
axons 38, 40

Babiak, Paul 199
Baddeley, A. D. 8
Balconi, M. 189
Bales, R. F. 199
Balthazard, P. A. 194
Banaji, Mahzarin 140
bar fights, and aggression 87–88, *88*
basal ganglia 34, 45, **46**, 72, 88, 91, 139, 170, 177
basic research 2–3, 11
Bass, B. M. 199
Bass, R. 199
Bechara, A. 172
Beer, J. 202
Beer, R. D. 248
behavioral economics 163–164, 166, 172
behavioral genetics 186
behavioral inhibition 114
behavioral neuroscience 3; applied, challenges in 6–11; disputes between academic researchers and practitioners 11–12; methods in 13–22; see also nervous system
benzedrine sulfate 61
Berger, Hans 17
Berns, G. S. 134
Berson, Y. 187
beta waves 17, 18, 148
big data 215, 245

Big 5 personality traits 195
binge-eating disorder 229
biomarkers 215, 219, *220*, 230
biopsychosocial model of health 212
bipolar disorder: diagnosis of 55–56; treatment of 61
bisphenol A (BPA) *70*, 84, 228
blood–brain barrier (BBB) 39, 48, 221
blood oxygenation level dependent (BOLD) contrast 20
body, and mind 211–212
Boto, E. 19
Bowers, J. S. 105
Boyatzis, R. E. 199, 200
Bradley, Charles 61
Brady, James 78
brain 31; adolescent 227; aging, and nutrition 229–230; areas, of psychopaths 91; atrophy 78; and behavior, relationship between 3–4, 5–6, 72; biomarkers 215; blood–brain barrier 39, 48, 221; and choice behavior 165–166; and COVID-19 virus 221–222; damage 192, 222, 246; function, lateralization of 10, 33, 149–150; functional connectivity 195–196; hierarchy 87; images, effect on truthiness of statements 7; and leadership 188–193; left brain/right brain neuromyth 104; lesions 192, 246; lobes of *33*; measures of brain activity 145–146; and mental arithmetic 111–112; microstates 18, 148, *149*, 224; and mind 4; networks 190–191, 199, 246; neuroplasticity 68, 103, 119, 202, 222, 227; as an outcome/mediator, and physical activity 231–232; physical processes in 5; as a predictor, and physical activity 232–233; and psychotherapy 72; recording of brain activity 17–19; reverse inference 7–8; structure, and aggression 87–89; structures involved with assigning value to a choice **170**; synchrony 188–189; training 118–122, *119*; see also nervous system
Brain and Learning Project (OCED) 101–102
BrainGate *252*
brain imaging see neuroimaging
brainstem 31–32, 222
brainstem nuclei 31
brain-to-brain communication 253
Braitenberg, Valentino 247
Brenninkmeijer, Jonna 145, 146
bright narcissism 198
Brosnan, Sarah 176
Brown, James Gordon *137*
Bruer, J. T. 105
bulimia nervosa 229

C-3PO 254, *254*
Cacioppo, John 136–137, 175, 222, 223, 224, *224*
Cacioppo, Stephanie 18, 148, 222, 223
Cade, John 61
caffeine 45, 117–118, *118*
calcium channels 41–42
Campaign to Stop Killer Robots 257–258
Cannon, Walter 37, 216

INDEX

Caspi, Avshalom 83
Castel, A. D. 7
caudate nucleus 177
central nervous system (CNS) 30, *30*, 31–35
central pattern generators 248
cerebellum *29*, 32, 57
cerebral cortex 32–33, 87
cerebral hemispheres 32, 33–34, 149
cerebrospinal fluid (CSF) 32, 39
charisma 187
chemical signaling 41–44, *42*
children: with ADHD 117, 168; adverse childhood experiences 214, *214*; with autism spectrum disorder 255; consumption of caffeine 117–118; deception by 93; with dyslexia 107–108; executive function in 113, 114; headaches in 61; maltreatment 68, 70, 83; mathematics learning 109–110, *110*, 111, 112; multiple language learning 103–104; as neuroscience research participants 106; parent–child interactions 189, *190*; prenatal exposure to synthetic progesterone 89, *90*
cholecystokinin (CCK) **46**, 47
Chow, Tiffany 82
cingulate cortex 33, 35, 139
clinical assessments for violent behavior prediction 92
clinical psychologists 66–67
Clinton, Hillary 20, 147
Coca Cola 151
cognition 136, 194; computerized cognitive training 118–122, *119*; meta-cognition 162; and MIND diet 229–230; nootropics 116–118; and physical activity 231–232, 233; and poverty 214
cognitive behavioral therapy (CBT) 4, 72
cognitive flexibility 114–115
cognitive inhibition 114
cognitive neuroscience 244
cognitive psychology 164, 165, 174, 244
cohort effects 232
Cole, S. W. 211, 222
commissures 32, 34
communication: brain-to-brain 253; neural 39–49; and neuroeducation 105
compound eyes 248
computational neuroscience 245
computerized cognitive training (CCT) 118–122, *119*
computerized tomography (CT) 78
computer science 244–245
confidentiality 22
confirmation bias 161
conformity 161
consciousness 241–242, 257
consumer neuroscience 22, *133*, 134–135; autonomic arousal measures 143, 145; brain activity measures 145–146; consumer segmentation 153–154; electroencephalography 148–150, *149*; emotions 135–139; eye tracking 143, *144*; facial coding 142; functional magnetic resonance imaging 146–148; implicit attitudes 140–142; marketing 151–153; mixed methods 150–151
consumers 132–134
context-dependent memory 8–9
cooperation 176, 177, *177*
corpus callosum 32, 34
corrugator supercilii muscle 14
cortical atrophy, and psychopathy 198
cortisol: and aggression 89–90, 187; effects on health 220; and leadership 187; and stress 218–219, 220
COVID-19 pandemic 173, *210*, 212–213; and brain training 118–119; long COVID 221; neurological outcomes 221–222; practices, and immune system 211–212; stress management during 220
cranial nerves 31, 36, *36*, 63
crickets 248
criminal behavior: aggression 84–91; and nature–nurture interactions 82–84; see also forensic neuroscience
cross-sectional design 232
"Crying Indian" ad 138
CTRL-Labs 253
culture: and aggression 86–87; and deception 93
Cushing's disease 218

Damasio, Antonio 136, 170, 172, 173
dark leadership 196–199
dark triad of personality 196–198
Darth Vader *197*
de Boer, N. S. 116
deception 92–93
decision-making *see* neuroeconomics
deep brain stimulation (DBS) 62, *62*
deep learning 245

deep neural networks 245
default mode network (DMN) 35, 175, 199, 200–201, *200*
delayed gratification 168–169, *169*
delta waves 17
dementia 116, 222, 229
dendrites 38
depression 4, 11, 201; and aggression 89; and bipolar disorder 55–56; and cortisol 218–219; and loneliness 225; and neurogenesis 68; and stress 217; treatment of 63, 65
Descartes, René 4, *5*, 212
developmental dyscalculia (DD) 112
de Voogd, L. D. 65, 66
de Waal, Frans 176
Diablo Canyon Nuclear Power Plant *139*
diagnosis of psychological disorders 54–59; diagnostic categories 55–56; use of observation for 55–56
Diagnostic and Statistical Manual of Mental Disorders (DSM-5) 55, 56, 59
Diamond, A. 115
disordered eating 228–229
Dmochowski, J. P. 150
dopamine 45, **46**, 117, 168, 178, 188, 227
dorsolateral prefrontal cortex (DLPC) 114, 170, **170**
Dowdle, Drew 147
Dowdle, John 147
dragonflies 249
drift-diffusion model 171
Drummond, Edward 79
dualism 4, 211
Dweck, Carol 104
dyscalculia 112

dyslexia 107–108, *108*

e-cigarettes 226
ecological validity 8
economics 163; behavioral 163–164, 166, 172; mathematical models 163; paradoxes 163; *see also* neuroeconomics
educational neuroscience *see* neuroeducation
Eisenberger, N. I. 192
Ekman, Paul 142
Elaboration Likelihood Model (ELM) 136–137
electrical signaling 40–41
electrocardiogram (EKG) 15
electroconvulsive therapy (ECT) 11, 63
electroencephalography (EEG) 17–18, 123, 148–150, *149*, 189, 224, *251*
Elflein, John 173
emotions 14, 147; components of 136; and consumer behavior 135–139; control of 114; and decision-making 171–175; and EEG recordings 149, 150; and EMDR 66; facial electromyography 14; facial emotion recognition and empathy 192–193; and limbic system 34; negative 137, 139, *139*, 149; positive 149; processing, at subconscious level 138; related to aggression, and testosterone 89; role in advertising 133, 135–136, 137–138; somatic marker theory of 136
empathy 91, 176, 188, 192–193
endocrine system 31, 35, 37
endorphins **46**, 47

ENIGMA Consortium (Enhancing Neuroimaging Genetics through Meta Analysis) 215
enteric nervous system 31, 37
environmental transfer 121
ependymal cells 39
epidural stimulation 252–253
epigenetics 69–70, *70*, 84; and nutrition 228; and smoking 227; and stress 219
epinephrine 45
Erickson, K. I. 213, 230, 231, 233
Eslinger, P. J. 170
ethics: artificial intelligence 246; behavioral neuroscience methods 21–22; medications 61; neural interfaces 253; polygraph measures 94; sex robots 257
Eugene Goostman program 242
event-related potentials (ERPs) 17–18, 108, 148, 230
evidence-based practice (EBP) 12–13, *12*, 106, 108
evolutionary theory of loneliness (ETL) 223
excitatory synapses 43–44
executive function 113–115, 174; brain training 118–122, *119*; evaluation of cognitive training 123; non-invasive brain stimulation 115–116; nootropics 116–118, *118*; and physical activity 231; school programs 115; Tools of the Mind curriculum 115
exercise *see* physical activity (PA)
expert testimony 13, 81, 83
explicit memory 140

extroversion 196
eye movement desensitization and reprocessing (EMDR) 65–66
eye tracking 16, 143, *144*, 151, 153

Facebook 22, 251
facial coding 142
facial electromyography (fEMG) 14
facial recognition 245–246
fairness 176, *177*
Farah, Martha 58, 59
far transfer 121
fight-or-flight response 37, 87, 216, 218
Floreano, D. 247
focused thought 199–200
Fooks, N. 112
forced swim test 216, *217*
Ford, E. S. 226
forebrain 31, 32, 34
forensic neuroscience 80; aggression 84–91; assessments 80–82; lie detection 92–95, *94*; malleability of memory 82; *mens rea* (state of mind) 81–82; nature, nurture, and criminal behavior 82–84; number of judicial opinions including neuroscience data *81*; prediction of violent behavior 91–92
forensic psychology 80
forward inference 189–190, *191*
forward-span tasks 114
foundational traits of leadership 195, 196
frame-consistent choices 174, 175
frame-inconsistent choices 174
framing effects 173–174

Frank, G. K. W. 229
Freeman, William 61
freezing response 37
Freud, Sigmund 85, 89, 241
frontal lobe 32–33, 87, 88, 94, 168
Frontera, J. A. 221
Froyen, D. J. 109
fruit flies 248
functional fixedness 115
functional magnetic resonance imaging (fMRI) 8, 9, 20, 21, 123, 138, 189, 190; choice behavior 174; consumer neuroscience 146–148; cost of 10; during EMDR 65, 66; dyslexia *108*; leadership 198, 201; mathematics learning 109, 111; safety of 10, 20; taste reward task 229; use in neuroeducation 106
functional magnetic resonance spectroscopy (fMRS) 20
functional near-infrared spectroscopy (fNIRS) 20–21, 189
Furtner, M. R. 196

Gage, Phineas 3, 91
galvanic skin response (GSR) *see* skin conductance response (SCR)
gambling 161, 169, 172–173, *172*
game theory 176
gamma aminobutyric acid (GABA) **46**, 47
gamma waves 17, 116, 148, 150
gap junctions 41
gasotransmitters 45, **46**, 47–48
Gatling, Richard Jordan 258

gender, and psychoactive substances 48
gene–environment interactions, and criminal behavior 82–84
general adaptation syndrome (GAS) 216–217
general intelligence 245
genetics 70–71, 84, 215; and aggression 85–86, 91; and alcohol abuse 230; behavioral 186; and leadership 186, 195; and psychoactive substances 48; *see also* epigenetics
Ghostrobotics 258
Gillihan, Seth 58, 59
glia 37, 39
glutamate **46**, 47
glycine **46**, 47
Godden, D. R. 8
Golgi, Camillo 28
Google 22
Google Duplex 242
Gordon, D. S. 198
Gordon, I. 187
graded potential 40
Grau, C. 253
gray matter 31
Greenwald, Anthony 140, 141
group-to-individual (G2i) problem 13, 58–59, 94
Guilty Knowledge Test 94
Gul, F. 166
gut, and brain 31, 37

handedness 10, 149–150
Hanson Robotics 242, *243*
happiness, and executive function 115
Hare, Robert 91, 199
harm, avoidance of 22
Harmony (robotic head) 255–256
Harvey, P. D. 121

headaches in children 61
health: biopsychosocial model of 212; definition of 212
health neuroscience 212–214; alcohol use 230, *231*; definition of 212; exercise/physical activity 230–233; health behaviors 226–234; loneliness 222–225; methods of 215; model *213*; neurological outcomes of COVID-19 pandemic 221–222; nutrition 228–230; smoking 226–228; stress 216–221
heart rate 14–15, 143
heart rate sensors 15
heart rate variability (HRV) 15–16, 143
Her (film) 255
heritability 71, 195, 198
heuristics 164, 174–175
Hinckley, John 78
hindbrain 31
hippocampus 34, 68, 70, 88, 112, 116, **170**, 218–219, 231, 250
histamine **46**, 47
Hitler, Adolph 185, 196
Hobbes, Thomas 84, 85
Hoeft, F. 107
Holguin, Roberto 82–83
Holt-Lunstad, J. 222
homicide: cases, neuroscience evidence in 81; rates, and culture 86–87
honeybees 249
Hopper, Grace 244
hormones 31, 34, 37, 90, 178, 188
hot sauce paradigm 8, *9*
house flies 248
human research 13
human–robot relations 254–258
hunger 228

Huntington's disease 4
hyperscanning 188–189, *190*
hypothalamic-pituitary-adrenal axis (HPA axis) 217–219, *218*, 225
hypothalamus 35, 88, 89, 170, **170**

immune system: and loneliness 225; and perceptions of social connectivity 211–212; and stress 220
implicit associations 140–142
Implicit Association Test (IAT) 141–142, *141*
implicit bias training 140
implicit memory 140
impulse control 114
impulsive aggression 85, 87–88, *88*, 89
Individuals with Disabilities Education Act (IDEA) 55
informed consent 22
inhibitory control 87, 114
inhibitory synapses 44
insanity defense 78–79
insects, modeling of robot after 248
inspirational leaders 201
Institute for Applied Neuroscience 1
insula 33, 110, 139, 169, 176, 177
insulin **46**, 47
internal validity 8
International Classification of Diseases (ICD-11) 55, 59
intraparietal sulcus (IPS) 110, *110*, 111, 112
invertebrates, robot models of 247–248
Ioannidis, J. P. A. 10
Iowa Gambling Task 172–173, *172*
Iron Eyes Cody 138
Ishiguro, Hiroshi 242

Izquierdo, E. J. 248

Jack, A. I. 189, 191, 193, 194
Jackson, John Hughlings 87
James, William 4, 18, 121, 171
Jirtle, Randy *70*, 84

Kahneman, Daniel 136, 163, 172, 173, **174**, 175
Kanwisher, N. 92
Kätsyri, J. 257
Kedia, G. 7, 8
Keep America Beautiful 138
Keynes, John Maynard 163
Khan, Genghis 185, *185*
knee-jerk reflex 31
Kosfeld, M. 187
Krause, L. 192

laboratory studies 8
lamprey 249, *249*
Langleben, Daniel 94
language 149; learning to read 107–109; multiple language learning 103–104
Lashley, Karl 246
lateral intraparietal area (area LIP) 178
lateralization of brain function 10, 33, 149–150
leadership 184–185; analysis of neurochemicals 186–188; behavior 194–201; Big 5 personality traits 195; capacities 195, 196, 199; dark 196–199; development 201–202; foundational traits 195, 196; influencing the brain 192–193; leader characteristics 195–196; observation of brain 188–192; and organizational neuroscience 185–186; style 199–201; training 202; transformational 194, 201

learning 120; deep 245; disabilities 114; mathematics 109–112; multiple language learning 103–104; to read 107–109; reinforcement learning 168; styles 102–103; supervised/unsupervised 247
left brain/right brain neuromyth 104
left-handedness, people with 10, 149–150
left hemisphere 33, 149
Lewis, M. 93
Lieberman, M. D. 192
lie detection 92–95, *94*
lily pad problem 161–162, *162*
limbic system 34, *35*, 88–89
Lindamood Bell remediation program 107–108
Ling, D. S. 115
lithium carbonate 61
lobotomy 61
Locke, John 84, 85
Loftus, Elizabeth 69, 82
Lombroso, Cesare 83
loneliness 222–223; evolutionary aspects of 223–224; evolutionary theory of 223; and health neuroscience 224–225; referrals 225; remedies for 225; UCLA Loneliness Scale **223**
longitudinal designs 232
loss aversion 170

McCabe, D. P. 7
McCarthy, John 245
Maccoby, M. 197
Machiavelli, Niccolò 197
Machiavellianism 197, 198
machine learning 20, 82, 150, 215, 247
McLennan, A. K. 222
macroglia 39

magnetic resonance imaging (MRI) 8, 10, 20, 135, 222
magnetic seizure therapy (MST) 65
magnetoencephalography (MEG) 17, 18–19, *19*, 64, 148
magnitude, judgment of 109, 110–111
major depressive disorder *see* depression
malnourishment 228–229
MAOA gene 82
Mao Zedong 185, 196
marketing 151–153
Markett, S. 196
Maslow, Abraham 85
mathematics learning 109–112
Matsumoto, David 142
Meaney, Michael 70, 219
Medical College Admission Test (MCAT) 213–214
medications: antidepressants 47, 68; methods of administration 48; for OCD 72; psychoactive drugs 39, 43, 47, 48–49; for psychological disorders 60–61
melatonin **46**, 47
memory(ies) 34, 116; context-dependent 8–9; explicit 140; implicit 140; malleability of 82; and physical activity 231; reconsolidation 68–69; short-term 114; spatial memory task 231, 232; tasks 65–66; working 114, 115, 123
meninges 32
mens rea (state of mind) 81–82
Merzenich, Michael 222
meta-cognition 162

methods, behavioral neuroscience 13; central measures 17–21; ethics 21–22; peripheral measures 13–16, *15*; spatial/temporal resolution of 17, 21, *21*, 147, 148
methylphenidate (Ritalin) 61, 117
microstates, brain 18, 148, *149*, 224
microvascular damage 222
midbrain 31, 32, 87
mind: and body 211–212; and brain 4; *mens rea* (state of mind) 81–82; theory of 175
MIND diet 229–230
mindfulness training 115
MindSigns 147–148
mirror neurons 72, 175–176, 201, 250
mirror test *see* rouge test
Mischel, Walter 168, *169*
mixed-longitudinal designs 232
M'Naghton, Daniel 79
moderating variables 233
Moe, H. T. 187
Molenberghs, P. 193, 201
monism 4, 211
Moniz, Antonio Egas 61
monosodium glutamate (MSG) 47
Moore, S. E. 134
Mori, Masahito 256, *256*
Morris, M. C. 229–230
Morse, Stephen 82
movement primitives 250
Mullins, Gay 151
Munduruku people 111
murder–suicide 89
Musk, Elon 251, 254
myelin 38, 41

Nagle, Matt 252
NAO robot *243*, 244

narcissism 196–198
narcissistic personality disorder 197
National Institute of Mental Health (NIMH) 59
National Neuroscience Curriculum Initiative (NNCI) 67
nature–nurture interactions, and criminal behavior 82–84
near transfer 121
Necomimi cat ears 18, *251*
negative emotions 137, 139, *139*, 149
neocortex 33
nervous system 30–31, *30*, 164; central 30, *30*, 31–35; glia 37, 39; neural communication 39–49; neurons 37–38, *38*; peripheral 30, *30*, 31, 35–36, *36*; structure of 28–29
neural-and-behavioral economics program 166
neural communication 39; chemical signaling 41–44, *42*; electrical signaling 40–41; neurochemicals 44–45, **46**, 47–49
neural dust 252
Neuralink project 251
neural interfaces 251–253
neural networks 244–245
neurocellular economics 166
neurochemicals 37, 38, 40, 41, 42, 43, 44–45, **46**, 47–48; and aggression 88–89; and leadership 186–188; manipulation of 48–49
neurochips 253
neuroeconomics *160*, 163–166; emotion *vs.* reason 171–175; probability and decision-making 161–162, *162*; social decision-making 175–178; value 167–171
neuroeducation 104–105; and communication 105; executive function 113–123; managing expectations 106; mathematics learning 109–112; methodology 106; neuromyths 101–104, *102*; reading 107–109, *108*
neurofeedback 202
neurogenesis 68
neuroimaging 8, 9, 17, 19–21, 54, 199, 215; costs of 10; for diagnosis of psychological disorders 58; dyslexia 107, *108*; group-to-individual problem 58–59, 94; and lie detection 94–95; and neuroeconomics 166; and prediction of violent behavior 92; safety concerns 10; task dependency of 59; *see also specific entries*
neurolaw 80
neuroleptics 61
neuromyths 101–104, *102*
neurons 37–38, *38*; mirror 72, 175–176, 201, 250; neurogenesis 68
neuropeptides 47
neuroplasticity 68, 103, 119, 202, 222, 227
neuroprediction 92
neuropsychologists 66
neuroscience 3, 6; applied 1; cognitive 244; computational 245; data, number of judicial opinions including *81*; and evaluation of cognitive training 123; organizational 185–194; reductionism of 166; social 175; *see also* consumer neuroscience; forensic neuroscience; health neuroscience
Neurosynth 192, *192*, 195, 215
neuroticism 196
New Coke 151, *152*
Newsome, W. T. 167
nicotine 45, 226, 227–228
Nielsen 146, 150–151
9/11 attacks 164, *164*
nitric oxide (NO) 47–48
nodes of Ranvier 38
non-invasive brain stimulation 115–116
nootropics 116–118, *118*
noradrenalin *see* norepinephrine
norepinephrine 37, 45, **46**, 47
nucleus accumbens 34, 88, 91, 113, 170, **170**
number conservation task 109–110
Nummenmaa, L. 198, 199
nutrition 228; disordered eating 228–229; epigenetics 228; and healthy brain aging 229–230

obesity 228–229
obsessive–compulsive disorder (OCD) 72
occipital lobe 33
oligodendrocytes 39
O'Malley, Gerald 82–83
online shopping 153
open science 9, 106, 191
Opteran Technologies 249
optic flow 248
optogenetics 248–249
orbicularis oculi muscle 14
orbitofrontal cortex (OFC) 62, 170, **170**, 172–173, 176

organizational behavior 186, 194, 195
organizational neuroscience 199; analysis of neurochemicals 186–188; influencing the brain 192–193; and leadership 185–186; multiple methods 193; observation of brain 188–192; research designs 193–194
Organization for Economic Cooperation and Development (OECD) 101–102, 103
oxytocin 44, **46**, 47, 178, 187

P300 wave 18, 230, *231*
parasympathetic nervous system 15, 16, 30–31, 36–37
parietal lobe 33, 94, 111
Parkinson's disease 34, 45
Paro (robot) 255, *255*
patellar reflex *see* knee-jerk reflex
Patton, George S. 174
Peel, Robert 79
Pegna, A. J. 138
peptide neurochemicals 45
perceptual choices 167
perceptual mismatch hypothesis 256–257
periaqueductal grey 87, 88, 89
period effects 232
peripheral nervous system (PNS) 30, *30*, 31, 35–36, *36*
personality: dark triad of 196–198; instruments 11–12; traits, and leadership 195–196
personal-oriented leaders 201
persuasion 136–137, 138
Pesendorfer, W. 166
Petty, Richard 136–137

phosphenes 253
photoplethysmography (PPG) 15
physical activity (PA) 230; brain as an outcome or mediator 231–232; brain as a predictor 232–233; motivation to engage in 233
Piaget, Jean 109, 110, *110*
plasticity *see* neuroplasticity
Platek, S. M. 198
Poirel, N. 109
Poldrack, R. A. 92
polygraph measures 93–94, *94*, 145
positive emotions 149
positron emission tomography (PET) 19–20
Posit Science 222
posterior cingulate cortex (PCC) 33, 170, **170**
postsynaptic cell 43
posttraumatic stress disorder (PTSD) 65, *67*
Poughkeepsie Tapes, The 147–148
power, statistical 10
prediction of violent behavior 91–92
prefrontal cortex 111; and executive function 113, 116, *116*, 117; of psychopaths 91
premeditated aggression 85, 86, 88, 89, 91
presynaptic cell 43
primates, robot models of 250
prisoner's dilemma 177
proactive aggression 85, 86, 88, 89, 91
probability, and decision-making 161–162, *162*
procedural strategies for arithmetic problems 112
progesterone (synthetic), prenatal exposure to 89, *90*

propranolol 69
prosthetics 252, *252*, 253
psychiatrists 66–67, 79–81
psychoactive drugs 39, 43, 47, 48–49
psychological assessments in courtroom 80–82
psychometrics 11–12
psychopathy 91, 176, 197, 198–199
psychopharmacology 58
psychosurgery 61–62
psychotherapy, and brain 72
public service announcement (PSA) 146, 150
pulse rate 15
punishment 81, 93, 168, 177
pupil dilation 16
pupillometry 16, 143
Purkinje cell *29*
Putin, Vladimir 258

Quizmania 147

Raine, Adrian 84
Ramón y Cajal, Santiago 28, *29*
raphe nuclei 47
rats 170, 216, 250
reactive aggression 85, 87–88, *88*, 89
Read, J. 11, 12
reading 107–109, *108*
Reagan, Ronald 78
RealDoll 255–256
reason, and decision-making 171–175
recreational drugs 48
reductionism of neuroscience 166
reinforcement learning 168
relationship-oriented leadership 199–200
re-ordering span tasks 114
repeated transcranial magnetic stimulation

(rTMS) 64–65, *64*, 115, 192–193
Research Domain Criteria Initiative (RDoC) 59, *60*
resting potential 40
reticular formation 31–32
retinal implants 252
retrieval strategies for arithmetic problems 112
reuptake 43
reuptake inhibitors 43
reverse inference 7–8, 147, 190, *191*, 232–233
reward prediction errors 168, 229
reward systems 168
right hemisphere 33–34, 149
robots 242; Aibo 255; human–robot relations 254–258; and invertebrates 247–248; models for 247–250; NAO *243*, 244; Paro 255, *255*; and primates 250; self-awareness of 242, *243*, 244; social 255–257; Sophia 242, *243*; uncanny valley hypothesis 256, *256*; and vertebrates 249–250; and war 257–258
Rogers, Carl 85
Rorschach Inkblot Test 11–12, 81
Ross, D. 166
rouge test 242
Rousseau, Jean-Jacques 84, 85

sampling 9–11
satellite cells 39
schizophrenia 61, 222; diagnosis of 55, 56; insanity defense 78; and smoking 213, 227–228
Schwann cells 39
sciatic nerve 40
Scutt, T. 248

seed method 195
Seghier, M. L. 106
selective attention 114, 115
selective breeding and aggression *86*
self-control 114
self-deception 93
self-preservation 224
self-reports 13, 142
Selye, Hans 216
serotonin **46**, 47, 89, 178, 187–188, *189*, 227
serotonin reuptake inhibitors 47
Serra, D. 166
sex robots 255–257
Shapiro, Francine 65
Shaywitz, B. A. 107, 108
Sherman, G. D. 187
short-term memory 114
signal detection theory 94, *94*, 165, **165**, 167
Simon, Herbert 171, 174
Simons, D. J. 120
Simonton, D. K. 198
simple practice 121
single photon emission computerized tomography (SPECT) 19–20, 53
size constancy 112, *113*
skin conductance 143, 145
skin conductance response (SCR) 16, 143, 145
Skinner, B. F. 161, 164, 168, 177
sleep 71–72
small molecule neurochemicals 45
smart drugs *see* nootropics
Smith, Adam 163
Smith, C. 216
Smith, E. E. 150
smoking 213, 226–227; cessation 232; developmental course of tobacco use 227; and

psychopathology 227–228; and psychosis 213
social connectivity: perceptions, and immune system 211–212; for stress management 221
social decision-making 175–178
social games 176–177, 178
social neuroscience 175
social robots 255–257
SoftBank Robotics 244
somatic marker theory 136
somatic nervous system 30, 35–36
Sophia (robot) 242, *243*
spatial memory task 231, 232
Special Purpose Unmanned Rifle (SPUR) 258
Sperry, Roger 6
spinal cord 31, 252–253
spinal nerves 31, 36, *36*
SQUIDs (superconducting quantum interference devices) 18, 19
Stalin, Josef 185, 196
Star Trek 258
Star Wars 197, 254, *254*
Stillman, C. M. 230, 231, 233
stimulants 117
stream of consciousness 18
stress 216; biomarker for 219, *220*; chronic, health impacts of 220; classic models of 216–217; coping with 220–221; and epigenetics 219; forced swim test 216, *217*; general adaptation syndrome 216–217; HPA axis and SAM 217–219, *218*
stressors 216
striatum 88, 91, 170–171, **170**, 177
strong artificial intelligence 242

Stroop task 116, *116*
substance P **46**, 47
substantia nigra 32
subventricular zone (SVZ) 68
suicide 89
Sullivan, Louis 13
supervised learning 247
sweat glands 16
SWORD International 258
sympathetic adrenal-medullary system (SAM) 217–219, *218*, 225
sympathetic nervous system 15, 16, 30–31, 36–37, 87, 143, 216
synaptic pruning 39
Szucs, D. 10

Talon *257*
task-oriented leadership 199–200
task-related networks 199–200, *200*, 201
taste reward task 229
tattoo inks, and fMRI 10
Tedder, Ryan *134*
temporal lobe 33
temporal summation 44
testosterone 178; and aggression 89–90, 187; and leadership 186–187, 188
tetanus 44
tetanus toxin 44
thalamus 34, 87
theory and practice, negotiation between 11–13
theory of mind 175
theta waves 17, 150
Thomas, M. S. C. 105
Thorndike, Edward 121
tobacco use *see* smoking
Tools of the Mind curriculum 115
trait anxiety 196
transcranial direct current stimulation (tDCS) 193
transcranial electrical stimulation (tES) 64, 115, 116
transfer of practice effects 120
transformational leadership 194, 201
traumatic brain injury (TBI) 66
treatment of psychological disorders: clinician's perspective 66–72; deep brain stimulation 62, *62*; and diagnosis 57–58; electroconvulsive therapy 63; eye movement desensitization and reprocessing 65–66; magnetic seizure therapy 65; medications 60–61; psychosurgery 61–62; repeated transcranial magnetic stimulation 64–65, *64*; transcranial electrical stimulation 64; vagus nerve stimulation 63; virtual reality therapy 66
Trivers, Robert 93
Turing, Alan 242
Turing test 242
Tuskegee Syphilis Study 21–22
Tversky, Amos 163, 173, **174**
Type 1 decisions 172, 175
Type 2 decisions 172, 175

UCLA Loneliness Scale **223**
Ulijaszek, S. J. 222
ultimatum game 176, 177, 178
uncanny valley hypothesis 256, *256*
unfocused thought 199–200
UNIVAC 244
unsupervised learning 247
"use it or lose it" hypothesis 119

user experience (UX) designers 143, *144*
user experience (UX) experts 153
utility model/theory 166, 171

vagus nerve 36, 63
vagus nerve stimulation (VNS) 63
valence model of frontal asymmetry 149
value-based decisions 167–171
Van der Meij, L. 187
vaping 226
vasopressin **46**, 47, 187
ventricles, cerebral 32
ventromedial prefrontal cortex 170–171, **170**
vertebrates, robot models of 249–250
vesicles 41, 42–43
vestibular system 251
Vilares, Iris 82
Virtual Iraq 67
virtual reality (VR) 202, *203*
virtual-reality gaming 215
virtual reality therapy (VRT) 66
volunteerism 22
vomiting reflex 48
voxels 20

Waldman, D. A. 189, 201, 202
Walter, William Grey 247
Waorani people 86
war, and robots 257–258
Watson, John B. 132–133, 135
weak artificial intelligence 242
wearable interfaces 251
wearable technology 16, 19, 143, 202
Webb, B. 248, 249

Weisberg, D. S. 6, 80
whiskers, robot models of 250
white matter 31, 34
WHOOP 15
Wiener, Norbert 245
winner takes all model 171

withdrawal reflex 31
working memory 114, 115, 123
World Health Organization 55, 212

Yamins, Daniel 246, 247
Yanomamö people 86
yoga 115
Yoon, C. 190
youth violence 83, 90

zebrafish 188, *189*
zygomatic major muscle 14